Wilkie Collins

Within the Maze

A Novel. Sixth Edition

Wilkie Collins

Within the Maze
A Novel. Sixth Edition

ISBN/EAN: 9783337039516

Printed in Europe, USA, Canada, Australia, Japan

Cover: Foto ©ninafisch / pixelio.de

More available books at **www.hansebooks.com**

PREPARING FOR MR. CATTACOMB.

WITHIN THE MAZE.

A Novel.

BY

MRS. HENRY WOOD,

AUTHOR OF
"EAST LYNNE," "THE CHANNINGS," ETC.

SIXTH EDITION.

LONDON:
RICHARD BENTLEY & SON, New Burlington Street.
Publishers in Ordinary to Her Majesty.
1880.

CONTENTS.

CHAPTER	PAGE
I. Mrs. Andinnian's Home	1
II. Lucy Cleeve	13
III. Done at Sunset	26
IV. The Trial	33
V. Unable to Get Strong	43
VI. An Atmosphere of Mystery	51
VII. At the Charing-cross Hotel	61
VIII. In the Avenue D'Antin	66
IX. Down at Foxwood	67
X. Mrs. Andinnian's Secret	87
XI. At the Gate of the Maze	99
XII. Taking an Evening Stroll	110
XIII. Miss Blake Gets in	121
XIV. Miss Blake on the Watch	131
XV. Revealed to Lady Andinnian	142
XVI. A Night at the Maze	157
XVII. Before the World	167
XVIII. A Night Alarm	178
XIX. In the Same Train	192
XX. Only One Fly at the Station	203
XXI. Hard to Bear	213
XXII. With His Brother	221
XXIII. The Maze Invaded	228
XXIV. Recognised	238
XXV. A New Lodger in Paradise-row	244
XXVI. Nurse Chaffen on Duty	249
XXVII. Watching the House	263
XXVIII. At Afternoon Service	274
XXIX. At Lawyer St. Henry's	283
XXX. Another Kettle-drum	295

Contents.

CHAPTER		PAGE
XXXI.	Only a Night Owl	309
XXXII.	One Day in Her Life	321
XXXIII.	Mrs. Chaffen Disturbed	330
XXXIV.	Baffled	337
XXXV.	At Scotland Yard	344
XXXVI.	Ill-Omened Chances	354
XXXVII.	Ann Hopley Startled	364
XXXVIII.	Up the Spouts and Down the Drains	373
XXXIX.	Taken from the Evil to Come	382
XL.	News for Mr. Tatton	391
XLI.	Mrs. Cleeve at Fault	400
XLII.	At the Red Dawn	413
XLIII.	Laid to His Rest	424
XLIV.	Repentance	429
XLV.	Only a Man Like Other Men	436
Conclusion		441

WITHIN THE MAZE.

CHAPTER I.
MRS. ANDINNIAN'S HOME.

THE house was ugly and old-fashioned, with some added modern improvements, and was surrounded by a really beautiful garden. Though situated close upon a large market town of Northamptonshire, it stood alone, excluded from the noise and bustle of the world.

The occupant of this house was a widow lady, Mrs. Andinnian. Her husband, a post-captain in the Royal Navy, had been dead some years. She had two sons. The elder, Adam, was of no profession, and lived with her: the younger, Karl, was a lieutenant in one of Her Majesty's regiments. Adam was presumptive heir to his uncle, Sir Joseph Andinnian, a baronet of modern creation: Karl had his profession alone to look to, and a small private income of two hundred a year.

They were not rich, these Andinnians: though the late captain had deemed himself well-off, what with his private fortune, and what with his pay. The private fortune was just six hundred a year; the pay not great: but Captain Andinnian's tastes were simple, his wants few. At his death it was found that he had bequeathed his money in three equal parts: two hundred a year to his wife, and two hundred each to his sons. "Adam and his mother will live together," he said in the will; "she'd not be parted from him: and four hundred pounds, with her bit of pension, will be enough for comfort. When Adam succeeds his uncle, they can make any fresh arrangement that pleases them. But I hope that when that time shall come they will not forget Karl."

Mrs. Andinnian resented the will, and resented these words in it. Her elder boy, Adam, had always been first and foremost with her: never a mother loved a son more ardently than she loved him. For Karl she cared not. Captain Andinnian was not blind to the injustice, and perhaps thence arose the motive that induced him not to leave his wife's two hundred pounds of income at her own disposal: when Mrs. Andinnian died it would lapse to Karl. The captain had loved his sons equally: he would willingly have left them equally provided for in life, and divided the fortune that was to come sometime to Adam. Mrs. Andinnian, in spite of the expected rise for Adam, would have had him left better off from his father's means than Karl.

There had been nearly a life-long feud between the two family branches. Sir Joseph Andinnian and his brother the captain had not met for years and years: and it was a positive fact that the latter's sons had never seen their uncle. For this feud the brothers themselves were not in the first instance to blame. It did not arise with them, but with their wives. Both ladies were of a haughty, over-bearing, and implacable temper: they had quarrelled very soon after their first introduction to each other; the quarrel grew, and grew, and finally involved the husbands as well in its vortex.

Joseph Andinnian, who was the younger of the two brothers, had been a noted and very successful civil engineer. Some great work, that he had originated and completed, gained him his reward—a baronetcy. While he was in the very flush of his new honours, an accident that he met with laid him for many months upon a sick-bed. Not only that: it incapacitated him for future active service. So, when he was little more than a middle-aged man, he retired from his profession, and took up his abode for life at a pretty estate he had bought in Kent, called Foxwood Court, barely an hour's railway journey from London: by an express train not much more than half-an-hour's. Here, he and his wife had lived since: growing more and more of an invalid as the years went on. They had no children; consequently his brother, Captain Andinnian was heir to the baronetcy: and, following on Captain Andinnian, Adam, the captain's eldest son.

Captain Andinnian did not live to succeed. In what seemed the pride of his health and strength, just after he had landed from a three years' voyage, and was indulging in ambitious visions of a flag, symptoms of a mortal disease manifested themselves. He begged of his physicians to let him know the truth; and they complied—he must expect but a very few weeks more of life. Captain Andinnian, after taking a day or two to look matters fully in the face, went up to London, and thence down to Sir Joseph's house in Kent. The brothers once face to face, met as though no ill-blood had ever separated them: hands were locked in hands, gaze went out to gaze. Both were simple-minded, earnest-hearted, affectionate-natured men; and but for their wives—to whom, if the truth must be avowed, each lay in subjection—not a mis-word would ever have arisen between them.

"I am dying, Joseph," said the captain, when some of their mutual emotion had worn away. "The doctors tell me so, and I feel it to be true. Naturally, it has set me on the thought of many things—that I am afraid I have been too carelessly putting off. What I have come down to you chiefly for, is to ask about my son—Adam. You'll tell me the truth, won't you, Joseph, as between brothers?"

"I'll tell you anything, Harry," was Sir Joseph's answer. "The truth about what?"

"Whether he is to succeed you or not?"

"Why, of course he must succeed: failing yourself. What are you thinking of, Harry, to ask it? I've no son of my own: it's not likely I shall have one now. He will be Sir Adam after me."

"It's not the title I was thinking of, Joseph. Failing a direct heir, I know that must come to him. But the property?—will he have that? It is not entailed; and you could cut him out absolutely."

"D'ye think I'd be so unjust as that, Harry?" was the half indignant reply. "A baronet's title, and nothing to keep it up upon! I have never had an idea of leaving it away from you; or from him if you went first. When Adam succeeds to my name and rank, he will succeed to my property. Were my wife to survive me, she'd have this place for life, and a good part of the income: but Adam would get it all at her death."

"This takes a weight off my mind," avowed Captain Andinnian. "Adam was not brought up to any profession. Beyond the two hundred a year he'll inherit from me——"

"A bad thing that—no profession," interrupted Sir Joseph. "If I had ten sons, and they were all heirs to ten baronetcies, each one should be brought up to use his brains or his hands."

"It's what I have urged over and over again," avowed the captain. "But the wife—you know what she is—set her face against it. 'He'll be Sir Adam Andinnian of Foxwood,' she'd answer me with, 'and he shall not soil his hands with work.' I have been nearly always afloat, too, Joseph: not on the spot to enforce things: something has lain in that."

"I wonder the young man should not have put himself forward to be of use in the world!"

"Adam is idly inclined. I am sorry for it, but it is so. One thing has been against him, and that's his health. He's as tall and strong a young fellow to look at as you'd meet in a summer's day, but he is, I fear, anything but sound in constitution. A nice fellow too, Joseph."

"Of good disposition?"

"Very. We had used to be almost afraid of him as a boy; he would put himself into such unaccountable fits of passion. Just as—as—somebody else used to do, you know, Joseph," added the sailor, with some hesitation.

Sir Joseph nodded. The somebody else was the captain's wife, and Adam's mother. Sir Joseph's own wife was not exempt from the same kind of failing: but in a less wild degree than Mrs. Andinnian. With her, the defects of temper partook more of the nature of sullenness.

"But Adam seems to have outgrown all that: I've seen and heard nothing of it since he came to manhood," resumed the captain. "I wish from my heart he had some profession to occupy him. His mother always filled him up with the notion that he would be your heir and not want it."

"He'll be my heir, in all senses, safe enough, Harry: though I'd rather have heard he was given to industry than idleness. How does he get through his time? Young men naturally seek some pursuit as an outlet for their superfluous activity."

"Adam has a pursuit that he makes a hobby of; and that is his love of flowers; in fact his love of gardening in any shape. He'll be out amidst the plants and shrubs from sunrise to sunset. Trained to it, he'd have made a second Sir Joseph Paxton. I should like you to see him: he is very handsome."

"And the young one—what is he like? What's his name by the way? Henry?"

"No. Karl."

"*Karl?*" repeated Sir Joseph in surprise, as if questioning whether he heard aright.

"Ay, Karl. His mother was in Germany when he was born, it being a cheap place to live in—I was only a poor lieutenant then, Joseph, and just gone off to be stationed before the West Indies. A great friend of hers there, some German lady, had a little boy named Karl. My wife fell in love with the name, and called her own infant after it."

"Well, it sounds an outlandish name to me," cried the baronet, who was entirely unacquainted with every language but his own.

"So I thought, when she first wrote me word," assented Captain Andinnian. "But after I came home and got used to call the lad by it, you don't know how I grew to like it. The name gains upon your favour in a wonderful manner, Joseph: and I have heard other people say the same. It is Charles in English, you know."

"Then why not call him Charles?"

"Because the name is really Karl, and not Charles. He was baptized in Germany, but christened in England, and in both places it was done as 'Karl.' His mother has never cared very much for him."

"For him or his name, do you mean?"

"Oh, for him."

Sir Joseph opened his eyes. "Why on earth not?"

"Because all the love her nature's capable of—and in her it's tolerably strong—is given to Adam. She can't spare an atom from him: her love for him is as a kind of idolatry. For one thing, she was very ill when Karl was born, and neither nursed nor tended him: he was given over to the care of her sister who lived with her, and who had him wholly, so to say, for the first three years of his life."

"And what's Karl like?" repeated Sir Joseph.

"You ought to see him," burst forth the captain with animation. "He's everything that's good and noble and worthy. Joseph, there are not many young men of the present day so attractive as Karl."

"With a tendency to be passionate, like his brother?"

"Not he. A tendency to patience, rather. They have put upon him at home—between ourselves; kept him down, you know; both mother and brother. He is several years younger than Adam; but they are attached to each other. A more gentle-natured, sweet-tempered lad than Karl never lived: all his instincts are those of a gentleman. He will make a brave soldier. He is ensign in the — regiment."

"The — regiment," repeated Sir Joseph. "Rather a crack corps that, is it not?"

"Yes: Karl has been lucky. He will have to make his own way in the world, for I can't give him much. But now that I am assured of your intentions as to Adam, things look a trifle brighter. Joseph, I thank you with all my heart."

Once more the brothers clasped hands. This re-union was the pleasantest event of their later lives. The captain remained two days at Foxwood. Lady Andinnian was civilly courteous to him, but never cordial. She did not second her husband's pressing wish that he should prolong his stay: neither did she once ask after any of his family.

Captain Andinnian's death took place, as anticipated. His will, when opened, proved to be what was mentioned above. Some years had gone by since. Mrs. Andinnian and her son Adam had continued to live together in their quiet home in Northamptonshire; Karl, lieutenant now, and generally with his regiment, paying them an occasional visit. No particular change had occurred, save the death of Lady Andinnian. The families had continued to be estranged as heretofore: for never a word of invitation had come out of Foxwood. Report ran that Sir Joseph was ailing much; very much indeed since the loss of his wife. And, now, that so much of introduction is over, we can go on with the story.

A beautiful day in April. At a large window thrown open to the mid-day sun, just then very warm and bright, sat a lady of some five and fifty years. A tall, handsome, commanding woman, resolution written in every line of her haughty face. She wore a black silk gown with the slightest possible modicum of crape on it, and the guipure cap—or, rather, the guipure lappets, for of cap there was not much to be seen—had in it some black ribbon. Her purple-black hair was well preserved and abundant still; her black eyes were stern, and fearlessly honest. It was Mrs. Andinnian.

She was knitting what is called a night-sock. Some poor sick pensioner of hers or her son's—for both had their charities—needed the comfort. Her thoughts were busy; her eyes went fondly out to the far end of the garden, where she could just discern her son against the shrubs: the fairest and dearest sight to Mrs. Andinnian that earth had ever contained for her, or ever would contain.

"It is strange Sir Joseph does not write for him," ran her thoughts—and they very often did run in the same groove. "I cannot imagine why he does not. Adam ought to be on the spot and get acquainted with his inheritance: his uncle must know he ought. But that I have never stooped to ask a favour in my life, I would write to Sir Joseph, and proffer a visit for Adam, and—for—yes, for me. During that woman's lifetime Adam was not likely to be welcomed there: but the woman's gone: it is two months this very day since she died."

The woman, thus unceremoniously alluded to, was Lady Andinnian: and the slight mourning, worn, was for her. Some intricacy in the knitting caused Mrs. Andinnian to bend her head: when she looked up again, her son was not to be seen. At the same moment, a faint sound of distant conversation smote her ear. The work dropped on her lap; with a look of annoyance she lifted her head to listen.

"He is talking to that girl again! I am sure of it."

Lift her head and her ears as she would, she could not tell positively whose voices they were. Instinct, however, that instinct of suspicion we all feel within us on occasion, was enough.

A very respectable man-servant of middle age, thoughtful in face, fair in complexion, with a fringe of light hair round the sides of his otherwise bald head, entered the room and presented a note to his mistress. "Who is it from?" she asked as she took it off the silver waiter. An old waiter, bearing the Andinnian crest.

"Mrs. Poole's housemaid has brought it, ma'am. She is waiting for an answer."

It was but a friendly note of invitation from a neighbour, asking Mrs. Andinnian and her two sons to go in that evening. For Karl, the second son, had come home for a two days' visit, and was just then writing letters in another room.

"Yes, we will go—if Adam has no engagement," said Mrs. Andinnian to herself, but half aloud. "Hewitt, go and tell Mr. Andinnian that I wish to speak with him."

The man went across the garden and through the wilderness of shrubs. There stood his master at an open gate, talking to a very pretty girl with bright hair and rosy cheeks

"My mistress wishes to see you, Mr. Adam."

Adam Andinnian turned round, a defiant expression on his haughty face, as if he did not like the interruption. He was a very fine man of some three-and-thirty years, tall and broad-shouldered, with his mother's cast of proud, handsome features, her fresh complexion, and her black hair. His eyes were dark grey, deeply set in the head, and rarely beautiful. His teeth also were remarkably good; white, even, and prominent, and he showed them very much.

"Tell my mother I'll come directly, Hewitt."

Hewitt went back with the message. The young lady who had turned to one of her own flower-beds, for the gardens joined, was bending over some budding tulips.

"I think they will be out next week, Mr. Andinnian," she looked round to say.

"Never mind the tulips," he answered after a pause, during which he had leaned on the iron railings, looking dark and haughty. "I want to hear more about this."

"There's nothing more to hear," was the young lady's answer.

"That won't do, Rose. Come here."

And she went obediently.

The house to which this other garden belonged was a humble, unpretending dwelling, three parts cottage, one part villa. A Mr. Turner lived in it with his wife and niece. The former was in good retail business in the town: a grocer: and he and his wife were as humble and unpretending as their dwelling. The niece, Rose, was different. Her father had been a lawyer in small local practice: and at his death Rose—her mother also dead—was taken by her uncle and aunt, who loved both her and her childish beauty. Since then she had lived with them, and they educated her well. She was a good girl: and in the essential points of mind, manner and appearance, a lady. But her position was of necessity a somewhat isolated one. With the tradespeople of the town Rose Turner did not care to mix: she felt that, however worthy, they were beneath her; quite of another order altogether: on the other hand, superior people would not associate with Miss Turner, or put so much as the soles of their shoes over the door-sill of the grocer's private house. At sixteen she had been sent to a finishing school: at eighteen she came back as pretty and as nice a girl as one of fastidious taste would wish to see.

Years before, Adam and Karl Andinnian had made friends with the little child: they continued to be intimate with her as brothers and sister. Latterly it had dawned on Mrs. Andinnian's perception that Adam and Miss Turner were a good deal together; certainly more than they need be. Adam had even come to neglect his flowers, that he so much loved, and to waste his time talking to Rose. It cannot be said that height, with pale, clearly-cut features and a remarkably nice expression of countenance. He had the deeply set, beautiful grey eyes of his brother; but his hair, instead of being black and straight, was brown and wavy. An attractive looking man, this Karl Andinnian.

"I am going out to post these letters," said Karl. "Can I do anything for you in the town, mother?"

The voice was attractive too. Low-toned, clear, melodious, full of truth: a voice to be trusted all over the world. Adam's voice was inclined to be harsh, and he had a loud way of speaking.

"Nothing in the town," replied Mrs. Andinnian: and now that you notice it, *her* voice was harsh too. "But you can go and ask your brother why he keeps me waiting. He is behind the shrubbery."

Karl left his letters on the table, traversed the garden, and found Adam with Miss Turner. They turned to wait his approach. A half doubt, he knew not wherefore, dawned for the first time on his mind.

"How are you this morning, Rose?" he asked, raising his hat with the ceremony one observes to an acquaintance, rather than to an intimate friend. "Adam, the mother seems vexed: you are keeping her waiting, she says, and she wishes to know the reason of it."

"I forgot all about it," cried Adam. "Deuce take the thorn!"

For just at that moment he had run a thorn into his finger. Karl began talking with Miss Turner: there was no obligation on *him* to return forthwith to the house.

"Go back, will you, Karl, and tell the mother I am sorry I forgot it. I shall be there as soon as you are."

"A genteel way of getting rid of me," thought Karl, with a laugh, as he at once turned to plunge into the wide shrubbery. "Good day to you, Rose."

But when he was fairly beyond their sight Karl's face became as grave as a judge's. "Surely Adam is not drifting into anything serious in that quarter!" ran his thoughts. "It would never do."

"Well—have you seen Adam?" began Mrs. Andinnian, when he entered.

"Yes. He is coming immediately."

"*Coming!*"—and she curled her vexed lips. "He ought to come. Who is he with, Karl?"

"With Miss Turner."

"What nonsense! Idling about with a senseless child!"

"I suppose it *is* nothing but nonsense?" spoke Karl, incautiously. "She—Miss Turner—would scarcely be the right woman in the right place."

His mother glanced at him sharply. "In *what* place?—what woman?"

"As Lady Andinnian."

Karl had angered his mother before in his life-time, but scarcely ever as now. She turned livid as death, and took up the first thing that came to her hand—a silver inkstand, kept for show, not use—and held it as if she would hurl it at his head.

"How *dare* you, sir, even in supposition, so traduce your brother?"

"I beg your pardon, mother. I spoke without thought."

As she was putting down the inkstand, Adam came in. He saw that something was amiss. Mrs. Andinnian spoke abruptly about the invitation for the evening, and asked if he would go. Adam said he could go, and she left the room to give, herself, a verbal answer to the waiting servant.

"What was the matter, Karl?"

"The mother was vexed at your staying with Rose Turner, instead of coming in. It was nonsense, she said, to be idling about with a senseless child. I—unfortunately, but quite unintentionally—added to her anger by remarking that I supposed it *was* nonsense, for she, Miss Turner, would scarcely be suitable for a Lady Andinnian."

"Just attend to your own affairs," growled Adam. "Keep yourself in your place."

Karl looked up with his sweet smile; answering with his frank and gentle voice. The smile and the voice acted like oil on the troubled waters.

"You know, Adam, that I should never think of interfering with you, or of opposing your inclinations. In the wide world, there's no one, I think, so anxious as I am for your happiness and welfare."

Adam did know it, and their hands met in true affection. Few brothers loved each other as did Adam and Karl Andinnian. Seeing them together thus, they were undoubtedly two fine young men—as their sailor father had once observed to his brother. But Karl, with his nameless air of innate goodness and refinement, looked the greater gentleman.

CHAPTER II.

LUCY CLEEVE.

LINGERING under the light of the sweet May moon, arm within arm, their voices hushed, their tread slow, went two individuals, whom few, looking upon them, could have failed to mistake for anything but lovers. Lovers they were, in heart, in mind, in thought: with as pure and passionate and ardent a love as ever was felt on this earth. And yet, no word, to tell of it, had ever been spoken between them.

It was one of those cases where love, all unpremeditated, had grown up, swiftly, surely, silently. Had either of them known that they were drifting into it, they might have had sufficient prudence to separate forthwith, before the danger grew into certainty. For he, the obscure and nearly portionless young soldier, had the sense to see that he would be regarded as no fit match for the daughter of Colonel and the Honourable Mrs. Cleeve; both of high lineage and inordinately proud of it into the bargain; and she, Lucy Cleeve, knew that, for all her good descent, she was nearly portionless too, and that her future husband, whomsoever he might turn out to be, must possess a vast deal more of this world's goods than did Lieutenant Andinnian. Ay, and of family also. But, there it was: they had drifted into this mutual love unconsciously: each knew that it was for all time: and that, in comparison, "family" and "goods" were to them as nothing.

"And so Miss Blake is back, Lucy?"

The words, spoken by Mr. Andinnian, broke one of those long pauses of delicious silence, that in themselves seem like tastes of paradise. Lucy Cleeve's tones in answer were low and soft as his.

"She came to-day. I hardly knew her. Her hair is all put on the top of her head: and—and—"

Lucy stopped. "And is of another colour," she had been about to conclude. But it might not be quite good-natured to say it, even to one to whom she would willingly have given her whole heart's confidence. Reared in the highest of all high and true principles, and naturally gifted with them, Lucy had a peculiar dread of deceit: her dislike of it extended even to the changing of the colour of the hair. But she was also of that sweet and generous disposition that shrinks from speaking a slighting word of another. She resumed hastily and with a slight laugh.

"Theresa is in love with Rome; and especially with its cardinals. One of them was very civil to her, Karl."

"About this picnic to-morrow, Lucy. Are you to be allowed to go?"

"Yes, now Theresa's here. Mamma would not have liked to send me without some one from home: and the weather is scarcely hot enough for herself to venture. Do—you—go?" she asked timidly.

"Yes."

There was silence again: each heart beating in unison. The prospect of a whole day together, spent amidst glens, and woods, and dales, was too much for utterance.

For the past twelve months, Lieutenant Andinnian's regiment had been quartered at Winchester. On his arrival, he had brought with him a letter of introduction to one of the clergy there—a good old man, whose rectory was on the outskirts of the town. The Rev. Mr. Blake and his wife took a great fancy to the young lieutenant, and made much of him. Living with them at that time was a relative, a Miss Blake. This lady was an orphan: she had a small fortune, somewhere between two and three hundred a year: and she stayed sometimes with the Blakes, sometimes with the Cleeves, to whom she and the Blakes were likewise related.

A novel writer has to tell secrets: not always pleasant ones. In this case, it must be disclosed that the one secret wish of Theresa Blake's life, to which her whole energies (in a ladylike way) were directed, was—to get married, and to marry well. If we could see into the hearts of some other young ladies, especially when they have left the bloom of youth behind, we might find them filled with the same ardent longing. Hitherto Miss Blake's hopes had not been realized. She was not foolish enough to marry downright unwisely: and nothing eligible had come in her way. Considering that she was so very sensible a young woman—for good common sense was what Miss Blake prided herself upon—it was very simple of her to take up the notion she did—that the attractive young lieutenant's frequent visits to the rectory were made for her sake. She fell head over ears in love with him: she thought that his attentions (ordinary attentions in truth, and paid to her as the only young lady of a house where the other inmates were aged) spoke plainly of his love for her. Of what are called "flirtations" Theresa Blake had had enough, and to spare : but of true love she had hitherto known nothing. She ignored the difference in their years—for there was a difference —and she waited for the time when the young officer should speak out: her income joined to his and his pay, would make what she thought they could live very comfortably upon. Love softens difficulties as does nothing else in life ; before she knew Karl Andinnian, Miss Blake would have scorned the notion of taking any man who could not have offered her a settlement of a thousand pounds a year at least.

But now—what was Karl Andinnian's share in all this? Simply none. He had no more notion that the young lady was in love with him than that old Mrs. Blake was. If Miss Blake did not see the years that she had come to, he did; and would nearly as soon, as far as age went, have offered to marry his mother. To a young man of twenty-six, a woman of thirty-four looks quite old. And so, in this misapprehension —the one finding fresh food for her hopes day by day, the other at his ease in his utter unconsciousness—the summer and autumn had passed. At the close of autumn Miss Blake departed with some friends for the Continent, more particularly to visit Paris and Rome. But that it was a long-since-made engagement, and also that she had so wished to see those renowned places, she would not have torn herself away from the locality that contained Mr. Andinnian.

Shortly afterwards the Cleeves returned to Winchester, after a long absence. They resided without the town, just beyond Mr. Blake's rectory. Lucy Cleeve had been in the habit of spending nearly as much time at the rectory as at home: and it was from the never-tiring training of him and his good wife that Lucy had learnt to be the truly excellent girl she was. On the very day of her return, she and Karl Andinnian met: and—if it was not exactly love at first sight with them, it was something very like it; for each seemed drawn to the other by that powerful, sympathetic attraction that can no more be controlled than explained or accounted for. A few more meetings, and they loved for all time : and since then they had gone on living in a dream of happiness.

There they were, pacing together the rectory garden under the warm May moonlight. The rector had been called to a sick parishioner, and they had strolled out with him to the gate. Mrs. Blake, confined to her sofa, was unsuspicious as the day. Lucy, twenty years of age, was looked upon by her as a child still: and the old are apt to forget the sweet beguilements of their own long-past youth, and that the young of the present day can be drifting into the same.

"It is very pleasant; quite warm," spoke Mr. Andinnian. "Would you like another turn, Lucy?"

They both turned simultaneously without a word of assent from her, and paced side by side to the gate in a rapture of silence. Lucy quitted him to pluck a spray from the sweet-briar hedge; and then they turned again. The moon went behind a cloud.

"Take my arm, Lucy. It is getting quite dark."

She took it; the darkness affording the plea; and the night hid the blushes on her transparent cheeks. They were half-way down the walk, and Karl was bending his head to speak to her; his tones low, though their subject was nothing more than the projected party for the morrow; when some one who had approached the gate from the road, stood still there to look at them.

It was Miss Blake. She had that day returned from her Continental excursion, and taken up her abode, as arranged, at Colonel Cleeve's. Whether at the rectory or at Colonel Cleeve's, Miss Blake paid at the rate of one hundred a year for the accommodation; and then, as she said, she was independent. It was a private arrangement, one that she insisted on. Her sojourn abroad had not tended to cool one whit of her love for Mr. Andinnian; the absence had rather augmented it. She had come home with all her pulses bounding and her heart glowing at the prospect of seeing him again.

But—she saw him with some one else. The moon was out again in all her silvery brightness, and Miss Blake had keen eyes. She saw one on his arm, to whom he seemed to be whispering, to whose face his own was bent; one younger and fairer than she was—Lucy Cleeve. A certain possibility of what it might mean darted through her mind with a freezing horror that caused her to shiver. But only for a moment. She drove it away as absurd—and opened the gate with a sharp click. They turned at the sound of her footsteps and loosed arms. Mr. Andinnian doffed his hat in salutation, and held out his hand.

"Miss Blake!"

"I came with old John to fetch you, Lucy, wishing to see dear Mrs. Blake," she carelessly said in explanation, letting her hand lie in Karl's, as they turned to the house. "And it is a lovely night. John has gone round to the kitchens."

Coming into the light of the sitting-room, you could see what Miss Blake was like—and Lucy, also, for that matter. Miss Blake was tall, upright; and, if there was a fault in her exceedingly well-made figure, it was that it was too thin. Her features and complexion were very good, her eyes were watchful and had a green tinge; and the hair, originally red, had been converted into a kind of auburn that had more than one shade of colour on it. Altogether, Miss Blake was nice-looking; and she invariably dressed well, in the height of any fashion that might prevail. What with her well-preserved face, her large quantity of youthful hair, and her natty attire, she had an idea that she looked years and years less than her real age; as in fact she did.

And Lucy? Lucy was a gentle girl with a soft, sweet face; a face of intellect, and goodness, and sensibility. Her refined features were of the highest type; her clear eyes were of a remarkably light brown, the long eyelashes and the hair somewhat darker. By the side of the upright and always self-possessed Miss Blake—I had almost written self-asserting—she looked a timid shrinking child. What with Miss Blake's natural height, and the un-natural pyramid of hair on the top of her head, Lucy appeared short. But Lucy was not below the middle height of women.

"I wonder—I wonder how much he has seen of Lucy?" thought Miss Blake, beginning to watch and to listen, and to put in prompting questions here and there.

She contrived to gather that the lieutenant had been a tolerably frequent visitor at Colonel Cleeve's during the spring. She observed—and Miss Blake's observance was worth having—that his good-night to Lucy was spoken in a different tone from the one to herself: lower and softer.

"There *cannot* be anything between them! There cannot, surely, be!"

Nevertheless the very thought of it caused her face to grow cold as with a mortal sickness.

"I shall see to-morrow," she murmured. "They will be together at the picnic, and I shall see."

Miss Blake did see. Saw what, to her jealous eyes—ay, and to her cool ones—was proof positive. Lieutenant Andinnian and Miss Lucy Cleeve were lost in love the one for the other. In her conscientious desire to do her duty—and she did hope and believe that no other motive or passion prompted the step—Miss Blake, looking upon herself as a sort of guardian over Lucy's interests, disclosed her suspicions to Mrs. Cleeve. What would be a suitable match for herself, might be entirely unsuitable for Lucy.

Colonel Augustus and the Honourable Mrs. Cleeve were very excellent people, as people go : their one prominent characteristic—perhaps some would rather call it failing—being family pride. Colonel Cleeve could claim relationship, near or remote, with three lords and a Scotch duke; Mrs. Cleeve was a peer's daughter. Their only son was in India with his regiment : their only daughter, introduced and presented but the last year, was intended to make a good marriage, both as regards rank and wealth. They knew what a charming girl she was, and they believed she could not fail to be sought. One gentleman, indeed, had asked for her in London; that is, had solicited of the Colonel the permission to ask for her. He was a banker's son. Colonel Cleeve thanked him with courtesy, but said that his daughter must not marry beneath her own rank : he and her mother hoped she would be a peeress. It may therefore be judged what was the consternation caused, when Miss Blake dropped a hint of her observations.

The remark already made, as to Mrs. Blake's blind unsuspicion, held good in regard to Colonel Cleeve and his wife. They had likewise taken a fancy to the attractive young lieutenant and were never backward in welcoming him to their house. *And yet they never glanced at Lucy's interests in the matter;* they never supposed that she likewise could be awake to the same attractions; or that her attractions had charms for the lieutenant. How frequent these cases of blindness occur in the world, let the world answer. Colonel and Mrs. Cleeve would as soon have suspected that Lucy was falling in love with the parish clerk. And why? Because the notion that any one, so much beneath them in family and position as Mr. Andinnian, should aspire to her, or that she could stoop to think of him, never would have entered into their exclusive imaginations, unless put there.

Mrs. Cleeve, dismayed, sick, frightened, but always mild and gentle, begged of Lucy to say that it was a cruel mistake; and that there was "nothing" between her and Mr. Andinnian. Lucy, amidst her blinding tears, answered that nothing whatever had been spoken between them. But she was too truthful, too honest, to deny the implication that there existed love. Colonel Cleeve sent for Mr. Andinnian.

The young man was just coming in from a full-dress parade when the note arrived. It was a peremptory one. He walked up at once, not staying to put off his regimentals. Colonel Cleeve, looking the thorough gentleman he was, and wearing his customary blue frock with a white cambric frill at his breast, met him at the door of his library. He was short and slight, and had mild blue eyes. His white hair was cut nearly close, and his forehead and head were so fair that at first sight it gave him the appearance of being powdered. The servant closed the door upon them.

That Karl Andinnian was, as the phrase runs, "taken to" by the plain questioning of the Colonel, cannot be denied. It was plunged into without preface. "Is it true that there is an attachment between you and my daughter? Is it true, sir, that you have been making love to her?"

For a short while Karl was silent. The Colonel saw his embarrassment. It was only the momentary embarrassment of surprise, and, perhaps, of vexation: but Karl, guileless and strictly honourable, never thought of not meeting the matter with perfect truth.

"That there does exist affection between me and your daughter, sir, I cannot deny," he replied with diffidence. "At least, I can answer for myself—that the truest and tenderest love man is, or, as I believe, can be, capable of, I feel for her. As to making love to her, I have not done it consciously. But—we have been a great deal together; and I fear Miss Cleeve must have read my heart, as—as——"

"As what, Mr. Andinnian?" was the stern question.

"As I have read her, I was going to presume to say," replied Karl, his voice and eyes alike drooping. Colonel Cleeve felt confounded. He would have called this the very height of impudence, but that the young man, standing before him, was so indisputably refined, so modest, and spoke as though he were grieved to the heart.

"And, pray, what could you have promised yourself by thus presuming to love my daughter?"

"I promised myself nothing. On my word of honour as a gentleman, sir, I have not been holding out any kind of hopes or promises to myself. I believe," added the young man, with the open candour so characteristic of him, "that I have been too happy in the present, in Miss Cleeve's daily society—for hardly a day passed that we did not see each other—to cast so much as a thought to the future."

"Well, sir, what excuse have you to make for this behaviour? Do you see its folly?"

"I see it now. I see it for the first time, Colonel Cleeve. For—I—suppose—you will not let me aspire to win her?"

The words were given with slow deprecation: as if he hardly dared to speak them.

"What do you think, yourself, about it?" sharply asked the Colonel. "Do you consider yourself a suitable match for Miss Cleeve? In any way? In *any* way, Mr. Andinnian?"

"I am afraid not, sir."

"You are *afraid* not! Good heavens! Your family—pardon me for alluding to it, Mr. Andinnian, but there are moments in a life-time, and this is one, when plain speaking becomes a necessity. Your family have but risen from the ranks, sir, as we soldiers say, and not much above the ranks either. Miss Cleeve *is* Miss Cleeve: my daughter, and a peer's grand-daughter."

"It is all true, sir."

"So much for that unsuitability. And then we come to means. What are yours, Mr. Andinnian?"

The young man lifted his head and his honest grey eyes to the half-affrighted but generally calm face. He could but tell the truth at all times without equivocation.

"I fear you will consider my means even more ineligible than my family," he said. "I have my pay and two hundred pounds a year. At my mother's death another two hundred a year will come to me."

Colonel Cleeve drew down his lips. "And that is all—in the present and in the future?"

"All I can reckon upon with any certainty. When my brother shall succeed Sir Joseph Andinnian, he may do something more for me. My father suggested it in his last testamentary paper: and I think he will do it: I believe he will. But of this I cannot be certain; and in any case it may not be much."

Colonel Cleeve paused a moment. He wished the young man would not be so straightforwardly candid, so transparently single-minded, putting himself, as it were, in all honour in his hands. It left the Colonel—the mildest man in the world by nature—less loophole to get into a proper passion. In the midst of it all, he could not help liking the young fellow.

"Mr. Andinnian, every word you say only makes the case worse. Two barriers, each in itself insurmountable, lie, by your own showing, between you and my daughter. The bare idea of making her your wife is an insult to her; were it carried into a fact—I condemn myself to speak of so impossible a thing unwillingly—it would blight her life and happiness for ever."

Karl's pale face grew red as his coat. "These are harsh words, Colonel Cleeve."

"They are true ones, sir: and justifiable. Lucy has been reared in the notions befitting her rank. She has been taught to expect that when she marries her home will be at least as well-appointed as the one she is taken from. My son is a great expense to me, and my means are limited as compared with my position—I am plain with you, you see, Mr. Andinnian; you have been so with me—but still we live as our compeers live, and have things in accordance about us. But what could *you* offer Lucy?—allowing that in point of family you were entitled to mate with her. Why, a lodging in a barrack; a necessity to tramp with you after the regiment at home and abroad."

Karl stood silent, the pain of mortification on his closed lips. Colonel Cleeve put the case rather extremely; but it was near the truth, after all.

"And you would wish to bring this disgrace, this poverty, this blight on Lucy! If you——"

"No, sir, I would not," was the impulsive interruption. "What do you take me for? Lucy's happiness is a great deal dearer to me than my own."

"If you have one spark of honour, Mr. Andinnian—and until now I believed you had your full share of it—if you do care in ever so small a degree for my daughter's comfort and her true welfare; in short, if you are a man and a gentleman, you will aid me in striving to undo the harm that has been done."

"I will strive to do what is best to be done," replied Karl, knowing the fiat that must come, and feeling that his heart was breaking.

"Very well. Our acquaintance with you must close from this hour; and I must ask you to give me your word of honour never to attempt to hold future communication with my daughter in any way; never to meet her in society even, if it be possible for you to stay away and avoid it. In future you and Miss Cleeve are strangers."

There was a dead silence. Karl seemed to be looking at vacancy, over the Colonel's head.

"You do not speak, Mr. Andinnian."

He roused himself with a sort of shudder. "I believe I was lost in glancing at the blighted life *mine* will be, Colonel Cleeve." And the Colonel, in spite of his self-interest, felt a kind of pity for the feelings that he saw were stung to the quick.

"Do you refuse to comply with my mandate?"

"No, sir. Putting the affair before me in the light you have put it, no alternative is left me. I see, too, that circumstanced as I am—and as *she* is—my dream of love has been nothing but madness. On my word of honour, Colonel Cleeve, could I have looked at the matter at first as I look at it now, and foreseen that we were destined to—to care for each other, I would have flown Miss Cleeve's presence."

"These regrets often come late in the day, Mr. Andinnian," was the rather sarcastic answer.

"They have in this case."

"Then I may rely on your honour?"

"You may indeed, sir. But that I see how right and reasonable your fiat is; how essential for Lucy's sake; I could hardly have complied with it; for to part with her will be rending myself from every joy of life. I give you my sacred word of honour that I will not henceforth attempt to hold communication of any kind with her; I will not meet her if I can avoid it. That I should live to say this calmly!" added Karl to himself.

"I expected no less from you, Mr. Andinnian," spoke the Colonel, stiffly but courteously. "I am bound to say that you have met this most lamentable affair in a proper spirit. I see I may rely upon you."

"You may rely upon me as you would rely upon yourself," said the young officer earnestly. "Should the time ever come that my fortunes ascend—it seems next door to an impossibility now, but such things have been heard of—and Lucy be still free——"

"That could make no alteration: want of fortune is not the only bar," haughtily interrupted Colonel Cleeve. "The present is enough for us, Mr. Andinnian: let us leave the future."

"True. The present is greatly enough; and I beg your pardon, Colonel Cleeve. I will keep my word both in the spirit and the letter. And now, I would make one request to you, sir—that you will allow me to see Lucy for an instant before we finally part."

"That you may exact some foolish promise from her?—of waiting, or something of that kind?" was the angry rejoinder.

"I told you that you might rely upon me," replied Karl with sad emphasis. "Colonel Cleeve, don't you see what a bitter blow this is to me?" he burst forth, with an emotion he had not betrayed throughout the interview. "It may be bitter to Lucy also. Let us say a word of good-bye to each other for the last time."

Colonel Cleeve hardly knew what to do. He did not like to say No; he did not like to say Yes. That it was bitter to one, he saw; that it might be bitter to the other, he quite believed: and he had a soft place in his heart.

"I will trust you in this as I trust you in the other, Mr. Andinnian. It must be good-bye only, you understand: and a brief one."

He quitted the room, and sent Lucy in. Almost better for them both that he had not done so—for these partings are nearly as cruel as death. To them both, this severing asunder for all time seemed worse than death. Lucy, looking quiet and simple in her coloured summer muslin, stood shivering.

"I could not depart without begging you to forgive me, Lucy," Karl said, his tone less firm than usual with emotion and pain. "I ought to have exercised more thought; to have foreseen what must be the inevitable ending. Colonel Cleeve has my promise that I will never again seek you in any way: that from henceforth we shall be as strangers. Oh my darling! —I may surely call you so in this last hour!—this is painful I fear to you as to me."

She went quite close to him, her eyes cast up to his with a piteous mourning in their depths; eyes too sad for tears.

"They have told me the same, Karl. There is no hope at all for us. But I—I wish in my turn to say something to you. Karl"—and her voice sank to a whisper, and she put out her hand as if inviting him to take it—"I shall never forget you; I shall never care for you less than I do now."

He did not take her hand. He took her. Almost beside himself with the bitter pain, Karl Andinnian so far forgot himself as to clasp this young girl to his heart: as to rain down on her sweet face the sad kisses from his lips. But he remembered his promise to Colonel Cleeve, and said never a word of hope for the future.

"Forgive me, Lucy; this and all. Perhaps Colonel Cleeve would hardly grudge it to us when it is to be our last meeting on earth."

"In the years to come," she sobbed, her face lying under his wet tears, "when we shall be an old man and woman, they may let us meet again. Oh, Karl, yes! and we can talk together of that best world, Heaven, where there will be no separation. We shall be drawing near its gates then, looking out for it."

A slight tap at the door, and Miss Blake entered. She had come to summon Lucy. Seeing what she did see—the tears, the emotion, the intertwined hands, Miss Blake looked—looked very grim and stately.

"Lucy, Colonel and Mrs. Cleeve have sent me to request you to go to them."

"God bless you, Lucy," he whispered. "God bless you, my best and dearest. Good-bye, for ever."

With what seemed a cool bow to Miss Blake and never a word, for in truth he was unequal to speaking it, Lieutenant Andinnian passed into the hall, caught up his hat and sword that he had left there, and let himself out, buckling on the latter. Lucy had her hands to her face, hiding it. Miss Blake waited.

"My dear Lucy, what am I to say?"

"Tell them that I wish to stay here alone, for a few minutes. Tell them that Mr. Andinnian is gone."

Miss Blake, her hard, thin lips compressed with the cruellest pain woman can ever feel, took her way back again. Only herself knew, or ever would know, what this dreadful blow was to her—the finding that she had been mistaken in Karl Andinnian's love. For anguish, such as this, women have lost life. One small drop, taking from the bitterness, there was—to know that he and his true love had bidden each other adieu for ever.

"Perhaps—in a few weeks, or months to come—when he shall have recovered his folly—he and I may be friends again," she murmured. "Nay—who knows—may even become something warmer and dearer: his feeling for that child can only be a passing fancy. Something warmer and dearer," softly repeated Miss Blake, as she traversed the hall.

"Lucy will come to you presently, Mrs. Cleeve. There is no hurry now: Mr. Andinnian is gone."

"What is Lucy doing, Theresa?"

"Sobbing silently, I think: she scarcely spoke to me. Fancy her being so foolish!"

Mrs. Cleeve went at once to the library. She and her husband were as much alike as possible: mild, good, unemotional people who hated to inflict pain: with a great love for their daughter, and a very great sense of their own importance and position in the world, as regarded pride of birth.

"Oh, Lucy dear, it was obliged to be. You are reasonable, and must know it was. But, from my very heart, I am sorry for you: and I shall always take blame to myself for not having been more cautious than to allow you to become intimate with Mr. Andinnian. It seems to me as though I had been living with a veil before my eyes."

"It is over now: let it pass," was Lucy's faint answer.

"Yes, dear, it is over. All over for good. By this time twelvemonth, Lucy, I hope you will be happily married, and forget this painful episode in your life. Not, my child, that we shall like to part with you: only—it will be for your own welfare and happiness."

Lucy pressed her slender white fingers upon her brow, and looked at her mother. There was a puzzled, doubting expression in her eyes that spoke of bewilderment.

"Mamma," she said slowly, "I think perhaps I did not understand you. I have parted with Mr. Andinnian, as you and papa wished, and as—as I suppose it was right I should do; I shall never, I hope, do anything against your will. But —to try to make me marry will be quite a different thing. Were you and papa to tell me that you insisted on it, I could only resist. And I should resist to the end."

Mrs. Cleeve saw that she had not been wise. To allude to any such future contingency when Lucy was smarting under the immediate pain of separation, was a mistake. Sighing gently, she sat down and took her daughter's hand, stroking it fondly.

"Lucy, my dear, I will relate to you a little matter of my own early experience," she began in a hushed tone. "*I* once had one of the affairs of the heart, as they are called. The young man was just as attractive as Mr. Andinnian, and quite worthy. But circumstances were unfavourable, and we had to part. I thought that all worth living for in life was over. I said that I should never care for any one else, and never marry. Not so very long afterwards, Captain Cleeve presented himself. Before he said a word to me, Lucy, before I knew what he was thinking of, I had learnt to like and esteem him: and I became his wife."

"And did you love him?" questioned Lucy, in great surprise.

"Oh dear no. Not with the kind of love I had felt for another—the kind of love that I presume you are feeling for Mr. Andinnian. Such love never comes back to the heart a second time. But, Lucy, my married life has been perfectly successful and happy. Once that great passion is over, you see, the heart is at rest, calmness and reason have supervened. Rely on it, my dear, your married life will be all the happier for this experience connected with Mr. Andinnian."

Lucy said no more. *She* knew. And Mrs. Cleeve thought how dutiful her daughter was.

On the following day, a letter came to the Colonel from Karl. A well-written and sensible letter; not of rebellion, but of acquiescence. While it deplored his fate in separating from Lucy; it bowed to the necessity that enforced it. A note was enclosed for Lucy: it was unsealed, in case the Colonel should wish to read before giving it to her. The Colonel did so: he did not fear treason from Karl, but it was as well to be on the safe side and assure himself there was none. It contained only a few words, rather more coherent than Karl's emotion of the previous day had allowed him to speak: and it bade her adieu for ever. Colonel Cleeve sent both notes to his daughter, and then lost himself in a reverie: from which he was aroused by the entrance of his wife.

"Lucinda, that is really a most superior young man: high-principled, true-hearted. A pity but he had rank and money."

"Who is a superior young man?" asked Mrs. Cleeve, not having the clue.

"Lieutenant Andinnian."

CHAPTER III.

DONE AT SUNSET.

The June sun rode gaily in the bright-blue skies, and the sweet June Roses were in bloom. Mrs. Andinnian, entirely unconscious of the blight that had fallen on her younger son, was placidly making the home happiness (as she believed) of the elder. Had she known of Karl's sorrow, she would have given to it but a passing thought.

There was peace in the home again. The vexation regarding their young lady-neighbour had long ago subsided in Mrs. Andinnian's mind. She had spoken seriously and sharply to Adam upon the point—which was an entirely new element in his experience; telling him how absurd and unsuitable it was that he, one of England's future baronets, and three-and-thirty years of age already, should waste his hours in frivolous talk with a girl beneath him. Adam heard her in silence, smiling a little, and quite docile. He rejoined in a joking tone.

"All this means, I suppose, mother, that you would not tolerate Miss Turner as my wife?"

"Never, Adam, never. You would have to choose between myself and her. And I have been a loving mother to you."

"All right. Don't worry yourself. There's no cause for it."

From this time—the conversation was in April, at the close of Karl's short visit to them—the trouble ceased. Adam Andinnian either did not meet the girl so much: or else he timed his interviews more cautiously. In May Miss Turner went away on a visit: Adam seemed to have dismissed her from his mind: and Mrs. Andinnian forgot that she had ever been anxious.

Never a word of invitation had come from Sir Joseph. During this same month, May, Mrs. Andinnian, her patience worn out, had written to Foxwood, proffering a visit for herself and Adam. At the end of a fortnight's time, she received an answer. A few words of shaky writing, in Sir Joseph's own hand. He had been very ill, he told her, which was the cause of the delay in replying, as he wished to write himself. Now he was somewhat better, and gaining strength. When able to entertain her and her son—which he hoped would be soon—he should send for them. It would give him great pleasure to receive them, and to make the acquaintance of his heir.

That letter had reached Mrs. Andinnian the first day of June. Some three weeks had elapsed since, and no summons had come. She was growing just a little impatient again. Morning after morning, while she dressed, the question always crossed her mind: will there be a letter to-day from Foxwood? On this lovely June morning, with the scent of the midsummer flowers wafting in through the open chamber window, it filled her mind as usual.

They breakfasted early. Adam's active garden habits induced it. When Mrs. Andinnian descended, he was in the breakfast-room, scanning the pages of some new work on horticulture. He wore a new suit of grey, and looked well and handsome; unusually so in his mother's eyes, for he had only returned the past evening from a few days' roving absence.

"Good morning, Adam."

He advanced to kiss his mother: his even white teeth and his grey eyes as beautiful as they could well be. Mrs. Andinnian's fond and admiring heart leaped up with a bound.

"The nonsense people write whose knowledge is superficial!" he said, with a gay laugh. "I have detected half a dozen errors in this book already."

"No doubt. What book is it?"

He held it out to her, open at the title-page. "I bought it yesterday at a railway-stall."

"What a nice morning it is!" observed Mrs. Andinnian, as she was busy with the cups.

"Lovely. It is Midsummer Eve. I have been out at work these two hours."

"Adam, I think that must be the postman's step," she remarked presently. "Some one is going round to the door."

"From Karl, perhaps," he said with indifference, for he had plunged into his book again.

Hewitt came in; one letter only on the silver waiter. He presented it to his master. Adam, absorbed in his pages, took the letter and laid it on the table without looking up. Something very like a cry from his mother startled him. She had caught up the letter and was gazing at the address. For it was one that had never before been seen there.

"Sir Adam Andinnian, Bart."

"Oh, my son! It has come at last."

"*What* has come?" cried he in surprise. "Oh, I see:— Sir Joseph must be dead. Poor old fellow! What a sad thing!"

But it was not exactly Sir Joseph's death that Mrs. Andinnian had been thinking of. The letter ran as follows:—

FOXWOOD, June 22nd.

"DEAR SIR,—I am truly sorry to have to inform you of the death of my old friend, and many years' patient, Sir Joseph Andinnian. He had been getting better slowly, but we thought surely; and his death at last was sudden and quite unexpected. I have taken upon myself to give a few necessary orders in anticipation of your arrival here.

"I am, Sir Adam, very sincerely yours,
"Sir Adam Andinnian." "WILLIAM MOORE.

The breakfast went on nearly in silence. Mrs. Andinnian was deep in thoughts and plans. Sir Adam, poring over his book while he ate, did not seem to be at all impressed with the importance of having gained a title.

"When shall you start, Adam?"

"Start?" he returned, glancing up. "For Foxwood? Oh, in a day or two."

"*In a day or two!*" repeated his mother, with surprised emphasis. "Why, what do you mean?"

"Just that, mother."

"You should be off in half an hour. You must, Adam."

"Not I. There's no need of hurry," he added, with careless good-humour.

"But there is need of it," she answered.

"Why? Had Sir Joseph been dying and wished to see me, I'd not have lost a single moment: but it is nothing of the kind, poor man. He is dead, unfortunately: and, therefore, no cause for haste exists."

"Some one ought to be there."

"Not at all. The Mr. Moore who writes—some good old village doctor, I conclude—will see to things."

"But why should you not go at once, Adam?" she persisted. "What is preventing you?"

"Nothing prevents me. Except that I hate to be hurried off anywhere. And I—I only came back to the garden yesterday."

"The garden!—that's what it is," resentfully thought Mrs. Andinnian. He read on in silence.

"Adam, if you do not go, I shall."

"Do, mother," he said, readily. "Go, if you would like to, and take Hewitt. I hate details of all kinds, you know; and if you will go, and take them on yourself, I shall be truly obliged. Write me word which day the funeral is fixed for, and I will come for it."

Perhaps in all her life Mrs. Andinnian had never resented anything in her favourite son as she was resenting this. She had looked forward to this accession of fortune with an eager anxiety which none could suspect: and now that it was come, he was treating it with this cool indifference! Many a time and oft had she indulged a vision of the day when she should drive in to take possession of Foxwood, her handsome son, the inheritor, seated beside her.

"One of my sons ought to be there," she said, coldly. "If you will not go, Adam, I shall telegraph to Karl."

"I will telegraph for you," he replied, with provoking good-humour. "Karl will be the very fellow: he has ten times the head for business that I have. Let him act for me in all things, exactly as though it were he who succeeded: I give him carte blanche. It will save all trouble to you."

Sir Adam Andinnian declined to be shaken out of his resolve and his inertness. In what might be called a temper, Mrs. Andinnian departed straight from the breakfast-table for the railway-station, to take the train. Her son duly accompanied her to see her safely away: she had refused to take Hewitt: and then he despatched a telegram to Karl, telling him to join his mother at Foxwood. Meantime, while these, the lady and the message, went speeding on their respective ways, the new baronet beguiled away the day's passing hours amongst his flowers, and shot a few small birds that were interfering with some choice seedlings just springing up.

Lieutenant Andinnian received the message promptly. But, following the fashion much in vogue amidst telegraphic messages, it was not quite as clear as daylight. Karl read that Sir Joseph was dead, that his mother was either going or gone to Foxwood; that she was waiting for him, and he was to join her without delay. But whether he was to join her at her own home and accompany her to Foxwood, or whether he was to proceed direct to Foxwood, lay in profound obscurity. The fault was not in Sir Adam's wording; but in the telegraph people's carelessness.

"Now which is it that I am to do?" debated Karl, puzzling over the sprawling words from divers points of view. The words did not help him: and he decided to proceed *home;* he thought his mother must be waiting for him there. "It must be that," he said: "Adam has gone hastening on to Foxwood, and the mother is staying for me to accompany her. Poor Uncle Joseph! And to think that I never once saw him in life!"

Mr. Andinnian had no difficulty in obtaining leave of absence: and he started on his journey. He was somewhat changed. Though only a month had gone by since the severance from Lucy Cleeve, the anguish had told upon him. His brother officers, noting the sad abstraction he was often plunged in, the ultra-strict fulfilment of his duties, as if life were made up of parades and drill and all the rest of it, told him in joke that he was getting into a bad way. They knew naught of what had happened; of the fresh spring love that had made his heart and this earth alike a paradise, or of its abrupt ending. "My poor horse has had to be shot, you know"—which was a fact; "and I can't forget him," Mr. Andinnian one day replied, reciprocating the joke.

The shades of the midsummer night were gathering as Karl neared the house of his mother. He walked up from the terminus, choosing the field-path, and leaving his portmanteau to be sent after him. The glowing fires of the departed sun had left the west, but streaks of gold where he had set illumined the heavens. The air was still and soft, the night balmy; a few stars flickered in the calm blue firmament: the moon was well above the horizon. This pathway over the fields ran parallel with the highroad. As Mr. Andinnian paced it, his umbrella in his hand, there suddenly broke upon his ears a kind of uproar, marring strangely the peaceful stillness of the night. Some stirring commotion, as of a mass of people, seemed to be approaching.

"What is it, I wonder?" he said to himself: and for a moment or two he halted and stared over the border of the field and through the intervening hedge beyond. By what his sight could make out, he thought some policemen were in front, walking with measured tread; behind came a confused mob, following close on their heels: but the view was too uncertain to show this distinctly.

"Some poor prisoner they are bringing in from the country," thought Mr. Andinnian, as the commotion passed on towards the town, and he continued his way.

"This is a true Midsummer Eve night," he said to himself, when the hum of the noise and the tramping had died away, and he glanced at the weird shadows that stood out from hedges and trees. "Just the night for ghosts to come abroad, and—— Stay, though: it is not on Midsummer Eve that ghosts come, I think. What is the popular superstition for the night? Young girls go out and see the shadowy forms of their future husbands? Is that it? I don't remember. What matter if I did? Such romance has died out for me."

He drew near his home. On the left lay the cottage of Mr. Turner. Its inmates seemed to be unusually astir within it, for lights shone from nearly every window. A few yards further Karl turned into his mother's grounds by a private gate.

Their own house looked, on the contrary, all dark. Karl could not see that so much as the hall lamp was lighted. A sudden conviction flashed over him that he was wrong, after all; that it was to Foxwood he ought to have gone.

"My mother and Adam and all the world are off to it, no doubt," he said as he looked up at the dark windows, after knocking at the door. "Deuce take the telegraph!"

The door was opened by Hewitt: Hewitt with a candle in his hand. That is, the door was drawn a few inches back, and the man's face appeared in the aperture. Karl was seized with a sudden panic: for he had never seen, in all his life, a face blanched as that was, or one so full of horror.

"What is the matter?" he involuntarily exclaimed, under his breath.

Ay, what was the matter? Hewitt, the faithful serving man of many years, threw up his hands when he saw Karl, and cried out aloud before he told it. His master, Sir Adam, had shot Martin Scott.

Karl Andinnian stood against the doorpost inside as he listened; stood like one bereft of motion. For a moment he could put no questions: but it crossed his mind that Hewitt must be mad, and was telling some fable of an excited brain.

Not so. It was all too true. Adam Andinnian had deliberately shot the young medical student, Martin Scott. And Hewitt, poor Hewitt, had been a witness to the deed.

"Is he dead?" gasped Karl. And it was the first word he spoke.

"Stone dead, sir. The shot entered his heart. 'Twas done at sunset. He was carried into Mr. Turner's place, and is lying there."

A confused remembrance of the lights he had seen arose to Karl's agitated brain. He pressed his hand on his brow and stared at Hewitt. For a moment or two, he thought he himself must be going mad.

"And where is he—my brother?"

"The police have taken him away, Mr. Karl. Two of them happened to be passing about the time of the commotion."

And Karl knew that the prisoner he had met in custody, with the guardians of the law around and the trailing mob behind, was his brother, Sir Adam Andinnian."

CHAPTER IV.

THE TRIAL.

THE tidings of the unfortunate act committed by Adam Andinnian (most people said it must have been an accident) were bruited abroad far and wide. Circumstances conspired to give to it an unusual notoriety; and for more than the traditional nine days it remained a wonder in men's minds. Sir Adam's recent accession to the family honours; the utter want of adequate motive; the name of the young lady said to be mixed up with it: all this tended to arouse the public interest. That a gentleman of peaceful tendencies, an educated man and new baronet should take up his gun and shoot another in calm deliberation, was well nigh incredible. All kinds of reports, true and untrue, were floating. Public interest was not allowed to flag. Before a sufficient space of time had elapsed for that, the period of the trial came on.

Sir Adam Andinnian was not fated, as too many prisoners are, to languish out months of suspense in prison. The calamity occurred towards the end of June; the assizes were held in July. Almost before his final examination by the magistrates had concluded, or the coroner's inquest (protracted after the fashion of inquests, but in this case without any sufficient reason) had returned its verdict, the summer assizes were upon the county. The magistrates had committed Sir Adam Andinnian to take his trial for wilful murder; the coroner's jury for manslaughter.

But now—what effect does the reader suppose this most awful blow must have had on Mrs. Andinnian? If any one ever deserved commiseration it was surely she. To every mother it would have been terrible. To her it was worse than terrible. She loved her son with the love only lavished on an idol; she had gone forth to his new inheritance in all the pride of her fond heart, counting every day, ay, and every hour, until **he** should gladden it with his presence. If any mortal man

D

stood on a pinnacle just then above all his fellows in her estimation, that man was her handsome son, Sir Adam Andinnian. And oh! the desolation that fell upon her when the son for whom she cared not, Karl, arrived at Foxwood to break the news.

And Karl? Hardly less keen, if any, was the blow upon him. Until then he did not know how very warm and true was his affection for his brother. Staggering back to the town the same night after his interview with Hewitt—and it seemed to Karl Andinnian that he did really stagger, under the weight of his affliction—he found the prisoner at the police station, and was allowed to see him. Adam did not appear to feel his position at all. Karl thought the passion —or whatever other ill feeling it might have been that prompted him to the fatal deed—was swaying him still. He was perfectly calm and self-possessed, and sat quite at ease while the chief of the station took down sundry reports in writing from the policeman who brought in the prisoner.

"I have done nothing that I regret," he said to Karl. "The man has but got his deserts. I should do it again to-morrow under the same provocation."

"But, Adam, think of the consequences to yourself," gasped Karl, aghast with dismay at this dangerous admission in the hearing of the officers.

"Oh, as to consequences, I shall be quite ready to take them," returned the prisoner, drawing himself up haughtily. "I never yet did aught that I was ashamed to acknowledge afterwards."

The Inspector ceased writing for a moment and turned round. "Sir Adam Andinnian, I would advise you for your own sake to be silent. Least said is soonest mended, you know, sir. A good rule to remember in all cases."

"Very good indeed, Wall," readily assented Sir Adam— who had previously been on speaking terms with the Inspector. "But if you think I shall attempt to disown what I've done, you are mistaken."

"It must have been an accident," urged poor Karl in a low tone, almost as though he were suggesting it. "I told Hewitt so."

"Hewitt knows better: he saw me take up the gun, level it, and shoot him," was the reply of Sir Adam, asserted openly. "Look here, Wall. The fellow courted his fate; *courted* it. I had assured him that if he dared to offend in a certain way again, I would shoot him as I'd shoot a dog. He set me at defiance and did it. Upon that, I carried out my promise and shot him. I could not break my word, you know."

Just then a doubt crossed the Inspector's mind—as he related afterwards—that Sir Adam Andinnian was not in his right senses.

"And the mother?" breathed Karl.

"*There's* the worst of it," returned Sir Adam, his tone quickly changing to grave concern. "For her sake I could almost regret it. You must go off to Foxwood to-morrow, Karl, and break it to her."

What a task it was! Never in all Karl's life had one like unto it been imposed upon him. With the early morning he started for Foxwood; and it seemed to him that he would rather have started to his grave.

It was perhaps somewhat singular that during the short period of time intervening before the trial, Lieutenant Andinnian should have been gazetted to his company. It gave Karl no pleasure. The rise he had hoped for, that was to have brought him so much satisfaction, could now but be productive of pain. If the trial resulted in the awful sentence—Condemnation—Karl would not of course continue in the army. No, nor could he with any inferior result; save and except acquittal. Karl felt this. It was a matter that admitted of no alternative. To remain one amidst his fellow officers with his only brother disgraced and punished, was not to be thought of. And Karl would rather have remained the nameless lieutenant than have been gazetted captain.

The truest sympathy was felt for him, the utmost consideration evinced. Leave of absence was accorded him at his request, until the result of the trial should be known. He wanted his liberty to stand by his brother, and to make efforts for the defence. Make efforts! When the accused persisted in openly avowing he was guilty, what efforts could be made with any hope of success?

One of the hottest days that July has ever given us was that of the trial. The county town was filled from end to end; thousands of curious people had thronged in, hoping to get a place in court; or, at least, to obtain a sight of the baronet-prisoner. It was reported that but for the earnest pleadings of his mother there would have been no trial—Sir Adam would have pleaded guilty. It was whispered that she, the hitherto proud, overbearing, self-contained woman, went down on her knees to entreat him not to bring upon his head the worst and most extreme sentence known to England's law —as the said pleading guilty would have brought—but to give himself a chance of a more lenient sentence: perhaps of an acquittal. It was said that Captain Andinnian would have taken his place in the dock to countenance and stand by his brother, but was not permitted.

The trial was unusually short for one involving murder, and unusually interesting. Immediately after the judge had taken his seat in the morning, the prisoner was brought in. The crowded court, who had just risen to do homage to the judge, rose again amidst stir and excitement. Strangers, straining their eager eyes, saw, perhaps with a momentary feeling of surprise, as grand a gentleman as any present. A tall, commanding, handsome man, with a frank expression of countenance when he smiled, but haughty in repose; his white teeth, that he showed so much, and his grey eyes beautiful. He wore deep mourning for his uncle, Sir Joseph; and bowed to the judge with as much stately ceremony as though he were bowing before the Queen. On one of his fingers flashed a ring of rare beauty: an opal set round with diamonds. It had descended to him from his father. Captain Andinnian, in deep mourning also, sat at the table with the solicitors.

The chief witnesses, it may be said the only ones of consequence, were Thomas Hewitt the man servant, and Miss Rose Turner. A surgeon spoke to the cause of death — a shot through the heart—and a policeman or two gave some little evidence. Altogether not much. The story that came out to the world through the speeches of counsel, including those for the defence as well as for the prosecution, may be summed up as follows:

Mr. Andinnian (now Sir Adam) had a great friendship for a young lady neighbour who lived close by, with whom he and his mother had been intimate, and for whose best interests he had a lively regard. This was a Miss Rose Turner: a young lady (the counsel emphatically said) worthy of every consideration, and against whom not a breath of slight had been, or could be whispered. Some few months ago Miss Turner was introduced at a friend's house, to a medical student (the deceased) named Martin Scott. It had been ascertained, from inquiries set on foot since Martin Scott's death, that this man's private pursuits and character were not at all reputable; but that was of course (the counsel candidly added) no reason why he should have been killed.

In spite of Miss Turner's strong objection, Martin Scott persisted in offering her his attentions; and two or three times, to the young lady's great disgust, he had forcibly kissed her. These facts became known to Mr. Andinnian: and he, being of a hasty, passionate nature, unfortunately took up the matter warmly. Indignant that the young lady should have been subjected to anything so degrading, he sought an interview with the offender, and told him that if ever he dared to repeat the insult to Miss Turner, he, Mr. Andinnian, would shoot him. It appeared, the counsel added, that Mr. Andinnian avowed this in unmistakable terms; that the unfortunate deceased fully understood him to mean it, and that Mr. Andinnian would certainly do what he said if provoked. Proof of which would be given. In spite of all this, Martin Scott braved his fate the instant he had an opportunity. On the fatal evening, June the twenty-third, Miss Turner having only just returned home from an absence of some weeks, Martin Scott made his appearance at her uncle's house, followed her into the garden, and there, within sight of Mr. Andinnian (or, rather, Sir Adam Andinnian, for he had then succeeded to his title, said the counsel, stopping to correct himself), he rudely took the young lady in his arms, and kissed her several times. Miss Turner, naturally startled and indignant, broke from him, and burst into a fit of hysterical sobs. Upon this, the prisoner caught up his loaded gun and shot him dead: the gun, unhappily, lying close to his hand, for he had been shooting birds during the day. Such was the substance of the story, as told to the court.

Thomas Hewitt, the faithful serving man, who deposed that he had lived in the Andinnian family for many years, and who could hardly speak for the grief within him, was examined. Alas! he was called for the prosecution: for all his evidence told against his master, not for him.

"That evening," he said, "about eight o'clock, or from that to half-past, I had occasion to see my master, Sir Adam, and went across the garden and beyond the shrubbery of trees to find him. He was standing by the gate that divides his grounds from Mr. Turner's; and all in the same moment, as I came in view, there seemed to be a scuffle going on in Mr. Turner's wide path by the rose bushes. Just at first I did not discern who was there, for the setting sun, then going below the horizon, shone in my face like a ball of fire. I soon saw it was Miss Turner and Martin Scott. Scott seemed to be holding her against her will. She broke away from him, crying and sobbing, and ran towards my master, as if wanting him to protect her."

"Well?—go on," cried the examining counsel, for the witness had stopped. "What did you see next?"

"Sir Adam caught up his gun from the garden-seat close by, where it was lying, presented it at Martin Scott, and fired. The young man sprang up into the air, a foot or two, and then fell. It all passed in a moment. I ran to assist him, and found he was dead. That is all I know."

But the witness was not to be released just yet, in spite of this intimation. "Wait a bit," said the counsel for the prosecution. "You saw the prisoner take up the gun, point it at the deceased and fire. Was all this done deliberately?"

"It was not done hurriedly, sir."

"Answer my question, witness. Was it *deliberately* done?"

"I think it was. His movements were slow. Perhaps," added poor Hewitt, willing to suggest a loophole of escape for his master, "perhaps Sir Adam had forgotten the gun was loaded, and only fired it off to frighten Scott. It was in the morning he had been shooting the birds: hours before; he could easily have forgotten that it was loaded. My master is not a cruel man, but a humane one."

"How came he to leave the gun out there for so many hours, if he had done with it?" asked the judge.

"I don't know, my lord. I suppose he forgot to bring it in when he came in to dinner. Sir Adam is naturally very careless indeed."

One of the jury spoke. "Witness, what was it that you wanted with your master when you went out that evening?"

"A telegram had come for him, sir, and I went to take it to him."

"What did the telegram contain? Do you know?"

"I believe it came from Foxwood, sir."

"From Foxwood?"

"The telegram was from my mother, Mrs. Andinnian," spoke up the prisoner, in his rather loud, but perfectly calm voice, thereby electrifying the court. "It was to tell me she had arrived safely at Foxwood Court: and that the day for my uncle Sir Joseph's funeral was not then fixed."

The prisoner's solicitor, in a great commotion, leaned over and begged him in a whisper to be silent.

"Nay," said the prisoner aloud, "if any information that I can give is required, why should I be silent?" Surely there had never before been a prisoner like unto this one!

The next witness was Rose Turner. She was accompanied by her uncle and a solicitor; was dressed handsomely in black, and appeared to be in a state of extreme nervous agitation. Her face was ashy pale, her manner shrinkingly reluctant, and her voice was so low that its accents could not always be caught. In the simple matter of giving her name, she had to be asked it three times.

Her evidence told little more than had been told by the opening counsel.

Mr. Scott had persecuted her with his attentions, she said. He wanted her to promise to marry him when he should be established in practice, but she wholly refused, and she begged him to go about his business and leave her alone. He would not; and her aunt had rather encouraged Mr. Scott; they did not know what kind of private character he bore, but supposed, of course, it was good. Martin Scott had twice kissed her against her will, very much to her own annoyance; she had told Mr. Andinnian of it—who had always been very kind to her, quite like a protector. It made Mr. Andinnian very angry; and he had then threatened Martin Scott that if he ever again attempted to molest her, he would shoot him. She was sure that Martin Scott understood that Mr. Andinnian was not joking, but meant to do what he said. So far the witness spoke with tolerable readiness: but after this not a word would she say that was not drawn from her. Her answers were given shrinkingly, and some of them with evident reluctance.

"You went out on a visit in May: where was it to?" questioned the counsel.

"Birmingham."

"How long did you stay there?"

"I was away from home five weeks altogether."

"When did you return home?—You must speak a little louder, if you please."

"On the evening of the twenty-second of June."

"That was the day before the murder?"

"It was not a murder," returned the witness, with emotion. "Sir Adam Andinnian was quite justified in what he did."

The judge interposed. "You are not here to state opinions, young lady, but to answer questions." The counsel resumed

"Did the deceased, Martin Scott, come to your uncle's residence on the evening of the twenty-third?"

"Yes. My uncle was at home ill that evening, and he kept Mr. Scott in conversation, so that he had no opportunity of teasing me."

"You went later into the garden?"

"Yes. Martin Scott must have seen me pass the window, for I found he was following me out. I saw Sir Adam standing at his gate, and went towards him."

"With what motive did you go?"

A pause. "I intended to tell him that Mr. Scott was there."

"Had you seen Sir Adam at all since you came home the previous evening?"

Whether the young lady said Yes or No to this question could not be told. Her answer was inaudible.

"Now this won't do," cried the counsel, losing patience. "You must speak so that the jury can hear you, witness; and you must be good enough to lift your head. What have you to be ashamed of?"

At this sting, a bright flush dyed the young lady's cheeks: but she evidently did not think of resisting. Lifting her face, she spoke somewhat louder.

"I had seen Sir Adam in the morning when he was shooting the birds. I saw him again in the afternoon, and was talking with him for a few minutes. Not for long: some friends called on my aunt, and she sent for me in."

"Was anything said about Martin Scott that day, between you and Sir Adam?"

"Not a word. We did not so much as think of him."

"Why, then, were you hastening in the evening to tell Sir Adam that Scott was there?"

The witness hesitated and burst into tears. Her answer was impeded by sobs.

"Of course it was a dreadful thing for me to do—as things have turned out. I had no ill thought in it. I was only going to tell him that Scott had come and was sitting with my uncle. There was nothing in that to make Sir Adam angry."

"You have not replied to my question. *Why* did you hasten to tell Sir Adam?"

"There was no very particular cause. Before I left home in May, I had hoped Mr. Scott had ceased his visits: when I found, by his coming this evening, that he had not, I thought

I would tell Sir Adam. We both disliked Martin Scott from his rudeness to me. I began to feel afraid of him again."

"Afraid of what?"

"Lest he should be rude to me as he had been before."

"Allow me to ask—in a case of this sort, would it not have been your uncle's place to deal with Mr. Scott, rather than Sir Adam Andinnian's?"

The witness bent her head and sobbed. While the prisoner, without affording her time for any answer, again spoke up.

"When Martin Scott insulted Miss Turner before, I had particularly requested her to inform me at once if he ever attempted such a thing again. I also requested her to let me know of it if he resumed his visits at her uncle's house. I wished to protect Miss Turner as efficiently as I would have protected a sister."

The prisoner was ordered to be silent. Miss Turner's examination went on.

"You went out on this evening to speak to the prisoner, and Martin Scott followed you. What next?"

"Martin Scott caught me up when I was close to the bed of rose bushes: that is, about half-way between the house and the gate where Sir Adam was standing. He began reproaching me; saying I had not given him a word of welcome after my long absence, and did I think he was going to stand it. Before—before—"

"Before what? Why do you hesitate?"

The witness's tears burst forth afresh: her voice was pitiable in its distress. A thrill of sympathy moved the whole court; not one in it but felt for her.

"Before I was aware, Martin Scott had caught me in his arms, and was kissing my face. I struggled to get away from him, and ran towards Sir Adam Andinnian for shelter. It was then he took up his gun."

"What did Sir Adam say?"

"Nothing. He put me behind him with one hand, and fired. I recollect seeing Hewitt standing beside me then, and for a few moments I recollected no more. At first I did not know any harm was done: only when I saw Hewitt kneeling down in the path over Martin Scott."

"What did the prisoner do, then?"

"He put the gun back on the seat again, quite quietly, and walked down the path towards where they were. My uncle and aunt came running out, and—and that ended it."

With a burst of grief that threatened to become hysterical, she covered her face. Perhaps in compassion, only two or three further questions of unimportance were asked her. She had told all she knew of the calamity, she said; and was allowed to retire: leaving the audience most favourably impressed with the pretty looks, the innocence, and the modesty of Miss Rose Turner.

A young man named Wharton was called; an assistant to a chemist, and a friend of the late Martin Scott. He deposed to hearing Scott speak in the spring—he thought it was towards the end of April—of Mr. Andinnian's threat to shoot him. The witness added that he was sure Martin Scott took the threat as a serious one and knew that Mr. Andinnian meant it as such; though it was possible that with the lapse of weeks the impression might have worn away in Scott's mind. He was the last witness called on either side; and the two leading counsel then addressed the jury.

The judge summed up carefully and dispassionately, but not favourably. As many said afterwards, he was "dead against the prisoner." The jury remained in deliberation fifteen minutes only, and then came back with their verdict.

Wilful murder: but with a very strong recommendation to mercy.

The judge then asked the prisoner if he had anything to urge against the sentence of Death that was about to be passed upon him.

Nothing but this, the prisoner replied, speaking courteously and quietly. That he believed he had done only his duty; that Martin Scott had deliberately and defiantly rushed upon his own fate: and that if young, innocent, and refined ladies were to be insulted by reprobate men with impunity, the sooner the country went back to a state of barbarism the better. To this the judge replied, that if for trifling causes men might with impunity murder others in cold blood, the country would already be in a state of barbarism, without going back to it.

But the trial was not to conclude without one startling element of sensation. The judge had put the black cap on his head, when a tall, proud-looking, handsome lady stepped forward and demanded to say a word in stay of the sentence. It was Mrs. Andinnian. Waving the ushers away who would have removed her, she was, perhaps in very astonishment, allowed to speak.

Her son had inherited an uncontrollable temper, she said; *her* temper. If anything occurred greatly to exasperate him (but this was very rare) his transitory passion was akin to madness. In fact it was madness for the short time it lasted, which was never more than for a few moments. To punish him by death for any act committed by him during this irresponsible time would be, she urged, murder. Murder upon him.

Only these few words did she speak. Not passionately; calmly and respectfully; and with her dark eyes fixed on the judge. She then bowed to the judge and retired. The judge inclined his head gravely to her in return, and proceeded with his sentence.

Death. But the strong recommendation of the jury should be forwarded to the proper quarter.

The judge, as was learnt later, seconded this recommendation warmly: in fact, the words he used in passing sentence as good as conveyed an intimation that there might be no execution.

Thus ended the famous trial. Within a week afterwards the fiat was known: and the sentence was commuted into penal servitude for life!

Penal servitude for life! Think of the awful blight to a man in the flower of his age and in the position of Adam Andinnian! And all through one moment's mad act!

CHAPTER V.

UNABLE TO GET STRONG.

IN an invalid's chair by the side of a fire, at mid-day, reclined Lucy Cleeve. Her face was delicate and thin; her sweet brown eyes had almost an anxious look in them; the white wrapper she wore was not whiter than her cheeks. Mrs. Cleeve was in the opposite chair reading. At the window sat Miss Blake, working some colours of bright silks on a white satin ground.

As Mrs. Cleeve turned the page, she chanced to look up, and saw in her daughter a symptom of shivering.

"Lucy! My darling, surely you are not shivering again!"

"N—o, I think not," was the hesitating answer. "The fire is getting dull, mamma."

Mrs. Cleeve stirred the fire into brightness, and then brought a warm shawl of chenille silk, and folded it over Lucy's shoulders. And yet the August sun was shining on the world, and the blue skies were dark with heat.

The cruel pain that the separation from Karl Andinnian had brought to Lucy was worse than any one thought for. She was perfectly silent over it, bearing all patiently, and so gave no sign of the desolation within. Colonel and Mrs. Cleeve said in private how reasonable Lucy was, and how well she was forgetting the young man. Miss Blake felt sure that she had never really cared for him: that the love had been all child's play. All through the month of June Lucy had gone about wherever they chose to take her: to flower-shows, and promenades, and dances, and picnics. She talked and laughed in society as others did; and no mortal wizard or witch could have divined she was suffering from the effects of a love-fever, that had been too rudely checked.

Very shortly she was to suffer from a different fever: one that sometimes proves to be just as difficult of cure. In spite of the gaiety and the going-out, Lucy seemed to be somewhat ailing: her appetite failed, and she grew to feel tired at nothing. In July these symptoms had increased, and she was palpably ill. The medical man called in, pronounced Miss Cleeve to be suffering from a slight fever, combined with threatenings of ague. The slight fever grew into a greater one, and then became intermittent. Intervals of shivering coldness would be succeeded by intervals of burning heat; and they in their turn by intense prostration. The doctor said Miss Cleeve must have taken cold; probably, he thought, had sat on damp grass at some picnic. Lucy was very obedient. She lay in bed when they told her to lie, and got up when they told her to get up, and took all the medicine ordered without a word, and tried to take the food. The doctor, at length, with much self-gratulation, declared the fever at an end; and that Miss Cleeve might come out of her bedroom for some hours in the day. Miss Cleeve did so come: but somehow she did not gain strength, or improve as she ought to have done. Seasons of chilling coldness would be upon her still; the white cheeks would sometimes be bright with a very suspicious-looking dash of hectic. It would take time to re-establish her, said the doctor with a sigh: and that was the best he could make of it.

Whether Colonel and Mrs. Cleeve would have chosen to speak much before their daughter of the lover she had been obliged to resign, cannot be said. Most probably not. But circumstances over which they had no control led to its being done. When, towards the close of June, the news of that strange tragedy enacted by Adam Andinnian broke upon the world, all the world was full of it. Not a visitor, calling to see them, but went over the marvellous wonders of the tale in Lucy's hearing, and, as it seemed to her, for her own special benefit. The entirely unprovoked (as was at first said and supposed) nature of the crime; the singular fact that it should have been committed the very day of his assuming his rank amidst the baronetage of the kingdom; the departure of Mrs. Andinnian on the journey that he ought to have taken, and the miserable thought, so full of poignancy to the Andinnian family, that if *he* had gone, the calamity could not have happened; the summons to the young lieutenant at Winchester, his difficulty with the telegram, and his arrival at night to find what had happened at the desolate house! All these facts, and very many more details, some true, some untrue, were brought before Lucy day after day. To escape them was impossible, unless she had shut herself up from society, for men and women's mouths were full of them; and none had the least suspicion that the name of Andinnian was more than any other name to Lucy Cleeve. It was subsequent to this, you of course understand, that she became ill. During this period, she was only somewhat ailing, and was going about just as other people went.

The subject—it has been already said—did not die out quickly. Before it was allowed to do so, there came the trial; and *that* and its proceedings kept it alive for many a day more. But that the matter altogether bore an unusua interest, and that a great deal of what is called romance, by which public imagination is fed, encompassed it, was undeniable. The step in rank attained by Lieutenant Andinnian, his captaincy, was discussed and re-discussed as though no man had ever taken it before. So that, long ere the period now arrived at, August, Colonel and Mrs. Cleeve talked of the Andinnian affairs before their daughter with as little thought of reticence as they would have given to the most common questions of every-day life, and perhaps had nearly forgotten that there had ever been a cause why they should observe it.

A word of Miss Blake. That the perfidy—she looked upon it as such—of Lieutenant Andinnian in regard to herself, was a very bitter blow and tried her heart nearly as the separation was trying Lucy's, may at once be admitted. Nothing, in the world or out of it, would have persuaded her that the young man did not at an early period love her, that he would have

ultimately married her but for the stepping in between them
of Lucy Cleeve : and there lay a very angry and bitter feeling
against Lucy at the bottom of her heart. Not against Mr.
Andinnian. The first shock over, she quite exonerated him,
and threw all the weight of blame on Lucy. Is it not ever so
—that woman, in a case of rivalry such as this, detests and
misjudges the woman, and exempts the man ?

But Miss Blake had a very strict conscience. In one of
more gentle and tender nature, this would have been an admirable thing; in her, whose nature was exceptionally hard, it
might cause her to grow into something undesirably stern.
There was a chance for her yet. Underlying her every thought,
word, action, her witty sallies in the ballroom, her prayers in
church, remained ever the one faint hope—that Karl Andinnian would recover his senses and return to his first allegiance.
If this ever came to pass, and she became Mrs. Andinnian, the
little kindness existing in Theresa Blake's nature would assert
itself. For though she was very just, or strove to be, she was
not kind.

With this strict conscience, Miss Blake could not encourage
her ill-feeling towards Lucy. On the contrary, she put it
resolutely from her, and strove to go on her way in a duteous
course of life and take up her own sorrow as a kind of appointed cross. All very well, this, so far as it went : but there
was one dreadful want ever making itself heard—the want to
fill the aching void in her lonely heart. After a disappointment
to the affections, all women feel this need; and none, unless
they have felt it, can know or imagine the intense need of it.
When the heart has been filled to the uttermost with a beloved
object, every hour of the day gladdened with his sight, every
dream of the night rejoicing with the thought of the morning's
renewed meeting, and he is compulsorily snatched away for
ever, the awful blank left is almost worse than death. Every
aim and end and hope in life seems to have died suddenly
out, leaving only a vacuum : a vacuum that tells of nothing
but pain. But for finding some object which the mind can
take up and concentrate itself upon, there are women who
would go mad. Miss Blake found hers in religion.

Close upon that night when you saw Mr. Andinnian and
Lucy Cleeve pacing together the garden of the Reverend Mr.
Blake's rectory, Mr. Blake was seized with a fit. The attack
was not in itself very formidable, but it bore threatening
symptoms for the future. Perfect rest was enjoined by his

medical attendants, together with absence from the scene of his labours. As soon, therefore, as he could be moved, Mr. Blake departed; leaving his church in the charge of his many-years curate, and of a younger man who was hastily engaged to assist him. This last was a stranger in the place, the Reverend Guy Cattacomb. Now, singular to say, but it was the fact, immediately after Mr. Blake's departure, the old curate was incapacitated by an attack of very serious illness, and he also had to go away for rest and change. This left the church wholly in the hands of the new man, Mr. Cattacomb. And this most zealous but rather mistaken divine, at once set about introducing various changes in the service; asking nobody's permission, or saying with your leave, or by your leave.

The service had hitherto been conducted reverently, plainly, and with thorough efficiency. The singing was good; the singers—men and boys—wore white surplices: in short, all things were done decently and in order: and both Mr. Blake and his curate were excellent preachers. To the exceeding astonishment of the congregation, Mr. Cattacomb swooped down upon them the very first Sunday he was left to himself, with what they were pleased to term "vagaries." Vagaries they undoubtedly were, and not only needless ones, but such as were calculated to bring a wholesome and sound Protestant church into disrepute. The congregation remonstrated, but the Reverend Guy persisted. The power, for the time being, lay in his hands, and he used it after his own heart.

"Man, proud man, dressed in a little brief authority,
Plays such fantastic tricks before high heaven as make the angels weep."

How applicable are those lines of Shakspeare's to some of the over-zealous young divines of the present day!

The progress of events in Mr. Blake's church need not be traced. It is enough to say that the Reverend Mr. Cattacomb—whose preaching was no better than the rest of him: a quarter of an hour's rant, of which nobody could make any sense at all—emptied the church. Nearly all the old congregation left it. In their places a sprinkling of young people began to frequent it. We have had examples of these things. The Reverend Guy led, and his flock (almost the whole of them ardent young girls of no experience) followed. There were banners and processions, and images of saints and angels, and candlesticks and scrolls and artificial flowers, and thrown-up incense, and soft mutterings coming from nowhere, and all kinds of odd services at all kinds of hours, and risings-up and sittings-down, and bowings here and bowings there, and private confessions and public absolutions. Whether the worship, or, in fact, the church, itself was meant to represent the Roman Catholic faith or the Protestant faith no living soul could tell. It was ultra-foolish—that is really the only name for it—and created some scandal. People took to speak of its frequenters slightingly and disrespectfully as "Mr. Cattacomb and his tail." The tail being the ardent young ladies who were never away from his heels.

Never a one amidst them more ardent than Miss Blake. In the Rev. Guy and his ceremonies she found that outlet for the superfluous resources of her heart that Karl Andinnian had left so vacant. Ten times a day, if the church had ten services, or scraps of services, was Miss Blake to be seen amid the knot of worshippers. At early morning she went to Matins; at sunset she went to Vespers. Once a week she was penned up in a close box which the Reverend Guy had put up as a confessional, confessing her sins. Some ladies chose the Reverend Mr. Cattacomb as their father priest in this respect; some chose his friend and coadjutor the Reverend Damon Puff, a very zealous young man also, whom the former had appointed to his assistance. One confessional box was soon found quite insufficient, and a second was introduced. Lookers-on began to wonder what would come next. Miss Blake did not neglect the claims of society in her new call to devotion; so that, what with the world and what with the church, she had but little spare time on her hands. It was somewhat unusual to see her, as now, seated quietly at her needle. The work was some beauteous silken embroidery, destined to cover a cushion for Mr. Cattacomb's reverend knees to rest upon when at his private devotions. The needle came to a sudden pause.

"I wonder if I am wrong," she exclaimed, after regarding attentively the leaf that had been growing under her hands. "Mrs. Cleeve, do you think the leaves to this rose should be *brown?* I fancy they ought to be green."

"Do not ask me anything about it, Theresa."

Mrs. Cleeve's answer wore rather a resentful accent. The fact was, both herself and Colonel Cleeve were sadly vexed at Miss Blake's wholesale goings in for the comprehensive proceedings of Mr. Cattacomb. They had resigned their pew in church themselves, and now walked regularly to the beautiful services in the cathedral. Colonel Cleeve remonstrated with Miss Blake for what he called her folly. He told her that she was making herself ridiculous; and that these ultra innovations could but tend to bring religion itself into disrepute. It will therefore be understood that Mrs. Cleeve, knowing what the embroidery was destined for, did not regard it with approbation.

"Theresa, if I thought my dear child here, Lucy, would ever make the spectacle of herself that you and those other girls are doing, I should weep with sorrow and shame."

"Well, I'm sure!" cried Miss Blake. "Spectacle!"

"What else is it? To see a parcel of brainless girls running after Guy Cattacomb and that other one—Puff? Their mothers ought to know better than to allow it. God's pure and reverent and holy worship is one thing: this is quite another."

Lucy asked for some of the cooling beverage that stood near: her mouth felt always parched. As her mother brought it to her, Lucy pressed her hand and looked up in her face with a smile. Mrs. Cleeve knew that it was as much as to say "There is no fear of *me*."

Colonel Cleeve came in as the glass was being put down. He looked somewhat anxiously at his daughter: he was beginning to be uneasy that she did not gain strength more quickly.

"How do you feel now, my dear?"

"Only a little cold, papa."

"Dear me—and it is a very hot day!" remarked the colonel, wiping his brows, for he had been walking fast.

"Is there any news stirring in the town?" asked Mrs. Cleeve.

"Nothing particular. Captain Andinnian has sold out. He could not do anything else under the circumstances."

"It is a dreadful blight upon the young man's career," said Mrs. Cleeve.

"There was no help for it, Lucinda. Had he been a general he must have done the same. A man who has a brother working in chains cannot remain an officer in the Queen's service. Had the brother been hanged, I think the Commander-in-chief would have been justified in cashiering Captain Andinnian, if he had not taken the initiative," added the colonel, who was very jealous of his order.

Miss Blake turned with a flush of emotion. This news fell

E

on her heart like lead. Her first thought, when the colonel spoke, had been—If he has left the army, there will be nothing to bring him again to Winchester.

"Captain Andinnian cannot be held responsible for what his brother did," she said.

"Of course not," admitted the colonel.

"Neither ought it to be visited upon him."

"The worst of these sad things you see, Theresa, is, that they *are* visited upon the relatives: and there's no preventing it. Captain Andinnian must go through life henceforth as a marked man; in a degree as a banned one: liable to be pointed at by every stranger as a man who has a brother a convict."

There was a pause. The last word grated on their ears. Miss Blake inwardly winced at it: should she become the wife of Karl Andinnian——

"Will Sir Adam be sent to Australia?" asked Mrs. Cleeve of her husband, interrupting Theresa's thoughts.

"No. To Portland Island. It is said he is already there."

"I wonder what will become of his money? His estate, and that?"

"Report runs that he made it all over to his mother before the trial. I don't know how far that may be true. Well, it is a thousand pities for Captain Andinnian," summed up the colonel: "he was a very nice young fellow."

They might have thought Lucy, sitting there, her face covered by her hand, was asleep, so still was she. Presently, Colonel and Mrs. Cleeve were called away to receive some visitors; and Miss Blake began folding her silks and white satin in tissue paper, for the hour of some service or other was at hand. Halting for a moment at the fire to shake the ends of silk from her gown into the hearth, she glanced at Lucy.

"Suppose you had been married to Karl Andinnian, Lucy!"

"Well?"

"What an awful fate it would have been for you!"

"I should only have clung to him the closer, Theresa," was the low answer. And it must be premised that neither Lucy nor any one else had the slightest notion of Miss Blake's regard for Karl.

Miss Blake glanced at her watch. She had two minutes yet. She turned and stood before Lucy. In her unselfish judgment—and she did try to judge unselfishly always—a union with Captain Andinnian now, though she herself might stoop to put up with it in her great love, would be utterly beneath Lucy Cleeve.

"You—you do not mean to imply that you would marry Captain Andinnian, as things are?"

"I would. My father and mother permitting."

"You unhappy girl! Where's your pride?"

"I did not say I was going to do it, Theresa. You put an imaginary proposition; one that is altogether impossible, and I replied to *that*. I do not expect ever to see Karl Andinnian again in this world."

Something in the despairing accent touched Miss Blake, in spite of her wild jealousy. "You seem very poorly to-day, Lucy," she gently said. "Are you in pain?"

"No," replied Lucy, with a sigh: "not in pain. But I don't seem to get much better, do I, Theresa? I wish I could for papa and mamma's sake."

CHAPTER VI.

AN ATMOSPHERE OF MYSTERY.

It seemed to Mrs. Andinnian and to her son, Karl, that trouble like unto theirs had never yet fallen upon man. Loving Adam as they did, for his sake it was more than they knew how to bear. The disgrace and blight to themselves were terrible; to Karl especially, who was, so to say, only entering on life. There are some calamities that can never be righted in this world; scarcely softened. This was one. Calamities when we can only *bear*, bear always here; when nothing is left us but to look forward to, and live on for the next world, where no pain will be. In Karl's mind this was ever present.

The bare fact of the selling-out was to Karl Andinnian a bitter blow. He was attached to his profession: and he had been looking forward to finding, in the active discharge of its duties, a relief from the blank left by the loss of Lucy Cleeve. Now he must be thrown utterly upon himself; an idle man. Everyone was very kind to him; from the Commander-in-chief, with whom he had an interview, downwards; evincing for him the truest respect and sympathy: but not one of them said, "Won't you reconsider your determination and remain with us?" His Royal Highness civilly expressed regret at the loss Her Majesty would sustain in so good a servant; but he took the withdrawal as a matter that admitted of no question. There could be none. Captain Andinnian's only brother, escaping the gallows by an accorded favour, was working in chains on Portland Island: clearly the captain, brave and unsullied man though he individually was, could but hasten to hide his head in private life.

It was a happy thing for Karl that he had plenty of business on his hands just now. It saved him in a degree from thought. Besides his own matters, there were many things to see to for his mother. The house in Northamptonshire was given up, its furniture sold, its household, except Hewitt, discharged. Karl was on the spot and saw to it all. Whilst there, he had rather a struggle with himself. His natural kindliness of feeling prompted him to call and see Miss Turner: personally he shrank from it, for he could not forget that it was through her all the misery had happened. He did violence to his inclination, and called. The young lady seemed to be in very depressed spirits, and said but little. The event seemed to have tried her much, and she was pale and thin. During the interval that had elapsed since the trial, her uncle, to whom she was much attached, had died. She told Karl that her aunt, Mrs. Turner, intended to remove at once to her native place, a remote district of Cumberland: Rose supposed she should have to remove with her. Mr. Turner had left a very fair amount of property. His wife was to receive the interest of it for her life; at her death the whole of it would come to Rose. As Karl shook hands with her on leaving, and wished her well, something he said was taken by her as alluding to the unhappy tragedy, though he had intended nothing of the sort. It had a strange effect upon her. She rose from her seat, her hands trembling; her face became burning red, then changed to a ghastly whiteness. "Don't speak of it, Captain Andinnian," she exclaimed in a voice of horror; "don't hint at it, unless you would see me go mad. There are times when I think that madness will be my ending." Again wishing her well, he took his departure. It was rather unlikely, he thought, that their paths would cross each other again in life.

Hewitt was sent to Foxwood. It would probably be made the future home of Mrs. Andinnian and her younger son; but at present they had not gone there. For some little time, while Karl was busy in London, Northamptonshire, or elsewhere, he had lost sight of his mother. She quitted the temporary home she occupied, and, so to say, disappeared. While he was wondering what this meant, and where she could be, he received a letter from her dated Weymouth. She told him she had taken up her abode there for the present, and she charged him not to disclose this to any one, or to let her address be known. Just for a moment, Karl was puzzled to imagine what her motive could be in going to a place that she knew nothing of. All at once the truth flashed upon him—she would be as near as possible to that cruel prison that contained her ill-fated son.

It was even so. Adam Andinnian was on Portland Island; and his mother had taken up her residence at Weymouth to be near him. Karl, who knew not the place, or the rules observed, wondered whether a spectator might stroll about on the (so-called) island at will, or ever get a chance glimpse of the gangs at their labour.

In the month of October, Captain Andinnian—to call him by this title for a short while longer—went to Weymouth. He found his mother established in a small, mean, ready-furnished house in an obscure part of the town. It was necessary for him to see her on matters connected with the Foxwood estate, of which he had now the management; but she had charged him to come to her in as private a manner as he well could, and not to make himself or his name known at the station or elsewhere, unless under necessity. "She is right," thought Karl; "the name of Andinnian is notorious now." That was true; and he did not suppose she had any other motive for the injunction.

"But, my dear mother, why are you *here?*" he asked within five minutes of his entrance, as he looked at the confined walls of the mean abode. "You might at least have been more comfortably and suitably lodged."

"What I choose to do, I do," she answered, in the distant tones of former days. "It is not for you to question me."

Mrs. Andinnian was altered. Mental suffering had told upon her. The once fresh hues of her complexion had given place to a fixed pallor; the large dark eyes had acquired a fierce and yet restless look. In manner alone was she unaltered, at least to Karl: and as to her pride, it seemed to be more dominant than ever.

"I was only thinking of your comfort, mother," he replied to her fierce rejoinder. "This is so different from what you have been accustomed to."

"Circumstances are different," she said, curtly.

"Have you but one servant in the whole house? For everything?"

"She is enough for me: she is a faithful woman. I tell you that circumstances are not what they were."

"*Some* are not—unhappily," he answered. "But others, pecuniary ones, have changed the other way. You are rich now."

"And do you think I would touch a stiver of the riches that are my dear Adam's?" she retorted, her eyes blazing. "Save what may be necessary to keep up Foxwood, and to—to— No," she resumed, after the abrupt breaking off, "I hoard them for him."

Karl wondered whether trouble had a little touched her brain. Poor Adam could have no further use for riches in this world. Unless, indeed, in years to come, he should obtain what was called a ticket of leave. But Karl fancied that in a case like Adam's—condemnation commuted—it was never given.

Mrs. Andinnian began asking the details of the giving-up of her former home. In answering, Karl happened to mention incidentally the death of their neighbour, Mr. Turner, and his own interview with Rose. The latter's name excited Mrs. Andinnian beyond all precedent: it brought on one of those frightful fits of passion that Karl had not seen of late years.

"I loathe her," she wildly said. "But for her wicked machinations, my darling son had not fallen into this dreadful fate that is worse than death. May my worst curses light upon the head of Rose Turner!"

Karl did what he could to soothe the storm he had unwittingly evoked. He told his mother that she would never, in all probability, be grieved with the sight of the girl again, for she was removing to the out-of-the-world district of Cumberland.

The one servant, alluded to by Karl, was a silent-mannered, capable woman of some forty years. Her mistress called her "Ann," but Karl found she was a Mrs. Hopley, a married woman. That she appeared to be really attached to her mistress, to sympathise with her in her great misfortune, and to be solicitous to render her every little service that could soothe her, Captain Andinnian saw and felt grateful for.

"Where is your husband?" he one day inquired.

"Hopley's out getting his living, sir," was the answer. "We have had misfortunes, sir: and when they come to people such as us, we must do the best we can to meet them. Hopley's working on his side, and me on mine."

"He is not in Weymouth then?"

"No, he is not in Weymouth. We are not Weymouth people, sir. I don't know much about the place. I never lived at it till I came to Mrs. Andinnian."

By this, Karl presumed that his mother had brought Mrs. Hopley with her when she came herself: but he asked no further. It somewhat explained what he had rather wondered at—that his mother, usually so reticent, and more than ever so now, should have disclosed their great calamity to this woman. He thought the servant must have been already cognisant of it.

"What misfortune was it of your own that you allude to?" he gently asked.

"It was connected with our son, sir. I and my husband never had but him. He turned out wild. While he was quite a lad, so to say, he ruined us, and we had to break up the home."

"And where is he now?"

She put her check apron before her face to hide her emotion. "He is dead," was the low answer. "He died a dreadful death, sir, and I can't yet bear to talk of it. It's hardly three months ago."

Karl looked at the black ribbon in her cap, at the neat black-and-white print gown she did her work in: and his heart went out to the woman's sorrow. He understood better now—she and her mistress had a grief in common. Later, he heard somewhat more of the particulars. Young Hopley, after bringing his parents to beggary, had plunged into crime; and then, to avoid being taken, had destroyed himself.

But, as the days went on, Karl Andinnian could not help remarking that there was an atmosphere of strangeness pervading the house; he could almost have said of mystery. Frequently were mistress and maid closeted together in close conference; the door locked upon them, the conversation carried on in whispers. Twice he saw Ann Hopley go out so be-cloaked and be-large-bonneted that it almost looked as though she were dressed for disguise. Karl thought it very strange.

One evening, when he was reading to his mother by candlelight, the front door was softly knocked at, and some one was admitted to the kitchen. In the small house, all sounds were plainly heard. A minute or two elapsed, and then Ann came in to say a visitor wished to speak to her mistress. While Karl was wondering at this—for his mother was entirely unknown in the place—Mrs. Andinnian rose without the least surprise, looked at her son, and hesitated.

"Will you step into another room, Karl? My interview must be private."

So! she had expected this visit. Captain Andinnian went into his bed-room. He saw—for his curiosity was excited, and he did not quite close the door—a tall, big, burly man, much wrapped up, and who kept his hat on, walk up the passage to the sitting-room, lighted thither by Ann. It seemed to the captain as though the visitor wished his face not to be looked at. The interview lasted about twenty minutes. Ann then showed the man out again, and Karl returned to the parlour.

"Who was it, mother?"

"A person to see me on private business," replied Mrs. Andinnian, in a voice that effectually checked further inquiries.

The days passed monotonously. Mrs. Andinnian was generally buried in her own thoughts, scarcely ever speaking to him; and when she did speak, it was in a cold or snappish manner. "If she would but make a true son of me, and give me her confidence!" Karl often thought. But, to do anything of the kind was evidently not the purpose of Mrs. Andinnian.

He one day went over to Portland Island. The wish to make the pilgrimage, and see what the place was like, had been in his mind from the first; but in the midst of the wish, a dreadful distaste to it drew him back, and he had let the time elapse without going. October was in its third week, and the days were getting wintry.

It is a dreary spot—and it struck with a strange dreariness on Captain Andinnian's spirit. Storms, that seemed to fall lightly on other places, rage out their fury there. Half a gale was blowing that day, and he seemed to feel its roughness to the depth of his heart. The prospect around, with its heaving sea, romantic enough at some times, was all too wild to-day; the Race of Portland, that turbulent place which cannot be crossed by vessel, gave him a fit of the shivers. As to the few houses he saw, they were as poor as the one inhabited by his mother.

In one of the quarries, amidst its great masses of stone Captain Andinnian halted, his eyes fixed on the foaming sea, his thoughts most bitter. Within a few yards of him, so to say, worked his unfortunate brother; chained, a felon; all his hopes in this world blighted; all his comforts in life gone out for ever. Karl himself was peculiarly susceptible to physical discomfort, as sensitive-natured men are apt to be; and he never thought without a shudder of what Adam had to undergo in this respect.

"Subjected to endless toil; to cruel deprivation; to isolation from all his kind!" groaned Karl aloud to the wild winds. Oh, my brother, if——"

His voice died away in very astonishment. Emerging from behind one of the blocks, at right angles with him, but not very near, came two people walking side by side, evidently conversing in close whispers. In the cloaked-up woman, with the large black bonnet and black crape veil over her face, Karl was sure he saw their servant, Ann Hopley. The other must be, he thought, one of the warders; and, unless Karl was greatly mistaken, he recognized in his strong, burly frame the same man who had come a night or two before to his mother's house. They passed on without seeing him, but he saw the man's face distinctly.

A light dawned on his mind. His mother was striving to make a friend of this warder, with a view to conveying messages, perhaps also, it might be, physical comforts, to Adam: yes, that was undoubtedly the solution of the mystery. But why need she have hidden it from him, Karl?

When he got home that night—for he stayed out until he was tired and weary—Ann Hopley, in her usual home attire, was putting the tea-tray on the table.

"I fancied I saw Ann out to-day," he observed to his mother, when they were alone.

"She went out on an errand for me," replied Mrs. Andinnian.

"I have been over to the Island," continued Karl. "It was there I thought I saw her."

Mrs. Andinnian was pouring some cream into the tea-cups when he spoke. She put down the small frail glass jug with a force that smashed it, and the cream ran over the tea-board.

"You have been to the Island?" she cried in a voice that betrayed some dreadful terror. "To the *Island?*"

Karl was rising to see what he could do towards repairing the mishap. The words arrested him. He had again been so unlucky as to raise one of her storms of passion: but this time he could see no reason in her anger: neither did he quite understand what excited it.

"To-day is the first time I have been to the Island, mother. I could not before summon up the heart to go."

"How *dared* you go?"

"I am thinking of going again," he answered, believing her question to relate to physical bravery. "And of getting—if it be possible to obtain it—permission to see *him*."

The livid colour, spreading itself over Mrs. Andinnian's face, grew more livid. "*I forbid it, Karl.* I forbid it, do you hear? You would ruin everything. I forbid you to go again on the Island, or to attempt to see Adam. Good heavens! you might be recognized for his brother."

"And if I were?" cried Karl, feeling completely at sea.

Mrs. Andinnian sat with her two hands on the edge of the tea-tray, staring at him, in what looked like dire consternation.

"Karl, you must go away to-morrow. To think that you could be such a fool as to go *there!* This is worse than all: it is most unfortunate. To-morrow you leave."

"Mother, why will you not place trust in me?" he asked, unable to fathom her. "Do you think you could have a truer confidant? or Adam a warmer friend? I guess the object of Ann's visits to the Island. I saw her talking with one of the warders to-day—the same man, or I fancied it, that came here the other night. That moment solved me the riddle, and——"

"Hush—sh—sh—sh!" breathed Mrs. Andinnian, in a terrified voice, ringing the bell, and looking round the walls of the room as if in dread that they had ears. "Not another word, Karl; I will not, dare not, hear it."

"As you please, mother," he rejoined, feeling bitterly hurt at her lack of trust.

"Have you more cream in the house, Ann?" said Mrs. Andinnian, calmly, when the woman appeared. "And you had better change the tray."

The meal was concluded in silence. Karl took up a newspaper he had brought in; Mrs. Andinnian sat moodily gazing into the fire. And so the time went on.

Suddenly there arose the distant sound of guns, booming

along on the still night air. To Captain Andinnian it suggested no ulterior thought; brought no cause for agitation: but his mother started up in wild commotion.

"The guns, Karl! the guns!"

"What guns are they?" he exclaimed, in surprise. "What are they firing for?"

She did not answer; she only stood still as a statue, her mouth slightly open with the intensity of listening, her finger lifted up. In the midst of this, Ann Hopley opened the door without sound, and looked in with a terror-stricken face.

"It's not *him*, ma'am; don't you be afeared. It's some other convicts that are off; but it can't be him. The plan's not yet organized."

And Karl learnt that these were the guns from Portland Island, announcing the escape, or attempted escape, of some of its miserable prisoners.

Well for him if he had learned nothing else. The true and full meaning of what had been so mysterious flashed upon him now, like a sheet of lightning that lights up and reveals the secrets of the darkness. It was not Adam's comforts they were surreptitiously seeking to ameliorate; they were plotting for his escape.

His escape! As the truth took possession of Captain Andinnian, his face grew white with a sickening terror; his brow damp as with a death sweat.

For he knew that nearly all these attempted escapes result in utter failure. The unhappy, deluded victims are re-captured, or drowned, or shot. Sitting there in his shock of agony, his dazed eyes gazing out to the fire, a prevision that death in one shape or other would be his brother's fate, if he did make the rash venture, seated itself firmly within him, as surely and vividly as though he had seen it in some fortune-teller's magic crystal.

"Mother," he said, in a low tone, as he took her hand, and the door closed on Ann Hopley, "I understand it all now. I thought, simple that I was, that I had understood it before: and that you were but striving to find a way of conveying trifles in the shape of comforts to Adam. This is dreadful."

"What is the matter with you?" cried Mrs. Andinnian. "You look ready to die."

"The matter is, that this has shocked me. I pray Heaven that Adam will not be so foolhardy as to attempt to escape!"

"And *why* should he not?" blazed forth Mrs. Andinnian.

Karl shook his head. "In nine cases out of ten, the result is nothing but death."

"And the tenth case results in life, in liberty!" she rejoined, exultantly. "My brave son does well to try for it."

Karl hid his eyes. The first thought, in the midst of the many tumultuously crowding his brain, was the strangely different estimation different people set on things. Here was his mother glorying in that to-be-attempted escape as if it were some great deed dared by a great general: *he* saw only its results. They could not be good; they must be evil. Allowing that Adam did escape and regain his liberty: what would the "liberty" be? A life of miserable concealment; of playing at hide-and-seek with the law; a world-wide apprehension, lying on him always, of being retaken. In short, a hunted man, who must not dare to approach the haunts of his fellows, and of whom every other man must be the enemy. To Karl the present life of degrading labour would be preferable to that.

"Do you wish to keep him there for life—that you may enjoy the benefit of his place at Foxwood and his money?" resumed Mrs. Andinnian, in a tone that she well knew how to make contemptuously bitter. The words stung Karl. His answer was full of pain: the pain of despair.

"I wish life had never been for him, mother. Or for me, either. If I could restore Adam to what he has forfeited by giving my own life, I would do it willingly. I have not much left to live for."

The tone struck Mrs. Andinnian. She thought that even the reflected disgrace, the stain on his name, scarcely justified it. Karl said a few words to her then of the blight that had fallen on his own life—the severance from Lucy Cleeve. She told him she was sorry; but it was quite evident that she was too much pre-occupied with other things to care about it. And the sad evening passed on.

With the morning, Weymouth learnt the fate of the poor convict—it was only one—who had attempted to escape, after whom the guns were let loose like so many bloodhounds. He was retaken. It was a man who had attempted escape once before, and unsuccessfully.

"The plans were badly laid," calmly remarked Mrs. Andinnian.

She did not now insist upon Karl's quitting her; he knew all; and, though he could not approve, she knew he would not do anything to frustrate. The subject was not again brought up: Mrs. Andinnian avoided it: and some more days wore on. Karl fancied, but could not be sure, that the other attempt at escape caused the action of this to be delayed: perhaps entirely abandoned. His mother and Ann Hopley seemed to be always in secret conference, and twice again there came stealthily to the house at night the same warder, or the man whom Karl had taken for one.

CHAPTER VII.

AT THE CHARING CROSS HOTEL.

On All Saints' Day, the first of November—and it was as bright a day for the festival as the saints, whether in that world or this, could wish—Captain Andinnian took leave of his mother, and went to London. His chief business there was to transact some business with the family lawyers, Plunkett and Plunkett. Their chambers were within the precincts of the Temple, and for convenience' sake he took up his quarters at the Charing Cross Hotel.

In the course of the afternoon, as he was turning out of Essex Street, having come through the little court from Plunkett and Plunkett's, he ran against a gentleman passing down the Strand. "I beg your pardon," Karl was beginning, and then became suddenly silent. It was Colonel Cleeve.

But, instead of passing on, as Karl might have expected him to do, the Colonel stopped and shook him cordially by the hand. To pass him would have jarred on every kindly instinct of Colonel Cleeve's nature. As to the affair with his daughter, he attached no importance to it now, believing it had made no permanent impression on Lucy, and had himself three-parts forgotten it.

"You have sold out, Captain Andinnian. I—I have been so very sorry for the sad causes that induced the step. Believe me, you have had all along my very best sympathy."

Karl hardly knew what he answered. A few words of murmured thanks; nothing more.

"You are not well," returned the Colonel, regarding the slender form that looked thinner than of yore, very thin in its black attire. "This has told upon you."

"It has; very much. There are some trials that can never be made light in this life," Karl continued, speaking the thoughts that were ever uppermost in his mind. "This is one of them. I thank you for your sympathy, Colonel Cleeve."

"And that's true, unfortunately," cried the Colonel warmly in answer. "You don't know how you are regretted at Winchester by your brother officers."

With another warm handshake, the Colonel passed on. Karl walked back to his hotel. In traversing one of its upper passages, a young lady came out of a sitting-room to cross to an opposite chamber. Captain Andinnian took a step back to let her pass in front of him; she turned her head, and they met face to face.

"Lucy!"

"Karl!"

The salutation broke from each before they well knew where they were or what had happened, amidst a rush of bewildering excitement, of wild joy. They had, no doubt, as in duty bound, been trying to forget each other; this moment of unexpected meeting proved to each how foolish was the fallacy. A dim idea made itself heard within either breast that tehy ought, in that duty alluded to, to pass on and linger not: but we all know how vain and weak is the human heart. It was not possible: and they stood, hand locked within hand.

Only for an instant. Lucy, looking very weak and ill, withdrew her hand, and leaned back against the door-post for support. Karl stood before her.

"I have just met Colonel Cleeve," he said: "but I had no idea that *you* were in London. Are you staying here?"

"Until to-morrow," she answered, her breath seeming to be a little short. "We came up yesterday. Papa chose this hotel, as it is convenient for the Folkestone trains. Mamma is here."

"Lucy, how very ill you look!"

"Yes. I had fever and ague in the summer, and do not get strong again. We are going to Paris for change. You do not look well either," added Lucy.

"I have not had fever: but I have had other things to try me," was his reply.

"Oh, Karl! I have been so grieved!" she earnestly said. "I did not know your brother, but I—I seemed to feel all the dreadful trouble as much as you must have felt it. When we are not strong, I think we do feel things."

"You call it by its right name, Lucy—a *dreadful* trouble. No one but myself can know what it has been to me."

They were gazing at each other yearningly: Lucy with her sweet brown eyes so full of tender compassion; Karl's grey-blue ones had a world of sorrowful regret in their depths. As she had done in their interview when they were parting, so she did now again—put out her hand to him, with a whisper meant to soothe.

"You will live it down, Karl."

He slightly shook his head: and took her hand to hold it between his.

"It is only since this happened that I have become at all reconciled to—to what had to be done at Winchester, Lucy. It would have been so greatly worse, had you been tied to me by—by any engagement."

"Not worse for you, Karl, but better. I should have helped you so much to bear it."

"My darling!"

The moment the words had crossed his lips, he remembered what honour and his long-ago-passed word to Colonel Cleeve demanded of him—that he should absolutely abstain from showing any tokens of affection for Lucy. Nay, to observe it strictly, he ought not to have stayed to talk with her.

"I beg your pardon, Lucy," he said, dropping her hand.

She understood quite well: a faint colour mantled in her pale face. She had been as forgetful as he.

"God bless you, Lucy," he whispered. "Farewell."

"O Karl—a moment," she implored with agitation, hardly knowing, in the pain of parting, what she said. "Just to tell you that I have not forgotten. I never shall forget. My regret, for what had to be, lies on me still."

"God bless you," he repeated, in deep emotion. "God bless and restore you, Lucy!"

Once more their fingers met in a brief handshake. And then they parted; he going one way, she the other; and the world had grown dim again.

Later in the day Karl heard it incidentally mentioned by some people in the coffee-room, that Colonel and Mrs. Cleeve with their daughter and two servants were going to make a prolonged stay on the Continent for the benefit of the young lady's health, who had been suffering from fever. Little did they think that the quiet, distinguished looking man in mourning, who had but come in to ask for some information, and was waiting while the waiter brought it, had more to do with the young lady's failing health than any fever.

Captain Andinnian took his breakfast next morning in private: as he sat down to it, the waiter brought him a newspaper. While listlessly unfolding it, he took the opportunity to ask a question.

"Have Colonel Cleeve and his family left the hotel?"

"Yes, sir. Just gone off for Folkestone. Broiled ham, sir eggs; steak with mushrooms," continued the man, removing sundry covers.

"Thank you. You need not wait."

But—ere the man had well closed the door, a startled sound like a groan of agony burst from Karl's lips. He sprang from his seat at a bound, his eyes riveted on the newspaper in one stare of disbelieving horror. The paragraph had a heading in the largest letters—

"ATTEMPTED ESCAPE FROM PORTLAND ISLAND. DEATH OF THE PRISONER, SIR ADAM ANDINNIAN."

Karl let the newspaper fall, and buried his face on the tablecloth to shut out the light. He had not courage to read more at once. He lay there praying that it might not be true.

Alas! it was too true. Two prisoners had attempted to escape in concert; Sir Adam Andinnian and a man named Cole. They succeeded in reaching the water, and got off in a small boat lying ready in wait. Some warders pursued them in another boat; and after an exciting chase in the dark night, came up with them as they reached the Weymouth side. Sir Adam was shot dead by a pistol; the small boat was upset and one of the warders drowned. Cole was supposed to have made his escape.

Such was the statement given in the newspapers. And, however uncertain the minor details might be at this early stage, one part appeared to admit of no doubt—Adam Andinnian was dead.

"I seemed to foresee it," moaned Karl. "From the very first, the persuasion has lain upon me that this would be the ending."

Ere many minutes elapsed, ere he had attempted to touch a morsel of breakfast, a gentleman was shown in. It was Mr. Plunkett: a stout man in spectacles, with a large red nose. He had the *Times* in his hand. Captain Andinnian's paper lay open on the breakfast table: Captain Andinnian's face, as he rose to receive his visitor, betrayed its own story.

"I see; you have read the tidings," began Mr. Plunkett, sitting down. "It is a dreadful thing."

"Do—do you think there's any chance that it may not be true?" he rejoined in an imploring tone.

"There's not the slightest as to the main fact—that Sir Adam is dead," replied the lawyer, decisively. "What *could* he have been thinking of, to hazard it?"

Karl sat shading his face.

"I'll tell you what it is, sir—there was a spice of madness in your brother's composition, I said so when he shot Scott. There must have been. And who, but a madman, would try to get away from Portland Island?"

"Nay. A rash act, Mr. Plunkett; but not one that implies madness."

There ensued a silence. These interviews are usually attended by embarrassment.

"I have intruded on you this morning to express my best sympathy, and to ask whether I can be of any service to you, Captain Andinnian," resumed the lawyer. "I beg your pardon: Sir Karl, I ought to say. If——"

Karl had raised his head in resentment—in defiance. It caused the lawyer's break.

"Nay, but you are Sir Karl, sir. You succeed to your brother."

"The reminder grated on me, Mr. Plunkett."

"The title's yours, and the estates are yours. Every earthly thing is yours."

"Yes, yes; I suppose so."

"Well, if we can do anything for you, Sir Karl, down there"—indicating with a nod of his head the direction in which Portland Island might be supposed to lie—"or at Foxwood, you have only to send to us. I hope you understand that I am not speaking with a view to business, but as a friend," concluded Mr. Plunkett. "I'll say no more now, for I see you are not yourself."

"Indeed I am not," replied Karl. "I thank you all the same As soon as I can, I must get down to my mother."

The lawyer said good morning, and left him to his breakfast. But Karl had no appetite: then, or for many a day to come. Calling for his bill, he took his departure.

Never had Karl imagined distress and anguish so great as

F

that which he witnessed on his arrival at Weymouth. For once all his mother's pride of power had deserted her. She flung herself at the feet of Karl, demanding *why* he did not persist in his objection to the contemplated attempt, and interfere openly, even by declaring all to the governor of Portland prison, and so save his brother. It was altogether too distressing for Karl to bear.

The first account was in the main correct. Adam Andinnian and the warder were both dead: the one shot, the other drowned.

It was understood that the body might be given up to them for burial. Though whether this was a special favour, accorded to the entreaties of Mrs. Andinnian, or a not-unusual one, Karl knew not. He was glad of this, so far: but he would have thought it better that the place of interment should be Weymouth, and the ceremony made one of the utmost privacy. Mrs. Andinnian, however, ruled it otherwise. She would have her unfortunate son taken to Foxwood, and she at once despatched Karl thither to make arrangements.

On the day but one after Karl reached Foxwood, all that remained of poor Sir Adam arrived. Mrs. Andinnian came in company. She could not bear to part even with the dead.

"I wish I could have seen him," remarked Karl, sadly, as he stood with his hand on the coffin.

"I have seen him, Karl," she answered amid her blinding tears. "They suffered me to look at him. His face was peaceful."

They, and they only, saving Hewitt, attended the funeral. He was buried in the family vault, in Foxwood churchyard, side by side with Sir Joseph and Lady Andinnian.

What an ending, for a young man who, but a few short months before, had been full of health and hope and life!

But the world, in its cold charity, said it was better so.

CHAPTER VIII.

IN THE AVENUE D'ANTIN.

NEW YEAR'S DAY. Or, as the French more emphatically term it, the Jour de l'An. Gay groups went strolling along the Boulevards in the glowing sunshine, gazing at the costly étrennes displayed in the tempting shops: women glancing at the perfect attire of other women that passed; men doffing their hats so perpetually that it almost seemed they might as well have kept them off altogether; children in their fantastic costumes chattering to their mothers, and turning their little heads on all sides: all, men, women, and children, apparently free from every care, save that of pleasure, which constitutes so observable a feature in Parisian life.

Amidst the crowd, passing onwards with a listless step, as if pleasure had no part in his heart and he had no use for étrennes, was a solitary individual: a distinguished-looking man of pleasing features and altogether refined face, whom few of the traversers could have mistaken for aught but an Englishman. His mourning apparel and a certain air of sadness that pervaded his face seemed to be in unison. Several women—ingrained coquettes from their birth, as French women are often born to be—threw glances of admiration at the handsome man, in spite of the fact that their husbands—for that one day—were at their side; and wondered what near relative he had lost. But the gentleman passed on his listless way, seeing them not, and utterly unconscious that any answering glances from his own eyes were coveted. It was Sir Karl Andinnian.

Close upon the burial of his ill-fated brother Adam, Mrs. Andinnian, prostrate with grief and trouble, took to confine herself to her own apartment at Foxwood Court: for it was at that residence she thenceforth took up her abode. Karl found himself nearly altogether excluded from her presence. Even at meals she declined to join him, and caused them to be served for herself apart. "Do you wish me away from Foxwood?" Karl one day asked her. "I do; I would be entirely alone," was her reply. "I am aware that Foxwood is yours now, Karl, and you may think I have no right even to express a hint that you might for a time leave it; but I feel that the chance of my regaining strength and spirits would be greater if left entirely to myself; your presence here is a strain upon me."

The answer was to Karl welcome as sunshine in harvest. He had been longing to travel; to try and find some relief from his thoughts in hitherto untrodden scenes: consideration for his mother—the consciousness that it would be wrong both in duty and affection to leave her—had alone prevented his proposing it. Within four-and-twenty hours after this he had quitted Foxwood.

But Karl was not soon to quit England. Various matters had to be settled in regard to the estate; and when he reached London his lawyers, Plunkett and Plunkett, said they should want him for a little while. The crime committed by Sir Adam so immediately upon the death of Sir Joseph, had caused a vast deal of necessary business to remain in abeyance. Certain indispensable law proceedings to be gone through, had to be gone through now. So Karl Andinnian perforce took up his temporary abode in London; and at the end of a week or two, when he found himself at liberty, he crossed over the water, Vienna being his first halting-place. The sojourn there of a former brother officer, Captain Lamprey, who had been Karl's chiefest friend and stuck to him in his misfortunes, induced it. Captain Lamprey was staying in Vienna with his newly-married wife, and he wrote to ask Karl to join them. Karl did so. Captain Lamprey's term of leave expired the end of December. He and his wife were going home to spend the Christmas, and Karl accompanied them as far as Paris. Mrs. Andinnian, in answer to a question from Karl, whether she would like him to return to her for Christmas, had written back to him a resolute and ungracious No.

So here he was, in Paris. It was all the same to him; this resting-place or that resting-place. His life had been blighted in more ways than one. Of Lucy Cleeve he thought still a great deal too much for his peace. She was far enough removed from him in all senses of the word. In a letter received by Captain Lamprey from some friends at Winchester, it was stated that the Cleeves were wintering in Egypt. Where Karl's own place of sojourn was next to be, he had not decided, but his thoughts rather turned towards every chief continental city that was famed for its gallery of paintings. He thought he would make a pilgrimage to all of them. Karl had the eye of a true artist; to gaze at good paintings was now the only pleasure of his life. He had not yet done with those in Paris and Versailles.

On, upon his course along the Boulevards, passed he. Now and again his eyes turned towards the lovely étrennes with a longing: once in a way, when the throngs allowed him, he halted to look and admire: a longing to buy étrennes himself, and that he had some one to give them to, when bought. It was not well possible for any body to feel more completely isolated from the happy world than did Karl Andinnian.

"How d'ye do, Sir Karl? Charming day for the holiday, is it not?"

Sir Karl made some answering assent, raised his hat, bowed, and passed on. The remark had come from an Englishman with whom he had a slight acquaintance, who had come out shop-gazing with his flock of daughters.

He went straight home then to his hotel—Hôtel Montaigne, Rue Montaigne. As he crossed the courtyard, the landlord—a ponderous gentleman with a ponderous watch-chain—came out and gave him some letters. From some cause the English delivery had been late that morning.

One of the letters was from Captain Lamprey, the other from Plunkett and Plunkett. Neither contained any news of interest; neither thought to wish him happiness for the New Year. It was all the same to Karl Andinnian: the New Year could not have much happiness in store for him.

He strolled out again, turning his steps towards the Champs Elysées. It was but one o'clock yet, and the brightest part of the day. At one of the windows of the palace he fancied he caught a transient glimpse of the Empress. Shortly afterwards, the peculiar clatter of the Prince Imperial's escort was heard advancing, surrounding the young prince in his carriage.

The Champs Elysées were bright to-day. Children attired in silks and satins were playing in the sun, their bonnes sitting by in their holiday costume. New Year's Day and All Saints' Day are the two most dressy epochs of the year in France—as everybody knows. Invalids sat in the warmth: ladies flitted hither and thither like gay butterflies. By a mere chance, Karl thought it so then, his eyes fell on two ladies seated alone on a distant bench. Involuntarily his steps halted; his heart leaped up with a joyous bound. They were Mrs. and Miss Cleeve.

But, ah! how ill she looked—Lucy. The bounding heart fell again as though some dead weight were pressing it. Thin, worn, white; with dark circles round the eyes, and lips that seemed to have no life in them. For a moment Karl wondered whether he might not approach and question her: but he remembered his bargain with Colonel Cleeve.

They did not see him: they were looking at some children in front of them, playing at "Malborough s'en va-t-en guerre." Karl pursued the path he was on, which would carry him away from their bench at right angles. He resolved that if they saw him he would go up and speak: if they did not, he must continue his way.

And he had to continue it. Mrs. Cleeve, who did not look to be in strong health either, seemed absorbed by the play and the childish voices chanting the chanson; Lucy had now bent her forehead upon her hand, as though some ache were there. Karl went on, out of sight, his brow aching too.

"Bon jour, monsieur."

The salutation, which had a touch of surprised pleasure in its tone, came from a natty-looking little Frenchwoman, with a thin red face and shrewd grey eyes. She might have been given five-and-thirty years: but in the register of her native *Mairie* she would have been found hard upon forty. Sir Karl stopped. She was Lucy's maid: formerly Lucy's nurse.

"C'est vous, Aglaé!"

"Mais oui, monsieur."

"I thought I saw Mrs. and Miss Cleeve sitting on a bench just now," continued Karl, changing his language. "Are you staying in Paris?"

"Oh, very long since," replied Aglaé, to whom both languages were nearly alike. "Our apartment is close by, sir—a small house in the Avenue d'.... .n. The delight to find myself in my proper land again, where I can go about without one of those vilain bonnets and hear no street gamins hoot at me for it, is untellable."

"I understood that Colonel Cleeve and his family had gone to Egypt for the winter," observed Karl.

"To Egypt, or to some other place of barbarism: so it was projected, sir. But my young lady, Miss Lucy, is not strong enough to be taken."

"What is the matter with her?" asked Karl, with assumed quietness.

"The matter? Oh! The matter is, that she has got no happiness left in her heart, sir," cried Aglaé, explosively, as if in deep resentment against things in general. "It's dried up. And if they don't mind, she will just go unwarningly out of life. That's my opinion: and, mind, sir, I do not go to say it without reason."

A slight blush mantled in Karl's face. He seemed to be watching a red paper kite, that was sailing beneath the blue sky.

"They see it now, both of them; the Colonel and Madame; they see that she's just slipping away from them, and *they* are ill. Ah, but the senseless—what you call it?—distinctions—that the English set up!"

"But what is the cause?" asked Karl. Though it seemed to him that he could discern quite well without being answered.

Aglaé threw her shrewd eyes into his.

"I think, sir, you might tell it for yourself, that. She has not been well since that fever. She was not well before the fever, since—since about the month of May."

He drew in his lips. Aglaé, with native independence, continued to stare at him.

"Why don't you call and see her, sir?"

"Because—well, I suppose you know, Aglaé. I should not be welcome to Colonel and Mrs. Cleeve."

"And the poor young lady, who never did harm to living soul, is to be let sink down into her grave for the sake of English prejudice! *I* can see. I've got my wits about me, and have seen it all along. My service to you, sir. Bon jour."

The maid went on in a rage, her dainty cap nodding, her smart boots going down rather more noisily than was needful. Sir Karl passed on his way, thinking deeply. He walked about until the daylight was fading, and then strode back rapidly to his hotel, with the air of a man who is about to carry out some resolution that will not wait. *He* was. A resolution that had been floating in his mind before he saw Lucy or encountered her maid.

Colonel Cleeve was seated alone that evening in his dining-room in the Avenue d'Antin, when a letter was delivered to him. For a few minutes he let it lie unheeded. The thoughts he was buried in were very sad ones—they ran on the decaying strength of his only daughter. It seemed to him and Mrs. Cleeve that unless some wonderful change—say a miracle, for instance—interposed, Lucy's life was not worth many weeks' purchase. They knew now—he and his wife—that the parting with Karl Andinnian had been too cruel for her.

Arousing himself from his gloomy visions, the Colonel opened the note—which had been left by hand. Why here was a strange thing!—he started in surprise. Started when he saw the contents of the letter and the signature appended. Had the miracle come?

It was one of the plain, candid, straightforward letters, so characteristic of Karl Andinnian. He said that he had chanced to see Miss Cleeve that day; that he had been shocked by her appearance; that he had happened to hear from Aglaé subsequently how very alarmingly she was failing. He went on to add with shrinking deprecation, every word of which told of the most sensitive refinement, that he feared the trouble of last May might have had something to do with it, and be still telling upon her. He then put a statement of his affairs, as to possessions and income, before Colonel Cleeve, and asked whether he might presume again to address Lucy now that he could offer a good settlement and make her Lady Andinnian.

Three times over Colonel Cleeve read the note, pausing well to reflect between each time. Then he sent for his wife.

"He is of no family—and there's that dreadful slur upon it besides," remarked the Colonel, talking it over. "But it may be the saving of Lucy's life."

"It is a good letter," said Mrs. Cleeve, reading it through her eye-glass.

"It's as good and proper a letter as any young man could write. All his instincts are honourable. Some men might have written to Lucy herself. Putting aside his lack of family and the other disrepute, we could not wish a better son-in-law than Sir Karl Andinnian."

"Yes," deliberated Mrs. Cleeve, after a pause. "True. The disadvantages are great: but they seem little when balanced against the chance of restoring Lucy's life. She will be a baronet's wife; she will be sufficiently rich; and—I think —she will be intensely happy."

"Then I'll send for him," said Colonel Cleeve.

The interview took place on the following morning. It was a peculiar one. Just as plainly open as Karl had been in his letter, so was the Colonel now.

"I think it may be the one chance for saving my child's life," he said; "for there's no denying that she was very much attached to you, Sir Karl. Sitting alone after dinner last evening, I was telling myself that nothing short of a miracle could help her: the doctors say they can do nothing, the malady is on her mind—though for my part I think the chief ill is the weakness left by that ague-fever. Your letter came to interrupt my thoughts; and when I read it I wondered whether that was the miracle."

"If you will only give me Lucy, my whole life shall be

devoted to her best comfort, sir," Karl said in a low tone. "My happiness was wrecked equally with hers: but I am a man and therefore stronger to bear."

"Nothing would have induced me to give her to you had your brother lived," resumed the Colonel. "If I am too plain in what I say I must beg you to excuse it; but it is well that we should understand each other thoroughly. Yourself I like; I always have liked you; but the disgrace inflicted upon you was so great while your brother was living, a convict, that to see Lucy your wife then would I think have killed both me and Mrs. Cleeve. Take it at the best, it would have embittered our lives for ever."

"Had my unfortunate brother lived, I should never have attempted to ask for her, Colonel Cleeve."

"Right. I have observed that on most subjects your ideas coincide with my own. Rather than that—the disgrace to her and to us; and grievous though the affliction it would have brought to me and to her mother—we would rather have laid our child to rest."

The deep emotion with which Colonel Cleeve spoke—the general self-contained man whose calmness almost bordered upon apathy—proved how true the words were, and how terribly the sense of disgrace would have told upon him.

"But your unhappy brother has paid the forfeit of his crimes by death," he continued, "and it is to be hoped and expected that in time the remembrance of him and of what he did will die out of people's minds. Therefore we have resolved to trust to this hope, and give you Lucy. It will be better than to let her die."

Sir Karl Andinnian drew in his slender lips. But that he had passed through a course of most bitter humiliation—and *that*, wherever it falls, seems for the time to wash out pride—he might have shown resentment at the last words. The Colonel saw he felt the sting; and he wished it had not been his province to inflict it.

"It was best to explain this, Sir Karl. Pardon me for its sound of harshness. And now that it is over and done with, let me say that never for a moment have I or Mrs. Cleeve blamed you. It was not your fault that your brother lost himself; neither could you have helped it: and we have both felt almost as sorry for you as though you had been a relative of our own. I beg that henceforth his name may never be mentioned between you and us: the past, so far as regards him, must be as though it had never been. You will observe this reticence?"

"Unquestionably."

"The affair is settled then, Andinnian. Will you see Lucy?"

"If I may," replied Karl, a bright smile succeeding to the sadness on his face. "Does she know I am here?"

"She knows nothing. Her mother thought it might be better that I should speak to you first. You can tell her all yourself. But mind you do it quietly, for she is very weak."

Lucy happened to be alone in the salon. She sat in a red velvet arm-chair as big as a canopy, looking at the pretty étrenne her mother had given her the previous day—a bracelet of links studded with turquoise and a drooping turquoise heart. A smile of gratitude parted her lips, though tears stood in her eyes; for she believed she should not live to wear it long.

"Lucy," said her father, looking in as he opened the door. "I have brought you a visitor who has called—Sir Karl Andinnian."

Lucy rose in trembling astonishment; the morocco case, which had been on her lap, falling to the ground. She wore a dress of violet silk, and Aglaé had folded about her a white shawl—for chillness was present with her still. Karl advanced, and the Colonel shut them in together.

He took both her hands in his, slipping the bracelet on to her attenuated wrist,—and quietly held them. The poor wan face and the hectic colour his presence had called up, had all his attention just then.

"I saw you in the Champs Elysées yesterday, Lucy. It pained me very much to see you so much changed."

"Did you see me? I was there with mamma. It is the fever I had in the summer that hangs about me and does not let me yet get strong."

"Is it *nothing* else, Lucy?"

The hectic deepened to crimson. The soft brown eyes drooped beneath the gaze of his.

"I fancied there might be another cause for it, Lucy, and I have ventured to say so to Colonel Cleeve. He agrees with me."

"You—you were not afraid to call here!" she exclaimed, as if the fact were a subject of wonder.

"What I had to say to Colonel Cleeve I wrote by letter. After that, he invited me to call."

Karl sat down on the red sofa opposite the chair, and put Lucy by him, his arm entwining her waist. "I want you," he said, "to tell me exactly what it is that keeps you from getting strong, Lucy."

"But I cannot tell you, for I don't know," she answered with a little sob. "I wish I could get well, Karl—for poor papa and mamma's sake."

"Do you think I could do anything towards the restoration, Lucy?" he continued, drawing her closer to his side.

"What could you do?"

"Watch you, and tend you, and love you, And—and make you my wife."

"Don't jest, Karl," she said, whispering and trembling. "You know it may not be."

"But if Colonel and Mrs. Cleeve say that it may be?"

The tone of his voice was redolent of anything but jesting; it was one of deep, truthful emotion. Lucy looked questioningly up at him.

"Oh Karl, don't play with me! What do you mean?"

He caught the sweet face, and held it to his. His own hands were trembling, his face as pale as hers. But she could not mistake his grave earnestness.

"It means, my darling, that you are to be mine for ever. My wife. They are going to give you to me: your father brought me here that I might, myself, break it to you."

A minute's doubting look; a slight shiver as if the joy were too great; and then with a sigh she let her head fall on his breast—its future resting-place.

"And what's this that you were looking at, Lucy?" he asked after a while, turning the pretty bracelet round and round her wrist.

"Mamma bought it me yesterday for my New Year's étrenne. I was thinking—before you came—that I might not live to wear it."

"I was thinking yesterday, Lucy, as I walked along the Boulevards, that I would give a great deal to have some one to buy étrennes for. It is not too late, is it? Meanwhile——"

Breaking off his sentence, he took a very rare ring from his finger, one of the most brilliant of opals encompassed by diamonds. She had never seen him wear it before.

"Oh, how very beautiful!" she exclaimed, as it flashed in a gleam of reflected sunlight.

"I do not give it you, Lucy," he said, putting it upon her finger. "I lend it you until I can find another, fit to replace it. That may be in a day, or so. This ring was my father's: made a present of to him by an Eastern Sultan, to whom he was able to render an essential service. At my father's death it came to my brother: and—later—to me."

Karl's voice dropped as he was concluding. Lucy Cleeve felt for him; she knew what *he* must feel at the allusion. She glided her hand into his, unsought.

"So until then this ring shall be the earnest of our betrothal, Lucy. You will take care of it and of my love."

The ring was the same that had been seen on Sir Adam's finger at the trial. On that same day, after his condemnation, he had taken it off, and caused it to be conveyed to Karl—his, from henceforth. But Karl had never put it on his own finger until after his brother's death.

CHAPTER IX.

DOWN AT FOXWOOD.

As Sir Karl Andinnian was leaving the house, he saw Colonel and Mrs. Cleeve in the dining-room. The latter held out her hand to Karl. He clasped it warmly.

"I am glad it is settled," she said, in a low, impressive tone. "You will take good care of her, I know, and make her happy."

"With the best energies of my heart and life," was his earnest answer. "Dear Mrs. Cleeve, I can never sufficiently thank you."

The voices penetrated to a dressing-chamber at the end of the short passage, the door of which was ajar. A lady in travelling attire peeped out. It was Miss Blake, who had just arrived from England somewhat unexpectedly. Karl passed out at the front door. Miss Blake's eyes, wide open with astonishment, followed him.

"Surely that was Captain Andinnian!" she exclaimed, advancing towards the dining-room.

"Captain Andinnian that used to be, Theresa," replied Colonel Cleeve. "He is Sir Karl Andinnian now."

"Yes, yes; but one is apt to forget new titles," was her impatient rejoinder. "I heard he was staying in Paris. What should bring him in *this* house? Is he allowed to call at it?"

"For the future he will be. He is to have Lucy. Mrs.

Cleeve will tell you about it," concluded the Colonel. "I must write my letters."

Mrs. Cleeve was smiling meaningly. Theresa Blake, utterly puzzled, looked from one to the other.

"Have Lucy!" she cried. "Have her for what?"

"Why, to be his wife," said Mrs. Cleeve. "Could you not have guessed, Theresa?"

"To—be—his—wife!" echoed Miss Blake. "Karl Andinnian's wife!" No, no; it cannot be."

"But it *is*, Theresa. It has been settled to-day. Sir Karl has now gone out from his first interview with her. Why, my dear, I quite believe that if we had not brought it about, Lucy would have died. They are all the world to each other."

Miss Blake went back to her room with her shock of agony. From white to scarlet, from scarlet to white, changed her face, as she sat down to take in the full sense of the news, and what it inflicted on her. A cry went up aloud to Heaven for pity, as she realized the extreme depth of her desolation.

This second blow was to Miss Blake nearly, if not quite, as cruel as the first had been. It stunned her. The hope that Karl Andinnian would return to her had been dwelt on and cherished as the weeks had gone on, until it became as a certainty in her inmost heart. Of course his accession to wealth and honours augmented the desirability of a union with him, though it could not augment her love. She had encouraged the secret passion within her; she had indulged in sweet dreams of the future; she had rashly cherished an assurance that she should, sooner or later, become Sir Karl's wife. To find that he was indeed to have Lucy was terrible.

Miss Blake had undergone disappointment on another score. The new modes of worship in Mr. Blake's church, together with the Reverend Guy Cattacomb, had collapsed. Matters had gone on swimmingly until the month of December. Close upon Christmas the rector came home: it should, perhaps, be mentioned that his old curate had died. Mr. Blake was hardly fit to return to his duties; but the reports made to him of the state of things in his church (they had been withheld during his want of strength), brought him back in grief and shame. His first act was to dismiss the Rev. Guy Cattacomb: his second to sweep away innovations and restore the service to what it used to be. Miss Blake angrily resented this: but she was unable to hinder it. Her occupation in Winchester was gone; she was for the present grown tired of the place, and considered whither her steps should be next directed. She had a standing invitation to visit the Cleeves, and felt inclined to do so; for she loved the gay Parisian capital with all her heart. Chance threw her in the way of Captain Lamprey. She heard from him that Sir Karl Andinnian was in Paris; and it need not be stated that the information caused the veering scale to go down with a run. Without writing to apprise Colonel and Mrs. Cleeve, she started. And, in the first few minutes of her arrival at their house, she was gratified by the sight of Karl; and heard at the same time the startling tidings that destroyed her hopes for ever.

It was like a fate. *Comme un sort*, as Mademoiselle Aglaé might have phrased it. Only a few months before, when Miss Blake got home to Winchester from Paris, her heart leaping and bounding with its love for Karl Andinnian, and with the prospect of again meeting him, she had been struck into stone at finding that his love was Lucy's; so now, hastening to Paris from Winchester with somewhat of the same kind of feelings, and believing he had bade adieu to Lucy for ever, she found that the aspect of matters had altered, and Lucy was to be the wife of his bosom. Miss Blake's state of mind under this shock was not an enviable one. And—whereas she had hitherto vented her silent anger on Lucy, woman fashion, she now turned it on Karl. What right, she asked herself, forgetting the injustice of the question, what right had he to go seeking Lucy in Paris, when she had been so unequivocally denied to him for ever? It was a worse blow to her than the first had been.

Waiting until the trace of some of the anguish had passed from her white face, until she had arranged her hair and changed her travelling dress, and regained composure of manner, she went into the presence of Colonel and Mrs. Cleeve. They were yet in the dining-room, talking of Lucy's future prospects; getting, in fact, with every word more and more reconciled to them.

"The alliance will be an everlasting disgrace to you," quietly spoke Miss Blake. "It will degrade Lucy."

"I do not see it, Theresa," said the Colonel. "I do not think any sensible people will see it in that light. And consider Lucy's state of health! Something had to be sacrificed to that. This may, and I believe will, restore her; otherwise she would have died. The love they bear for each other is marvellous—quite out of the common."

Theresa bit her pale lips to get a little colour in them. "A man whose brother was tried and condemned for wilful murder, and who died a convict, striving to escape from his lawful fetters! He is no proper match for Lucy Cleeve."

"The man *is* dead, Theresa. His crimes and mistakes have died with him. Had he lived, the convict, we would have followed Lucy to the grave, rather than allowed one of the Andinnian family to enter ours."

Theresa played with a tremendously big wooden cross of black wood, that she wore appended to a long necklace of black beads—the whole thing most incongruously unbecoming, and certainly not in the best of taste in any point of view. That she looked pale, vexed, disturbed, Colonel and Mrs. Cleeve saw: and they set it down in their honest and simple hearts to her anxiety for Lucy.

"Against Sir Karl Andinnian nothing can be urged, Theresa: and his brother, as I say, is dead," pursued the Colonel. "In himself he is everything that can be desired: a sweet-tempered, honourable gentleman. He is a baronet now, you know; and his proposed settlement on Lucy is good."

"I don't call him rich," doggedly returned Miss Blake. "Compare him with some baronets."

"And compare him, on the other hand, with others! His income averages about seven thousand a year, I believe. Out of that he will accord his mother a good portion while she lives. Compare that with my income, Theresa—as we are on the subject of comparisons; I cannot count anything like *two* thousand."

"Are you sure that he is worthy of Lucy in other ways?" resumed Miss Blake, her tone unpleasantly significant. "I have heard tales of him."

"What tales?"

"Words dropped from the officers at Winchester. To the effect that he is *wild*."

"I can hardly believe that he is," said the Colonel, uneasily, after a pause. "I should dislike to give Lucy to any man of that kind."

"Oh, well, it may not be true," returned Miss Blake, her suggestive conscience reminding her that she was saying more than she ought: or, rather, giving a colouring to it that she was not altogether justified in. "You know little Dennet. More than a year ago—it was before I went abroad —he was talking at the rectory one day about the officers generally, hinting that they were unsteady. I said—of course it was an absurd thing for me to say—that I felt sure Mr. Andinnian was steady: and Dennet rejoined, in a laughing kind of way, that Andinnian was as wild as the rest. That's the truth," concluded Miss Blake honestly, in obedience to her conscience.

Not very much, you will think; but Colonel Cleeve did not like the doubt it implied; and he resolved to set it at rest, if questioning could do it. That same evening, when Karl arrived to dinner, as invited, the Colonel caused him to be shown into a little apartment, that was as much a boot-closet as anything else: but they were cramped for room in the Avenue D'Antin. Colonel Creeve was standing by the fire. He and Karl were very much alike in one particular— that of unsophistication. In his direct, non-reticent manner, he mentioned the hint he had received, giving as nearly as possible the words Theresa had given.

"Is it true, or is it not, Sir Karl?'

"It is not true: at least, in the sense that I fear you may have been putting upon it," was the reply: and Karl Andinnian's truthful eyes went straight out to the Colonel's. "When I was with the regiment I did some foolish things, sir, as the others did, especially when I first joined: a young fellow planted down in the midst of careless men can hardly avoid it, however true his own habits and principles may be. But I soon drew in. When my father lay on his dying bed, he gave me some wise counsel, Colonel Cleeve."

"Did you follow it?"

"If I did not always quite follow it, I at any rate mostly tried to. Had I been by inclination one of the wildest of men, events would have surely sobered me. My acquaintance with Lucy, the love for her that grew up in my heart, would have served to keep me steady; and since then there has been that most dreadful blow and its attendant sorrow. But I was not wild by inclination: quite the contrary. On my word, Colonel Cleeve, I have not gone into the reckless vice and folly that some men go into; no, not even in my days of youth and carelessness. I can truly say that I have never in my life done a wrong thing but I have been bitterly

ashamed of it afterwards, whatever its nature; and—and—
have asked forgiveness of God."

His voice died away with the last hesitating sentence.
That he was asserting the truth as before Heaven, Colonel
Cleeve saw, and judged him rightly. He took Karl's hands
in his: he felt that he was one amid a thousand.

"God keep you, for a true man and a Christian!" he
whispered. "I could not desire one more worthy than you
for my daughter."

When they reached the drawing-room, Lucy was there:
Lucy, who had not joined in the late dinner for some time
past. She wore pink silk; she had a transient colour in her
face, and her sweet brown eyes lighted up at sight of Karl.
As he bent low to speak to her, Theresa Blake covered her
brow, as though she had a pain there.

"Madame est servie."

Sir Karl advanced to Mrs. Cleeve, as in duty bound. She
put him from her with a smile. "I am going on by myself,
Karl. Lucy needs support, and you must give it her. The
Colonel has to bring Miss Blake."

And as Karl took her, nothing loth, under his arm, and
gave her the support tenderly, Miss Lucy blushed the rosiest
blush that had been seen in her face for many a month.
Mademoiselle Aglaé, superintending the arrangement of the
round table, had taken care that their seats should be side
by side. Theresa's fascinated eyes, opposite, looked at them
more than there was any need for.

"Lucy has got a prize," whispered the Colonel to her, as
she sat on his right hand. "A prize if ever there was one.
I have been talking to him about that matter, Theresa, and
he comes out nobly. And—do you see how changed Lucy is,
only in this one day? how well and happy she looks? Just
think! it was only this time last night that his note was
brought in."

Miss Blake did see. Saw a great deal more than was agreeable; the unmistakable signs of mutual love amidst the
rest. Her own feelings were changing; and she almost felt
that she was not far off hating her heart's cherished idol,
Karl Andinnian, with a jealous, and bitter, and angry hatred.
But she must wait for that. Love does not change to hate so
quickly.

It was decided that the marriage should take place without
delay; at least, with as little delay as Lucy's health should

allow. Perhaps in February. Day by day she grew better; appetite returned, spirits returned, the longing to get well returned: all three very essential elements in the case. At a week or two's end Lucy was so much stronger that the time was finally fixed for February, and Sir Karl wrote to tell Plunkett and Plunkett to prepare the deeds of settlement. He also wrote to his mother—which he had somewhat held back from doing: for instict told him the news would terribly pain her; that she would accuse him of being insensible to the recent loss of his brother. And he found that he had judged correctly; for Mrs. Andinnian did not vouchsafe him any answer.

It grieved him much: but he did not dare to write again. It must be remembered that the relations between Karl and his mother were quite exceptional ones. She had kept him at a distance all his life, had repressed his instincts of affection; in short, had held him in complete subjection. If she chose not to accord him an answer, Karl knew that he should only make matters worse by writing to ask why she would not.

"He has forgotten his ill-fated brother: he casts not a thought to my dreadful sorrow; he is hasting with this indecent haste to hear the sound of his own gay wedding bells!" As surely as though he had heard her speak the complaints, did Karl picture to himself the manner of them. In good truth, he would not have preferred to marry so soon himself; but it was right that private feelings should give way to Lucy. They were in a hurry to get her to a warmer place; and it was deemed better that Karl should go with her as her husband than as her lover. In the latter case, Colonel and Mrs. Cleeve must have gone—and he, the Colonel, wanted to be in England to attend to some matters of business. Sir Karl and his wife were to stay away for a year; perhaps more; the doctors thought it might be well for Lucy. Karl was only too glad to acquiesce: for the arrangement, as he candidly avowed, would leave him at liberty to allow his mother a year's undisturbed possession of Foxwood. And so the month of January came to an end, Lucy gaining ground regularly and quickly. As to Miss Blake, she stayed where she was, hardening her heart more and more against Karl Andinnian.

On the 6th of February Sir Karl went to London. The marriage was to take place in Paris on the 12th. He had various matters to transact, especially with his lawyers. The deeds of settlement on Lucy, previously despatched to Paris by Plunkett and Plunkett, had been already signed. When in London Karl wrote a short note to his mother, saying he was in town, and should run down to Foxwood to see her. In her reply, received by return of post, she begged he would *not* go down to Foxwood, as it might "only upset her"—if, the words ran, she might so far presume to deny his entrance to his own house.

It was rather a queer letter. Karl thought so as he studied it. By one of the sentences in it, it almost seemed as though Mrs. Andinnian were not aware of his projected marriage. The longer he reflected, the more desirable did it appear to him that he should see her. So he wrote again, craving pardon for disobeying her, but saying he must come down.

About six o'clock in the evening he reached Foxwood. It was the last day of his stay; on the following one he must depart for Paris. A servant-maid admitted him, and Hewitt came out of the dining-room. The man's face wore a look of surprise.

"I suppose my mother is expecting me, Hewitt."

"I think not, Sir Karl. I took a telegram to the station this morning, sir, to stop your coming," he added in a confidential tone, as he opened the door to announce his master.

Mrs. Andinnian was dining in solitary state in the solitary dining-room. She let fall her knife and fork, and rose up with an angry glare. Her dress was of the deepest mourning, all crape. Save the widow's cap, she had not put on mourning so deep for her husband as this that she wore for her ill-fated son.

"How did you dare to come, after my prohibitory telegram, Karl?" she exclaimed, imperiously.

"I have had no telegram from you, mother," was the reply. "None whatever."

"One was sent to you this morning."

"I missed it, then. I have been about London all day, and did not return to the hotel before coming here."

He had been standing close to her with his hand extended. She looked fixedly at him for a few moments, and then allowed her hand to meet his.

"It cannot be helped, now; but I am not well enough to entertain visitors," she remarked. "Hewitt, Sir Karl will take some dinner."

"You surely do not look on me as a visitor," he said, smiling, and taking the chair at table that Hewitt placed. But, for all the smile, there was pain at his heart. "My stay will be a very short one, mother," he added, "for I must be away long before dawn to-morrow morning."

"The shorter the better," answered Mrs. Andinnian. And Sir Karl could not help feeling that it was scarcely the thing to say to a man, coming to his own house.

He observed that only Hewitt was waiting at table: that no one else was called to bring in things required by the fact of his unexpected intrusion. Hewitt had to go backwards and forwards. During one of these absences Karl asked his mother *why* she should have objected to his coming.

"You have been told," she answered. "I am not in a state to bear the least excitement or to see any one. No visitor whatever is welcomed at Foxwood. My troubles are great, Karl."

"I wish I could lighten them for you, mother."

"You only increase them. But not willingly, I am sure, Karl. No fault lies with you."

It was the kindest thing she had said to him. As they went on talking, Karl became more and more convinced, from chance expressions, that she was in ignorance of his engagement and approaching marriage. When Hewitt had finally left them together after dinner, Karl told her of it. It turned out that Mrs. Andinnian had never received the letter from Paris: though where the fault lay, Karl could not divine. He remembered that he had given it to the waiter of the Hôtel Montaigne to post—a man he had always found to be very exact. Whether he had neglected it, or whether the loss lay at the door of the post itself, the fact was the same—it had never reached Mrs. Andinnian.

She started violently when Karl told her. He noticed it particularly, because she was in general so cold and calm a woman. After staring at Karl for a minute or two she turned her gaze to the fire and sat in silence, listening to him.

"Married!" she exclaimed, when he had stopped. "Married!—and your brother scarcely cold in his dishonoured grave! It must not be, Karl."

Karl explained to her why it must be. Lucy's health required a more genial climate, and he had to take her to one without delay. When respect for the dead and consideration for the living clash, it was right and just that the former should give way, he observed. Mrs. Andinnian did not interrupt him; and he went on to state the arrangements he had completed as to Lucy's settlement. He then intimated, in the most delicate words he could use, that their proposed prolonged residence abroad would afford his mother at present undisturbed possession of Foxwood; and he mentioned the income (a very liberal one) he had secured to her for life.

She never answered a word. She made no comment whatever, good or bad; but sat gazing into the fire as before. Karl thought she was hopelessly offended with him.

He said that he had a letter to write. Mrs. Andinnian gave a dash at the bell, and ordered Hewitt to place ink and paper before Sir Karl. When tea came in she spoke a few words—asking whether he would take sugar, and such like—but, that excepted, maintained her silence. Afterwards, she sat at the fire, again in her arm-chair; buried in disturbed thought; and then she rose to pace the room with uncertain steps, like one who is racked by anxious perplexity. At first Karl felt both annoyed and vexed, for he thought she was making more of the matter than she need have done; but soon he began to doubt whether she had not some trouble upon her, apart from him and his concerns. A word, that unwittingly escaped her, confirmed him in this.

"Mother," he said, "you seem to be in great distress of your own: for I cannot believe that any proceedings of mine would thus disturb you."

"I am, Karl. I am."

"Will you not let me share it, then?—and, if possible, soothe it? You will find me a true son."

Mrs. Andinnian came back to her seat and replied calmly. "If you could help me in any way, Karl, you should hear it. But you cannot—you cannot, that I can see. Man is born to trouble, you know, as the sparks fly upwards."

"I thought that *I* had offended you: at least, pained you by my coming marriage. It grieved me very much."

"My trouble is my own," she answered.

Karl could not imagine what it could be. He tried to think of various causes—just as we all do in a similar case—and rejected them again. She had always been a strangely independent, secretive woman: and such women, given to act with the daring independence of man, but possessing not man's freedom of power, may at times drift into troubled seas. Karl greatly feared it must be something of this kind.

Debt? Well, he did *not* think it could be debt. He had never known of any outlets of expense: and surely, if this were so, his mother would apply to him to release her. But, still the idea kept coming back again: for he felt sure she had not given the true reason for wishing to keep him away from Foxwood, and he could not think of any other trouble. Sunk in these thoughts, he happened to raise his glance and caught his mother's sharp eyes inquisitively fixed on him.

"What are you deliberating upon, Karl?"

"I was wondering what your care could be?"

"Better not wonder. *You* could not help me. Had my brave Adam been alive, I might have told him. He was daring, Karl; you are not."

"Not daring, mother? I? I think I am sufficiently so. At any rate, I could be as daring as the best in your interests."

"Perhaps you might. But it would not serve me, you see. And sympathy—the sympathy that my poor lost Adam gave me—I have never from you sought or wished for."

She was plain at any rate. Karl felt the stab, just as he had felt many other of her stabs during his life. Mrs. Andinnian shook off her secret thoughts with a kind of shiver; and, to banish them, began talking with Karl of ordinary things.

"What has become of Ann Hopley?" he inquired. "She was much attached to you: I thought perhaps you might have kept her on."

"Ann Hopley?—oh, the servant I had at Weymouth. No, I did not keep her on, Karl. She had a husband, you know."

At ten o'clock Mrs. Andinnian wished him good-night and good-bye, and retired. Karl sat on, thinking and wondering. He was sorry she did not place confidence in him, and so give him a chance of helping her: but she never had placed it, and he supposed she never would. At times—and this was one—it had almost seemed to Karl as though she could not be his mother.

CHAPTER X.

MRS. ANDINNIAN'S SECRET.

"WILL you take anything, Sir Karl?"

The question came from Hewitt, who had looked in to ask for orders for the morning, rousing his master from a curious train of thought.

"I don't mind a drop of hot brandy and water, Hewitt. Half a glass. Something or other seems to have given me the shivers. Is it a cold night?"

"No, Sir Karl; the night's rather warm than cold."

"Has my mother any particular trouble or worry upon her, Hewitt, do you know?" Karl asked, as he mechanically watched the mixing of the spirit and water. "She seems to be very much put out."

"I have noticed it myself, sir; but I don't know what the cause is," was the answer. "For my part, I don't think she has been at all herself since Sir Adam's death. Loving him as she did—why, of course, sir, it was a heavy blow; one not to be got over easily."

"And that's true, Hewitt. How many servants have you here?" resumed Karl, asking the question not really with any particular care to know, but simply to turn the subject.

"There's me and two maids, sir."

"You and two maids!" echoed Karl, in surprise.

"Yes, sir, me and two maids. That's all; except the out o' door gardeners."

"But that's not enough for Foxwood. It is only what we had in Northamptonshire. How does the work get done? Why does my mother not keep more?"

"My mistress says she can't afford more, Sir Karl," returned Hewitt, who seemed sore upon the point, and spoke shortly.

"But she can afford more," returned Karl impulsively; "a great many more. Her income is a large one now."

Hewitt rubbed his bald head with an air of perplexity. Karl spoke to him of things that he would not have entered on with any less esteemed and faithful servant. Hewitt had been so long in the family that he seemed like an old confidential friend. From his boyhood's days Karl had looked up to Hewitt with respect. The man stood before his master, as if intending to wait and see him drink the brandy-and-water.

"There can be no debts, you know, Hewitt," spoke Sir Karl, hastily.

Hewitt did not evince any surprise whatever at the implied suggestion. It seemed to be rather the contrary.

"I have fancied that my mistress had some embarrassment on her mind, sir, such as debt might cause," was the rejoinder, much to Karl's astonishment. "I have fancied her money goes somewhere—though I should never hint at such a thing to anybody but you, sir; nor to you if you had not asked me. Perhaps Sir Adam left some debts behind him."

"No, he did not, Hewitt. Any debts left by Sir Adam would have been paid out of the estate before it came to me. Plunkett and Plunkett informed me at once that there were no debts at all: except the costs of the trial."

"Then it must be some that have cropped up since: that is, the claim for them," surmised Hewitt. "It is what I've thought myself, Sir Karl."

"But why have you thought it?"

"Well, sir, one can't help one's thoughts," answered Hewitt, falling away from the question—but not intentionally. "One evening, sir, when my mistress seemed fit to die with trouble, I asked her if anything had happened to vex her: and she answered—after looking at me sternly in silence—No, nothing fresh; only some sorrow of a good many years ago. It was the evening after that gentleman called, Sir Karl: a gentleman who came and stayed with her ever so long."

"What gentleman?" asked Karl.

"Some stranger, sir; I didn't know him. He came up to the house and asked for Mrs. Andinnian. I told him (they were my general orders) that Mrs. Andinnian was not well enough to see visitors. Oh, indeed, he said, and asked to come in and write a note. I was standing by when he began to write it, and he ordered me to the other end of the room: I suppose he feared I might look over. It seemed to me that he wrote but one or two words, Sir Karl; not more: quite in a minute the paper was folded and sealed—for he told me to light the taper. 'There,' said he, 'take that to Mrs. Andinnian: I think she'll see me.' My mistress was very angry when I took it to her, asking why I disobeyed orders;

but when she opened it, her face went deadly white, and she bade me show the gentleman up to her sitting-room. He was there about two hours, sir."

Karl thought this rather strange. "What sort of man was he, Hewitt?"

"A well-dressed gentleman, sir; tall. He had had a hurt to his left arm, and wore it in a black silk sling. When he took it out of the sling to seal the note, he could hardly use it at all. It was that same evening after he had been, sir, that my mistress seemed so full of trouble: a great deal more so than usual."

"Did you hear his name?"

"No, sir, I didn't hear his name. A tray of luncheon was ordered up for him; and by the little that I heard said when I took it in and fetched it away, I gathered that he was a gentleman applying for the agency of your estate."

"But I do not require an agent," cried Karl in some wonder.

"Well, sir, I'm sure that's what the gentleman was talking of. And my mistress afterwards said a word or two to me about the place being neglected now Sir Karl was absent, and she thought she should appoint an agent to look after it."

"But the place is not neglected," reiterated Karl. "How long was this ago?"

"About three weeks, Sir Karl. I've not heard anything of it since, or seen the gentleman. But my mistress seems to have some secret care or uneasiness, apart from the death of Sir Adam. She seems always to be in an inward worry——and you know how different from that she used to be. It has struck me, Sir Karl, that perhaps that stranger came to prefer some claims left by Sir Adam."

Karl did not think this likely, and said so. But neither of them could be at any certainty.

"I wish you would write to me from time to time during my absence, Hewitt, and let me know how my mother is," resumed Karl, dropping the unsatisfactory subject.

"And that I will with pleasure, Sir Karl, if you will furnish me with an address to write to."

"And be sure, Hewitt, that you send to me in any trouble or sickness. I wish my poor mother's life was a less lonely one!"

Hewitt shook his head as he left the room. He felt sure that his mistress would never more allow her life to be anything but a lonely one: the light of it had gone out for ever with her beloved son.

Sir Karl went up to his chamber shortly. Before he had well closed his door, a maid knocked at it, and said Mrs. Andinnian wished to see him. Karl had supposed his mother to be in bed: instead of that, he found her standing by the fire in her little sitting-room, and not undressed.

"Shut the door, Karl," she said—and he saw that her face was working with some painful emotion. "I have been debating a question with myself the better part of this evening, downstairs and up—whether or no I shall disclose to you the trouble that is upon us: and I have resolved to do so. Of two evils, it may, perhaps, be the least."

"I am very glad indeed, my mother."

"Hush!" she solemnly said, lifting a warning hand. "Speak not before you know. Glad! It has been consideration for you, Sir Karl," she added, in that stern and distant tone that so pained him, "that has alone kept me silent. You have no doubt been thinking me unnaturally cold and reserved; but my heart has been aching. Aching for you. If I have not loved you with the passionate love I bore for your poor brother—and oh, Karl, he was my first-born!—I have not been so neglectful of you as you may imagine. In striving to keep you away from Foxwood, I was but anxious that your peace should not be imperilled earlier than it was obliged to be."

"Let me hear it, mother. I can bear it, I daresay."

"You may *bear* it, Karl. A man can bear most things. But, my son, I dread to tell it you. You will regard it as an awful calamity, a frightful perplexity, and your spirit may faint under it."

Karl smiled sadly. "Mother, after the calamities I have undergone within the past year, I do not think Fate can have any worse in store for me."

"Wait—and judge. Your anger will naturally fall on me, Karl, as the chief author of it. Blame me, my son, to your heart's content: it is my just due. I would soften the story to you if I knew how: but it admits not of softening. What is done cannot be undone."

Mrs. Andinnian rose, opened the door, looked up and down the corridor, shut it again, and bolted it. "I do not need to fear eaves-droppers in the house," she observed, "and the doors are thick: but this secret is as a matter of life or death. Sit down there, Karl," pointing to a chair opposite her own.

"I would rather stand, mother."

"Sit down," she reiterated: and Karl took his elbow from the mantel-piece, and obeyed her. He did not seem very much impressed with what he was about to hear: at least, not to the extent that her preparation seemed to justify. Each leaned forward, looking at the other. Mrs. Andinnian had her arms on the elbows of her chair; Karl's were crossed.

"First of all, Karl, you will take an oath, a solemn vow to God, that you will never disclose this secret to any human being without my consent."

"Is this necessary, mother?"

"It is necessary for you and for me," she sharply answered, as if the question vexed her. "I tell you nothing unless you do."

Karl rose, and took the oath. Resuming his seat as before, he waited.

No, she could not say it. They sat, gazing at each other, she in agitation, he in expectancy; and for a minute or two she literally could not say what she had to say. It came forth at last. Only four words.

Only four words. But Karl Andinnian as he heard them sprang up with a cry: almost as the ill-fated man Martin Scott had sprung, when shot to death by his brother.

"Mother! This cannot be true!"

Mrs. Andinnian went over to him and pushed him gently into his chair. "Hush, Karl; make no noise," she soothingly whispered. "It would not do, you see, for the household to be alarmed."

He looked up at his mother with a kind of frightened gaze. She turned away and resumed her seat. Karl sat still, tumultuous ideas crowding on him one after another.

"You should have disclosed this to me before I engaged myself to marry," he cried at last with a burst of emotion.

"But don't you see, Karl, I did not know of your intended marriage. It is because you have informed me of it to-night that I disclose it now."

"Would you have kept it from me always?"

"That could not have been. You must have heard it some time. Listen, Karl: you shall have the story from beginning to end."

It was one o'clock in the morning, before Karl Andinnin quitted his mother's room. His face seemed to have aged years. Any amount of perplexity he could have borne to himself, and borne it calmly; but he did not know how to grapple with this. For, what had been disclosed to him ought to do away with his proposed marriage.

He did not attempt to go to bed. The whole of the rest of the night he paced his room, grievously tormented as to what course he should take. The wind, howling and raging around the house—for it was one of the most turbulent of nights—seemed but an index of his turbulent mind. He knew that in honour he was bound to disclose the truth to Colonel Cleeve and Lucy; but this might not be. Not only was he debarred by his oath; but the facts themselves did not admit of disclosure. In the confusion of his mind he said to his mother, "May I not give a hint of this to Lucy Cleeve, and let her then take me or leave me?" and Mrs. Andinnian had replied by demanding whether he was mad. In truth, it would have been nothing short of madness.

What to do? what to do? In dire distress Karl Andinnian strode the carpet as he asked it. He might make some other excuse, if indeed he could invent one, and write to break off the marriage—for, break it off to their faces he could not. But, what would be the effect on Lucy? Colonel Cleeve had not concealed that they gave her to him to save her life. Were he to abandon her in this cowardly and heartless manner, now at the eleventh hour, when they were literally preparing the meats for the breakfast table, when Lucy's wedding robe and wreath were spread out ready to be worn, it might throw her back again to worse than before, and verily and indeed kill her. It was a dilemma that has rarely fallen on man. Karl Andinnian was as honest and honourable a man as any in this world, and he could see no way out of it: no opening of one. He might not impart to them so much as a hint of the dreadful secret, neither could he inflict the stab that might cost Lucy's life: on the other hand, to make Lucy his wife, knowing what he now knew, would be dishonour unutterable. What was he to do? What was he to do? There was absolutely no loophole of escape, no outlet on either side.

Karl Andinnian knelt down and prayed. Man, careless, worldly man, rarely does these things. He did. In his dire distress he prayed to be guided to the right. But all the uncertainty came back as he rose up again, and he could not see his course at all. Very shortly Hewitt knocked at his door: saying it was time for Sir Karl to get up, if he would catch the passing train. When Sir Karl came forth Hewitt thought how very quickly he had dressed.

"It is a rough morning, sir," said Hewitt, as he opened the hall door.

"Ay, I can hear that. Farewell, Hewitt."

Delayed a tide by the non-controllable winds and waves, Sir Karl reached Paris only on the evening of the eleventh. He drove at once from the station to the Avenue d'Antin, and asked to see Lucy in private. Torn by conflicting interests, he had at length resolved to sacrifice his own sense of honour to Lucy's life. At least, if she should not decide against it.

She was looking radiant. She told him (in a jest) that they had considered him lost, that all had prophesied he had decamped and deserted her. Karl's smile in answer to this was so faint, his few words were so spiritless and subdued, that Lucy, a little sobered, asked whether anything was the matter. They were standing on the hearth-rug: Karl a few steps apart from her.

"What should you say if I had deserted you, Lucy?"

"I should just have said Bon voyage, monsieur," she answered gaily, never believing the qustion had a meaning.

"Lucy, my dear, this is no time for jesting. I have come back with a great care upon me. It is a fact, believe it or not as you will, that I had at one time determined to desert you: to write and give you up."

There was no immediate answer, and Karl turned his eyes on her. The words told home. Her blanched face had a great terror dawning on it.

"Sit down, Lucy, while you listen to me," he said, placing her in a chair. "I must disclose somewhat of this to you, but it cannot be much."

Remaining standing himself, he told her what he could. It was a most arduous task to speak at all, from the difficulties that surrounded it. A great and unexpected misfortune had fallen upon him, he said; one that from its nature he might not further allude to. It would take away a good deal of his substance; it ought in short to debar his marriage with her. He went on to tell of the conflict he had passed through, as to whether he should quit her or not, and of his final resolve to disclose so much to her, and to leave with her the decision.

If she decided against him, he would invent some other plea to Colonel and Mrs. Cleeve for breaking off the marriage; or let the act appear to come from her, as she should will. If she decided for him, why then——

"Tell me one thing, Karl," she said as he broke down. "Has this matter had its rise in any dishonour or ill-doing of yours?"

"No," was the emphatic rejoinder. "I am as innocent in it, and until a day or two ago, was as unconscious of it as you can be. You need not fear that, Lucy."

"Then on your part, you need not have doubted me, Karl," she said, the glad tears rising to her eyes with the intensity of her relief. "It was cruel of you to think of a separation now. I am yours."

"Lucy, look fully into the future. At least as fully as these indefinite words of mine will admit of. I hope—I trust—that no further complication may come of it; that it may be never known to the world. But it may, and probably will, be otherwise. A great calamity may fall upon us; in the world's eyes we should both be dishonoured—*dishonoured*, Lucy; I through others, you through me."

"I am yours; yours for all time," was the reiterated answer.

"Very well, Lucy. So be it. But, my darling, if that blow should fall, you may repent of your marriage with me. I know your parents would repent it for you."

"Hush, Karl!" she whispered, rising from her seat to the arms opening to receive her. "*I* repent? That can never be. My dearest friend, my almost husband, I am yours for weal or for woe. Have you forgotten the vows I shall take to you to-morrow in the sight of God? For richer for poorer, for better for worse."

"God bless you, Lucy! May God bless and protect us both." And as Sir Karl held her to him, his frame shook with its own emotion, and a scalding tear fell on her face from an aching heart.

The second week in March, just as nearly as possible a month after the marriage, Sir Karl Andinnian received at Florence, where he and his wife were staying, a telegram from Hewitt at Foxwood. It stated that Mrs. Andinnian was ill with some kind of fever; it had taken a dangerous turn, and her life might be a question of a few hours.

As quickly as it was practicable for them to travel, Sir Karl and Lady Andinnian reached Paris. Mrs. Cleeve and Miss Blake were still there; the Colonel was in London. The Cleeves had let their house at Winchester, and could not yet get back to it. Sir Karl left Lucy with her mother: not daring, as he said, to take her on to Foxwood, lest the fever should be infectious. The change in Lucy was wonderful: her cheeks were plump and rosy, her eyes told their own unmistakable tale of happiness. Mrs. Cleeve could do nothing but look at her.

"We did well to give her to him," said she to Theresa. But, for answer, Miss Blake only drew in her lips. The sting had not left her.

"O Karl, my darling, don't stay long away from me!" whispered Lucy, clinging to him in the moment of his departure. "And be sure take care of yourself, Karl, and do not run any risk, if you can help it, of the fever."

With many a sweet word of reassurance murmured between his farewell kisses of passionate tenderness, Karl answered her. To part with one another, even for this short and temporary space of time, seemed a great trial.

A change for the better had taken place in Mrs. Andinnian when Karl arrived at Foxwood. She was in no immediate danger. Mr. Moore, the surgeon at Foxwood, informed him that he must not trust to this improvement. The fever had in a degree subsided, but her state of prostration was so great that he feared she might yet die of the weakness. Karl inquired the nature of the illness: Mr. Moore replied that it was a species of low fever more than anything else, and appeared to have been induced chiefly by the sad state of mind Mrs. Andinnian had been brought into, grieving over the fate of her elder son. Dr. Cavendish of Basham (the neighbouring market town) had attended regularly with Mr. Moore. Sir Karl at once telegraphed to London for a physician of worldwide reputation. When this great doctor arrived, he only confirmed the treatment and opinion of the other two; and said that nothing could well be more uncertain than the recovery of Mrs. Andinnian.

Karl wrote these various items of information to his wife in Paris, and showed her how impossible it was that he could quit his mother during the uncertainty. Lucy replied by saying she should think very ill of him if he could; but she begged him to allow her to come to Foxwood and help him in the nursing, saying she was not afraid of the fever. She added a pretty and affectionate message to Mrs. Andinnian—that she would find in her a loving daughter. The same post brought Karl a letter from Mrs. Cleeve, who evidently *was* afraid of the fever. "*Do* you take precautions for yourself, dear Sir Karl, and *do* you fumigate all letters before you send them out?"

Such was its chief burthen.

Karl believed there was no danger from the fever: but, alas, he dared not have Lucy. He had reached Foxwood only to find more complication than ever in the unhappy secret disclosed to him by his mother. Only a word or two dropped by her—and in her weak, and sometimes semi-lucid state, he could not be sure she would not drop them—and Lucy might know as much as he did. Besides, there was no establishment at Foxwood sufficient to receive Lady Andinnian.

Hour after hour, day after day, he sat by his mother's bedside. When they were alone, she could only whisper of the trouble she had disclosed to him. Karl felt that it was wearing her out. He told her so, and she did not deny it. Never for a moment did she let the subject rest: it filled her mind to the exclusion of everything else in the world.

Karl felt that death would inevitably end it: and he watched her grow weaker. The strain upon his own mind was great. Brooding over the matter as he did—for, in truth, to think of any other theme was not practicable—he saw what a wrong he had committed in marrying Lucy. Sir Karl's only interludes of change lay in the visits of the medical men. Dr. Cavendish came once a day; Mr. Moore twice or thrice. The latter was rather brusque in his manner, but kindly, keen, and sensible. He was plain, with a red face, and nose that turned up; and brown hair tinged with grey. The more Karl saw of him, the more he liked him: and he felt sure he was clever in his calling.

"It is a great misfortune that Mrs. Andinnian should have taken poor Sir Adam's death so much to heart," Mr. Moore one day observed to Karl, when he found his patient exhausted, restless, in all ways worse. "While she cultivates this unhappy frame of mind, we can do nothing for her."

"Her love for my brother was a great love, Mr. Moore quite passing the ordinary love of mothers."

"No doubt of that. Still, Sir Karl, it is not right to let regret for his death kill her."

Karl turned the conversation. He knew how wrong were the surgeon's premises. Her regret for his brother's death had been terrible: but it was not that that was killing Mrs. Andinnian.

The days went on, Mrs. Andinnian growing weaker and weaker. Her mind had regained unfortunately all its activity: unfortunately because she had not strength of body to counterbalance its workings. Karl had a great deal to do for her; consultations to hold with her and letters to write: but even yet he was not admitted to her full confidence. During that night's interview with her, when he had learned so much, he had enquired who the gentleman was that had called and taken luncheon. Mrs. Andinnian had declined to answer him, further than it was a Mr. Smith, who had applied for the agency of Sir Karl's estate. Hewitt informed him that Mr. Smith had called again the very day succeeding Sir Karl's departure. He had held a long interview with Mrs. Andinnian, and she had never been well since that hour.

It was very strange: strange altogether. Karl now found out that Mr. Smith had been appointed the agent, and had had a small house, side by side with Foxwood Court, assigned to him as his residence. The information nearly struck Karl dumb. He felt sure there was more behind, some inexplicable cause for this: but no more satisfactory explanation could he obtain from his mother. "*She* was ill, *he* was going to live abroad, therefore it was necessary some responsible person should be on the spot to look after things," was all she said. And Mr. Smith arrived at Foxwood and took up his abode: and Sir Karl did not dare to forbid it.

To Karl's intense surprise, the next letter he had from his wife was dated London. They had left Paris and come over. With his whole heart Karl hoped they would not be coming to Foxwood; and in his answering letter he talked a good deal about the "fever."

As to himself, he was wearing to a shadow. One might surely have thought *he* had a fever, and a wasting one. In writing to Mrs. Cleeve he admitted he was not well; and she wrote him back four pages full of instructions for fumigation, and beseeching him not to come to them. There is nothing like trouble to wear out a man.

The event that had been prognosticated by the doctors and

H

feared by Karl took place—Mrs. Andinnian died. In the midst of praying for a few days' longer life, she died. Only a few days, had run her incessant prayer; a few days! Karl's anguish, what with the death, and what with the weight of other things, seemed more than he could bear. Mrs. Andinnian's grave was made close to that of her son Adam: and the funeral was a very quiet one.

Karl remained at Foxwood, ostensibly fumigating the house and himself, preparatory to joining his wife in town. He looked as much like a skeleton as a man. Mr. Moore noticed it, and asked what was coming to him.

One day Mr. Smith, the agent, called, and was shown in to Sir Karl. The interview lasted about twenty minutes, and then the bell was rung.

"Is the gentleman going to remain here as your agent, sir," enquired Hewitt, with the familiarity of an old servant, when he had closed the door on the guest.

"Why, yes, Hewitt, while I am away. My mother appointed him. She thought it better some one should be here to act for me—and I suppose it is right that it should be so."

Freely and lightly spoke Karl. But in good truth Mr. Smith fairly puzzled him. He knew no more who he was or whence he came than he had known before; though he did now know what his business was at Foxwood. Mr. Smith's conversation during the interview had turned on the Foxwood estate: but he must have been aware Sir Karl saw all the while that his agency was only a blind—a blind to serve as a pretext for his residence at Foxwood. The two were playing a shallow part of pretence with one another. Mrs. Andinnian had fixed the amount of salary he was to receive, and Sir Karl meant to continue the payment of it. Why?—the reader may ask. Because Sir Karl dared not refuse; for the man knew too much of Mrs. Andinnian's dangerous secret: and it lay in his power to render it more dangerous still.

At length Sir Karl went up to London to rejoin his wife. Lucy gave a startled cry when she saw him—he was looking so ill; and Mrs. Cleeve accused him of having had the fever. Karl turned it off lightly: it was nothing, he said, but the confinement to his mother's sick-room.

But Miss Blake, who was growing very keen in her propensity for making the world better than it is, could not understand two things. Why Karl need have lingered so long at Foxwood, or why he could not have had his wife there.

CHAPTER XI.

AT THE GATE OF THE MAZE.

A MORE charming place than Foxwood Court presented in the summer months when the rare and sweet flowers by which it was surrounded were in bloom, could not have been found in the Kentish county. The mansion was not very large, but it was exceedingly gay and pretty to look upon; a white building with a goodly number of large windows, those on the lower floor mostly opening to the ground, so that the terrace could be gained from the rooms at will. The terrace—a gravel walk with brilliant flower beds on either side—ran along the front and the two sides of the house. A marble step or two in four places descended to a lower walk, or terrace, and from thence there was spread out the level lawn, a wide expanse, dotted with beds of flowers, and bounded with groves of beautiful trees. The chief entrance to the house was in its centre: a pillared portico, surmounting a flight of steps that led down to the broad walk dividing the lawn. At the end of this walk between the bank of trees were the large iron gates and the lodge; and there were also two or three small private gates of egress in the iron palisades that enclosed the grounds beyond the trees. If there was a fault to be found with the locality altogether, it perhaps was that it had too many trees about it.

The iron gates opened upon a broad highway: but one that from circumstances, now to be explained, was not much used, except by visitors to Foxwood Court. To the left of the gates a winding road led round to the village of Foxwood; it lay in front, distant about a quarter of a mile. To the right the road went straight to the little railway station: but as there was also a highway from the village to the station direct, cutting off all the round by Foxwood Court, it will readily be understood why that part of the road was rarely used. In the village of Foxwood there were a few good and a few poor houses; some shops; a church and parsonage, the incumbent an elderly man named Sumnor; Mr. Moore, the surgeon; and a solicitor, Mr. St. Henry, who was universally called in the place Lawyer St. Henry. Some good mansions were scattered about in the vicinity; and it was altogether a favoured and attractive neighbourhood.

In a small but very pretty room of Foxwood Court, at the side of the house that looked towards the railway station, and faced the north, sat Mrs. Cleeve and Miss Blake at breakfast. It was a warm and lovely June morning. The table, set off with beautiful china from the Worcester manufactories, with silver plate, and with a glass of choice flowers, was drawn close to the window, whose doors were wide open. By Mrs. Cleeve's hand lay a letter just received from her daughter, Lady Andinnian, saying that she and Karl were really commencing their journey home.

But for interference, how well the world might get on! After Karl Andinnian quitted Foxwood to rejoin his wife in London—as was related previously—Lucy had so far regained her health and strength that there was really no need for her to go, as had been arranged, to another climate. She herself wished not to go, but to take up her abode at once at Foxwood Court, and Colonel and Mrs. Cleeve, seeing her so well, said they would prefer that she should remain in England. Karl, however, ruled it otherwise; and to the Continent he went with his wife.

Nothing more would have been thought of this, but for Miss Blake. She was very keen-sighted, and she was fond of interference. Somewhat of love still, anger, and jealousy rankled in her heart against Karl Andinnian. Anything she could say against him she did say: and she contrived to impress Mrs. Cleeve with a notion that he, in a sort, had kidnapped Lucy and was taking her abroad for some purposes of his own. She boldly averred that Sir Karl had been *keeping his wife away from Foxwood* by statements of the fever, and such like, false and plausible: and that he probably meant to hide her away from them in some remote place for ever.

This served to startle Mrs. Cleeve—though she only half believed it. She wrote to Sir Karl, saying that both herself and the Colonel wished to see Lucy home, and begged of him to return and take up his abode at Foxwood. Karl replied that Foxwood was not ready for them; there was no establishment. Mrs. Cleeve wrote again—urging that she and Theresa should go down and engage two or three servants, just enough to receive himself and Lucy: afterwards they could take on more at will. A few days' delay and Karl's second answer came. He thanked Mrs. Cleeve for the trouble she offered to take, and accepted it: specifying a wish that the servants should be natives of the locality—and who had always lived in it.

"Karl wishes to employ his poor neighbours," observed Mrs Cleeve. "He is right, Theresa. You must see how good and thoughtful he is."

Theresa could find no cause to confute this much. But she was more and more persuaded that Sir Karl would have kept Lucy away from Foxwood if he could. And we must admit that it looked like it.

Mrs. Cleeve lost no time in going down with Miss Blake to Foxwood Court. Hewitt, who had been left in charge, with an elderly woman, received them. They thought they had never seen a more respectable or thoroughly efficient retainer than Hewitt. The gardeners were the only other servants employed. They lived out of doors: the chief one, Maclean, inhabiting the lodge with his wife.

While Miss Blake was looking out for some young women servants, two or three of whom were speedily found and engaged, she made it her business to look also after the village and its inhabitants. That Miss Blake had a peculiar faculty for searching out information, was indisputable: never a better one for the task than she: and when an individual is gifted with this quality in a remarkable degree, it has to be more or less exercised. Miss Blake might have been a successful police detective: attached to a private enquiry office she would have made its fortune.

And what she learnt gave her a profound contempt for Foxwood. We are speaking of the village now: not the Court. In the first place, there was no church: or, at least, what Miss Blake chose to consider as none. The vicar, Mr. Sumnor, set his face against views of an extreme kind, and that was enough for Miss Blake to wage war with. Old Sumnor, to sum him up in Miss Blake's words, might be conscientious enough, but he was as slow as a tortoise. She attended his church the first Sunday, and found it unbearably tame. There were no candles or flowers or banners or processions: and there was no regular daily service held. Miss Blake thought one might as well be without breakfast and dinner. Foxwood was a benighted place and nothing less.

Mr. Sumnor's family consisted of an invalid daughter left him by his first wife; a second wife and two more daughters. Mrs. Sumnor kept him in subjection, and her two daughters were showy and fast young ladies. The surgeon, Mr. Moore, a widower, had four blooming girls, and a sister, Aunt Diana, a kind of strong-minded female, who took care of them. The young ladies were pretty, but common-place. As to the lawyer, St. Henry, he had no children of his own, but had taken to a vast many of his dead brother's. There were many other young ladies in the vicinity; but it was an absolute fact that there were no gentlemen—husbands and fathers of families excepted; for the few sons that existed were gone out to make their way in the world. Miss Blake considered it not at all a desirable state of things, and accorded it her cool contempt. But the place showed itself friendly, and came flocking in its simple manners and hearty good will to see the Hon. Mrs. Cleeve, Lady Andinnian's mother, and to ask what it could do for her. So that Miss Blake, whether she liked it or not, soon found herself on terms of sociability with Foxwood.

One morning an idea dawned upon her that seemed like a ray from heaven. Conversing with the Miss St. Henrys, those ladies—gushing damsels with enough brown hair on their heads to make a decent-sized hayrick, and in texture it was nearly as coarse as hay—informed her confidentially that they also considered the place dead, in the matter of religion. Often visiting an aunt in London—whose enviable roof-top was cast within the shadow of a high ritualistic establishment, boasting of great hourly doings and five charming curates—it might readily be imagined the blight that fell upon them when doomed to return to Foxwood Church and plain old Sumnor: and they breathed a devout wish that a church after their own hearts might be established at Foxwood. This was the ray of light that flashed upon Miss Blake. She started at its brightness. A new church at Foxwood! If the thing were possible to be accomplished, *she* would accomplish it. The Rev. Guy Cattacomb, what with prejudiced bishops and old-world clergyman, did not appear to be appreciated according to his merits, and had not yet found any active field for his views and services. Miss Blake was in occasional correspondence with him, and knew this. From being a kind of dead-and-alive creature under the benighting torpidity of Foxwood, Miss Blake leaped at once into an energetic women. An object was given her: and she wrote a long letter to Mr. Cattacomb telling him what it was. This morning his answer had been delivered to her.

She chirped to the birds as she sat at breakfast: she threw them crumbs out at the window. Mrs. Cleeve was quitting

Foxwood that day, but hoped to be down again soon after
Karl and her daughter reached it.

"You are sure, Theresa, you do not mind being left alone
here?" cried Mrs. Cleeve, eating her poached egg.

But Theresa, buried in her own active schemes, and in the
letter she had just had from Mr. Cattacomb—though she did
not mention aloud the name of the writer—neither heard nor
answered. Mrs. Cleeve put the question again.

"Mind being left here? Oh dear no, I shall like it. I
hated the place the first few days, but I am quite reconciled
to it now."

"And you know exactly what there is to do for the arrival
of Sir Karl and Lucy, Theresa?"

"Why of course I do, Mrs. Cleeve. There's Hewitt, too:
he is a host in himself."

Breakfast over, Miss Blake, as was customary, went out.
Having no daily service to take up her time, she hardly knew
how to employ it. Mr. Cattacomb's letter had told her that
he should be most happy to come to officiate at Foxwood if a
church could be provided for him: the difficulty presenting
itself to Miss Blake's mind was—that there was no church to
provide. As Miss Blake had observed to Jane St. Henry
only yesterday, she knew they might just as well ask the
Dean of Westminster for his abbey, as old Sumnor for his
church, or the minister for his Dissenting chapel opposite the
horse-pond.

Revolving these slight drawbacks in her brain, Miss Blake
turned to the right on leaving the gates. Generally speaking
she had gone the other way, towards the village. This road
to the right was more solitary. On one side of it were the
iron palisades and the grove of trees that shut in Foxwood;
on the other it was bounded by a tall hedge that had more
trees behind it. A little farther on, this tall hedge had a
gate in the middle, high and strong, its bars of iron so closely
constructed that it would not have been well possible for ill-
intentioned tramps to mount it. The gate stood back a little,
the road winding in just there, and was much shut in by
trees outside as well as in. Opposite the gate, over the road,
stood a pretty red-brick cottage villa, with green venetian
shutters, creeping clematis around its parlour windows, and
the rustic porch between them. It was called Clematis Cottage, and may be said to have joined the confines of Foxwood
Court, there being only a narrow side lane between, which

led to the Court's stables and back premises. Miss Blake had before noticed the cottage and noticed the gate: she had wondered in her ever-active curiosity who occupied the one; she had wondered whether any dwelling was enclosed within the other. This morning as she passed, a boy stood watching the gate, his hands in his pockets and whistling to a small dog, which had contrived to get its one paw into the gate and seemed to be in a difficulty as to getting it back again. Miss Blake, after taking a good look at Clematis Cottage, crossed the road; and the boy, in rustic politeness, turned his head and touched his shabby cap.

"Where does this gate lead to?" she asked. "To any house?"

"Yes, 'um," replied the boy, whose name, as he informed Miss Blake in reply to her question, was Tom Pepp. "It's the Maze."

"The Maze," she repeated, thinking the name had an odd sound. "Do you mean that it is a house, boy?—a dwelling place?"

"It be that, 'um, sure enough. Old Mr. Throcton used to live in't. Folks said he was crazy."

"Why is it called the Maze."

"It is a maze," said the boy, patting his dog, which had at length regained its liberty. "See that there path, 'um"—pointing to the one close within the gate—"and see them there trees ayont it?"

Miss Blake looked through the interstices of the gate at the trees beyond the path. They extended on all sides farther than she could see. Thick, clustering trees, and shrubs full of leafy verdure, with what looked like innumerable paths amidst them.

"That's the maze," said the boy, "and the place is called after it. Once get among them there trees, 'um, and you'd never get out again without the clue. The house is in the middle on't; a space cleared out, with a goodish big garden and grass plat. I've been in there three or four times when old Mr. Throcton lived there."

"Did you get in through the maze?" asked Miss Blake.

"Yes, 'um; there ain't no other way. 'Twere always along of mother; she knowed the housekeeper. The man servant he'd take us through the trees all roundabout and bring us out again."

"Where does this path lead to?" was the next question

speaking of the one inside between the labyrinth and the gate.

"He goes round and round and round again," was the lucid answer. "I've heard say that a door in it leads right to the house, 'um, but nobody can find the door save them that know it."

"What an extraordinary place!" exclaimed Miss Blake, much impressed with the narration. "One would think smugglers lived there—or people of that k'nd."

The boy's eyes—and intelligent eyes they were—went up to Miss Blake's. He did not particularly understand what a smuggler might be, but felt sure it could not apply to Mr. Throcton.

"Mr. Throcton was a rich gentleman that had always lived here," he said. "There warn't nothing wrong with him—only a bit crazy. For years afore he died, 'um, he'd never see nobody; and the house, mother said, were kept just like a prison."

Miss Blake, very curious, looked at the lock and tried to shake the gate. She might as well have tried to shake the air.

"Who lives in it now, Tom Pepp?"

"A young lady, 'um."

"A young lady?" echoed Miss Blake. "Who else?"

"Not nobody else," said the boy.

"Why, you don't mean to say a young lady lives alone there?"

"She do, 'um. She and a old servant or two."

"Is she married or single?"

Tom Pepp could not answer the last question. Supposed, now he came to think of it, she must be single, as no husband was there. He did not know her name.

"What is she like?" asked Miss Blake.

"I've never see'd her," said Tom Pepp. "I've never see'd her come out, and never see'd nobody go in but the butcher's boy. He don't go in, neither: he rings at the gate and waits there till they come to him. A woman in a poke bonnet comes out and does the other errands."

"Well, it must be a very lively place for a young lady!" mentally observed Miss Blake with sarcasm. "She must want to hide herself from the world."

"Mother see'd her at church once with her veil up. She'd never see'd nothing like her so pretty at Foxwood."

Turning to pursue her walk, Tom Pepp, who worked for Farmer Truefit, and who was in fact playing truant for half an hour and thought it might be policy not to play it any longer, turned also, the farm lying in that direction. At that moment, Miss Blake, happening to cast her eyes across the road, saw the head and shoulders of a gentleman stretched out of one of the sash windows of Clematis Cottage, evidently regarding her attentively.

"Who is that gentleman, Tom Pepp?"

"Him! Well, now, what did I hear his name was again?" returned the lad, considering. "Smith. That's it. It's Mr. Smith, 'um. He be a stranger to the place, and come here just afore Mrs. Andinnian died. It's said he was some friend of her'n."

"Rather a curious person, that Mrs. Andinnian, was she not?" remarked Miss Blake, invited to gossip by the intelligence of the boy.

"I never see'd her," was the reiteration. "I've never yet see'd the new master of Foxwood, Sir Karl Andinnian. It's said Sir Karl is coming home himself soon," added the boy; "him and his lady. Hope he'll be as good for the place as Sir Joseph was."

They passed on; the opposite gentleman's eyes following Miss Blake: of which she was quite conscious. Soon they came to the road on the left hand that led direct to the village. Miss Blake glanced down it, but continued her walk straight onwards, as if she had a mind to go on to the railway station. Casting her eyes this way and that, she was attracted by a pile of ruins on the other side the road, with what looked like a kind of modern room amidst them.

"Why, what's that?" she cried to Tom Pepp, standing still to gaze.

"Oh, them be the ruins, 'um," answered Tom Pepp. "It had used to be the chapel belonging to the grey friars at the monastery."

"What friars?—what monastery?" eagerly returned Miss Blake, much interested.

The friars were dead years ago, and the monastery had crumbled to pieces, and Mr. Truefit's farm was built upon where it used to stand, was the substance of the boy's answer; delivered in terrible fright, for he caught sight of his master, Mr. Truefit, at a distance.

The farmhouse lay back beyond the first field. Miss Blake

glanced at it; but all her interest was concentrated in these ruins close at hand.

"Surely they have not desecrated sacred ruins by putting up a barn amidst them!" she exclaimed, as she crossed the road to explore. There were half-crumbled walls around, part of an ivied stone block that she thought must have been the basement of a spire, and other fragments.

"It's not a barn," said Tom Pepp; "never was one. They mended some o' the old walls a few years ago, and made it into a school-room, and the children went to school in it—me for one. Not for long, though. Lady Andinnian and Sir Joseph—it was more her than him—fell out with Parson Sumnor and the trusts; and my lady said the children should never come to it again. After that, the trusts built 'em a school-room in the village; and 'twas said Sir Joseph sent 'em a five-hundred pound in a letter and never writ a word to tell where it come from. He was a good man, he was, when my lady 'ud let him be."

Miss Blake did not hear half; she was lost in an idea that had taken possession of her, as she gazed about inside the room. It was narrow, though rather long, with bare whitewashed walls and rafters above, the windows on either side being very high up.

"If this place was the chapel in the old times, it must have been consecrated!" cried she breathlessly.

"Very like, um," was the lad's answer, in blissful ignorance of her meaning. "Them grey friars used to eat their meals in it, I've heard tell, and hold jollifications."

Preoccupied, the sinful insinuation escaped Miss Blake. The conviction, that this consecrated place would be the very thing needed for Mr. Cattacomb's church, was working in her brain. Tom Pepp was ensconced in a dark corner, his dog in his arms, devoutly hoping his master would not come that way until he had made his escape. The ruins belonged to Farmer Truefit, the boy said. The fact being, that they stood on the land the farmer rented; which land was part of the Andinnian estate.

"Has nothing been done with the room since it was used for the school?" asked Miss Blake.

"Nothing," was the boy's reply. It was kept locked up until Lady Andinnian's death: since then, nobody, so far as he knew, had taken notice of it.

"What a beautiful little chapel it will make!" thought

Miss Blake. "And absolutely there's a little place that will do for a vestry! I'll lose no time."

She went off straight to an interview with Mr. Truefit; which was held in the middle of a turnip field. The farmer, a civil man, stout and sturdy, upon hearing that she was a relative of his new landlord's wife, the young Lady Andinnian, and was staying at Foxwood Court, took off his hat and gave her leave to do what she liked to the room and to make it into a place of worship if she pleased; his idea being that it was to be a kind of Methodist chapel, or a mission-room.

This sublime idea expanding within her mind, Miss Blake walked hurriedly back to Foxwood—for Mrs. Cleeve was to depart at midday. In passing the Maze, the interest as to what she had heard induced her to go up to the gate again, and peer in. Turning away after a good long look, she nearly ran against a rather tall gentleman, who was slowly sauntering amid the trees outside the gate. A gentleman in green spectacles, with a somewhat handsome face and black whiskers—the same face and whiskers, Miss Blake thought, that had watched her from the opposite window. He wore grey clothes, had one black glove on and his arm in a sling.

Mr. Smith took off his hat and apologised. Miss Blake apologised. Between them they fell into conversation. She found him a very talkative, pleasant man.

"Curious place, the Maze?" he echoed in answer to a remark of Miss Blake's. "Well, yes, I suppose it may be called so, as mazes are not very common."

"I have been told a young lady lives in it alone."

"I believe she does. In fact, I know it, for I have seen her, and spoken with her."

"Oh, have you!" cried Miss Blake, more curious than ever.

"When I went to receive the premium for Sir Karl Andinnian—due on taking the house," quietly explained Mr. Smith.

"And who is she?"

"She is a Mrs. Grey."

"Oh—a married woman."

"Certainly. A single lady, young as she is, would scarcely be living entirely alone."

"But where is her husband?"

"Travelling, I believe. I understood her to say so."

"She is quite young, then?"

"Quite."

"Is she good-looking?" continued Miss Blake.

"I have rarely seen anyone so pretty."

"Indeed! What a strange thing that she should be hiding herself in this retired place!"

"Do you think so? It seems to me to be just the spot a young lady might select, if obliged to live apart for a time from her husband."

"Of course there's something in that," conceded Miss Blake. "Does she visit at all in the neighbourhood?"

"I think not. I am sure not. If she did I should see her go in and out. She takes a walk occasionally, and sometimes goes to church on Sundays. But she mostly keeps in her shell, guarded by her two old domestics."

In talking, they had crossed the road, and now halted again at the little gate of Clematis Cottage. Miss Blake asked if he knew anything about the ruins she had noticed further up: and Mr. Smith (who had introduced himself to her by name in a light, gentlemanly manner) said he did not, but he had a book of the locality indoors which he would refer to, if she would do him the honour of stepping into his little drawing-room.

Rather fascinated by his courteous attentions, Miss Blake did so: and thought what a bright-looking, pretty drawing-room it was. The gentleman took off his green glasses (casually mentioning that he wore them out of doors as a protection against the sun, for his eyes were not strong) and searched for the guide-book. The book, however, proved to be chiefly a book of roads, and said very little more of the monastery and the ruins than Miss Blake had heard from Tom Pepp.

"You have hurt your arm," she at length ventured to observe, as he slowly drew it once or twice out of the sling, and seemed to use it with trouble. "Any accident?"

"An accident of long standing, madam. But the wrist continues weak, and always will continue so, next door to useless; and I wear the sling for protection."

Miss Blake took her departure; the gentleman escorting her to the garden gate with much ceremony. In fact, it almost seemed as though he wished to make a favourable impression on her.

"He is a gallant man," was Miss Blake's mental comment—"and a well-informed and pleasant one. I wonder who he is?"

But her thoughts, veering round to many other matters, at

length settled themselves upon the Maze and its young lady inmate. They quite took hold of her mind and held possession of it, even to the partial exclusion of Mr. Cattacomb and the promising ruins.

In later days, Miss Blake said this must have been nothing less than instinct.

CHAPTER XII.

TAKING AN EVENING STROLL.

MISS BLAKE carried her point. In a very short space of time the little wayside room in the ruins—call it chapel, schoolroom, barn, what you will—was converted into a church and styled "St. Jerome." Setting to work at once with a will, Miss Blake had left not a stone unturned to accomplish her purpose. She pressed several of the young ladies in the village into the service. Nothing loth, they. Having heard of the divers merits of the Reverend Guy Cattacomb, they could but be desirous so shining a light should be secured amidst them. Miss Blake herself brought all her rare energy, her unflagging perseverance to the task. When she took a cause to heart, no woman was so indomitable as she. As may readily be supposed, a good deal had to be done to the room before it could be made what was wanted; but contrivance worked wonders. All the money Miss Blake could spare she freely applied: it was not sufficient, and she wrote to sundry friends, begging contributions. She next went, with Miss St. Henry and Miss Moore, to some of the houses in the vicinity, to every one where it might be safe to go, asking for aid. This personal canvass was not always successful. Some professed not to understand why a second church was required, and gave shillings instead of pounds. One old lady, however, had her generous instincts so worked upon by the eloquence of Miss Blake (as much as she could hear of it, for she was very deaf, and her companion declared afterwards that she believed all the while she was giving to a new industrial school possessing a resident chaplain), that she handed over a cheque for fifty guineas. Miss Blake could not believe her eyes when she saw it: and she assured the old lady that every blessing of heaven would be showered down on her in return. Miss Blake's personal friends also contributed well—and the matter was accomplished. Not only was the chapel itself set up, but the stipend of Mr. Cattacomb assured for the first few months. To do Miss Blake justice, she wished all things to be religiously right, and she never entertained a doubt that the place had once been duly consecrated. Her whole heart was in the work—always excepting a slight small corner of it that was still filled with her wrongs and Karl Andinnian.

The early afternoon sun shone down on the bright flowers, the well kept lawns of Foxwood Court, as Miss Blake stepped out of one of its windows, her walking costume perfect. She was always well dressed: but to-day her toilet was more elaborate than usual. Standing for a moment to look round at the beautiful place, at its complete order, there rose up in her heart one wild, angry thought—"But for Lucy, this would have been my own." A very mistaken assumption on Miss Blake's part, but who was to convince her of that? Banishing the thought resolutely, she walked along at a brisk pace, as if running a race with time. It was a great day this. Two events were coming off in it that stirred Miss Blake to the core. The Reverend Mr. Cattacomb was expected by the four o'clock train; and Sir Karl and Lady Andinnian would arrive at home for dinner.

Miss Blake took the way to St. Jerome's Church, a very choice bouquet of hot-house flowers in her hand. Glancing at the gate of the Maze—in regard to which place her interest had not in the least abated—she bore onwards, and soon joined some groups of ladies, who were advancing to St. Jerome's by the more direct route from the village. They had appointed to meet that afternoon and put the finishing touches to the room ere it should be seen by its pastor—if indeed any touches remained to be done. A matter such as this could not but have excited much comment at Foxwood ever since the first day that Miss Blake took it in hand. Prudent mothers, full of occupation themselves, warned their daughters against being "led away." The daughters, whose hands were idle, rushed to the new attraction, stealthily at first, openly afterwards. They grew to be as energetic as Miss Blake herself, and were in a fervour of eagerness for the arrival of Mr. Cattacomb.

Miss Blake opened the door and allowed the rest to file in. She stayed looking at something that did not please her—a wheel-barrow full of earth lodging right against St. Jerome's outside walls.

"I should not wonder but it's that Tom Pepp who has left it there!" said Miss Blake severely. "The boy is for ever dodging about here—and brings other boys in his train. When Mr. Cattacomb——"

"Good afternoon, madam!"

Miss Blake turned at the address, and recognized Mr. Smith —his green spectacles on and his arm in a sling as usual. She had seen him once or twice since that first meeting, but he had only bowed in passing.

"May I be permitted to enter?" he asked, waving his hand at the church door.

"Oh, certainly," she replied. "Indeed, I hope you will become one of St. Jerome's constant worshippers." So he went in with the crowd of ladies.

It certainly looked a sweet little place—as Jane St. Henry remarked aloud. Candles, flowers, crosses, scrolls—for Miss Blake knew exactly what would please Mr. Cattacomb. The common white-washed walls were nearly hidden: mottoes, a painting or two, and prints lay thickly on them, all of course of a sacred character. The plain segged-seated chairs stood pretty thickly. The other arrangements were as good as funds, time, and space had allowed. Leading off on one side at the upper end, was a small vestry; with a sort of corner box in it that was to serve as a confessional. This vestry— which used to be the place where the school children put their hats and bonnets—had an objectionable modern window in it; before which was hung a blind of printed calico, securing the vestry's privacy from sun and gazers.

Mr. Smith might have been a travelled man, but in all his travels he had seen no place of worship like unto this. He was saying so to himself as he turned and gazed about through his green glasses. He took them off and gazed again.

"Is it not charming, sir?" asked Jane St. Henry.

"It is rather small," was the response.

"Oh, that's the worst," said the young lady. "One cannot have everything at the beginning: there must always be some drawbacks. I know a church in London, not very much larger than this, where there are three sweet little private sanctuaries: here we have only one."

"Sanctuaries?" repeated the agent, evidently not understanding.

"Confessionals. For confession, you know. We have only one here, and that is obliged to be in the vestry."

"Oh, then the place *is* Roman Catholic!" said Mr. Smith, quietly. "I thought so."

He had no intention to offend: it was simply what he inferred: but Miss St. Henry gave a little shriek and put her two hands to her ears. Martha Sumnor, a free, showy girl, stepped up.

"For goodness' sake don't call it that," she said. "Papa would go on at us, for coming here, worse than he does."

Mr. Smith bowed and begged pardon. He could not help thinking this was a daughter of the vicar of the old church, but was not sure: and he wondered much.

Even so. The two daughters of Mr. Sumnor had joined St. Jerome's. They and their mother had long set the vicar at defiance.

Foxwood was deemed to be a particularly healthy place; in the summer months, invalids were wont to resort to it from the neighbouring town of Basham. To meet requirements, lodgings being scarce, a row of houses had been run up in the heart of the village, near where the old pound used to stand. They were called Paradise Row. Very pretty to look at; perhaps not quite so good to wear; stuccoed white fronts outside, lath and plaster within. If the door of one banged, the whole of the houses shook; and the ringing of a sitting-room bell was heard right and left throughout the Row.

It was in the middle house of these favoured dwellings, No. 5, kept by Mrs. Jinks, that the ladies had secured apartments for the Reverend Guy Cattacomb. The bow-windowed front parlour, and the bed-room behind it. Mrs. Jinks, familiarly called by her neighbours and friends the Widow Jinks, was beyond the middle age — to speak politely — with a huge widow's cap nearly as black as the chimney, and a huge black bonnet generally tilted on the top of it. She had deemed herself very lucky to find her rooms taken by the ladies for the new clergyman, boasting to her neighbours that it was of course a "permanent let:" but before the clergyman arrived, she had grown somewhat out of conceit of the "let," so worried was she by the young ladies. Parties of them were always coming, bringing this, that, and the other for the comfort of their expected pastor, and calling the Widow Jinks to the door a dozen times in a day.

Upon leaving St. Jerome's this afternoon, the ladies went in a body to Paradise Row, intending to await the advent of the Reverend Guy, and to see that butter and other essentials

I

had been got in for him. Miss Blake could have dispensed with so large a party—but what was she to do?—There they were, and stuck to her. All the way to the house they had been talking of Mr. Smith; wondering who he was and why he had come to live at Foxwood. Miss St. Henry at length remembered to have heard he was a friend of the Andinnian family, and had been looking after things as agent during the absence of Sir Karl.

"An agent!" exclaimed Miss Blake, drawing herself up.

"Not a common agent, of course. Does what he does out of friendship. Here we are."

"Oh, that's very different," returned Miss Blake, giving a loud, long, important knock at the Widow Jinks's door.

"Well, that *is* a shame of old Jinks!" cried Jemima Moore, in an undertone to the rest as they got admittance and went into the parlour.

For the Widow Jinks had not deemed it necessary to smarten herself up to receive her new lodger. She answered the door in her ordinary working costume: rusty black gown, huge cap and bonnet. Her face and hands were black too, as if she had been disturbed in cleaning the pots and kettles.

"She ought to be told of it. And did you see how sour she looked?"

Miss Blake put the beautiful bouquet of hothouse flowers—which she had been guarding carefully—into a vase of water, for it was for Mr. Cattacomb they had been destined. Some light refreshment in the shape of wine and cake stood ready on the table; and Mrs. Jinks was examined as to other preparations. All was in readiness, and the ladies waited with impatience.

An impatience that at length subsided into doubt, and that into disappointment. The clock had gone ticking on; the train must have been in long ago, and it became evident that Mr. Cattacomb had not come. Miss Blake walked home slightly vexed: and there she found Sir Karl and Lady Andinnian.

Things often go cross and contrary. *They* had not been expected until later, and Miss Blake had intended to preside —if it may be called so—at both arrivals. As it happened, she had presided at neither. It was in crossing the lawn, that Lucy, radiant, blooming, joyous, ran out to meet her.

"Good gracious!" cried Miss Blake.

"Oh, Theresa, how beautiful and happy everything is!" cried the young wife, pushing back her bonnet to give and take the kiss of greeting. "Karl has been showing me the rooms. Hewitt said you would not be long."

"But when did you come, Lucy?"

"We came in by the four o'clock train, and took a fly. Here's my husband. Karl, do you see Theresa?"

Karl was coming down the terrace steps to greet her. Miss Blake advanced coldly.

"How do you do, Sir Karl?" and the hand she put into his seemed limp and cold. *He* did not look blooming; but worn, ill, and depressed.

They entered the hall together, the rays from the coloured windows shining on them and on the tesselated floor, lighting all up with a cheerful brightness. The reception-rooms were on either side the hall: they were what Sir Karl had been showing to his wife. Lucy declared it was the prettiest house she was ever in.

"I like this room better than any of the grand ones," spoke Miss Blake, leading to the little north room she generally sat in, where we saw her breakfasting with Mrs. Cleeve.

"It shall be called your room, then, Theresa," said Lucy. "Oh yes, it is very pretty," she continued, looking at the light paper, flecked with gold, the light furniture with its crimson satin coverings, the various tasty objects scattered about, and the glass doors, wide open to the terrace, to the sweet flowers, and to the smooth lawn beyond.

"I believe this was the late Lady Andinnian's favourite room," observed Karl.

"Let me see," said Lucy, stepping outside, "this must look towards the railway station. Oh yes; and Foxwood lies the other way."

Opposite to this window, some steps descended to the lawn from the terrace. In very lightness of heart, she ran down and up them. Karl was talking to Miss Blake.

"There's a room answering to this in size and position on the other side of the house; as of course you know," he observed. "Sir Joseph, I hear, made it his business room."

"Hewitt calls it Sir Karl's room, now," interrupted Miss Blake. "You smoke in it, don't you, Sir Karl?"

"I did smoke in it once or twice when I was staying down here during the time of my mother's illness," he replied. "But I am not a great smoker. Just one cigar at night: and not always that."

"Did I see that room, Karl?" asked his wife.

"No, Lucy. It was hardly worth showing you."

"Oh, but I shall like it better than all the rest, if it's yours."

"Come and see it then."

She put her arm within his, and he looked down on her with a smile as they went through the house. Miss Blake walked behind with drawn-in lips. Sir Karl was greatly altered in manner she thought; all his life and spirits had left him: and he did not seem in the least glad to see *her*.

The room on the other side had grey walls and looked altogether rather dowdy. Books and maps were on the shelves, a large ink-stand stood on the table, and the chimney-piece was ornamented with a huge Chinese tobacco-box.

"Now, Karl, that great arm-chair shall be yours, and this little one mine," said Lucy. "And you must let me come in when I please—although I can see it is to be your business room, just as it was Sir Joseph's."

"As often as you will, my darling."

He threw open the glass doors as he spoke, stepped across the terrace, and down the steps to the lawn—for this room answered in every respect to the other. This room faced the south; the front of the house the west, and Miss Blake's favourite room the north. The sun came slantwise across the flower-beds. Sir Karl plucked one of the sweetest roses, and brought it to his wife. Lucy said nothing as she took it; but Miss Blake, observant Miss Blake, saw the lingering touch of their hands; the loving glance from Lucy's eyes to his.

"Shall I show you your rooms upstairs, Lady Andinnian? If you have not been up."

"Thank you, I'll take Lucy myself," said Karl. "No, we have not been up."

The rooms they were to occupy lay in front, towards the northern end of the corridor. The bed-room was large and beautifully fitted up. Just now Aglaé had it in confusion, unpacking. Two dressing-rooms opened from it. Sir Karl's on the right—the last room at that end; Lucy's on the left: and beyond Lucy's was another bed-room. These four rooms all communicated with each other: when their doors stood open you might see straight through all of them: each one could also be entered from the corridor.

"But what do we want with this second bed-room?" asked Lucy, as she stood in it with her husband.

A full minute elapsed before he answered her, for it was the room where that strange communication, which was o'ershadowing his life, had been made to him by his mother. The remembrance of the turbulent night and its startling disclosures was very present with him, and he turned to the window, and put his head out, as though gasping for a breath of air.

"They have not made any change, you see, Lucy: I did not give orders. It was my mother's chamber during her short span of residence here. The next, that little dressing-room of yours, she made her up-stairs sitting-room. Perhaps you would like to have this made into a sitting-room for yourself."

"Nay, Karl, if I want to sit upstairs, there's my dressing-room. We will let this be as it is. Is that Foxwood?" she added, pointing to the roofs of houses and a church-spire in the distance.

"Yes, that's Foxwood."

"And what are all those trees over the way?" turning her finger rather towards the right: in fact to the Maze. "There are some chimneys amidst them. Is it a house?"

"Yes."

"A gentleman's house? It must be pleasant to have neighbours so near, if they are nice people. Is it occupied, Karl?"

"I—I fancy so. The truth is, Lucy,"—breaking into rather a forced laugh—"that I am as yet almost as much of a stranger here as yourself. Shall I call Aglaé. I'm sure you must want to get your bonnet off?"

"Aglaé's there, you know; I am going to her. But first of all"—clasping her arms fondly round him and lifting her sweet face to his—"let me thank you for this beautiful home. Oh, Karl! how happy we shall be in it."

"God willing!" he answered in a beseeching tone of exquisite pain. And, as he held her to him in the moment's tenderness, his chest heaved with a strange emotion.

"How he loves me," thought Lucy, passing to her own rooms. For she put the emotion down to that. "I wonder if there ever was such love before in the world as his and mine? Aglaé, I must wear white to-day."

She went down to dinner in white muslin and white ribbons, with a lily in her hair, a very bride to look at. Poor girl! it was a gala-day with her, this coming home, almost like her wedding-day. Poor wife!

The only one to talk much at dinner was Lucy. Miss Blake was not in one of her amiable moods: Sir Karl and Lucy had both dressed for dinner: she had not, not supposing they would, and that helped to put her out. In this retired spot, and with her head filled with Mr. Cattacomb and St Jerome's, Miss Blake had been almost forgetting that there existed such a thing as dressing for dinner. Karl was silent and grave as usual, just like a man preoccupied. His wife had become used to his air of sadness. She set it down, partly to the cause of the mysterious communication he had made to her the night before their marriage, and which had never since been mentioned between them, and partly to his ill-fated brother's trouble and shocking death. Therefore Lucy took the sadness as a matter of course, and never would appear to notice it.

Miss Blake began to converse at last. She spoke of St. Jerome's: telling with much exultation all that had been done. But Sir Karl looked grave. The good sound doctrines and worship of what used to be called High-Church were his own: but he did not like these new and extreme movements that caused scandal.

"You say that this St. Jerome's is on my land, Miss Blake?"

"On your land, Sir Karl: but in Farmer Truefit's occupation. The consent lay with him and he gave it."

"Well, I hope you will have the good sense not to go too far."

Miss Blake lifted her head, and asked Hewitt for some bread. Lucy's pretty face had flushed, and she glanced timidly at her husband. Remembering past days, she had not much faith in Theresa's moderation.

"When Mrs. Cleeve, knowing Lucy's inexperience and youth, suggested that I should stay here for some time after her return home, Sir Karl, if agreeable to you and to her, and I acquiesced, wishing to be useful to both of you in any way that might be, I had no conception there was not a church open for daily worship in the place. I must go to daily worship, Sir Karl. It is as essential to me as my bread and cheese."

"I'm sure I can say nothing against daily worship—to those who can make the time for it," rejoined Karl. "It is not *that* I fear, Miss Blake: think how beautiful the daily service was in Winchester Cathedral!"

"Oh, of course; yes," replied Miss Blake, in a slighting tone; "the cathedral service was very well as far as it went. But you need not fear, Sir Karl."

"Thank you," he replied; "I am glad to hear you say so." And the subject dropped.

The two ladies were alone for a few minutes after dinner in the North room. Lucy was standing at the open window.

"Of course you know all about the place by this time, Theresa," she suddenly said. "There's a house over there amidst those trees: who lives in it?"

"Some lady, I believe, who chooses to keep herself very retired," replied Miss Blake.

"Oh, I asked Karl, but he could not tell me: he says he is nearly as much a stranger here as I am. Theresa! I do think that's a nightingale! Listen."

"Yes, we have nightingales here," said Miss Blake indifferently.

Lucy crossed the lawn, and paced before the clusters of trees. The bird was just beginning its sweet notes. Karl came out, drew her hand within his arm, and walked with her until Miss Blake called out that the tea was waiting.

But Lucy yet was not very strong. She began to feel tired, and a sudden headache came on. When tea was over Karl said she must go to bed.

"I think I will," she answered, rising. "If you will pardon my leaving you, Theresa. Good night."

Karl went up with her and stayed a few minutes talking. In coming down he went straight to his smoking room and shut the door.

"Very polite, I'm sure!" thought Miss Blake, resentfully.

But the next moment she heard him leave it and come towards the sitting-room.

"I will wish you good night too, Miss Blake," he said offering his hand. "Pray ring for anything you may require; you are more at home, you know, than we are," he concluded with a slight laugh.

"Are you going to bed also, Sir Karl?"

"I? Oh no. I am going into my smoking-room. I have a letter to write."

Now Miss Blake resented this frightfully. Lucy might go to bed; it was best for her as she was fatigued; but that Sir

Karl should thus unceremoniously leave her to her own company at nine o'clock, she could not pardon. As to letter writing, the post had gone out. It was evident he thought nothing of her, even as a friend; nothing.

Dropping her forehead upon her hands, she sat there she knew not how long. When she looked up it was nearly dark. Her thoughts had wandered to Mr. Cattacomb, and she wondered whether he would be arriving by the last train.

Throwing a shawl over her shoulders, Miss Blake went into the garden, and thence by one of the small private gates into the lonely road. It was still and solitary. The nightingales were singing now, and she paced along, lost in thought, past the Maze and onwards.

She had reached nearly as far as the road to Foxwood, not having met a soul, when the advance of two or three passengers from the station told her the train was in. They turned off to the village, walking rapidly: but neither of them was the expected clergyman.

"What can have kept him?" she murmured, as she retraced her steps.

There was no moon, but the summer sky was light: not much of it, however, penetrated to the sides of the road through the over-shadowing trees. Miss Blake had nearly gained the Maze when she heard the approach of footsteps. Not caring to be seen out so late alone, she drew back between the hedge and the clump of trees at the gate, and waited.

To her vexation, peeping forth from her place of shelter, she recognised Sir Karl Andinnian. He was stealing along under shadow of the hedge too—*stealing* along, as it seemed to Miss Blake, covertly and quietly. When he reached the gate he looked up the road and down the road, apparently to make sure that no one was within sight or hearing: then he took a small key from his pocket, unlocked the strong gate with it, entered, locked it after him again, and disappeared within the trees of the veritable maze.

To say that Miss Blake was struck with amazement would be saying little. What could it mean? What could Sir Karl want there? He had told his wife he knew not who lived in it. And yet he carried a private key to the place, and covertly stole into it on this, the first night of his return! The queer ideas that floated through Miss Blake's mind, rapidly chasing each other, three parts bewildered her. They culminated in one emphatically spoken sentence.

" I should like to get inside too!"

Softly making her way across the road to enter the Court's grounds by the nearest gate, she chanced to lift her eyes to Clematis Cottage. The venetian shutters were closed. But, peering through one of them from the dark room, was a face that she was sure was Mr. Smith's. It looked just as though he had been watching Sir Karl Andinnian.

CHAPTER XIII.

MISS BLAKE GETS IN.

STILL no signs of the Rev. Guy Cattacomb. The morning, following the night told of in the last chapter, rose bright and sunny. Miss Blake rose with it, her energetic mind full of thought.

"I wonder how I am to begin to keep house?" said Lucy with a laugh, when she got up from the breakfast table, her cheeks as bright as the pink summer muslin she wore. "Do I go into the kitchen, Theresa?"

"You go with the cook to the larder," replied Theresa, gravely. "See what provisions remain in it from yesterday, and give your orders accordingly. Shall I go with you this morning, Lady Andinnian?"

"I wish you would! I wish you'd put me in the way of it. In Paris, when I was going to be married, mamma regretted she had not shown me more of housekeeping at home."

"You have, I believe, a careful and honest cook: and that is a great thing for an inexperienced mistress," said Miss Blake.

"As if cooks were ever dishonest in the country!" cried Sir Karl, laughing—and it was the first laugh Miss Blake had heard from his lips. "You must go to your grand London servants for that—making their perquisites out of everything, and feeding their friends and the policeman!"

"And then, Karl, when I come back, you will take me about everywhere, won't you?" whispered Lucy, leaning fondly over his shoulder as Miss Blake went on. "I want to see all about the grounds."

He nodded and let his cheek rest for a moment against hers. "Go and order your roast beef. And—Lucy?"

His manner had changed to seriousness He turned in his chair to face her, his brow flushing as he took her hands.

"You will not be extravagant, Lucy—" his voice sinking to a whisper lower than hers. "When I told you of that—that trouble, which had fallen upon me and might fall deeper, I said that it would cost me a large portion of my income. You remember?"

"Oh Karl! do you think I could forget? We will live as quietly and simply as you please. It is all the same to me."

"Thank you, my dear wife."

Theresa stood at the open hall door, looking from it while she waited. "I was thinking," she said, when Lady Andinnian's step was heard, "that it really might be cheaper in the end if you took a regular housekeeper, Lucy, as you are so inexperienced. It would save you a great deal of trouble."

"The trouble's nothing, Theresa; and I should like to learn. I would not think of a housekeeper. I should be afraid of her."

"Oh, very well. As you please, of course. But when you get your whole staff of servants, the house full of them, the controlling of the supplies for so many will very much embarrass you."

"But we don't mean to have our house full of servants, Theresa. We do not care to set up on a grand scale, either of us. Just about as papa and mamma live, will be enough for us indoors."

"Nonsense," said Miss Blake.

"We must have a coachman—Karl thinks he shall take on Sir Joseph's; the man has asked to come—and, I suppose, one footman to help Hewitt, and a groom. That's all. I think we have enough maids now."

"You should consider that Sir Karl's income is a large one, Lucy," spoke Miss Blake in a tone of lofty reproach. "It is absurd to take your papa's scale of living as a guide for yours."

"But Sir Karl does not mean to spend his income: he has a reason for saving it."

"Oh that's another thing," said Miss Blake. "What is his reason?"

The young Lady Andinnian could have punished her rebellious tongue. She had spoken the hasty words, "he has a reason for saving it" in the heat of argument, without thought. What right, either as a wife or a prudent woman, had she to allow allusion to it to escape her lips? Her rejoinder was given slowly and calmly.

"My husband is quite right not to begin by spending all his income, Theresa. We should both of us think it needless extravagance. Is this the kitchen? Let us go in here first. I must get acquainted with all my places and people."

The business transacted, Lucy went out with Karl. Theresa watched them on to the lawn and thence round the house, Lucy in her broad-brimmed straw hat, and her arm within her husband's. Miss Blake then dressed herself and walked rapidly to St. Jerome's. Some faint hope animated her that Mr. Cattacomb might have arrived, and be already inaugurating the morning service. But no. St. Jerome's was closely shut, and no Mr. Cattacomb was there.

She retraced her steps, lingering to rob the hedges of a wild honeysuckle or a dog-rose. This non-arrival of Mr. Cattacomb began to trouble her, and she could not imagine why, if he were prevented coming, he had not written to say so. Reaching the Maze, Miss Blake woke up from these thoughts with quite a start of surprise: for the gate was open and a woman servant stood there, holding colloquy with the butcher's boy on horseback: a young man in a blue frock, no hat, and a basket on his arm. A middle-aged and very respectable looking servant, but somewhat old-fashioned in her appearance: a spare figure straight up and down, in a black-and-white cotton gown and white muslin cap tied with black ribbon strings. In her hand was a dish with some meat on it, which she had just received from the basket, and she appeared to be reproaching the boy on the score of the last joint's toughness.

"This hot weather one can't keep nothing properly," said the boy, in apology. "I was to ask for the book, please, ma'am."

"The book!" returned the woman. "Why I meant to have brought it out. Wait there, and I'll get it."

The boy, having perhaps the spirit of restlessness upon him, backed his steed, and turned him round and round in the road like a horse in a mill. Miss Blake saw her opportunity and slipped in unseen. Gliding along the path, she concealed herself behind a huge tree-trunk near the hedge, until the servant should have come and gone again. Miss Blake soon caught sight of her skirts amid the trees of the maze.

"Here's the book," said she to the boy. "Ask your master

to make it up for the month, and I'll pay." And shutting and locking the gate, she retreated into the maze again and disappeared.

When people do covert things in a hurry, they can't expect to have all their senses about them, and Miss Blake had probably forgotten that she should be locked in. However—here she was in the position, and must make the best of it.

First of all, she went round the path, intending to see where it led to. It was fenced in by the garden wall, the high hedge and shrubs on one side, by the trees of the maze on the other. Suddenly she came to what looked like a low vaulted passage built in the maze, which probably communicated with the house: but she could not tell. Its door was fast, and Miss Blake could see nothing.

Pursuing her way along the walk, it brought her round to the entrance gate again, and she remembered Tom Pepp's words about the path going round and round and leading to nowhere. Miss Blake was not one to be daunted. She had come in to look about her, and she meant to do it. She plunged into the maze.

Again had she cause to recall Master Pepp's account,—" Once get into that there maze and you'd never get out again without the clue." Miss Blake began to fear there was only too much truth in it. For a full hour in reality, and it seemed to her like two hours, did she wander about and wander again. She was in the maze and could not get out of it.

She stood against the back of a tree, her face turning hot and cold. It took a great deal to excite that young woman's pulses: but she did not like the position in which she had placed herself.

She must try again. Forward thither, backward hither, round and about, in and out. No; no escape; no clue; no opening: nothing but the same interminable trees and the narrow paths so exactly like one another.

"What will become of me?" gasped Miss Blake.

At that moment a voice very near rose upon her ear—the voice of the servant she had seen. "Yes, ma'am, I'll do it after dinner."

Unconsciously Miss Blake had wandered to the confines of the maze that were close on the house. A few steps further and she could peep out of her imprisonment.

A small, low, pretty-gabled house of red brick. A sitting-room window, large and thrown open, faced Miss Blake; the porch entrance, of which she could get a slanting glimpse, fronted a grass-plat, surrounded by most beautiful flower-beds, with a greenhouse at the end. It was a snug, compact spot, the whole shut in by a high laurel hedge. On the grass stood the woman servant, spreading some bits of linen to dry: Miss Blake made them out to be cambric handkerchiefs: her mistress had probably been speaking to her from the porch, and the answer was what she heard. An old man, with either a slight hump on his back or a dreadful stoop, was bending over a distant flower-bed. He wore a wide, yellow straw hat, and a smock-frock, similar to that of the butcher's boy, only the latter's was blue and the old man's white. His hair was grey, and he appeared to be toothless: but in his prime he must have been tall and powerful. Miss Blake made her comments.

"What an extraordinary solitude for a young person to live in! But what choice flowers those look to be! That toothless old man must be the gardener! he looks too aged and infirm for his work. *Why* does she live here? There must be more in it than meets the eye. Perhaps——"

The soliloquy was arrested. The door of the sitting-room opened, and a young lady entered. Crossing to the window, she stood looking at something on the table underneath, in full view of Miss Blake. A fair girl, with a delicate face, soft damask cheeks, blue eyes, and hair that gleamed like threads of light gold.

"Good gracious! how lovely she is!" was Miss Blake's involuntary thought. Could this young girl be Mrs. Grey?

The young lady left the window again. The next minute the keys of a piano were touched. A prelude was played softly, and then there rose a verse of those lines in the "Vicar of Wakefield" that you all know so well, the voice of the singer exceedingly melodious and simple:

> "When lovely woman stoops to folly,
> And finds too late that men betray——"

Miss Blake had never in her life cared for the song, but it bore now a singular charm. Every word was distinct, and she listened to the end. A curious speculation crossed her.

Was this young girl singing the lines in character? "Heaven help her then!" cried Miss Blake—for she was not all hardness.

But how was she, herself, to get away? She might remain there unsought for ever. There was nothing for it but boldly showing herself. And, as the servant was then coming back across the lawn with some herbs which she had apparently been to gather, Miss Blake wound out of the maze, and represented herself before the woman's astonished eyes.

She made the best excuse she could. Had wandered inside the gate, attracted by the mass of beautiful trees, and lost herself amidst them. After a pause of wondering consideration, the servant understood how it must have been—that she had got in during her temporary absence from the gate when she went to fetch the butcher's book; and she knew what a long while she must have been there.

"I'll let you out," she said. "It's a pity you came in."

Very rapidly the woman walked on through the maze, Miss Blake following her. There were turnings and twistings, amid which the latter strove to catch some clue to the route. In vain. One turning, one path seemed just like another.

"Does your mistress live quite alone here?" she asked of the servant.

"Yes, ma'am," was the reply, more civilly spoken—for, that the servant had been at first much put out by the occurrence, her manner testified. "She's all alone, except or me and my old man."

"Your old man?" exclaimed Miss Blake, questioningly.

"My husband," explained the woman, perceiving she was not understood. "He's the gardener."

"Oh, I saw him," said Miss Blake. "But he looks quite too old and infirm to do much."

"He's not as old as he looks—and he has a good deal of work in him still. Of course, when a man gets rheumatics, he can't be as active as before."

"How very dull your mistress must be!"

"Not at all, ma'am. She has her birds, and flowers, and music, and work. And the garden she's very fond of: she'll spend hours in the greenhouse over the plants."

"Mrs. Grey, I think I have heard her called."

"Yes, Mrs. Grey."

"Well now—where's her husband?"

"She's not got a hus— At least,—her husband's not here."

The first part of the answer was begun in a fierce, resentful tone: but at the break the woman seemed to recollect herself and calmed down. Miss Blake was silently observant, pondering all in her inquisitive mind.

"Mr. Grey is travelling abroad just now," continued the woman. "Here we are."

Yes, there they were, escaped from the maze, the iron gate before them. The woman took a key from her pocket and unlocked it—just as Sir Karl had taken a key from his pocket the previous night. Miss Blake saw now what a small key it was, to undo so large a gate.

"Good morning," she said. "Thank you very much. It was exceedingly thoughtless of me to stroll in."

"Good day to you, ma'am."

Very busy was Miss Blake's brain as she went home. The Maze puzzled her. That this young and pretty woman should be living alone in that perfect seclusion with only two servants to take care of her, one of them at least old and decrepid, was the very oddest thing she had ever met with. Miss Blake knew the world tolerably well; and, so far as her experience went, a man whose wife was so young and so lovely as this wife, would wish to take her travelling with him. Altogether, it seemed very singular: and more singular still seemed the stealthy and familiar entrance, that she had witnessed, of Sir Karl Andinnian.

Meanwhile, during this bold escapade of Miss Blake's, Lady Andinnian had gone out on a very different expedition. It could not be said that Lucy had no acquaintance whatever at Foxwood before she came to it. She knew the vicar's eldest daughter, Margaret, who had occasionally stayed with Mr. and Mrs. Blake at Winchester: the two clergymen were acquainted, having been at college together. On this morning Lucy had started to see Miss Sumnor; walking alone, for Karl was busy. The church, a very pretty one, with a tapering spire, stood in its churchyard, just through the village. The vicarage joined it: a nice house, with a verandah running along the front; a good garden and some glebeland.

On a couch in a shaded room, lay a lady of some thirty, or more, years of age; her face thin, with upright lines between the eyebrows, telling of long-standing trouble or pain, perhaps of both; her hands busy with some needle-work. Lady Andinnian, who had not given her name, but simply asked to see Miss Sumnor, was shown in. She did not recognize her at the first moment.

"Margaret! It cannot be you."

Margaret Sumnor smiled her sweet, patient smile, and held Lady Andinnian's hand in hers. "Yes it is, Lucy—if I may presume still to call you so. You find me changed. Worn and aged."

"It is true," candidly avowed Lucy, in the shock to her feelings. "You look altogether different. And yet, it is not three years since we parted. Mrs. Blake used to tell me you were ill, and had to lie down a great deal."

"I lie here always, Lucy. Getting off only at night to go to my bed in the next room. Now and then, if I am particularly well, they draw me across the garden to church in a hand-chair: but that is very seldom. Sit down. Here, close to me."

"And what is the matter with you?"

"It has to do with the spine, my dear. A bright young girl like you need not be troubled with the complication of particulars. The worst of it is, Lucy, that I shall be as I am for life."

"Oh, Margaret!"

Miss Sumnor raised her work again and set a few stitches, as if determined not to give way to any kind of emotion. Lady Andinnian's face wore quite a frightened look.

"*Surely* not for always, Margaret!"

"I believe so. The doctor says so. Papa went to the expense of having a very clever man down from London; but he only confirmed what Mr. Moore had feared."

"Then, Margaret, I think it was a cruel thing to let you know it. Hope and good spirits go so far to help recovery, no matter what the illness may be. Did the doctors tell you?"

"They told my father, not me. I learnt it through—through a sort of accident, Lucy," added Miss Sumnor: who would not explain that it was through the carelessness—to call it by a light name—of her stepmother. "After all, it is best that I should know it. I see it is now, if I did not at the time."

"How it must have tried you!"

"Oh it did: it did. What I felt for months, Lucy, I cannot describe. I had grown to be so useful to my dear father: he had begun to need me so very much; to depend upon me for so many things: and to find that I was suddenly cut off from being of any help to him, to be instead only a burden! —even now I cannot bear to recal it. It was that, that changed me, Lucy: in a short while, I had gone, in looks, from a young woman into an aged one."

"No, no, not that. And you have to bear it always!"

"The bearing is light now," said Miss Sumnor, looking up with a happy smile. "One day, Lucy, when I was in a sad mood of distress and inward repining, papa came in. He saw a little of what I felt; he saw my tears, for he had come upon me quickly. Down he sat in that very chair that you are sitting in now. 'Margaret, are you realizing that this calamity has come upon you from God—that it is His will?' he asked: and he talked to me as he had never talked before. That night, as I lay awake thinking, the new light seemed to dawn upon me. 'It is, it is God's will,' I said; 'why should I repine in misery?' Bit by bit, Lucy, after that the light grew greater. I gained—oh such comfort!—in a few weeks more I seemed to lie right under God's protection: to be, as it were, always in His sheltering Arms: and my life is happier now than I can tell you of, in spite of very many and constant trials."

"And you manage to amuse yourself, I see," resumed Lucy, breaking the pause that had ensued.

"Amuse myself! I can assure you my days are quite busy and useful ones. I sew—as you perceive, resting my elbows on the board; see, this is a pillow-case that I am darning. I read, and can even write a note; I manage the housekeeping; and I have my class of poor children here, and teach them as before. They are ten times more obedient and considerate, seeing me as I am, than when I was in health."

Lucy could readily believe it. "And now tell me, Margaret, what brought this illness on?"

"Nothing in particular. It must have been coming on for years, only we did not suspect it. Do you remember that when at the rectory I never used to run or walk much, but always wanted to sit still, and dear Mrs. Blake would call me idle? It was coming on then. But now, Lucy, let me hear about yourself. I need not ask if you are happy."

Lucy blushed rosy red: she was only too happy: and gave an account of her marriage and sojourn abroad, promising to bring her husband some day soon to see Miss Sumnor. Next, they spoke of the new place—St. Jerome's, and the invalid's brow wore a look of pain.

"It has so grieved papa, Lucy. Indeed, there is no want of another church in the place; even if it were a proper church, there's no one to attend it: our own is too large for the population. Papa is grieved at the movement, and at the

K

way it is being done; it is anything but orthodox. And to think that it should be Theresa Blake who has put it forward!"

"The excuse she makes to us is that she wanted a daily service."

"A year ago papa took to hold daily service, and he had to discontinue it, for no one attended. Very often there would be only himself and the clerk."

"I do not suppose this affair of Theresa's will last," said Lucy, kindly, as she took her leave and went home.

Karl was out at luncheon, but they all three met at dinner: he, Lucy, and Miss Blake. Lucy told him of her visit to Margaret Sumnor, and asked him to go there with her on his return from London, whither he was proceeding on the morrow. Miss Blake had not heard of the intended journey before, and inquired of Sir Karl whether he was going for long.

"For a couple of days; perhaps three," he answered. "I have several matters of business to attend to."

"I think I might as well have gone with you, Karl," said his wife.

"Not this time, Lucy. You have only just come home from travelling, you know, and need repose."

Miss Blake, having previously taken her determination to do it, mentioned, in a casual, airy kind of way, her adventure of the morning: not however giving to the intrusion quite its true aspect, and not saying that she had seen the young lady. She had "strolled accidentally" into the place called the Maze, she said, seeing the gate open, and lost herself. A woman servant came to her assistance and let her out again; but not before she had caught a glimpse of the interior: the pretty house and lawn and flowers, and the infirm old gardener.

To Miss Blake's surprise—or, rather, perhaps not to her surprise—Sir Karl's pale face turned to a burning red. He made her no answer, but whisked his head round to the butler, who stood behind him.

"Hewitt," he cried sharply, "this is not the same hock that we had yesterday."

"Yes, Sir Karl, it is. At least I—I believe it is."

Hewitt took up the bottle on the sideboard and examined it. Miss Blake thought he looked as confused as his master. "He plays tricks with the wine," was the mental conclusion she drew.

Hewitt came round, grave as ever, and filled up the

glasses again. Karl began talking to him about the wine in the cellar: but Miss Blake was not going to let her subject drop.

"Do you know this place that they call the Maze, Sir Karl?"

"Scarcely."

"Or its mistress, Mrs. Grey?"

"I have seen her," shortly replied Karl.

"Oh, have you! When?"

"She wrote me a note relative to some repairs that were required, and I went over."

"Since you were back this time, do you mean?"

"Oh no. It was just after my mother's death."

"Don't you think it very singular that so young a woman should be living there alone?"

"I suppose she likes it. The husband is said to be abroad."

"You have no acquaintance with the people?" persisted Miss Blake.

"Oh dear no."

"And going in with a key from his own pocket!" thought Miss Blake, as she drew in her lips.

"Foxwood and its inhabitants, as I told Lucy, are tolerably strange to me," added Sir Karl. "Lucy, you were talking of Margaret Sumnor. How old is she?"

He was resolute in turning the conversation from the Maze: as Miss Blake saw. What was his motive? All kinds of comical ideas were in her mind, not all of them good ones.

"I'll watch," she mentally said. "In the interests of religion, to say nothing of respectability, *I'll watch.*"

CHAPTER XIV.

MISS BLAKE ON THE WATCH.

"LUCY, you will come with me to the opening service?"

Lady Andinnian shook her head. "I think not, Theresa."

"Why, it would be quite a distraction for you," urged Miss Blake, using the word in the French sense.

Sir Karl had been in London some three or four days now; and Lucy, all aweary without him, was longing and looking for his return every hour of the live-long summer's day. But she was proof against this offered temptation.

"I don't think Karl would like me to go to St. Jerome's, Theresa. Thank you all the same."

"Do you mean to make Sir Karl your guide and model through life, Lucy?"—— and Lady Andinnian, sincere and simple herself, detected not the covert sarcasm.

"I hope I shall never do, or wish to do, anything that he would object to," was her answer, a sweet blush dyeing her cheeks.

"Well, if you won't appear at church, will you attend the kettle-drum afterwards, Lucy?"

"The kettle-drum!" echoed Lucy. "What kettle-drum?"

"We are going to hold one at Mrs. Jinks's—that is, in Mr. Cattacomb's rooms—for the purpose of introducing him to some of his friends, and to organize the parish work."

Lady Andinnian looked up in surprise. "The parish work? What can you be talking of, Theresa?"

"Oh, there will be district visiting, and that. It *must* all be arranged and organized."

"Will it not be interfering with Mr. Sumnor?" Lucy ventured to ask, after a pause of silence.

"Not at all," was the answer, given loftily. "Shall I come round this way and call for you as we return from the service?"

"Thank you, no, Theresa: I would rather not. I do ot think I should myself much care for the kettle-drum."

"Very well," coolly replied Miss Blake. "As you please, of course, Lady Andinnian."

The service at St. Jerome's was at length about to be inaugurated: for the Reverend Guy Cattacomb had duly appeared after a few days' delay, for which he satisfactorily accounted. It was to be held in the afternoon, *this* afternoon, he having arrived in the morning; and Miss Blake, while talking to Lady Andinnian, was already dressed for it. She started forth alone: just as other eager women, mostly young, some middle-aged, were starting for it, and flocking into St. Jerome's.

Much inward speculation had existed as to what the new parson would be like; and the ladies looked at him eagerly when he entered from the vestry to commence the service. They saw a tall young man in a narrow surplice, with a sheep-skin tippet worn hind before, and a cross at the back in the opening: spectacles; no hair on his face, and not over much on his head, a few tufts of it only standing up like young carrots; eyes very much turned up. Certainly, in regard to personal beauty, the new pastor could not boast great things; but he made up for it in zeal, and—if such a thing may be said of a clergyman—in vanity; for that he was upon remarkably good terms with himself and his looks, every tone and gesture betrayed. It was rather a novel service, but a very attractive one. Mr. Cattacomb had a good sonorous voice—though it was marred by an affected accent and a drawling kind of delivery that savoured of insincerity and was most objectionably out of place. Miss Jane St. Henry played the harmonium; the ladies sang: and their singing, so far as it went, was good, but men's voices were much wanted. There was a short sermon, very rapidly delivered, and not to be understood—quite after a new fashion of the day. During its progress, little Miss Etheridge happened to look round and saw Mr. Moore, the surgeon, at the back of the room.

"If you'll believe me, old Moore's here!" she whispered to Mary St. Henry.

Yes, the surgeon was there. He had laughed a little over this curious new place that was being called a church, and said at home that day that he should look in and see what its services were to be like. He was more surprised than pleased. Just as Mr. Smith, the agent, asked, Is it Roman Catholic or Protestant? so did Mr. Moore mentally ask the question now. The place was pretty full. Some few people had come over from Basham to be present. Mr. Moore's eyes went ranging amid the chairs, scanning the congregation. His daughters were not there. They are too sensible, thought the doctor: though he did not give them credit for over-much sense in general. The fact was, the Misses Moore had been afraid to come. Hearing their father say he should look in, they deemed it wise to keep away—and did so, to their own deep mortification and disappointment. Mr. Moore was an easy-tempered man, and an indulgent father; but if once in a way he did by chance issue an edict, they knew it might not be disobeyed—and had he seen them there with his own eyes, he might have prohibited their going for the future. So they allowed policy to prevail, and stayed at home.

What with the opening service, and what with the coming party at Mrs. Jinks's, Foxwood was that day stirred to its centre. The preparations for the kettle-drum were on an exhaustive scale, the different ladies having vied with each other in sending in supplies. Butter, cream, delicate bread and cakes, jam, marmalade, choice fruits, biscuits, and other things too numerous to mention. Miss Blake had taken a huge packet of tea, and some beautiful flowers, the latter offering cajoled out of old Maclean, the head gardener at the Court.

The walk to St. Jerome's and back, together with the excitement of the new service, had made them thirsty, and it was universally agreed to take tea first, though only four o'clock, and proceed to business afterwards. The table groaned under the weight of good things on it, and Miss Blake was president-in-chief. The room was too small for the company, who sat or stood as they could, elbowing each other, and making much of Mr. Cattacomb. Tongues were going fast, Mr. Cattacomb's amidst them, and Miss Blake was getting hot with the work of incessantly filling cups from the tea-pots, when a loud knock, announcing further visitors, shook the street door and Paradise Row.

"Who can it be? I'm sure we have no room for more."

Mrs. Jinks went to see. Throwing open the front door, there stood the Misses Moore. Though debarred of the opening service, they would not be done out of the kettle-drum.

"Are they here yet, Mrs. Jinks?" cried the young ladies eagerly.

"Yes, they are here," replied the Widow Jinks, her cap (clean for the occasion, and no bonnet) trembling with suppressed wrath.

"Oh dear! Has tea begun?"

"Begun, Miss Jemima! it's to be hoped it's three parts over. I'll tell you what it is, young ladies: when I agreed to let my parlours to the Reverend Cattakin, I didn't bargain to keep the whole parish in kettle-drumming. Leastways, not to wait on 'em, and bile kettles for 'em, and toast muffins for 'em by the hour at a stretch. I thought what a nice quiet lodger I should have—a single man, and him a minister! Instead of which I might just as well keep an inn."

The young ladies walked on, wisely giving no answer, and entered the parlour. There they were presented to Mr. Cattacomb, and joined the tea-table.

Kettle-drums, as we are all aware, cannot last for ever, and before six o'clock Miss Blake was on her way back to Foxwood Court. The discussion as to district visiting and other matters was postponed to another day, Mr. Cattacomb pleading fatigue (and no wonder); and Miss Blake—who was in point of fact the prime mover and prop and stay of it all—inwardly thinking that a less crowded meeting would be more conducive to business. As she was nearing the gate at Foxwood Court, she met Mr. Smith sauntering along, apparently out for an airing.

"Good afternoon, madam!"

He would have passed with the words, but she stopped to talk with him. The truth was, Miss Blake had taken, she knew not why or wherefore, a liking for Mr. Smith. From the first moment she saw him he had possessed a kind of attraction for her. It must be said that she believed him to be a gentleman.

"You were not at the opening service at St. Jerome's this afternoon, Mr. Smith?" she said, half-reproachfully.

"Well, to tell you the truth, I thought I should be out of place there, as the congregation was comprised only of ladies," was his reply. "Happening to be walking that way, I saw lots of them go in."

"Foxwood cannot boast of gentlemen in the middle of the day; the few who reside here are off to Basham for their different occupations. But you are an idle man, Mr. Smith."

"I am not always idle, I assure you, Miss Blake. I have Sir Karl Andinnian's interests to look after."

"Oh, indeed! As a friend, I presume?"

"Just so."

"Well, you would not have been quite solitary if you had come into the church. Mr. Moore was there."

"Ay. He looked in for five minutes, and came out laughing. I don't know what amused him, unless it was to see the Miss Sumnors there."

"I think you must have been watching us all—all who went in, and all who came out," said Miss Blake. The agent smiled as he disclaimed the imputation: and with that they parted.

"Those flowers were so much admired and appreciated, Maclean," said Miss Blake to the gardener as she passed the lodge—where he sat at tea with his wife—the door open. "There are no such hot-house flowers anywhere as yours."

Maclean rose and thanked her for the compliment. She passed rapidly on, and entered the house by the window of the North room.

"I wonder where Lucy is?—Dressing, perhaps; or seated

at the window looking out for her husband. Foolish child.
Does he deserve that love?"

Treading softly on the carpeted staircase, her knock at
Lady Andinnian's door and her entrance were simultaneous.
Lucy, in her white morning dress with its blue ribbons, was
standing up beside her husband. His arm was round her
waist, her face lay upon his breast, his own bent down
upon it.

It was an awkward moment for Miss Blake; she bit her
lips as she stammered an apology. Lucy, blushing and laughing, drew away. Karl stood his ground, laughing too.

"I did not know you had returned, Sir Karl."

"I have just come; three minutes ago," he said, holding
out his hand. "Lucy was telling me you had gone to a
kettle-drum, and I saucily assured her she must have dreamt
it. Fancy kettle-drums at Foxwood!"

They separated for the purpose of dressing, Miss Blake
biting her lips still as she went to her room. The little
matter had turned her hot and cold. Do as she would, she
could not get rid entirely of her love for Karl Andinnian, in
spite of the chronic resentment she indulged towards him.

"If this is jealousy," she murmured, sitting down to think,
and undoing her veil with fingers that thrilled to their extreme ends, "I must indeed school myself. I thought I had
learned to bear calmly."

At dinner Sir Karl seemed in better spirits than usual.
He told them he had been to the Opera to hear the new
singer, Ilma di Murska, in "Robert le Diable."

"Oh, Karl!—and not to have had me with you!" cried
Lucy.

"I will take you up on purpose, Lucy. You must hear her.
In the song 'Robert, toi que j'aime' she electrified us all. I
never heard anything like it in my life. And she is most
elegant on the stage. Her dresses are splendid."

"Was anyone there that you knew?"

"I hardly looked at the house at all. I was in the
stalls. The Prince and Princess of Wales were in the royal
box."

"I am sure, Karl, it is a wonder to hear that you went!"

"True, Lucy; but my evenings hung heavily on my hands.
What with Plunkett and Plunkett and other business matters,
the days were busy enough: I used to wish the evenings were.
I felt very dull."

"Just as I have been feeling here, Karl, without you."

His answer to his wife was but a look; but Miss Blake wished she had not caught it. What had she done, that his love should have missed her to be lavished on this girl-child?

"Sir Karl," she cried somewhat abruptly, "who is Mr. Smith?'

"I don't know," carelessly replied Sir Karl, whose thoughts were preoccupied.

"Not know! but is he not your agent?—and a friend also?"

Sir Karl was fully aroused now. "Know who Mr. Smith is?" he repeated—and he wished to heaven in his secret heart that he did know. "How do you mean, Miss Blake? He is Mr. Smith, and—yes—a kind of agent to me on the estate."

The latter part of the answer was given lightly, half merrily, as if he would pass it off with a laugh. Miss Blake resumed.

"Is he not an old friend of the Andinnian family?"

"Of some of them, I believe. I did not know him previously myself."

"Who gave him his appointment?"

"My mother. She considered it well to have some responsible person here to look after my interests, as I was living abroad."

"Do you not intend, Sir Karl, to make an acquaintance of him?—a friend?"

For a moment Sir Karl's brows were heavily knitted. "I do not suppose I shall," he quietly said.

"He seems a well-informed, agreeable man; and is, I conclude, a gentleman," returned Miss Blake, quite in a tone of remonstrance.

"I am glad to hear it," replied Sir Karl, his manner somewhat freezing. "And so, Lucy, you have had some of the neighbours calling here?" he continued, addressing his wife, and turning the conversation.

"Oh, Karl, yes! And you were not here to help me; and I did not know them, and confused their names hopelessly one with another."

"I should not have known them either," laughed Sir Karl.

Miss Blake had some letters to write, and got to them after

dinner: she had been too much engaged with other things during the day. Tea was taken in early to the drawing-room, and afterwards she went back to her own room, the North room, to finish her writing by what little light remained. She saw Sir Karl and Lucy in the garden arm-in-arm, conversing together in low, confidential tones. Evidently they were all-sufficient for each other and did not miss her.

Say what we will, it could but seem to Miss Blake a neglect and something worse, looking upon past matters in her own light; and it told upon her cruelly.

The evening dusk drew on. She heard Lucy at the piano in the drawing-room, seemingly alone, trying a bit of one song and a bit of another. There was no doubt that Lucy thought Theresa was still busy and would not interrupt her. Miss Blake put up her desk and sat at the open window. By and by, when it was nearly dark, she threw a shawl on her shoulders, stepped out, crossed the lawn, and lost herself amidst the opposite trees. Miss Blake was that night in no mood for companionship; she preferred her own company to that of Lucy or her husband. As we say by the cross little children, the black dog was on her back; she did not listen even to the sweet melody of the nightingales.

"But for St. Jerome's I would not stay another day here," ran her thoughts. "I almost wish now I had not stirred in the church matter, but let the benighted place alone. As it is—and Mr. Cattacomb's come—why, I must make the best of it, and do my duty. Stay! stay, Theresa Blake!" she broke off in self-soliloquising sternness, "Is this fulfilling your good resolution—to give up all and bear all? Let me put away these most evil thoughts and work bravely on, and stay here cheerfully for Lucy's sake. It may be that she will want a friend, and I—Oh, there he is!"

The last sentence related to Karl. She had gradually got round the house to the other side, which brought her in face of Sir Karl's room. The doors of the window stood wide open; a lamp was on the table, by the light of which he seemed to be reading a note and talking to Hewitt, who stood near. Crossing over on the soft grass she drew within earshot, not really with any intention of listening, but in her mind's abstraction—what was there likely to pass between Sir Karl and his servant that concerned her to hear? With the bright lamp inside and the darkness out, they could not see her.

"You must be very cautious, Hewitt," Sir Karl was saying. "Implicitly silent."

"I have been, sir, and shall be," was the answer. "There's no fear of *me*. I have not had the interests of the family at heart all these years, Sir Karl, to compromise them now."

"I know, I know, Hewitt. Well, that's all, I think, for to-night."

Miss Blake passed back again out of hearing, very slowly and thoughtfully. She *had* heard the words, and was dissecting them: it almost sounded as though Sir Karl and his man had some secret together. Stepping on to the terrace, she was about to go in, when she heard Sir Karl enter the drawing-room and speak to his wife.

"I think I shall take a bit of a stroll, Lucy."

"To smoke your cigar? Do so, Karl."

"I—wonder—whether it is an excuse to go where he went the other night?" thought Miss Blake, the idea striking her like a flash of lightning. "I'll watch him. I will. I said I would, and I will. His family may have interests of their own, but Lucy and her family have theirs, and for her sake I'll watch."

Drawing the shawl over her head, she passed out at one of the small gates, crossed the road, and glided along under cover of the opposite hedge as far as the Maze. There she stood, back amidst the trees, sheltered from observation. The dress she wore happened to be black, for it was one of St. Jerome's fast-days, the shawl was black, and she could not be seen in the shade.

It was a still night. The dew was rising, and there seemed to be some damp exhaled from the trees. The time passed, ever so many minutes, and she began to think she had come on a fruitless errand. Or was it that Sir Karl was only lingering with his wife?

"Good gracious! What was that?"

A shrill shriek right over Miss Blake's head had caused the words and the start. It must have been only a night bird; but her nerves—what few she had—were on the tension, and she began to tremble slightly. It was not a pleasant position, and she wished herself away.

"I'll go," she mentally cried. "I wish I had not come. I —hope—Mr. Smith's not looking out, or he will see me!" she added, slowly and dubiously.

The doubt caused her to stay where she was and strain her

eyes at the opposite cottage. Was it fancy? One of the windows stood open, and she thought she saw a head and eyes peeping from it. Peeping, not openly looking.

"He must have seen me come!" decided Miss Blake. "But surely he'd not know me, wrapped up like this! Hark!"

A very slight sound had dawned upon her ear. Was it Sir Karl advancing? Surely the sound was that of footsteps! At the same moment, there arose another and separate sound; and that was close to her, inside the gates by which she stood.

"Some one must be coming out!" breathed Miss Blake. "It's getting complicated. I wish I was safe away. Two pairs of eyes may see what one pair would not."

Sir Karl Andinnian—for the footsteps were his—advanced. Very quietly and cautiously. Miss Blake could see that he had changed his dress coat for another, which he had buttoned round him, though the night was close. Halting at the gate he drew the key from his pocket as before, unlocked it, and passed in. Some one met him.

"Karl! I am so glad you have come! I thought you would! I knew you had returned."

It was a soft, sweet voice: the same voice, Miss Blake could have laid a wager on it, that had sung "When lovely woman stoops to folly." Their hands met: she was sure of that. Perhaps their lips also: but she could not see."

"Why, how did you know I was back?" he asked.

"Oh, Ann came to the gate to answer a ring, and saw you pass by from the station."

"Why are you out here?" he resumed. "Is it prudent?"

"I was restless, expecting you. I have so much to say; and, do you know, Karl——"

The voice sank into too low a tone to be audible to the thirsty ears outside. Both had spoken but in whispers. Miss Blake cautiously stretched forth her head, so as to get a glimpse through the closely-barred gate. Yes: it was the lovely girl she had seen during that stealthy visit of hers: and she had taken Sir Karl's arm while she talked to him. Another minute, and they both disappeared within the trees of the Maze.

Whether Miss Blake was glued to the trunk of the tree she stood at, or whether it was glued to her, remains a problem to be solved. It was one of the two. There she stood; and leave it she could not. That the flood-gates of a full tide of iniquity had suddenly been opened upon her was as clear to her mind as the light of day. Much that had been incomprehensible in the Maze and its inmates admitted of no doubt now. An instinct of this had been playing in her fancy previously: but she had driven it away *as* fancy, and would not allow herself to dwell on it. And now—it seemed as though she stood at the edge of a yawning precipice, looking down on a gulf of almost unnatural evil, from the midst of which Sir Karl Andinnian shone prominently out, the incarnation of all that was wicked and false and treacherous. But for the necessity of stillness and silence, Miss Blake could have groaned aloud.

A few minutes, and she stole away. There was nothing to wait or watch for: she knew all. Forgetting about Clematis Cottage and the eyes that might be peeping from it, she got back into the grounds of Foxwood and sat down on the bare terrace in the night to commune with herself. What should her course be? Surely she ought to impart the secret to that poor girl, Lucy, whom the man had dared to make his wife.

Let us render justice to Miss Blake. Hard though she was by nature, she strove to do her duty in all consciousness at all times and in all places. Sin she detested, no matter of what nature; detested it both *as* sin and for its offence against God. That Sir Karl Andinnian was living in secret, if not open sin, and was cruelly deceiving his innocent and unsuspicious wife, was clearly indisputable. It must not be allowed to go on—at least so far as Lucy was concerned. To allow her to remain the loving and unsuspicious partner of this man would be almost like making her a third in the wickedness, thought Miss Blake in her anger. And she decided on her course.

"And I—if I did not enlighten her, knowing what I know —should be countenancing and administering to the sin," she said aloud. "Good heavens! what a pit seems to be around us! may I be helped to do right!"

Rising, and shaking the night dew from her hair, she passed upstairs to her own chamber. Lady Andinnian was moving about her dressing-room. Impulse induced Miss Blake to knock at the door. Not that she intended to speak then.

"Are you undressing, Lucy?" she asked, an unconscious pity in her voice for the poor young wife.

"Not yet, Theresa. Aglaé's coming up, though, I think. It was dull downstairs by myself, and I thought I might as well come up. I could not find you anywhere. I thought you must have gone to bed."

"I was out of doors."

"Were you? I called to you outside on the terrace, but no one answered."

"Sir Karl is out, then?"

"He is strolling about somewhere," replied Lucy. "He does not sleep well, and likes to take half an hour's stroll the last thing. It strikes me sometimes that Karl's not strong, Theresa: but I try to throw the fear off."

Miss Blake drew in her lips, biting them to an enforced silence. She was burning to say what she could say, but knew it would be premature.

"I will wish you good-night, Lucy, my dear. I am tired, and—and out of sorts."

"Good night, Theresa: dormez bien," was the gay answer.

"To waste her love and solicitude upon *him!*" thought Miss Blake, as she stepped across the corridor with erect head and haughty brow. "I told Colonel Cleeve before the marriage that he was wild—little Dennet had said so—but I was put down. No wonder Sir Karl cannot spend his income on his home! he has other ways and means for it. Oh, how true are the words of holy writ! 'The heart of man is deceitful above all things, and desperately wicked.'"

CHAPTER XV.

REVEALED TO LADY ANDINNIAN.

THE morning sun had chased away the dew on the grass, but the hedge-rows were giving out their fragrance, and the lark and blackbird sang in the trees. Miss Blake was returning from early service at St. Jerome's, or, as St. Jerome's people called it, Matins.

In spite of the nearly sleepless night she had passed, Miss Blake looked well. Her superabundance of hair, freshly washed up with its cunning cosmetics and adorned to perfection, gleamed as if so many golden particles of dust were shining on it: her morning robe was of light muslin, and becoming as fashion could make it. It was very unusual for Miss Blake to get little sleep: she was of too equable a temperament to lie awake: but the previous night's revelation of iniquity had disturbed her in no common degree, and her head had ached when she rose. The headache was passing now, and she felt quite ready for breakfast. A task lay before her that day: the disclosure to Lady Andinnian. It was all cut and dried: how she should make it and when she should make it: even the very words of it were already framed.

She would not so much as turn her eyes on the gate of the Maze: had she been on that side of the road she would have caught up her flounces as she passed it. Never, willingly, would she soil her shoes with that side of the way again by choice—the place had a brand on it. It was quite refreshing to turn her eyes on Clematis Cottage, sheltering the respectable single bachelor who lived there.

Turning her eyes on the cottage, she turned them on the bachelor as well. Mr. Smith, in a light morning coat, and his arm as usual in a black sling, was out of doors amidst the rose trees on the little lawn, gazing at one of them through his green spectacles. Miss Blake stopped as he saluted her, and good mornings were exchanged.

"I am no judge of flowers," he said, "have not lived among them enough for that; but it appears to me that this rose, just come out, is a very rare and beautiful specimen."

Obeying the evident wish—given in manner alone, not in words—that she should go in and look at the rose, Miss Blake entered. It was a tea-rose of exquisite tint and sweetness. Miss Blake was warm in her admiration; she had not noticed any exactly like it at the Court. Before she could stop the sacrilege Mr. Smith had opened his penknife, cut off the rose, and was presenting it to her.

"Oh, how could you!" she exclaimed. "It was so beautiful here, in your garden."

"Madam, it will be more beautiful there," he rejoined, as she began to put it in her waistband.

"I should be very sorry, but that I see other of the buds will soon be out."

"Yes, by to-morrow. Earth does not deal out her flowers to us with a niggardly hand."

Accompanying the resolution Miss Blake had come to the previous evening and perfected in the night—in her eyes a very righteous and proper resolution; namely, to disclose what she knew to Lady Andinnian—accompanying this, I say, was an undercurrent of determination to discover as many particulars of the ill-savoured matter as she possibly could discover. Standing at this moment on Mr. Smith's grass-plat, that gentleman beside her and the gates of the Maze in full view opposite, an idea struck Miss Blake that perhaps he knew something of the affair.

She began to question him. Lightly and apparently carelessly, interspersed with observations about the flowers, she turned the conversation on the Maze, asking this, and remarking that.

"Lonely it must be for Mrs. Grey? Oh, yes. How long has she lived there, Mr. Smith?"

"She came—let me see. Shortly, I think, before Mrs. Andinnian's death."

"Ah, yes. At the time Sir Karl was staying here."

"Was Sir Karl staying here? By the way, yes, I think he was."

Miss Blake, toying with a spray of the flourishing clematis, happened to look suddenly at Mr. Smith as he gave the answer, and saw his glance turned covertly on her through his green glasses. "He knows all about it," she thought, "and is screening Sir Karl. That last answer, the pretended non-remembrance, was an evasion. Men invariably hold by one another in matters of this kind." Just for a moment there was a silence.

"Mr. Smith, you may trust me," she then said in a low tone. "I fancy that you and I both know pretty well *who* it was brought the lady here, and why she lives in that seclusion. But I could never have believed it of Sir Karl Andinnian."

Mr. Smith in his surprise—and it looked like very genuine surprise—took off his glasses and gazed at Miss Blake without them. He had rather fine brown eyes, she noticed. Not a word spoke he.

"You wonder that I should speak of this, Mr. Smith—I see that."

"I don't understand you, ma'am, and that's the truth."

"Oh, well, I suppose you will not understand. Sir Karl ought to be ashamed of himself."

Whether it was her tart tone that suddenly enlightened Mr. Smith, or whether he had but been pretending before, there could be no mistake that he caught her meaning now. He put on his green spectacles with a conscious laugh.

"Hush," said he, making believe playfully to hide his face. "We are content, you know, Miss Blake, to ignore these things."

"Yes, I do know it, dear sir: it is the way of the world. But they cannot be ignored in the sight of Heaven."

The striking of nine o'clock inside the house reminded Miss Blake that the morning was getting on, and that she had best make haste if she wanted any breakfast. Mr. Smith held the gate open for her, and shook her offered hand. She stepped onwards, feeling that a mutual, if silent, understanding had been established between them—that they shared the disgraceful secret.

Had Miss Blake wanted confirmation in her belief, this admission of Mr. Smith's would have established it. But she did not. She was as sure of the fact as though an angel had revealed it to her. The sight of her own good eyes, the hearing of her true ears, and the exercise of her keen common sense had established it too surely.

"My task lies all plain before me," she murmured. "It is a disagreeable one, and may prove a thankless one, but I will not shrink from it. Who am I that I should turn aside from an appointed duty? That it *has* been appointed me, events show. I have been guided in this by a higher power than my own."

An appointed duty! Perhaps Miss Blake thought she had been "appointed" to watch the Maze gates in the shade of the dark night, appointed to track the private steps of her unsuspicious host, Karl Andinnian! There is no sophistry in this world like self-sophistry; nothing else so deceives the human heart: more especially when it is hidden under a guise of piety.

Miss Blake found her opportunity in the course of the morning. A shade of pity crossed her for the happiness she was about to mar, as she saw the husband and wife out together after breakfast, amid the flowers. Now, Lucy's arm entwined fondly in his; now, tripping by his side; now, calling his attention to some rare or sweet blossom, as Mr. Smith had called Miss Blake's in the morning, went they. In Lucy's bright face, as she glanced perpetually at her lord and husband, there was so much of love, so much of trust: and in his, Sir Karl's, there was a whole depth of apparent tenderness for her.

"Men were deceivers ever," angrily cried Miss Blake, recalling a line of the old ballad. "It's enough to make one sick. But I am sorry for Lucy; it will be a dreadful blow. How I wish it could be inflicted on him instead of her! In a measure it will fall on him—for of course Lucy will take active steps."

Later, when Sir Karl, as it chanced, had gone over to Basham, and Lucy was in her pretty little dressing-room, writing to some girl friend, Miss Blake seized on the opportunity. Shutting herself in with Lady Andinnian, she made the communication to her. She told it with as much gentle consideration as possible, very delicately, and, in fact, rather obscurely. At first Lady Andinnian did not understand, could not understand; and when she was made to understand, her burning face flashed forth its indignation, and she utterly refused to believe.

Miss Blake only expected this. She was very soothing and tender.

"Sit down, Lucy," she said. "Listen.——On my word of honour, I would not have imparted this miserable tale to inflict on you pain so bitter, but that I saw it *must* be done. For your sake, and in the interests of everything that's right and just and seemly, it would not have done to suffer you to remain in ignorance, a blind victim to the dastardly deceit practised on you by your husband."

"He could not so deceive me, Theresa; he could not deceive any one," she burst forth passionately.

"My dear, I only ask you to listen. You can then judge for yourself. Do not take my word that it is or must be so. Hear the facts, and then use your own common sense. Alas, Lucy, there can be no mistake: but for knowing that, should I have spoken, think you? It is, unfortunately, as true as heaven."

From the beginning to the end, Miss Blake told her tale. She spoke out without reticence now. Sitting beside Lucy on the sofa, and holding her hands in hers with a warm and loving clasp, she went over it all. The mystery that appeared to encompass this young lady, living alone at the Maze in strict seclusion with her two old servants, who were man and wife, she spoke of first as an introduction. She said how curiously it had attracted her attention, unaccountably to herself at the time, but that *now* she knew a divine inspiration had guided her to the instinct. She avowed how she had got in, and that it was done purposely; that she had seen the girl, who was called Mrs. Grey, and was "beautiful as an angel," and heard her sing the characteristic song (which might well indeed have been written of *her*), "When lovely woman stoops to folly." Next, she described Sir Karl's secret visits; the key he let himself in with, taken from his pocket; the familiar and affectionate words interchanged between him and the girl, who on the second occasion had come to the gate to wait for him. She told Lucy that she had afterwards had corroborative evidence from Mr. Smith, the agent: he appeared to know all about it, to take it as a common matter of ordinary course, and to be content to ignore it after the custom of the world. She said that Sir Karl had brought Mrs. Grey to the Maze during the time he was staying at Foxwood in attendance on his sick mother: and she asked Lucy to recall the fact of his prolonged sojourn here, of his unwillingness to leave it and rejoin her, his wife; and of the very evident desire he had had to keep her altogether from Foxwood. In short, as Miss Blake put the matter—and every syllable she spoke did she believe to be strictly true and unexaggerated—it was simply impossible for the most unwilling listener not to be convinced.

Lady Andinnian was satisfied: and it was as her death-blow. Truth itself could not have appeared more plain and certain. After the first outburst of indignation, she had sat very calm and quiet, listening silently. Vexatious trifles excite the best of us, but in a great calamity heart and self alike shrink into stillness. Save that she had turned pale as death, there was no sign.

"Lucy, my poor Lucy, forgive me! I would have spared you if I could: but I believe the task of telling you was *laid* on me."

"Thank you, yes; I suppose it was right to tell me, Theresa," came the mechanical answer from the quivering lips.

"My dear, what will be your course? You cannot remain here, his wife."

"Would you please let me be alone, now, Theresa? I do not seem to be able to think yet collectedly."

The door closed on Miss Blake, and Lady Andinnian bolted it after her. She bolted the other two doors, so as to make sure of being alone. Then the abandonment began. Kneel-ing on the carpet, her head buried on the sofa-pillow, she lay realizing the full sense of the awful shock. It shook her to the centre. Oh, how dreadful it was! She had so loved Karl, so believed in him: she had believed that man rarely loved a maiden and then a wife as Karl had loved her. This, then, must

have been the secret trouble that was upon him!—which had
all but induced him to break off his marriage! So she reasoned,
and supposed she reasoned correctly. All parts of the supposition, had she thought them well out, might not perhaps
have fitted in to one another: but in a distress such as this,
no woman—no, nor man either, is capable of working out
problems logically. She assumed that the intimacy must
have been going on for years: in all probability long before
he knew her.

An hour or so of this painful indulgence, and then Lady
Andinnian rose from the floor and sat down to think, as well
as she could think, what her course should be. *She* was truly
religious, though perhaps she knew it not. Theresa Blake
was ostensibly so, and very much so in her own belief; but
the difference between them was wide. The one had the real
gold, the other but the base coin washed over. She, Lucy,
strove to think and to see what would be right and best to do;
for herself, for her misguided husband, and in the sight of
God.

She sat and thought it out, perhaps for another hour. Aglaé
came to the door to say luncheon was served, but Lady Andinnian said Miss Blake was to be told that she had a headache
and should not take any. To make a scandal and leave her
husband's home—as Theresa seemed to have hinted—would
have gone well-nigh to kill her with the shame and anguish it
would entail. And oh, she hoped, she trusted, that her good
father and mother, who had yielded to her love for Karl and
so sanctioned the marriage, might never, never know of this.
She lifted her imploring eyes and hands to Heaven in prayer
that it might be kept from them. She prayed that she might
be enabled to do what was right, and to *bear:* to bear silently
and patiently, no living being, save Sir Karl, knowing what
she had to endure.

For, while she was praying for the way to be made clear
before her and for strength to walk in it, however thorny it
might be, an idea had dawned upon her that this matter might
possibly be kept from the world,—might be held sacred between
herself and Sir Karl. *Could* she? could she continue to live
on at the Court, bearing in patient silence—nay, in impatient
—the cruel torment, the sense of insult? And yet, if she did
not remain, how would it be possible to conceal it all from her
father and mother? The very indecision seemed enough to
kill her.

Visitors drove up to the house in the course of the afternoon —the county families were beginning to call—and Lady Andinnian had to go down. Miss Blake was off to one of St. Jerome's services—of which the Reverend Guy Cattacomb was establishing several daily. Sir Karl came home while the visitors were there. After their departure, when he came to look round for his wife, he was told she had hastily thrown on her bonnet and mantle and gone out. Sir Karl rather wondered.

Not only to avoid her husband, but also because she wanted to see Margaret Sumnor, and perhaps gain from her a crumb of comfort in her utter wretchedness, had Lady Andinnian run forth to gain the vicarage. Margaret was lying as before, on her hard couch, or board; doing, for a wonder, nothing. Her hands were clasped meekly before her on her white wrapper, her eyelids seemed heavy with crying. But the eyes smiled a cheerful greeting to Lady Andinnian.

"Is anything the matter, Margaret?"

It was but the old story, the old grievance; Margaret Sumnor was pained by it, more or less, nearly every day of her life —the home treatment of her father: the contempt shown to him by his second family; ay, and by his wife.

"It is a thing I cannot talk of much, Lucy. I should not speak of it at all, but that it is well known to Foxwood, and commented on openly. Caroline and Martha set papa at naught in all ways: the insolence of their answers to him, both in words and manner, brings the blush of pain and shame to his face. This time the trouble was about that new place of Miss Blake's, St. Jerome's. Papa forbade them to frequent it; but it was just as though he had spoken to a stone—in fact, worse; for they retorted and set him at defiance. They wanted daily service, they said, and should go where it was held. So now papa, I believe, thinks of resuming his daily services here at Trinity, hoping it may counteract the other. There, that's enough of home and my red eyes. Lucy, you don't look well."

Lady Andinnian drew her chair quite close to the invalid, so that she might let her hand rest in the one held out for her. "I have a trouble, too, Margaret," she whispered. "A dreadful, sudden trouble, a blow; and I think it has nearly broken my heart. I cannot tell you what it is; I cannot tell any one in the world——"

"Except your husband," interposed Miss Sumnor. "Never have any concealments from him, Lucy."

Lady Andinnian's face turned red and white with embarrassment. "Yes, him; I shall have to speak to him," she said, in some hesitation: and Miss Sumnor's deep insight into others' hearts enabled her to guess that the trouble had something to do with Sir Karl. She suspected it was that painful thing to a young wife—a first quarrel.

"I am not like you, Margaret—ever patient, ever good," faltered poor Lady Andinnian. "I seem to be nearly torn apart with conflicting thoughts—perhaps I ought to say passions—and I thought I would come to you for a word of advice and comfort. There are two ways in which I can act in this dreadful matter; and indeed that word is no exaggeration, for it is very dreadful. The one would be to make a stir in it, take a high tone, and set forth my wrongs; that would be revenge, proper, just revenge; but I hardly know whether it would be right, or bring right. The other way would be to put up with the evil in silence, and *bear;* and leave the future to God. Which must I do?"

Margaret Sumnor turned as much as she could turn without assistance, and laid both her hands imploringly on Lady Andinnian's.

"Lucy! Lucy! choose the latter. I have seen, oh, so much of this revenge, and of how it has worked. My dear, I believe in my honest heart that this revenge was never yet taken but it was repented of in the end. However grave the justifying cause and cruel the provocation, the time would come when it was heartily and bitterly regretted, when its actor would say, Oh that I had not done as I did, that I had chosen the merciful part!"

There was a brief silence. Miss Sumnor resumed.

"'Vengeance is mine; I will repay;' you know Who says that, Lucy: but you cannot know what I have seen and marked so often—that when the vengeance is taken into human hands it somehow defeats itself. It may inflict confusion and ruin on the adversary; but it never fails to tell in some way on the inflictor. It may be only in mental regret: regret that may not set in until after long years, but rely upon it, he never fails, in his remorseful heart, to wish the past could be undone. A regret, such as this, we have to carry with us to the grave; for it can never be remedied, the revengeful act cannot be blotted out. It has been done, and it stands with its consequences for ever; consequences, perhaps, that we never could have foreseen."

Lady Andinnian sat listening with drooping face. A softer expression stole over it.

"There is one thing we never can repent of, Lucy; and that is, of choosing the path of mercy—of leniency. It brings a balm to the sorely-chafed spirit, and heals in time. Do *you* choose it, my dear. I urge it on you with my whole heart."

"I think I will, Margaret; I think I will," she answered, raising for a moment her wet eyes. "It will mortify my pride and my self esteem: be always mortifying them; and I shall need a great deal of patience to bear."

"But you will be able to bear; to bear all; you know where to go for help. Do this, Lucy; and see if in the future you do not find your reward. In after years, it may be that your heart will go up with a great bound of joy and thankfulness. 'I did as Margaret told me,' you will say, 'and bore.' Oh, if men and women did but know the future that they lay up for themselves according as their acts shall be!—the remorse or the peace."

Lucy rose and kissed her. "It shall be so, Margaret," she whispered. And she went away without another word.

She strove to keep the best side uppermost in her mind as she went home. Her resolution was taken; and perhaps because it was taken, the temptation to act otherwise and to choose revenge, rose up in all manner of attractive colours. She could abandon her ill-doing husband and start, even that night, for her parents' home; reveal the whole, and claim their protection against him. This would be to uphold her pride and her womanly self-respect: but oh, how it would pain them! And they had given their consent to the marriage against their better judgment for her sake; so to say, against their own will. No; she could not, for very shame tell them; and she prayed again that they might never know it.

"I *can* take all the pain upon myself, and bear it without sign for their sakes," she mentally cried. "Oh, yes, and for mine, for the exposure would kill me. I *can* bear this: I must take it up as my daily and nightly cross; but I could not bear that my own dear father and mother, or the dear friends of my girlhood, should know he is faithless to me—that he never could have loved me. Theresa, the only one cognisant of it, will be silent for my sake."

Bitter though the decision was, Lucy could but choose it. She had believed Karl Andinnian to be one of the few good men of the earth; she had made him her idol; all had seen it.

To let them know that the idol had fallen from its pedestal, and *so* fallen, would reflect its slighting disgrace on her, and be more than human nature could encounter.

Her interview with Sir Karl took place that evening She had managed, save at dinner, to avoid his presence until then. It was held in her dressing-room at the dusk hour. He came up to know why she stayed there alone and what she was doing. In truth, she had been schooling herself for this very interview, which had to be got over before she went to rest. The uncertainty of what she could say was troubling her, even the very words she should use caused her perplexity. In her innate purity, her sensitively refined nature, she could not bring herself to speak openly to her husband upon topics of this unpleasant kind. That fact rendered the explanation more incomplete and complicated than it would otherwise have been. He had come up, and she nerved herself to the task. As good enter on it now as an hour later.

"I—I want to speak to you, Sir Karl."

He was standing by the open window, and turned his head quickly. Sir Karl! "What's amiss, Lucy?" he asked.

"I—I—I know all about your secret at the Maze," she said with a great burst of emotion, her chest heaving, her breath coming in gasps.

Sir Karl started as though he had been shot. His very lips turned of an ashy whiteness.

"Lucy! You cannot know it!"

"Heaven knows I do," she answered. "I have learnt it all this day. Oh, how could you so deceive me?"

Sir Karl's first act was to dart to the door that opened on the corridor and bolt it. He then opened the two doors leading to the chambers on either side, looked to see that no one was in either of them, shut the doors again, and bolted them.

"Sir Karl, this has nearly killed me."

"Hush!" he breathed. "Don't talk of it aloud, for the love of God!"

"Why did you marry me?" she asked.

"Why, indeed," he retorted, his voice one of sad pain. "I have reproached myself enough for it since, Lucy."

She was silent. The answer angered her; and she had need of all her best strength, the strength she had so prayed for, to keep her lips from a cruel answer. She sat in her low dressing-chair, gazing at him with reproachful eyes.

He said no more just then. Well-nigh overwhelmed with the blow, he stood back against the window-frame, his arms folded, his face one of pitiful anguish. Lucy, his wife, had got hold of the dreadful secret that was destroying his own peace, and that he had been so cunningly planning to conceal.

"How did you learn it?" he asked.

"I shall never tell you," she answered with quiet firmness, resolved not to make mischief by betraying Theresa. "I know it, and that is enough. Put it down, if you choose, that it was revealed to me by accident—or that I guessed it."

"But, Lucy, it is necessary I should know."

"I have spoken, Sir Karl. I will *never* tell you."

The evening breeze came wafting into that room of pain; cooling, it might be, their fevered brows, though they were not conscious of it. Lady Andinnian resumed.

"The unpardonable deceit you practised on my father and mother——"

Sir Karl's start of something like horror interrupted her. "They must not know of it, Lucy. In mercy to us all, you must join with me in concealing it from them."

"It was very wicked in you to have concealed it from them at all. At least, to have married me with such a secret—for I conclude you could not have really dared to tell them. They deserved better at your hands. I was their only daughter: all they had to love."

"Yes, it was wrong. I have reproached myself since worse than you can reproach me. But I did not know the worst then."

She turned from him proudly. "I—I wanted to tell you, Sir Karl, that I for one will never forgive or forget your falsehood and deceit; and, what I am about to say, I say for my father and mother's sake. I will keep it from them, always if I can; I will bury it within my own breast, and remain on here in your home, your ostensible wife. I had thought of leaving your house for theirs, never to return; but the exposure it would bring frightened me; and, in truth, I shrink from the scandal."

"What do you mean?" he exclaimed. "My 'ostensible' wife?"

"I shall never be your wife again in reality. That can be your room"—pointing to the one they had jointly occupied;

"this one is mine," indicating the chamber on the other hand "Aglaé has already taken my things into it."

Sir Karl stood gazing at her, lost in surprise.

"No one but ourselves need know of this," she resumed, her eyes dropping before the tender, pitiful gaze of his. "The arrangements are looked upon by Aglaé as a mere matter of convenience in the hot weather; the servants will understand it as such. I would spare us both gossip. For your sake and for mine I am proposing this medium course—to avoid the scandal that otherwise must ensue. I shall have to bear, Karl—to bear—" her heart nearly failed her in its bitter grief—"but it will be better than a public separation."

"You *cannot* mean what you say," he exclaimed. "Live apart from me! The cause cannot justify it."

"It scarcely becomes you to say this. Have you forgotten the sin?" she added in a whisper.

"The sin? Well, of course it was sin—crime, rather. But that is of the past."

She thought she understood what he wished to imply, and bit her lips to keep down their bitter words. He was surely treating her as the veriest child, striving to hoodwink her still! That he was agitated almost beyond control, she saw: and did not wonder at.

"The sin is past," he repeated. "No need to recall it or talk of it."

"Be it so," she scornfully said. "Its results remain. *This*, I presume, was the great secret you spoke of the night before our marriage."

"It was. And you see now, Lucy, why I did not dare to speak more openly. I grant that it would have been enough to prevent our marriage had you then so willed it: but, being my wife, it is not any sufficient cause for you to separate yourself from me."

And, in answer to a question of mine, he could boast that night of his innocence! ran her indignant thoughts.

"I am the best judge of that," she said aloud, in answer. "Not sufficient cause! I wonder you dare say it. It is an outrage on all the proprieties of life. You must bring—them—to the Maze here, close to your roof and mine!"

In her shrinking reticence, she would not mention to him the girl in plain words; she would not even say "her," but substituted the term "them," as though speaking of Mrs. Grey and her servants collectively. Sir Karl's answer was a hasty one.

"That was not my doing. The coming to the Maze was the greatest mistake ever made. I was powerless to help it."

Again she believed she understood. That when Sir Karl had wished to shake off certain trammels, he found himself not his own master in the matter, and could not.

"And so you submitted?" she scornfully said.

"I had no other choice, Lucy."

"And you pay your visits there!"

"Occasionally. I cannot do otherwise."

"Does it never occur to you to see that public exposure may come?" she continued, in the same contemptuous tone. For the time, Lucy Andinnian's sweet nature seemed wholly changed. Every feeling she possessed had risen up against the bitter insult thrust upon her—and Sir Karl seemed to be meeting it in a coolly insulting spirit.

"The fear of exposure is killing me, Lucy," he breathed, his chest heaving with its painful emotion. "I have been less to blame than you imagine. Let me tell you the story from the beginning, and you will see that——"

"I will not hear a word of it," burst forth Lucy. "It is not a thing that should be told to me. At any rate, I will not hear it."

"As you please, of course; I cannot force it on you. My life was thorny enough before: I never thought that, even if the matter came to your knowledge, you would take it up in this cruel manner, and add to my pain and perplexity."

"It is for the Maze that we have to be economical here!" she rejoined, partly as a question, her hand laid upon her rebellious bosom.

"Yes, yes. You see, Lucy, in point of fact——"

"I see nothing but what I do see. I wish to see no further."

Sir Karl looked searchingly at her face, as though he could not understand her. Could this be his own loving and gentle Lucy? It was indeed difficult to think so.

"In a day or two, when you shall have had time to recover from the blow, Lucy—and a blow I acknowledge it to be— you will, I hope, judge me more leniently. You are my wife and I will not give you up: there is no real cause for it. When you shall be calmer, you may feel sorry for some things you have said now."

"Sir Karl, listen: and take your choice. I will stay on in your house on the terms I have mentioned, and they shall be perfectly understood and agreed to by both of us; or I will leave it for the protection of my father's home. In the latter case I shall have to tell him why. It is for you to choose."

"Have you well weighed what your telling would involve?"

"Yes; exposure: and it is that I wish to avoid. If it has to come, it will be your fault. The choice lies with you. My decision is unalterable."

Sir Karl Andinnian wiped his brow of the fever-drops gathered there. It was a bitter moment: and he considered that his wife was acting with most bitter harshness. But no alternative was left him, for he dared not risk exposure and its awful consequences.

And so, that was the decision. They were to live on, enemies, under the same roof-top: or at best, not friends. The interview lasted for some time; but no more explanation took place between them; and, when they parted, they parted under a mutual and total misapprehension which neither of the two knew or suspected. Misapprehension had existed throughout the interview—and was to exist. It was one of those miserable cases that now and then occur in the world—a mutual misunderstanding, for which no one is to blame. Sometimes it is never set right on this side the grave.

Her heart was aching just as much as his. She loved him passionately, and she was calming down from her anger to a softer mood, such as parting always brings. "Will you not send the—the people away?" she whispered in a last word, and with a burst of grief.

"If I can I will," was his answer. "I am hemmed in, Lucy, by all kinds of untoward perplexities, and I cannot do as I would. Good-night. I never could have believed you would take it up like this."

They shook hands and parted. The affair had been at last amicably arranged, so to say: the separation was begun. And so Sir Karl and Lady Andinnian were henceforth divided, and the household knew it not.

Miss Blake did not suspect a word of it. She saw no signs of any change—for outwardly Karl and his wife were civil and courteous to each other as usual, meeting at meals, present together in daily intercourse. After a few days Miss Blake questioned Lady Andinnian.

"Surely you have not been so foolishly soft as to condone that matter, Lucy?"

But Lucy wholly refused to satisfy her. Nay, she smiled; and she as good as tacitly let Miss Blake suppose that she might have been soft and foolish. Not even to her, or to any other living being, would Lucy betray what was sacred between herself and her husband.

"I am content to let it rest, Theresa: and I must request that you will do the same. Sir Karl and I both wish it."

Miss Blake caught the smile and the gently evasive words, and was struck mute at Lucy's sin and folly. She quite thought Lucy ought to have an atonement offered up for her at St. Jerome's. Surely Eve was not half so frail and foolish when she took the apple!

CHAPTER XVI.

A NIGHT AT THE MAZE.

THE Maze was an old-fashioned, curious house inside, full of angles and passages and nooks and corners. Its rooms were small, and not many in number, the principal ones being fitted up with dark mahogany wainscoting. The windows were all casement windows with the exception of two: into those, modern sashes of good size had been placed by the late owner and occupant, Mr. Throcton. At Mr. Throcton's death the property was put up for sale and was bought by Sir Joseph Andinnian, furniture and all, just as it stood. Or, it may rather be said, was bought by Lady Andinnian; for the whim to buy it was hers. Just after the purchase had been entirely completed, Lady Andinnian sickened and died. Sir Joseph, ill at the time, did nothing whatever with the new place; so that on his death it came into the possession of his heirs in exactly the same state as when it was purchased. They let it be also, and it remained shut up. According to what Mr. Smith informed Miss Blake—and he was in the main correct, though not quite—Mrs. Grey had come to it and taken possession while Mrs. Andinnian lay ill at Foxwood and her son Karl was in attendance on her. But the little fable the agent had made use of—that he had gone over to the Maze to receive the premium from Mrs. Grey on taking possession—had no foundation in fact. He had certainly gone to the Maze and seen the lady called Mrs. Grey, but not to receive a premium, for she paid none.

The two rooms into which sash windows had been placed were—the one that faced Miss Blake when she had penetrated to the confines of the Maze on that unlucky day, and within which she had seen the unconscious Mrs. Grey; and the one above it. They were at the end of the house, looking towards the entrance gates. Into this upper room the reader must pay a light visit. It was used as a sitting-room. The same dark mahogany wainscoting lined the walls as in the room below, the furniture was dark and heavy-looking; and, in spite of the sultry heat of the night, the shutters were closed before the window, and dull crimson curtains of damask wool were drawn across them. There was nothing bright in the appendages of the room, save the lighted lamp on the table and a crystal vase of hot-house flowers.

Seated at the table at work—the making of an infant's frock—was Mrs. Grey. Opposite to her, in the space between the table and the fire-place, sat Sir Karl; and by her side, facing him—Adam Andinnian.

It is more than probable that this will be no surprise; that the reader has already divined the truth of the secret, and all the miserable complication it had brought and was bringing in its train. It was not Adam Andinnian who had died in that fatal scuffle off Portland Island—or more strictly speaking, off Weymouth—but one of the others who had been concerned in it.

Yes, there he sat, in life and in health; his speech as free, his white and beautiful teeth not less conspicuous than of yore—Sir Adam Andinnian. Karl, sitting opposite with his grave, sad face, was not in reality Sir Karl, and never had been.

But Adam Andinnian was altered. The once fine black hair, which it had used to please him to wear long in the neck, was now short, scanty, and turned to grey; his once fine fresh colour had given place to pallor, and he was growing a beard that looked grey and stubbly. Decidedly old-looking now, as compared with the past, was Adam Andinnian. He wore evening dress: just as though he had been attired for a dinner party—say—at Foxwood Court. Mrs. Grey—as she was called, though she was in reality Lady Andinnian—wore a summer dress of clear white muslin, through which might be seen her white neck and arms. It was the pleasure of her husband, Sir Adam, that in the evening, when he only dared to come out of his hiding-shell, they should keep up, in attire at least, some semblance of the state that ought to have been theirs.

"I can tell you, Karl, that I don't approve of it," Sir Adam was saying, with all his old haughty bearing and manner. "It's a regular scandal. What business has any one to set up such a thing on my land?"

"It's Truefit's land for the time being, you know, Adam. He gave the consent."

"A parcel of foolish people—be-vanitied boys of self-called priests, and be-fooled girls, running and racing to the place four or five times a day under pretence of worship!" continued Sir Adam, getting up to pace the room in his excitement, as though he would have burst through its small confines. "I won't permit it, Karl."

He seemed to have got somewhat shorter, and his walk had a limp in it. But he was the same hasty, fiery, Adam Andinnian. A man cannot well change his nature.

"I do not see how it is to be prevented," was Karl's answer. "It will not do, in our position, to raise a stir over anything, or to make enemies. I daresay it will bring itself to an end some way or other."

"The whole parish is making fun of it, I find. Ann bears it talked of when she goes on errands. And it is a downright insult on Mr. Sumnor. What a curious-minded person that Miss Blake must be! Rose"—Sir Adam halted close to his wife—"if ever you put your foot inside this St. Jerome's I'll not forgive you."

She lifted her eyes to his from the baby's frock. "I am not likely to go to it, Adam."

"The empty-headed creatures that girls are, now-a-days! If bull-baiting came up, they'd run off to it, just as readily as the good girls of former days would run from any approach of evil to take shelter under their mother's wing. Does your wife frequent St. Jerome's, Karl?"

"Oh no."

"She shows her sense."

Karl Andinnian smiled. "You have not lost the old habit, Adam—the putting yourself into a heat for nothing. I came over this evening to have some serious talk with you. Do sit down."

"Yes do, Adam," added his wife, turning to him; "you

will get the pain in your hip again. Do you wish me to go away?" she added to Karl, as she prepared to gather up her working materials.

"No, no, Rose: it's only the old story, I know—the wanting to get rid of me," interposed Sir Adam, sitting down himself. "Stay where you are, wife. Now for it, Karl.—Wait a moment, though," he added, ringing the bell.

It was answered by the same staid, respectable-looking servant seen by Miss Blake; the same confidential woman who had lived with Mrs. Andinnian at Weymouth—Ann Hopley.

"Ann, I am as thirsty as a fish," said her master. "Bring up a bottle of soda-water and a dash of brandy."

"Yes, sir," she replied—not daring now or at any other time to give him his title.

He opened the soda-water himself when it was brought, put in the brandy, drank it, and sat down again. Karl Andinnian began to speak, feeling an innate certainty that his words would be wasted ones.

But some explanation of the past is necessary, and it may as well be given here.

When Karl Andinnian went down from London to Weymouth upon the news of his brother's attempted escape and death, he found his mother in a dreadful state of distress—as already related. This distress was not put on: indeed such distress it would not be possible to assume: for Mrs. Andinnian believed the public accounts—that Adam was dead. *After* she had despatched Karl to Foxwood to make arrangements for the interment, the truth was disclosed to her. Sir Adam had escaped with life, and was lying concealed in Weymouth; but he had been terribly knocked about in the scuffle, and in fact had been considered dead. By the careful stupidity of one of the warders, or else by his connivance, Mrs. Andinnian never entirely knew which, he was reported at the prison as being dead—and perhaps the prison thought itself well rid of so obstreperous an inmate. The warders had said one to another from the time he was first put there, that that Andinnian gentleman had "mischief" in him. Further explanation may be given later on in the story: at present it is enough to say that Adam Andinnian escaped.

When Mrs. Andinnian arrived at Foxwood with the body (supposed to be her son's, but in reality that of the other poor convict, Cole), she then knew the truth. Adam was not dead. He was lying somewhere in great danger; they would not, from motives of prudence, allow her to know where; but, dead he was not. Not a hint did she disclose of this to Karl; and he stood by her side over the grave, believing it was his brother that was placed in it; believing her when she falsely stated she had seen the face of the dead. All her efforts were directed to keep Karl from finding out the truth. She called him Sir Karl; she never gave him a hint that his succession to the title and estates was but a pseudo one. Perhaps she did not dare to speak of it, even to him. Karl went abroad, re-met Lucy Cleeve, and became engaged to her. He caused the marriage settlements to be drawn up and signed, still never dreaming that he had no legal right to settle, that the revenues were not his. Only when he went down to Foxwood, a day or two before his marriage, did he become acquainted with the truth.

That was the dread secret disclosed to him by his mother; that, in her fear, she had made him take an oath to keep— "Adam is not dead." Just at the first moment Karl thought her intellects must be wandering: but as she proceeded in a few rapid words to tell of his escape, of his dangerous illness, of his lying, even then, hidden away from the terrors of the law, all the dreadful position of his ill-fated brother rushed over Karl as in one long agony. He saw in vivid colours the hazard Adam was running—and must ever run, until either death or recapture should overtake him; he saw, as if portrayed in a mirror, the miserable future that lay before him, the lonely fugitive he must be.

To Karl Andinnian's mind, no fate in this world could be so miserable. Even death on the scaffold would to himself have been preferable to this life-time of living dread. He had loved his brother with a keen love; and he felt this almost as a death-blow: he could have died in his love and pity, if by that means his brother might be saved. Mingling with this regret had come the thought of his own changed position, and that he ought not to marry.

This he said. But Mrs. Andinnian pointed out to him that his position would not be so very materially altered. Such was her conviction. That she herself, by connivance with one of the warders, had mainly contributed to the step Adam had taken, that she had been the first to put it into his head, and set him on to attempt it, she was all too remorselessly conscious of. Now that he *had* escaped, and was entered in the prison rolls as dead, and lay hidden away in some hole or corner, not daring to come out of it, or to let into it the light of day, she saw what she had done. Not even to her might his hiding-place be disclosed. She saw that his future life must be, at the very best, that of a nameless exile—if, by good fortune, he could make his escape from his own land. If? His person was rather a remarkable one, and well known to his enemies the police force. Not one, perhaps, but had his photograph. A fugitive in some barren desert unfrequented by man, where he must drag on a solitary life of expatriation! Not much of his income would be needed for this.

"You will have to occupy Foxwood as its master; you must be Sir Karl to the world, as you are now," spoke Mrs. Andinnian; "and it is your children who will inherit after you. There is no reason whatever for breaking off your marriage, or for altering any of the arrangements. You will have to pay a certain sum yearly to Adam out of the estate. He will not need it long, poor fellow; a man's life, banned to the extent his will be, eats itself away soon."

Hemmed in by perplexities of all kinds, Karl's interview with his mother ended, and he went forth with his care and trouble. His own trouble would have been enough, but it was as nothing to that felt for his brother. He dared not tell the truth to Colonel Cleeve or to Lucy, or impart the slightest hint that his brother was alive; he almost as little dared, for Lucy's sake, to break off the marriage. And so it took place.

After that, he heard no more until he was again at Foxwood, summoned thither by his mother's illness. Mrs. Andinnian had fretted herself sick. Night and day, night and day was the fear of her son's discovery ever before her mind; she would see the recapture in her dreams: remorse wore her out, and fever supervened. She would have given all she possessed in the world could he be safely back at Portland Island without having attempted to quit it. Karl, on his arrival, found her in this sad state: and it was then she disclosed to him a further complication in the case, which she had but recently learnt herself. Sir Adam Andinnian was married.

It may be remembered that he was absent for a few days from his home in Northamptonshire, returning to it only on the eve of the day that news came of Sir Joseph's death, the fatal day when he killed Martin Scott. He had left home for the purpose of marrying Rose Turner, who was staying in Birmingham, a measure which had previously been planned between them. But for his mother's prejudices—as he called them—he would have married the young lady in the face of day; but he knew she would never consent, and he did not care openly to set her at naught. "We will be married in private, Rose," he decided, "and I will feel my way afterwards to disclose it to my mother." And Miss Rose Turner cared for him too much to make any objection. Alas, the time never came for him to disclose it. On the very day after his return to his home, the young lady returning also to hers, to her unsuspicious friends, he was thrown into prison on the charge of murder. It was not a time to speak; he wished to spare comment and annoyance to her; and she gave evidence at the trial—which she could not have done had she been his acknowledged wife. All this had been disclosed to Mrs. Andinnian the day after Karl left to celebrate his marriage. The stranger, Mr. Smith, spoken of by Hewitt as presenting himself again that day at Foxwood, and demanding an interview with its mistress, told her of it then. It was another bitter blow for Mrs. Andinnian, and the distress of mind it induced no doubt helped to bring on the fever. This, in her turn, she disclosed to Karl later from her sick-bed; and for him it made the complication ten times worse. Had he known his brother had a wife, nothing would have induced him to marry Lucy. Mrs. Andinnian told him more; that Adam had escaped safely to London, where he then lay hidden, and where his wife had joined him; and that they were coming to inhabit the Maze at Foxwood. The last bit of news nearly struck Karl dumb.

"Is Adam mad?" he asked.

"No, very sane," replied Mrs. Andinnian. "He wants to be at least on his own grounds: and we all think—he and I and —no matter—that he may be safer here than anywhere. Even were there a suspicion abroad that he is alive—which there is not, and I trust never will be,—his own place is the very last place that people would look into for him. Besides, there will be precautions used—and the Maze is favourable for concealment."

"It will be utter madness," spoke Karl. "It will be putting himself into the lion's mouth."

"It will be nothing of the sort—or Mr. Smith would not approve of it," retorted Mrs. Andinnian. "I *must* see my son, Karl: and how else am I to see him? I may not go to him where he is: it might bring suspicion on him: but I can go over to the Maze."

"Who is Mr. Smith?—and what has he to do with Adam?—and how comes he to be in the secret?" reiterated Karl.

But to this he could get no answer. Whether Mrs. Andinnian knew, or whether she did not know, she would not say. The one fact that Mr. Smith held the dangerous secret, and must be conciliated, was quite enough, she said, for Karl. Mr. Smith had Adam's safety and interest at heart, she went on to state; he wished to be near the Maze to watch over him; and she had given him the pretty cottage opposite the Maze gates to live in, calling him Sir Karl's agent, and appointing him to collect a few rents, so as to give a colouring of ostensibility to the neighbourhood. In vain Karl remonstrated. It was useless. The ground seemed slipping from under all their feet, but he could do nothing.

After all, poor Mrs. Andinnian did not live to see her most beloved son. Anxiety, torment, restlessness, proved too much for her, and brought on the crisis sooner than was expected. On the very day after she died, the tenants came to the Maze —at least, all the tenants who would be seen openly, or be suspected of inhabiting it. They arrived by the last evening train; Mrs. Grey and her attendants, the Hopleys; and took two flies, which were waiting in readiness, on to the Maze; the lady occupying one, Hopley and his wife the other. How Adam Andinnian reached the place, it is not convenient yet to state.

In the course of the next evening, Karl Andinnian went over to the Maze and saw his brother. Adam was much altered. In the fever, which had supervened on his injuries received at the escape, he had lost his hair and become pale and thin. But his spirits were undaunted. He should soon "pick up" now he was in the free open country air and on his own grounds, he said. As to danger, he seemed not to see it, and declared there was less risk of discovery there than anywhere else. Karl could play the grand man and the baronet for him at Foxwood—but he meant, for all that, to have a voice in the ruling of his own estate. Poor Karl Andinnian, on the contrary, saw the very greatest danger in the position of affairs. He would have preferred to shut up Foxwood, leaving only Hewitt to take care of it, that no chance of discovery should arise from either servants or other inhabitants there. But Sir Adam ruled it otherwise; saying he'd not have the Court left to stagnate. Hewitt was in the secret. It might have been neither expedient nor practicable to keep it from him: but the question was decided of itself. One evening just before Mrs. Andinnian's death, when Hewitt had gone to her sick-room on some errand at the dusk hour, she mistook him for Karl; and spoke words which betrayed all. Karl was glad of it: it seemed a protection to Adam, rather than not, that his tried old servant should be cognizant of the truth. So Karl went abroad again with his wife, and stayed until his keeping aloof from Foxwood began to excite comment in his wife's family; when he deemed it more expedient to return to it.

And now does the reader perceive all the difficulties of Karl Andinnian? There he was, in a false position: making believe to be a baronet of the realm, and a wealthy man, and the owner of Foxwood: and obliged to make believe. A hint to the contrary, a word that he was not in his right place, might have set suspicion afloat—and Heaven alone knew what would then be the ending. For Adam's sake he must be wary and cunning; he must play, so to say, the knave's part and deceive the world. But the dread of his brother's discovery lay upon him night and day, with a very-present awful dread: it was as a burning brand eating away his heart.

And again—you, my reader, can now understand the complication between Karl and his wife. *He* believed she had discovered the fact that Adam was alive and living concealed at the Maze; *she*, relying on Miss Blake's information, put down the Maze mystery to something of a very different nature. How could he suppose she meant anything but the dangerous truth? How could she imagine that the secret was any other than Miss Blake had so clearly and convincingly disclosed to her? In Lucy's still almost maidenly sensitiveness, she could not bring her lips to allude openly to the nature of her charge: and there was no necessity; for she assumed that Karl knew it even better than she did. In his reluctance to pronounce his brother's name, or to hint at the secret, lest even the very air should be treacherous and carry it abroad, he was perhaps less open than he might have been. When he offered to relate to her the whole story, she stopped him and refused to listen: and so closed up the explanation that would have set the cruel doubt right and her heart at rest.

Sitting there with Adam to-night, in that closely curtained room, Karl entered upon the matter he had come to urge— that his brother should get away from the Maze into some safer place. It was, as Sir Adam expressed it, but the old story—for Karl had never ceased to urge it from the first—and Adam wholly refused to listen. There was no risk, he said, no fear of discovery, and he should not go away from his own land. Either from this little particular spot of land which was individually his, or from the land of his birth. It was waste of words in Karl to speak further. Adam had always been of the most obstinate possible temperament. But the (supposed) discovery of his wife had frightened Karl worse than ever. He did not mention it to them, since he was not able to say how Lucy had made it.

"As sure as you are living, Adam, you will some day find the place entered by the officers of justice!" he exclaimed in pain.

"Let them enter it," recklessly answered Sir Adam. "They'll not find me."

"Oh, Adam, you don't know. They are lynx-eyed and crafty men."

"No doubt they are. I am all safe, Karl."

Karl had been there longer than usual, and he rose to say good night. Mrs. Grey—for convenience sake we must continue to call her by that name, and Lucy Lady Andinnian—folded up her work and went downstairs with him. She was changed too; but for the better. The very pretty, blooming-faced Rose Turner had come in for her share of the world's bitter trouble, and it had spiritualized her. The once round face was oval now, the lovely features were refined, the damask cheeks were a shade more delicate, the soft blue eyes had a sad light in them. Miss Blake's words were not misapplied to her—"beautiful as an angel."

"Karl," she whispered, "the dread of discovery is wearing me out. If we could but get away from England!"

"I am sure it will wear out me," was Karl's answer.

"Adam is afraid of Mr. Smith; I am sure he is. He thinks Smith would stop his going. Karl, I fully believe, as truly as I ever believed any great truth in my life, that Smith is keeping us here and will not let us go. Mr. Smith may appear to be a friend outwardly, but I fear he is an inward enemy. Oh, dear! it is altogether a dreadful situation."

Karl went on home, his brain active, his heart sinking. The manner in which his wife had taken up the matter, distressed him greatly. He supposed she was resenting it chiefly on the score of her father and mother. The colonel had told him that they would rather have followed Lucy to the grave than see her his wife had Sir Adam lived.

"I wonder how she discovered it?" ran his thoughts—but in truth the fact did not excite so much speculation in his mind, because he was hourly living in the apprehension that people must suspect it. When we hold a dangerous secret, this is sure to be the case. "Perhaps Hewitt let drop an incautious word," he went on musing, "and Lucy caught it up, and guessed the rest. Or—perhaps I dropped one in my sleep."

Crossing the lawn of the Court, he entered by the little smoking-room, his hand pressed upon his aching brow. No wonder that people found fault with the looks of Sir Karl Andinnian! He was wearing to a skeleton. Just as his mother, when she was dying, used to see the re-capture of Adam in her dreams, so did Karl see it in his. Night after night would he wake up from one of the dreadful visions. Adam, the re-taken convict, held fast by a heap of scowling, threatening warders, and a frightful scaffold conspicuous in the distance. He would start up in bed in horror, believing it all real, his heart quivering, and once or twice he knew that he had cried out aloud.

"Yes, yes, that's how it must have been," he said, the mystery becoming as apparently clear to his eyes as the light of day. "Hewitt is too cautious and true. I have betrayed it in my sleep. Oh, my brother! May heaven help and save him!"

CHAPTER XVII.

BEFORE THE WORLD.

FOXWOOD COURT was alive with gaiety. At least, what stood for gaiety in that inwardly sad and sober house. Colonel and Mrs. Cleeve had come for a fortnight's stay. Visits were being exchanged with the neighbours; dinner parties reigned. It was not possible for Sir Karl and Lady Andinnian to accept hospitality and not return it: and—at any rate during the sojourn of the Colonel and his wife—Sir Karl dared not shut themselves up as hermits lest comment should be excited. So the Court held its receptions, and went out to other people's: and Sir Karl and Lady Andinnian dressed, and talked, and comported themselves just as though there was no shadow between them.

Lady Andinnian was growing graver day by day: her very heart seemed to be withering. That Sir Karl paid his secret visits to the Maze two or three nights a week, she knew only too well. One of the most innocent and naturally unsuspicious persons in the world was she: but, now that her eyes had been opened, she saw all clearly. Without watching and tracking the movements of her husband as Miss Blake had tracked them; in her guileless honour she could never have done that; Lady Andinnian was only too fully awake now to the nightly strolls abroad of her husband; and instinct told her for what purpose they were taken.

Life for her at this present time seemed very hard to bear. The task she had imposed upon herself—to endure in patience and silence—seemed well nigh an impracticable one. The daily cross, that she had apportioned herself to take up, felt too heavy for mortal frame to carry. Humiliation, jealousy, love waged war with each other within her, and rendered her very wretched. It needed all the good and gentle and patient principles instilled into her from early childhood, it needed all the strength she was ever praying for, to hold on perseveringly in her bitter path, and make no sign. At times she thought that the silence to which she was condemned must eat away her heart; but a chance occurrence or two showed her that silence was not the worst phase she might have to bear.

On the day after Mrs. Cleeve's arrival, she was upstairs in her daughter's chamber. Miss Blake was also there. Lucy had come in, hot and tired, from an afternoon walk to Margaret Sumnor's, and Aglaé had been summoned to help her to change her silk dress for an unpretending muslin.

"I did not know it was so hot before I went out, or I would not have put on the silk," observed Lucy. "Sitting so quietly with you all the morning, mamma, in that cool drawing-room, talking of old times, I forgot the heat."

Mrs. Cleeve made no particular reply. She was looking about her; taking silent notice. The doors of communication to the further chamber stood open, as was usual during the day: Lucy took care of that, to keep down suspicion in the house of there being any estrangement between herself and her husband.

"And you have made this your sleeping-room, Lucy, my dear?" observed Mrs. Cleeve.

"Yes, mamma."

"And that further one is Sir Karl's! Well, I'm sure you are getting quite a fashionable couple—to have separate rooms. I and your papa never had such a thing in our lives, Lucy."

Lucy Andinnian grew crimson; as if a flush of the summer heat were settling in her face. She murmured, in reference to the remarks, some words about the nights being so very hot, and that she had felt a sort of fever upon her. The very consciousness of having the truth to conceal caused her to be more urgent in rendering some plea of excuse. Aglaé, whose national prejudice had been particularly gratified at the alteration, and who had lived too long in Mrs. Cleeve's service, to keep in whatever opinion might rise to her tongue's end, hastened to speak.

"But, and is it not the most sensible arrangement, madame, that my lady and Sir Karl could have made, when the summer is like an Afric summer for the hotness? Mademoiselle here knows that."

"Don't appeal to me, Aglaé," cried Miss Blake, in a frozen tone.

"Yes, yes, Aglaé; I say the fashion is coming up in England; and perhaps it induces to comfort," said Mrs. Cleeve.

"But certainly. And, as madame sees,"—pointing through the little sitting-room to the further chamber—" it is but like the same chamber. When Sir Karl is in that, and my lady in this, they can look straight at one another."

"Aglaé see to these shoulder-knots, sharply interposed Lady Andinnian. "You have not put them on evenly."

"And talk to each other, if they please," persisted Aglaé, ignoring the ribbons to uphold her opinion. "Madame ought to see that the arrangement is good."

"At any rate, Lucy, I think you should have kept to the large room yourself, and Sir Karl have come to the smaller one," said Mrs. Cleeve.

"It's the very remark I made to my lady," cried Aglaé, turning at length to regard the ribbons with a critical eye. "But my lady chose, herself, this. It is commodious; I say nothing to the contrary: but it is not as large as the other."

Oh, how Lucy wished they would be silent. Her poor flushed face knew not where to hide itself; her head and heart were aching with all kinds of perplexity. Taking up the eau-de-cologne flask, she saturated her handkerchief and passed it over her brow.

"Has my lady got ache to her head?"

"Yes. A little. Alter these ribbons, Aglaé, and let me go."

"It is because of this marvellous heat," commented Aglaé. "Paris this summer would not be bearable."

Aglaé was right in the main; for it was an unusually hot summer. The intense heat began with Easter, and lasted late into autumn. In one sense, it was favourable to Lucy, for it upheld her given excuse in regard to the sleeping arrangements.

Miss Blake had stood all the while with in-drawn lips. It was a habit of hers to show it in her lips when displeased. Seeing always the doors open in the day-time, no suspicion of the truth crossed her. She believed that what she had disclosed to Lucy was no more to her than the idle wind, once Sir Karl had made good his own false cause.

A question was running through Miss Blake's mind now—had been in it more or less since Mrs. Cleeve came: should she, or should she not, tell that lady what she knew? She had deliberated upon it; she had set herself to argue the point, for and against: and yet, down deep in her heart from the first had laid the innate conviction that she should tell. In the interests of religion and morality, she told herself that she ought not to keep silence; for the suppression of iniquity and deceit, she was bound to speak. Had Lucy but taken up the matter rightly, there would have been no necessity for her to have again interfered: neither should she have done it. But Lucy had set her communication at naught: and therefore, in Miss Blake's judgment, the obligation was laid upon her. Why—how could she, who was only second to the Rev. Guy Cattacomb in the management and worship at St. Jerome's, and might have been called his lay curate; who prostrated herself there in prayer ever so many times a day, to the edification and example of Foxwood—how could she dare to hold cognizance of a mine of evil, and not strive to put an end to it and bring it home to its enactors? Every time she went to that holy shrine, St. Jerome's, every time she came back from its sacred dust, as may be said, hallowing her shoes, she had to pass those iniquitous gates, and was forced into the undesirable thoughts connected with them!

If Miss Blake had wavered before, she fully made her mind up now; now, as she stood there in the chamber, the conversation dying away on her ears. Aglaé was attending to the shoulder-knots; Lucy was passive under the maid's hands; and Mrs. Cleeve had wandered into the little intermediate sitting-room. No longer a dressing-room; Lucy had given it up as such when she changed her chamber. She had some books and work and her desk there now, and sat there whenever she could. Miss Blake stood on, gazing from the window and perfecting her resolution. She thought she was but acting in the strict line of wholesome duty, just as disinterestedly as the Archbishop of Canterbury might have done; and she would have been very much shocked had anything told her she was only actuated by a desire of taking vengeance on Karl Andinnian. She wanted to bring home a little confusion to him; she hoped to see the young lady at the Maze turned out of the village amidst an escorting flourish of ironical drums and shrieking fifes, leaving Foxwood Court to its peace. But Miss Blake was in no hurry to speak: she must watch her opportunity.

They were engaged to dine on the following day at a distance, four or five miles off; a ball was to follow it. When the time came, Lady Andinnian, radiant in her white silk bridal dress, entered the reception room leaning on the arm of her good-looking husband. Who could have dreamt that they were living on ill terms, seeing them now? In public they were both cautiously courteous to each other, observing every little obligation of society: and, in truth, Karl at all times, at home and out, was in manner affectionate to his wife.

Two carriages had conveyed them: and, in going, Lucy had occupied one with her father; Karl, Mrs. Cleeve, and Miss Blake the other. Lucy had intended to return in the same order, but found she could not. Colonel Cleeve, unconscious of doing wrong, entered the carriage with his wife and Miss Blake: Lucy and her husband had to sit together. The summer's night was giving place to dawn.

"I fear you are tired, Lucy," he kindly said, as they drove off.

"Yes, very. I wish I was at home."

She drew her elegant white cloak about her with its silken tassels, gathered herself into the corner of the carriage, and shut her eyes, seemingly intending to go to sleep. Sleep! her heart was beating too wildly for that. But she kept them resolutely closed, making no sign; and never another word was spoken all the way. Sir Karl helped her out: the others had already arrived.

"Good-night," she whispered to him, preparing to run up stairs.

"Good-night, Lucy."

But, in spite of Lady Andinnian's efforts to make the best of things and show no sign, a mother's eye could not be deceived; and before Mrs. Cleeve had been many days in the house, she was struck with the underlying aspect of sadness that seemed to pervade Lucy. Her cheerfulness appeared to be often forced; this hidden sadness was real. Unsuspecting Mrs. Cleeve could come to but one conclusion—her daughter's health must be deranged.

"Since when have you not felt well, Lucy?" she asked her confidentially one day, when they were alone in Lucy's little sitting-room.

Lucy, buried in a reverie, woke up with a start at the question. "I am very well, mamma. Why should you think I am not?"

"Your spirits are unequal, Lucy, and you certainly do not look well; neither do you eat as you ought. My dear, I think—I hope there must be a cause for it."

"What cause?" returned Lucy, not taking her meaning.

"We should be so pleased to welcome a little heir, my dear. Is it so?"

Lucy—she had just dressed for dinner, and dismissed Aglaé—coloured painfully. Mrs. Cleeve smiled.

"No, mamma, I think there is no cause of that kind," she answered, in a low, nervous tone. And only herself knew the bitter pang that pierced her, as she remembered how certain it was that there could be no such cause for the future.

But Mrs. Cleeve held to her own private opinion. "The child is shy in these early days, even with me," she thought. "I'll say no more."

One morning during this time, Karl was sitting alone in his room, when Hewitt came to him to say Smith the agent was asking to see him. Karl did not like Smith the agent: he doubted, dreaded, and did not comprehend him.

"Will you see him, sir?" asked Hewitt, in a low tone, perceiving the lines on his master's brow.

"I suppose I must see him, Hewitt," was the reply—and the confidential faithful servant well understood the force of the must. "Show him in."

"Beg pardon for disturbing you so early, Sir Karl," said the agent, as Hewitt brought him in and placed a chair. "There's one of your small tenants dropping into a mess, I fancy. He has got the brokers in for taxes, or something of that kind. I thought I'd better let you know at once."

Hewitt shut the door, and Karl pushed away the old letters he had been sorting. Sir Joseph's papers and effects had never been examined yet; but Karl was settling to the work now. That Mr. Smith had spoken in an unusually loud and careless tone, he noticed: and therefore judged that this was but the ostensible plea for his calling, given lest any ears should be about.

"Which of my tenants is it, Mr. Smith?" he quietly asked.

Mr. Smith looked round to be sure that the door was closed, and then asked Sir Karl if he'd mind having the window shut; he felt a bit of a draught. And he shut the glass-doors himself with his one hand, before Karl could assent to the proposal, or rise to do it himself.

"It is Seaford the miller," he answered. "And"—dropping his voice to the lowest and most cautious tone—"it is a fact that he has the brokers in for some arrears of Queen's rates. But the man has satisfied me that it is but a temporary embarrassment; and I think, Sir Karl, your rent is in no danger. Still it was right that you should know of it; and it has served, just in the nick of time, to account for my object in coming."

"What is the real object?" inquired Karl, in a voice as cautious as the other voice.

Mr. Smith took a newspaper out of the pocket of his light summer coat; borrowed his disabled hand from the sling to help unfold it, and then pointed to a small paragraph. It ran as follows:—

"Curious rumours are afloat connected with a recorded attempt at escape from Portland Island, in which the unfortunate malefactor met his death. A mysterious whisper has arisen, we know not how or whence, that the death was but a fiction, and that the man is at large."

"What paper is it?" cried Karl, trying to force some colour into his white lips.

"Only one in which all kinds of stories are got up," rejoined Mr. Smith, showing the title of a sensational weekly paper. "The paragraph may have resulted from nothing but the imagination of some penny-a-liner, Sir Karl, at fault for real matter."

"I don't like it." observed Karl after a pause. "Assume

that it may be as you suggest, and nothing more, this very announcement will be the means of drawing people's thoughts towards it."

"Not it," spoke Mr. Smith. "And if it does?—nobody will think it points to Sir Adam Andinnian. Another prisoner has been killed since then, trying to escape."

"How do you know that?"

"I *do* know it," replied Mr. Smith, emphatically. But he advanced no further proof. "It was a curious thing, my getting this paper," he continued. "Yesterday I was over at Basham, mistook the time of the returning train, and found when I reached the station that I had to wait three-quarters of an hour. The only newspapers on the stand were these weekly ones; I bought this to while away the time, and saw the paragraph."

"These events, looked upon as chances and errors, are in reality ordained," spoke Karl dreamily. "What can be done, Mr. Smith?"

"Nothing; nothing, Sir Karl. There's nothing to do. He is safe enough where he is—even if the rumour did come to be looked into by the law's authorities. Rely upon it, the Maze will never be suspected.

"I wish to heaven he had never come to the Maze!" was Karl Andinnian's pained rejoinder.

"It might be better on the whole that he had not," acknowledged Mr. Smith. "The plan originated with himself and with the late Mrs. Andinnian—and they carried it out."

"I wish,' said Karl, speaking upon sudden impulse, "that you would allow me to know how you became connected with this affair of my unfortunate brother—and what you still have to do with it."

"How I became connected with it does not signify," was the short and ready answer. "As to what I have to do with it still, you know as well as I. I just watch over him—or rather the place that contains him—and if danger should arise I shall be at hand to, I hope, give him warning, and to protect him from it."

"He ought to be got away from the Maze," persisted Karl.

"He'd never get away in safety. Especially if there's anything in this"—striking his hand on the newspaper paragraph. "With my consent, he will never try to."

Karl did not answer; but he thought the more. That this man was the true impediment to his brother's escape; that he was in fact keeping him where he was, he believed with his whole heart. Once Sir Adam could be safe away from the kingdom, Mr. Smith no doubt foresaw that he might no longer enjoy Clematis Cottage to live in, or the handsome sum which he received quarterly. A sum that Mrs. Andinnian had commenced to pay, and Karl did not dare to discontinue. The words were but a confirmation of his opinion. Mr. Smith was Adam's enemy, not friend; he was keeping him there for his own self-interest: and Karl feared that if Adam attempted to get away in spite of him, he might in revenge deliver him up to justice. In dangers of this secret kind, fear has no limit.

"He could not be as safe anywhere in England as here," concluded Mr. Smith, as if he divined Karl's thoughts. "The police would suspect every hole and corner of the country, every town, little and big, before they would suspect his own home. As to the sailing away for another land, the danger of his recognition would be too great both on the voyage and on embarking for it, for him to dare it. He'd be discovered as sure as apple-trees grow apples."

"Will it be better to tell him of this?" cried Karl, alluding to the newspaper.

"I think not. Just as you please, though, Sir Karl. Rely upon it, it is only what I suggest—an emanation from some penny-a-liner's inventive brain."

"The paper had better be burnt," suggested Karl.

"The very instant I get home," said Mr. Smith, putting the paper in his pocket and taking his hat from the table. "I wish I could burn the whole impression—already gone forth to the world. I'll go out this way, Sir Karl, if you will allow me."

Opening the glass-doors again, he stepped across the terrace to the lawn, talking still, as though continuing the conversation. Other windows stood open, and the agent was cautious.

"I'll be sure to see Seaford in the course of the day. You may trust to me not to let any of them get behind-hand with their rents. Good-morning, Sir Karl."

The agent, however, did not turn into his house. Deep in thought, he strolled on, up the road, his free hand in his light coat pocket, his head bent in meditation. He wished he could obtain some little light as to this mysterious announcement; he fancied he might be able to. On he strolled, unthinkingly, until he came to St. Jerome's, the entrance door of which edifice was ajar.

"Holding one of their services," thought the agent. "I'll have a look in, and see Cattacomb surrounded by his flock of lambs."

Mr. Smith was disappointed: for the reverend gentleman was not there. It appeared to be the hour for cleaning the room, instead of one for holding service. Four or five young ladies, their gowns turned up round their waists and some old gloves on, were dusting, sweeping, and brushing with all their might and main; Miss Blake presiding as high priestess of the ceremonies.

"They'd not do such a thing in their own homes to save their lives," laughed the agent, coming softly out again unseen. "Cattacomb must be in clover among 'em!"

He went home then, looked attentively once more at the alarming paragraph, and burnt the newspaper. After that, he paced his little garden, as if in a fit of restlessness, and then leaned over the gate, lost in reflection. The trees of the Maze were perfectly still in the hot summer air; the road was dusty, and not a single passenger to be seen on it.

A few minutes, and footsteps broke upon his ear. They were Miss Blake's, bringing her home from St. Jerome's. She stopped to shake hands.

"Well," said he with a laugh, "all the scrubbing done?"

"How do you know anything about the scrubbing?" returned Miss Blake.

"I looked in just now, and saw you all at it, dusting and brushing, and thought what an enviable young priest that Cattacomb must be. Now, my lad! don't ride over us if you can help it."

The very same butcher-boy, in the same blue frock, had come galloping up to the Maze gate, rung the bell, and was now prancing backwards across the road on his horse, which was very restive. Something appeared to have startled the animal; and it was to the boy the last remark had been addressed. Miss Blake stepped inside the garden-gate, held open for her—for the horse seemed to think the path his own ground as well as the highway.

"He have been shoed this morning, and he's always in this dratted temper after it," spoke the boy gratuitously.

The woman-servant came out with her dish, received some meat, and disappeared again, taking care to lock the gate after her. She had never left it unlocked since the unlucky day when Miss Blake got in. Glancing over the road, she saw the lady and the agent watching her, and no doubt recognized the former. "Looks like a faithful servant, that," remarked Mr. Smith.

"Faithful," echoed Miss Blake—"well yes, she does. But to what a mistress! Fidelity to such a person does her no credit."

Mr. Smith turned as grave as a judge. "Hush!" said he, impressively. "Unless one has sure and good ground to go upon, it is better not to assume evil."

"No ground was ever surer than this."

"My dear young lady, you may be utterly mistaken." She liked the style of address from him—my dear *young* lady: it flattered her vanity. But she would not give way.

"I have seen what I have seen, Mr. Smith. Sir Karl Andinnian would not be stealing in there at night, if it were proper for him to be going in the open day."

"Never speak of it," cried Mr. Smith, his tone one of sharp, strong command. "What could you prove? I ask, Miss Blake, what you could prove—if put to it?"

She did not answer.

"Why, nothing, madam. Absolutely *nothing*. How could you?"

Miss Blake considered. "I think there's a good deal of negative proof," she said, at length.

"Moonshine," cried Mr. Smith. "Negative proof in a case of this kind always is moonshine. Listen, my dear Miss Blake, for I am advising you now as a good friend. Never breathe a word of this matter to living soul. You don't know what the consequences to yourself might be."

"Consequences to myself!"

"To yourself, of course: there's no one else in question—at least in my mind. You might be sued for libel, and get sentenced to pay heavy damages and to a term of imprisonment besides. For goodness sake, be cautious! Remember Jane Shore! She had to stand in the pillory in a white sheet, in the face and eyes of a gaping multitude, a lighted taper in her hand."

"Jane Shore!" cried Miss Blake, who at the above suggestion had begun to go as pale as she could well go. "Jane Shore! But that was not for libel. It was for—for—"

Miss Blake broke down.

"Shoreditch is named after her, you know," put in Mr. Smith. "Poor thing! she was very lovely: raven hair and eyes of a violet blue, say the old chronicles. Keep your own counsel, young lady, implicitly—and be silent for your own sake."

Miss Blake said good-morning, and walked away. The prospect suggested to her, as to the fine and imprisonment, looked anything but a pleasant one. She resolved henceforth to *be* silent; to Mrs. Cleeve and to all else: and, under the influence of this new and disagreeable suggestion, she wished to her heart she had never opened her lips to Lady Andinnian.

"Meddlesome tabby cat," aspirated the gallant Mr. Smith. "She might play up Old Beans with her tongue. Women are the very deuce for being ill-natured to one another."

CHAPTER XVIII.

A NIGHT ALARM.

COLONEL and Mrs. Cleeve had departed again, and the time went on. Foxwood Court was comparatively quiet. The opening visits on all sides had been paid and returned, and there was a lull in the dinner-parties. The weather continued most intensely hot; and people were glad to be still.

Never had poor Lucy Andinnian felt the estrangement from her husband so cruelly as now. At first, the excitement of resentment had kept her up, and the sojourn of her father and mother, together with the almost daily gaiety, had served to take her out of herself: it was only at night during the lonely hours, when trouble prevented sleep, that she had felt its keenest sting. But now: now when she and Karl were alone, save for Miss Blake: when she sat in her lonely room hour after hour, and had leisure to realize her true position, Lucy gave way to all the abandonment of grief her trial brought. It was indeed a bitter one; a fiery trial: and when she looked back to it in after days, she could never imagine how she had contrived to bear it.

Love is an all-powerful master: an over-ruling tyrant. In the first torments of awakened jealousy, it is all very well to take refuge in revengeful anger, and snap our fingers metaphorically at the beloved one, and say he may go promener. The reaction comes. Jealousy, alas, does not tend to extinguish love, but rather to increase it. Lucy Andinnian found it so to her cost. Her love for Karl had in no whit abated: and the very fact of knowing he paid these stolen night visits to the Maze, while it tortured her jealousy, in no way diminished her love. She was growing pale and thin; she questioned whether she had done wisely in undertaking this most cruel task of bearing in silence and patience, hoping it might bring him back to his true allegiance; for she knew not whether she could endure on to the end.

There were moments when in her desolation she almost wished she was reconciled to her husband on any terms, even to the extent of condoning the wrong and the evil. The strict reader must pardon her, for she was very desolate. The idea always went away at once, and she would arouse herself with a shiver. Perhaps, of all phases of the affair, the one that told most upon her, that she felt to be more humiliating than the rest, was the fact of its having been brought close to her home, to its very gates: and a thousand times she asked herself the ambiguous question—Why could not Sir Karl rid the Maze of its inmates, and convey them to a distance?

She might have schooled her heart to care for Karl less had they been separated: he at the North Pole, say: she at the South. But they were living under the same roof, and met hourly. They went to church together, and paid visits with each other, and sat at the same breakfast and dinner tables. For, their public intercourse was so conducted that no suspicion of the truth should get abroad, within doors or without. As to Karl, he was waiting, on his side, with what patience he might until his wife's mood should alter; in fact, he had no other alternative; but he treated her with the most anxious kindness and consideration. That she had taken the matter up with unjustifiable harshness, he thought; but he excused it, knowing himself to be the real culprit for having married her. And thus they went on; Lucy's spirit wounded to the core, and her anguished heart pining for the love that she believed was not hers.

She was sitting one Saturday evening under the acacia tree, in the delicate muslin she had worn in the day, when Karl came down from his dressing-room ready for dinner, and crossed the lawn to her. He had been to Basham, and she had not seen him since the morning.

"You are very pale, Lucy."

"My head aches badly: and it was so pleasant to remain

here in the cool that I did not go in to dress," she said to him in a tone of apology.

"And why should you?" returned Karl. "That is as pretty a dress as any you have. What has given you the headache?"

"I—always have it now, more or less," had been on the tip of her tongue; but she broke off in time. "The heat, I think. I got very hot to-day, walking to Margaret Sumnor's."

"It is too hot for walking, Lucy. You should take the carriage."

"I don't like the parade of the carriage when I go to Margaret's."

"Would you like a little pony-chaise? I would buy you one if you——"

"No, thank you," she interrupted hastily, her tone a cold one. "I prefer to walk when I go about Foxwood. The hot weather will pass away sometime."

"You were saying the other day, Lucy, to some one who called, that you would like to read that new book on the Laplanders. I have been getting it for you."

He had a white paper parcel in his hand, undid it, and gave her a handsomely bound volume. She felt the kindness, and her sad face flushed slightly.

"Thank you; thank you very much. It was good of you to think of me."

"And I have been subscribing to the Basham library, Lucy, and brought home the first parcel of books. It may amuse you to read them."

"Yes, I think it will. Thank you, Sir Karl."

She had never called him "Karl" when they were alone, since the explosion. Now and then occasionally before people, she did, especially before her father and mother. But he understood quite well that it was only done for appearance' sake.

The dinner hour was at hand, and they went in. Very much to the surprise of both, Mr. Cattacomb was in the drawing-room with Miss Blake. Lucy had neither heard nor seen him: but the acacia tree was out of sight of the front entrance.

"I have been telling Mr. Cattacomb—he came to me in the heat, on business of St. Jerome's—that you will be charitable enough to give him some dinner," said Miss Blake, introducing Mr. Cattacomb to Sir Karl in form—for it was the first time Karl had met that reverend man. Of course Karl could only return a civil answer; but he had not been at all anxious for the acquaintanceship of Mr. Cattacomb, and was determined not to treat him precisely as though he had been an invited guest.

"I think you may perhaps prefer to take in your friend Miss Blake, as Lady Andinnian is a stranger to you," he said, when Hewitt announced dinner. "We are not on ceremony now."

And Sir Karl caught his wife's hand in his. "I was not going to leave you to *him*, Lucy," he whispered.

So they went parading in to dinner arm-in-arm, this estranged man and wife, brushing past Hewitt and the tall new footman, who wore powdered hair.

"It is just as though he did care for me!" thought Lucy, glancing at her husband as he placed her in her seat at the table's head.

Mr. Cattacomb and Miss Blake, seated opposite each other, talked a great deal, Karl scarcely at all. When alone, the dinners at the Court were simply served, Sir Karl carving.

He was attentive to his impromptu guest, and sent him of the best: but he thought he had never in all his life been in company with so affected and vain a man as that belauded clergyman. Once, with the fish before him, Karl fell into a reverie. He woke up with a start, looking about him like a man bewildered.

"Some more fish, Lucy, my darling?"

Lucy's plate had gone away long before. They all saw that he had been, so to speak, unconscious of what he said. He rallied then; and did not lose himself again.

Dinner over, Mr. Cattacomb, making an apology, hurried away for some slight service at St. Jerome's, Miss Blake accompanying him as a matter of course. Lucy disappeared: and Karl, thus abandoned, went to his smoking-room. Not to smoke; but to muse upon the acute angles of his position —as he was too much given to do. Karl Andinnian was as a man in a net: as things looked at present, there seemed to be no chance of freedom from it; no hope of it, at present or in the future. And his ill-fated brother again! The past night he, Karl, had dreamt one of those ugly dreams. He thought he saw Adam fleeing from his pursuers; a number of them, and they all looked like warders of Portland Prison. Panting, crying, Adam rushed in, seized hold of Karl, and begged him, as he valued salvation hereafter, to hide and save him. But the warders burst in and surrounded them. Poor Karl woke up as usual in fright and agony. This dream had been recurring to his mind all day: it was very vivid now in the silent evening hour after sunset.

"I'd give my life to place him in safety," ran his thoughts. "Not much of a gift, either, for I verily believe this constant, distressing suspense will kill me. If he were but safe in some distant land! He might—Why, what is Lucy doing?"

Opposite this south window there was a beautiful vista, through the trees, of the grounds beyond. Sir Karl had seen his wife running swiftly from one walk to another, and suddenly stoop—as he fancied. Looking still, he found she did not get up again.

"She must have fallen," he exclaimed; and rushed out.

He was with her in a minute. She was getting up after her fall, but her ankle felt intolerably painful. Karl was very tender: he had her in his arms, and took her to a leafy arbour close by. There he put her to sit down, and held her to him for support.

"I have twisted my ankle," she said. "It's nothing."

But the tears of pain stood in her eyes. He soothed her as he would have soothed her in the bygone days; holding her in his firm protection, whispering terms of sweet endearment. What with the ankle's sharp twinges, what with his loving words, and what with her chronic state of utter wretchedness, poor Lucy burst into sobs, and sobbed them out upon his breast.

"My darling! The ankle is giving you pain."

"The ankle's nothing," she said. "It will soon be well." But she laid there still and sobbed pitiably. He waited in silence until she should grow calmer, his arm round her. A distant nightingale was singing its love-song.

"Lucy," began Karl, then, "I would ask you—now that we seem to be for the moment alone with the world and each other—whether there is any *sense* in living in the way we do? Is there any happiness for either of us? I want you to forgive all, and be reconciled: I want you to see the matter in its proper light, apart from prejudice. The past is past, and cannot be recalled: but it leaves no just reason in the sight of God or man for our living in estrangement."

Her head was hidden against him still. She did not lift her eyes as she whispered her answer.

"Is there no reason for it now, Karl? Now, at the present time. None?"

"No. As I see it, NO; on my word of honour as a gentleman. The notion you have taken up is an unsound and utterly mistaken one. You had grave cause to complain; granted: to resent; I admit it all: but surely it was not enough to justify the rending asunder of man and wife. The past cannot be undone—Heaven knows I would undo it if I could. But there is no just cause for your visiting the future upon me in this way, and making us both pay a heavy penalty. Won't you forgive and forget? Won't you be my own dear wife again? Oh, Lucy, I am full of trouble, and I want your sympathy to lighten it."

Her whole heart yearned to him. He drew her face to his and kissed her lips with the sweetest kisses. In the bliss and rest that the reconciliation brought to her spirit, Lucy momentarily forgot all else. Her kisses met his; her tears wet his cheeks. What with one emotion and another—pain, anguish, grief and bliss, the latter uppermost—poor Lucy felt faint. The bitter past was effaced from her memory: the change seemed like a glimpse of Paradise. It all passed in a moment, or so, of time.

"Oh, Karl, I should like to be your wife again!" she confessed. "The estrangement we are living in is more cruel for me than for you: there is no confidence between us, no pleasant interchange of mutual thought. Shall it be so?"

"Shall it," repeated Karl. "Is there need to ask me, Lucy?"

"It lies with you."

"With me! Why, how—how does it—lie with me? You know, my darling——"

A slight ruffle, as if some one were brushing past the shrubs in the opposite path, caused Sir Karl to withdraw his arm from his wife. Miss Blake came up: a note in her hand. Sir Karl politely, in thought, wished Miss Blake at York.

"As I was coming in, Sir Karl, I overtook a woman with this note, which she was bringing you. It was the servant at the Maze—or some one very like her."

Miss Blake looked full at Sir Karl as she spoke, wishing no doubt that looks were daggers. She had added the little bit of information, as to the messenger, for Lucy's especial benefit. Karl thanked her coolly, and put the note, unopened, into his pocket. Lucy, shy, timid Lucy, was limping away. Miss Blake saw something was wrong and held out her arm.

"What is the matter, Lucy? You are in pain! You have been crying!"

"I slipped and hurt my ankle, Theresa. It was foolish to cry, though. The pain is much less already."

Miss Blake helped her indoors in lofty silence. Anything like the contempt she felt for the weakness of Lucy Andinnian, she perhaps had never felt for any one before in all her life. Not for the weakness of crying at a hurt: though that was more befitting a child than a woman: but for the reprehensible weakness she was guilty of in living on terms of affection with her husband. "Must even sit in a garden arbour together hand in hand, listening to the nightingales," shrieked Miss Blake mentally, with rising hair. "And yet— she knows what I disclosed to her!"

The note was from Mrs. Grey. Had Miss Blake herself presided at its opening, she could not reasonably have found fault with it. Mrs. Grey presented her compliments to Sir Karl Andinnian, and would feel obliged by his calling to see her as soon as convenient, as she wished to speak with him on a little matter of business concerning the house.

There was nothing more. But Karl knew, by the fact of her venturing on the extreme step of writing to the Court, that he was wanted at the Maze for something urgent. It was several days since he had been there: for he could not divest himself of the feeling that some one of his nightly visits of his, more unlucky than the rest, might bring on suspicion and betrayal. To his uneasy mind there was danger in every surrounding object. The very sound of the wind in the trees seemed to whisper it to him as he passed; hovering shades, of phantom shape, glanced out to his fancy from the hedges.

He stayed a short while, pacing his garden, and then went indoors. It was getting dusk. Miss Blake had her things off and was alone in the drawing-room. The tea waited on the table.

"Where's Lucy?" he asked.

"She went to her room to have her ankle seen to. I would have done anything for her, but she declined my services."

Karl knocked at his wife's little sitting-room door, and entered. She was leaning on the window-sill, and said her ankle felt much better after the warm water, and since Aglaó had bound it up. Karl took her hand.

"We were interrupted, Lucy, when I was asking an important question," he began—"for indeed I think I must have misunderstood you. How does the putting an end to our estrangement lie with me?"

"It does lie with you, Karl," she answered, speaking feelingly and pleasantly, not in the cold tone of reserve she had of late maintained when they were alone. "The estrangement is miserable for me; you say it is for you; and the efforts we have to make, to keep up the farce before the household and the world, make it doubly miserable for both of us. We cannot undo our marriage: but to continue to live as we are living is most unsatisfactory and deplorable."

"But it is you who insisted on living so, Lucy—to my surprise and pain."

"Could I do otherwise?" she rejoined. "It is a most unhappy business altogether: and at times I am tempted to wish that it had been always kept from me. As you say—and I am willing to believe you, and do believe you—the past is past: but you know how much of the consequences remain. It seems to me that I must give way a little: perhaps, having taken my vows as your wife, it may be what I ought to do; a duty even in God's sight."

"Do you recollect your words to me on the eve of our wedding-day, Lucy, when I was speaking of the possibility that a deeper blow might fall: one that would dishonour us both in the world's eyes, myself primarily, you through me, and cause you to repent of our union? You should never repent, you said; you took me for richer for poorer, for better or for worse."

"But I did not know the blow would be of this kind," murmured Lucy. "Still, I will do as you wish me—forget and forgive. At least, if I cannot literally forget, for that would not be practicable, it shall be as though I did, for I will never allude to it by word or deed. That will be my concession, Karl. You must make one on your side."

"Willingly. What is it?"

"Clear the Maze immediately of its tenants."

He gave a slight start, knitting his brow. Lucy saw the proposal was unpalatable.

"Their being there is an insult to me, Karl," she softly said, as if beseeching the boon. "You must get them away."

"I cannot, Lucy," he answered, his face wrung with pain. "I wish I could! Don't you understand that I have no control over this?"

"I think I understand," she said, her manner growing cold. "You have said as much before. Why can you not? It seems to me, if things be as you intimate, that the matter would be easily accomplished. You need only show firmness."

He thought how little she understood. But he could not bear to enlarge upon it, and said nothing.

"There are houses enough, and to spare, in the world, Karl."

"Plenty of them."

"Then, why not let the Maze be left?"

"More things than one are against it, Lucy. There are wheels within wheels," he added, thinking of Smith, the mysterious agent. "One great element against it is the risk—the danger."

"Danger of exposure, do you mean?"

"Of discovery. Yes."

Never had Karl Andinnian and his wife been so near coming to an enlightenment on the misunderstanding that lay between them and their peace. It passed off—just as many another good word passes off, unsaid, in life.

"My hands are tied, Lucy. If wishing the Maze empty would effect it, it would be vacant to-morrow. I can do nothing."

"I understand," she said bitterly, even as she had said once before, all the old resentful indignation rising up within her. "I understand, Sir Karl. There are complications, entanglements; and you cannot free yourself from them."

"Precisely so."

"*Is* the sin of the past?" she asked with flashing eyes, and a rising colour; her voice betraying her frame of mind. He gazed at her unable to understand.

"Why, of course it is past, Lucy. What can you mean?"

"Oh, you know, you know. Never mind. We must go on again as we have been going on."

"No, Lucy."

"Yes, Sir Karl. As long as those people remain in the Maze, tacitly to insult me, I will never be more to you than I am now."

It was a strangely harsh decision; and one he could not account for. He asked for her reasons in detail, but she would not give any. All she said further was, that if he felt dissatisfied, she could—and should—seek the protection of her father and declare the truth.

So they parted again as they had parted before. Hemmed in on all sides, afraid to move an inch to the left or the right, Karl could only submit; he could do nothing.

"I was charged by Miss Blake to tell you that tea is ready," he said, turning on his heel to quit the room.

"Ask her to send me a cup by Aglaé, please. I shall stay here to rest my ankle." And as Karl closed the door upon her, poor Lucy burst into a flood of tears, and sobbed as though her heart would break. Underlying all else in her mind was a keen sense of insult, of slight, of humiliation: and she asked herself whether she ought to bear it.

Pacing the gravel path round the trees of the Maze after dark had fallen—as much dark as a summer's night ever gives us—were Karl Andinnian and Mrs. Grey. She, expecting him, went to wait for him just within the gate: as she did the evening Miss Blake had the satisfaction of watching and seeing. It was a still, hot night, and Mrs. Grey proposed that they should walk round the outer circle once, before going in: for she had things to say to him.

"Why have you kept away these last few days, Karl?" she asked, taking the arm he offered her. "Adam has been so vexed and impatient over it: but I should not have ventured to write to you for only that—I hope you were not angry with me."

He told her he was not angry. He told her why he had kept away—that an instinct warned him it might be imprudent to come in too often. It seemed to him, he added, that the very hedges had eyes to watch him. She shivered a little, as though some chill of damp had struck her; and proceeded to relate what she had to say.

By a somewhat singular coincidence, a copy of the same newspaper that contained the mysterious paragraph had been bought at the little newsvendor's in Foxwood by Ann Hopley, who was fond of reading the news when her day's work was over. She saw the paragraph, took alarm, and showed it to her master and mistress.

"It has nearly frightened me to death, Karl," said Mrs. Grey. "The paper was a week old when Ann bought it: and I am glad it was, or I should have been living upon thorns longer than I have been."

He told her that he had seen it. And he did what he could to reassure her, saying it was probably but an unmeaning assertion, put in from dearth of news.

"That is just what Mr. Smith says," she replied. "He thinks it is from the brain of some poor penny-a-liner."

"Mr. Smith!" exclaimed Karl. "How do you know?"

"Adam would see him about it, and I sent for him. He, Smith, says there's nothing for it now but staying here; and Adam seems to be of the same opinion."

"Were you present at their interview?"

"No. I never am. The man is keeping us here for purposes of his own. I feel sure of it. He has been a good friend to us in many ways: I don't know what we should have done without him; but it is his fault that we are staying on here."

"Undoubtedly it is."

"Adam is just as careless and gay as ever in manner, but I think the announcement in the newspaper has made him secretly uneasy. He is not well to-night."

"What is the matter with him?"

"It is some inward pain: he has complained of it more than once lately. And he has been angry and impatient of an evening because you did not come. It is so lonely for him, you know."

"I do know it, Rose. Nothing brings me here at all but that."

"It was he who at last made me write to you to-day. I was not sorry to do it, for I wanted to see you myself and to talk to you. I think I have discovered something that may be useful; at least that we may turn to use. First of all—Do you remember that a year or two ago there was a public stir about one Philip Salter?"

"No. Who is Philip Salter?"

"Philip Salter committed a great crime: forgery, I think: and he escaped from the hands of the police as they were bringing him to London by rail. I have nearly a perfect recollection of it," continued Mrs. Grey, "for my uncle and aunt took great interest in it, because they knew one of the people whom Salter had defrauded. He was never retaken. At least, I never heard of it."

"How long ago was this?"

"More than two years. It was in spring-time, I think."

Karl Andinnian threw his recollection back. The name, Philip Salter, certainly seemed to begin to strike on some remote chord of his memory; but he had completely forgotten its associations.

"What of him, Rose?" he asked.

"This, she answered, her voice taking even a lower tone: "I should not be surprised if this Mr. Smith is the escaped man, Philip Salter! I think he may be."

"This man, Smith, Philip Salter!" exclaimed Karl. "But what grounds have you for thinking it?"

"I will tell you. When Mr. Smith came over a day or two ago, it was in the evening, growing dusk. Adam saw him in the upstairs room. They stood at the window—perhaps for the sake of the light, and seemed to be looking over some memorandum paper. I was walking about outside, and saw them. All at once something fell down from the window. I ran to pick it up, and found it was a pocket book lying open. Mr. Smith shouted out, "Don't touch it, Mrs. Grey: don't trouble yourself,' and came rushing down the stairs. But I had picked it up, Karl; and I saw written inside it the name, Philip Salter. Without the least intention or thought of prying, I saw it: 'Philip Salter.' Mr. Smith was up with me the next moment, and I gave him the pocket-book closed."

"His Christian name is certainly Philip," observed Karl, after a pause of thought. "I have seen his signature to receipts for rent—'Philip Smith.' This is a strange thing, Rose."

"Yes—if it be true. While he is planted here, spying upon Adam, he may be hiding from justice himself, a criminal."

Karl was in deep thought. "Was the name in the pocket-book on the fly-leaf, Rose—as though it were the owner's name?"

"I think so, but I cannot be sure. It was at the top of a leaf certainly. If we could but find it out—find that it is so, it might prove to be a way of release from him," she added; "I mean some way or other of release might come of it. Oh, and think of the blessing of feeling free! I am sure that, but for him, Adam would contrive to escape to a safer land."

There was no time to say more. The night was drawing on, and Karl had to go in to his impatient brother. Impatient! What should we have been in his place? Poor Adam Andinnian! In his banned, hidden, solitary days, what interlude had he to look forward to but these occasional visits from Karl?

"I will think it over, Rose, and try and find something out," said Karl, as they went in. "Have you told Adam?"

"No. He is so hot and impulsive, you know. I thought it best to speak to you first."

"Quite right. Say nothing to him at present."

In quitting the Maze that evening, Adam, in spite of all Karl could say or do, would walk with him to the gate; only laughing when Karl called it dangerous recklessness. There were moments when the same doubt crossed Karl's mind that had been once suggested to him by Mr. Plunkett—Was Adam always and altogether sane? This moment was one. He absolutely stood at the gate, talking and laughing in an undertone, as Karl went through it.

"Rubbish, Karlo, old fellow," said he to the last remonstrance. "It's a dark night, and not a soul within miles of us. Besides, who knows me here?"

Karl had locked the gate and was putting the key in his pocket, when a sound smote his ear and he turned to listen. The tramp, tramp, as of policemen walking with measured steps was heard, coming from the direction of the railway-station, and with it the scuffle and hum of a besetting crowd. It brought into his mind with a rush and a whirl that fatal night some twelve months before, when he had heard the tramp of policemen on the other side the hedge—and their prisoner, though he knew it not, was his brother, Adam Andinnian.

"Adam, do you hear!" he cried hoarsely. "For the love of heaven hide yourself." And Sir Adam disappeared within the Maze.

What with the past recollection, what with his brother's near presence, what with the approach of these police—as he took them to be—what with the apprehension ever overlying his heart, Karl was seized with a panic of terror. Were they coming in search of Adam? He thought so: and all the agony that he often went over in his dreams, he suffered now in waking reality. The hubbub of exposure; the public disgrace; the renewed hard life for him at Portland Island; even perhaps—Karl's imagination was vivid just then—the scaffold in the distance as an ending! These visions surging through his brain, Karl flew to the other side of the road—lest his being on the side of the Maze might bring suspicion on it—and then walked quietly to his own entrance gates. There he stood, and turned to await the event, his head beating, his pulses leaping.

With a relief that no tongue could express, Karl saw

them pass the Maze and come onwards. Presently, in the night's imperfect light, he distinguished a kind of covered stretcher, or hand-barrow, borne by a policeman and other men, a small mob following.

"Is anything amiss?" he asked, taking a few steps into the road, and speaking in the quietest tones he could just then command.

"It's poor Whittle, Sir Karl," replied the policeman—who knew him. There were a few scattered cottages skirting the wood beyond the Court, and Karl recognized the name, Whittle, as that of a man who lived in one of them and worked at the railway-station.

"Is he ill?" asked Karl.

"He is dead, Sir Karl. He was missed from his work in the middle of the afternoon and not found till an hour ago: there he was, stretched out in the field, dead. We got Mr. Moore round, and he thinks it must have been a sun-stroke."

"What a sad thing!" cried Karl, in his pitying accents. "Does his wife know?"

"We've sent on to prepare her, poor woman! There's four or five little children, Sir Karl, more's the pity!"

"Ay; I know there are some. Tell her I will come in and see her in the morning."

A murmur of approbation at the last words arose from the bystanders. It seemed to them an earnest that the new baronet, Sir Karl, would turn out to be a kind and considerate man; as good for them, perhaps, as Sir Joseph had been.

He listened to the tramp, tramp, until it had died away, and then turned in home with all his trouble and care: determined to search the newspapers—filed by Sir Joseph—before he went to rest, for some particulars of this Philip Salter.

"Oh, that Adam were but safe in some less dangerous land!" was the refrain, ever eating itself into his brain

CHAPTER XIX

IN THE SAME TRAIN.

"You must step out sharp, Sir Karl. The train is on the move."

Sir Karl Andinnian had gone hastening into the railway-station late, on Monday morning, to catch the eleven o'clock express train, and was taking a ticket for London. It was the station-master who had addressed him, as he handed him his ticket. One of the porters held open the door of a first-class compartment, and Sir Karl jumped in.

A lady was gathered into the corner beyond him, her veil down: there was no one else in the carriage. Karl did not look round at her until the train had left the station. And when he saw who it was, he thought his eyes must be playing him false.

"Why, Rose!" he exclaimed. "Can it be you?"

She smiled and threw her veil back, leaning towards him at the same moment to explain why she was there. The whistle set up a shriek at the time, and though Sir Karl, his ear bent close to her, no doubt heard the explanation, the air of the carriage did not. "Slight accident—last night—quite useless—would have me come—Rennet—" were all the disconnected words *that* caught.

"I quite shrunk from the journey at first," she said, when the whistle had subsided. "I feel always shy and timid now: but I am not sorry to go, for it will give me the opportunity of making some needful purchases. I would rather do it in London than Basham; in fact, I should not dare go to Basham myself: and I did not care to trust Ann Hopley to buy these fine little things."

"Is Adam better?"

"Yes, I think so: he seemed pretty well yesterday. You did not come to the Maze last night, Karl. He was wishing for you."

Karl turned off the subject. The fright he had had, coming out on Saturday night, would serve to keep him away for some days to come. In his heart of hearts he believed that, in the interests of prudence, the less he went to the Maze the better: instinct was always telling him so.

"I suppose you will return to-night, Rose?"

"If I can," she answered. "It depends on Rennet. Should I be obliged to wait until to-morrow, I shall have to sleep at an hotel: Adam has directed me to one." And so the conversation innocently progressed, and the train went on.

But now, as capricious fortune had it, who should be in that self-same train but Miss Blake! Miss Blake was going up to London en cachette. That is to say, she had not intended Sir Karl and Lady Andinnian to know of the journey. Some grand piece of work, involving choice silks and much embroidery, was being projected by Miss Blake for Mr. Cattacomb's use at St. Jerome's: she had determined to get the silks at first hand, which she could only do in London; and took the train this morning for the purpose. "If I am not in to luncheon, don't think anything of it: I can get a biscuit out," she said to Lucy: and Miss Blake's general out-of-door engagements appeared to be so numerous—what with the church services, and the hunting-up little ragamuffins from their mothers' cottages for instruction—that Lucy would have thought nothing of it had she been away all day long. Miss Blake, however, intended to get back in the afternoon.

Seated in her compartment, waiting for the train to start, she had seen Sir Karl Andinnian come running on to the platform; and she drew her face back out of sight. She saw him put into a carriage just behind her own: and she felt a little cross that he should be going to London at all.

"What is taking him, I wonder?" she thought. "He never said a word about it at breakfast. I don't believe Lucy knows it."

Arrived at the terminus, Miss Blake, knowing that gentlemen mostly leap out of a train before it has well stopped, held back herself. Cautiously peeping to see him pass and get fairly off, she saw what she had not expected to see—Sir Karl helping out a lady. They passed on quickly: Sir Karl carrying a large clasped reticule bag, and the lady clinging to his arm. She was closely veiled: but Miss Blake's keen eyes knew her through the veil for Mrs Grey.

Miss Blake could have groaned the roof off the carriage. She was the only passenger left in it. "The deceitful villain!" she exclaimed: and then she burst on to the platform, and sheltered herself behind a projecting board to look after the criminals.

Sir Karl was putting Mrs. Grey into a four-wheeled cab. He handed in her reticule bag after her, shook hands, gave a direction to the driver, and the cab went off. Then he looked round for a hansom, and was driven away in his turn. Miss Blake, making good her own departure, believed she had not yet suspected half the tricks and turns there must be in this wicked world.

"Poor Lucy! poor wife!" she murmured, pityingly. "May Heaven look down and shield her!"

Karl's errand in London was to find out what he could about Philip Salter. On the Saturday night, patiently searching the file of newspapers—the "Times"—he at length came upon the case. One Philip Salter had been manager to a financial firm in London, and for some years managed it honestly and very successfully. But he got speculating on his own account, lost and lost, and continued to lose, all the while using the funds, that were not his, to prop him up, and prevent exposure. To do this, unsuspected, he was forced to resort to forgery: to fabricate false bonds: to become, in short, one of the worst of felons. The day of discovery came; but Mr. Salter had not waited for it. He was off, and left no trace, as he thought, behind him. Some clue, however, fancied or real, was obtained by a clever ordinary police officer. He went down to Liverpool, seized Philip Salter on board an American vessel just about to steam out of port, and started with him for London at once by the night train, disguised as he was. Midway on the road, Salter did what only a desperate man, fighting for very life, would have dared to do—he jumped from the carriage, and made his escape.

So much Karl read: but, though he searched onwards, he could see nothing else. Some of the newspapers were missing; had not been filed; and, it might be, that they were the very papers that spoke further. He then resolved to seek information elsewhere.

All day on the Sunday it had been floating through his mind. His wife's ankle was better. He walked to church with her as usual, sitting by her side in their conspicuous pew—placed sideways to the pulpit and exposed to the eyes of all the congregation. Throughout the service, throughout the sermon, Karl's mind was dwelling on the suspicion connecting Philip Smith with Philip Salter. Lucy thought him very still: as still and sad as herself. The only other conspicuous pew was opposite; it belonged to the vicarage. Margaret Sumnor was in it alone, in the half-reclining seat that had been made for her. Mrs. Sumnor rarely went to church in the morning: the younger daughters were of course at St. Jerome's.

"I will go to London to-morrow," decided Karl in his own mind that night. "Could Smith be got away from his post of espionage, it might be Adam's salvation." And that's what brought him taking the eleven o'clock train on Monday morning.

His hansom cab conveyed him to Plunkett and Plunkett's. That he must conduct this inquiry in the most cautiously delicate manner, he knew well; or he might only make bad worse, and bring the hornet's nest, that he was always dreading, about his brother's head. Once let Smith—if he were really Salter—suspect that inquiries were being made about himself, and he might in revenge denounce Sir Adam.

Mr. Plunkett, with whom Karl as well as the rest of the family had always transacted business, was not in town. Mr. George Plunkett saw him, but he was to Karl comparatively a stranger. Even this seemed to fetter him and make him feel more uneasily, but without reason, the necessity of caution. In a decidedly hesitating way, he said that he had a reason for wishing to learn some particulars about a man who had cheated the community a year or two ago and had made his escape, one Philip Salter: he wanted to know whether he had been re-caught; or, if not, where he was now supposed to be. Mr. George Plunkett immediately asked—not supposing there was any reason why he should not be told—for what purpose Sir Karl wished for the information. Was it that any of his friends had been sufferers and were hoping to get back what they had lost? And Karl contrived, without any distinct assertion, to leave this impression on the lawyer's mind. Mr. Plunkett, however, could give him no information about Salter, beyond the fact —or rather, opinion, for he was not sure—that he had never been retaken. The matter was not one they had any interest in, he observed; and he recommended Sir Karl to go to Scotland Yard.

"I will write a note of introduction for you to one of the head officers there, Sir Karl," he said. "It will insure you attention."

But Karl declined this. "If I went to Scotland Yard at all," he said, "it would be as an unknown, private individual, not as Sir Karl Andinnian. I don't much care to go to Scotland Yard."

"But why?" exclaimed Mr. George Plunkett. And then, all in a moment an idea flashed across him. He fancied that Sir Karl was shy of presenting himself there as the brother of the unfortunate man who had stood his trial for murder.

"I have reasons for not wishing it to be known that I am stirring in this," admitted Karl. "Grave reasons. At Scotland Yard they might recognize me, and perhaps put questions that at present I would rather not answer."

"Look here, then," said the lawyer. "I will give you a letter to one of the private men connected with the force—a detective, in fact. You can see him at his own house. He is one of the cleverest men they have, and will be sure to be able to tell you everything you want to know. There's not the least necessity for me to mention your name to him, and he'll not seek to learn it. I shall say you are a client and friend of ours, and that will be sufficient."

"Thank you, that will be best," replied Karl.

Mr. George Plunkett wrote the note there and then, and gave it to Karl. It was addressed to Mr. Burtenshaw, Euston Road. He took a cab and found the house—a middling-sized house with buff-coloured blinds to the windows. A maid servant came to the door, and her untidy, dirty cap flew off as she opened it.

"Can I see Mr. Burtenshaw?" asked Sir Karl.

"Mr. Burtenshaw's out, sir," she replied, stooping to pick up her "cap"—a piece of bordered net the size of a five-shilling piece. "He left word that he should be back at five o'clock."

"If I were a detective officer, my servants should wear caps on their heads," thought Karl, as he turned away, and went to get some dinner.

The church clocks were striking five when he was at the door again. Mr. Burtenshaw was at home; and Karl, declining to give his name, was shown to an upstairs room. A little man of middle age, with a sallow face and rather nice grey eyes, was standing by a table covered with papers. Karl bowed, and handed him Mr. George Plunkett's note.

"Take a seat, sir, pray, while I read it," said Mr. Burtenshaw, instinctively recognizing Karl for a gentleman and a noble one. And Karl sat down near the window.

"Very good; I am at your service, sir," said the detective, drawing a chair opposite Karl's. "What can I do for you?"

With less hesitation than he had shown to Mr. George

Plunkett, for he was gathering courage now the ice was broken, Karl frankly stated why he had come, and what he wanted—some information about the criminal, Philip Salter.

"Do you know much about the case?" continued Karl—for Mr. Burtenshaw had made no immediate reply, but sat in silence.

"I believe I know all about it, sir. I was wondering whether you had unearthed him and were come to claim the reward."

"The reward! Is there an offered reward out against him?"

"Five hundred pounds. It was offered after he had made his desperate escape, and it stands still."

"He has not been retaken, then?"

"No, never. We have failed in his case, I am ashamed to say. What particulars are they, sir, that you wish to hear of him? Those connected with his frauds and forgeries?"

"Not those: I have read of them in some of the old papers. I want to know where he is supposed to be; and what he is like in person."

"Our belief is that he is still in Great Britain; strange though it may sound to you to hear me say it. England or Scotland. After that escapade, all the ports were so thoroughly guarded and watched that I don't think he could have escaped. We have a more especial reason, which I do not speak of, for suspecting that he is here still: at least that he was three months ago."

"There are a hundred places in England where he may be hiding," spoke Karl impulsively. "Where he may be living as an ordinary individual, just like the individuals about him."

"Exactly so."

"Living openly as may be said, but cautiously. Perhaps wearing a disguise."

"No doubt of the disguise. False hair and whiskers, spectacles, and all that."

Karl remembered Mr. Smith's green spectacles. His hair might not be his own: he wished he had taken better note of it.

"And in person? What is he like?"

"That I cannot tell you," said Mr. Burtenshaw. "I never saw him. Some of us know him well. Grimley especially does."

"Who is Grimley?"

"The man who let him escape. He has been under a cloud since with us. My wonder is that he was not dismissed."

"Then, you don't know at all what Salter is like?"

"No."

"Are there no photographs?"

"I think not. I have seen none. Is it very essential your ascertaining this?"

"The most essential point of all. Is this Grimley to be got at? If I could see him to-day and get Salter's description from him, I should be more than glad."

Mr. Burtenshaw took some ivory tablets from his pocket and consulted them. I will send for Grimley here, sir. Will eight o'clock be too late for you?"

"Not at all," replied Karl, thinking he could get away by the half-past nine train.

Mr. Burtenshaw escorted him to the head of the stairs, and watched him down, making his mental comments.

"I wonder who he is? He looks too full of care for his years. But he knows Salter's retreat as sure as a gun—or thinks he knows it. Won't denounce him till he's sure."

When Karl got back at eight o'clock, some disappointment was in store for him. Grimley was not there. The detective showed the scrap of message returned to him, scribbled in pencil on a loose bit of paper. Karl read as follows:

"Can't get to you before eleven: might be a little later. Suppose it's particular? Got a matter on hand, and have to leave for the country at five in the morning."

"Will you see him at that late hour, sir?"

Karl considered. It would involve his staying in town for the night, which he had not prepared for. But he was restlessly anxious to set the question at rest, and resolved upon waiting.

He walked away through the busy London streets, seemingly more crowded than usual that Monday evening, and sent a telegraphic message to his wife, saying he could not be home until the morrow. Then he went into the Charing Cross Hotel and engaged a bed. Before eleven he was back again at Mr. Burtenshaw's. Grimley came in about a quarter past: a powerful, tallish man, with a rather jolly face, not dressed in his official clothes as a policeman, but in an ordinary suit of pepper-and-salt.

"You remember Philip Salter, Grimley?" began the superior man at once, without any circumlocution or introduction.

"I ought to remember him, Mr. Burtenshaw."

"Just describe his person to this gentleman as accurately as you can."

"He's not dropped upon at last, is he?" returned the man, his whole face lighting up.

"No. Don't jump to conclusions, Grimley, but do as you are bid." Upon which rebuke Grimley turned to Sir Karl.

"He was about as tall as I am, sir, and not unlike me in shape: that is, strongly made, and very active. His real hair was dark brown, and almost black—but goodness only knows what it's changed into now."

"And his face?" questioned Karl. As yet the description tallied.

"Well, his face was a fresh-coloured face, pleasant in look, and he was a free, pleasant man to talk to you. His eyes—I can't be sure, but I think they were dark brown: his eyebrows were thick and rather more arched than common. At that time his face was clean-shaved, whiskers and all: daresay it's covered with hair now."

"Was he gentlemanly in his look and manners?"

"Yes, sir, I should say so. A rather bustling, business-kind of gentleman: I used to see him often before he turned rogue. Leastways before it was known. You'd never have thought it of him: you'd have trusted him through thick and thin."

Smith at Foxwood was not bustling in his manners: rather quiet. But, as Sir Karl's thoughts ran, there was nothing down there for him to be bustling over: and, besides, the trouble might have tamed him. In other particulars the description might have well served for Smith himself, and Karl's hopes rose. Grimley watched him keenly.

"Have you a photograph of him?" asked Karl.

"No, sir. 'Twas a great pity one was never took. I might have had it done at Liverpool that day: but I thought I'd got him safe, and it didn't occur to me. Ah! live and learn. I never was *done* before; and I've not been since."

"You let him escape you in the train?"

"I *let* him: yes, sir, that's the right word; as things turned out. 'Don't put the handcuffs on me, Grimley,' says he, when we were about to start for the up-night train. 'It's not pleasant to be seen in that condition by the passengers who sit opposite you. I'll not give you any trouble: you've got me, and I yield to it.' 'On your honour, sir?' says I. 'On my word and honour,' says he. 'To tell you the truth, Grimley,' he goes on, 'I've led such a life of fear and suspense lately that I'm not sorry it's ended.' Well, sir, I put faith in him: you've heard me say it, Mr. Burtenshaw: and we took our seats in the carriage, me on one side, my mate, Knowles, on the other, and Salter, unfettered, between us. He had got a thick, fluffy, grey wrapper on, half coat, half cloak, with them wide hanging sleeves: we touched the sleeves on both sides, me and Knowles, with our arms and shoulders. There was one passenger besides; he sat opposite Knowles, and slept a good deal. Salter slept too—or seemed to sleep. Well, sir, we had got well on in our journey, when from some cause the lamp goes out. Soon after, the train shoots into a tunnel, and we were in utter darkness. Salter, apparently, was sleeping fast. A glimmer of light arose when we were half way through it, from some opening, I suppose, and I saw the opposite passenger, as I thought, leaning out at the far window, the one next Knowles. The next minute there was a sound and a rush of air. 'Good heavens, he has fell out,' I says to Knowles: and Knowles—I say he had been asleep too, though he denied it—rouses up and says, 'Why, the door's open.' Sir, when we got out of the tunnel, the rays of the bright lamp at its opening shone in; the opposite passenger was safe enough, his head nodding on his breast, but my prisoner was gone."

Karl caught up his breath; the tale excited him. "How could it have been done?" he exclaimed.

"The dickens knows. There was his thick, rough coat again our arms, but his arms was out of it. How he had managed to slip 'em out and make no stir, and get off his seat to the door, I shall never guess. One thing is certain—he must have had a railway key hid about him somewhere, and opened the door with it: he must have been opening it when I thought it was the passenger leaning out."

"What did you do?"

"We could do nothing, sir. Except shout to arouse the guard; we did enough of that, but the guard never heard us. When the next station was reached, a deal of good time had been lost. We told what had occurred, and got the tunnel searched. That Salter would be found dead, everybody thought. Instead of that he was not found at all; not a trace of him."

"He must have received injuries," exclaimed Karl.

"I should say so," returned Grimley. "Injuries that

perhaps he carries from that day to this.' And Karl half started as he remembered the arm always in a sling.

Just for a single moment the temptation to denounce this man came over him, in spite of his wish and will. Only for the moment: he remembered the danger to his brother. Besides, he would not really have betrayed Smith for the world.

"What age is Salter?" he resumed.

"He must be about five-and-thirty now, sir. He was said to be three-and-thirty when it happened."

That was the first check. Smith must be quite forty. "Did Salter look older than his years?" he asked.

"No, I think not. Ah, he was a cunning fox," continued Mr. Grimley, grating his teeth at the remembrance. "I've known since then what it is to trust to the word and honour of a thief. Can you tell me where to find him, sir?" he suddenly cried, after a pause. "To retake that man would be the most satisfactory piece of work I've got left to me in life."

"No, I cannot," replied Karl, gravely: which Mr. Grimley did not appear to like at all. So the interview came to an end without much result; and Karl departed for his hotel. Both Grimley and Mr. Burtenshaw, bowing him out, remained, firmly persuaded in their own minds that this unknown gentleman, who did not give his name, possessed some clue or other to the criminal Salter.

We must return for a few minutes to Foxwood Court. Miss Blake got back by an early afternoon train, as she had intended, and found some visitors with Lady Andinnian. It was old General Lloyd, from Basham, with two of his daughters. They were asking Lady Andinnian to take luncheon with them on the morrow, and accompany them afterwards to the flower-show that was to be held at the Guildhall. Sir Karl and Miss Blake were included in the invitation. Lucy promised: she seemed worn and weary with her solitude, and she loved flowers greatly. For Sir Karl she said she could not answer: he was in London for the day: but she thought it likely he would be able to accompany her. Miss Blake left it an open question: St. Jerome's was paramount just now, and to-morrow was one of its festival days.

They dined alone, those two, Sir Karl not having returned for it: and, in spite of the troubles, it seemed very dull to Lucy without her husband.

"Did you know Sir Karl was going to London?" asked Miss Blake.

"Yes," said Lucy; "he told me this morning. He had business with Plunkett and Plunkett."

Miss Blake suddenly pushed her hair from her forehead, as if it troubled her, and bit her lips to enforce them to silence.

After dinner Miss Blake went out. Tom Pepp, who was appointed bell-ringer to St. Jerome's, in his intervals of work, had played truant at Matins in the morning and wanted looking up; and so she went to do it. This bell was a new feature at St. Jerome's, and caused much talk. It was hung over the entrance-door, communicating with a stout string inside: which string Tom Pepp had to pull, to his intense delight.

When Miss Blake got back, Lucy was still alone. The evening passed on, and Sir Karl did not come. Soon after nine o'clock a telegraphic despatch arrived from him, addressed to Lady Andinnian. Lucy's heart beat a little faster as she opened and read it:

"I cannot get my business done to-night, and must sleep in town. Shall be home to-morrow."

"I wonder what business it is that is detaining him?" spoke Lucy mechanically, after handing the despatch to Theresa, her thoughts bent upon her absent husband.

Theresa Blake was trembling to her fingers' ends. She flung down the despatch after reading it, and flung after it a contemptuous word. The action and the word quite startled Lady Andinnian.

"I'll tell you, Lucy; I'll tell you because you ought to know it," she cried, scattering prudence to the winds in her righteous indignation; scattering even all consideration touching Jane Shore, the pillory, the white sheet, and the lighted taper. "The plea of business is good to assume: very convenient! Sir Karl did not go to London alone this morning. That girl was with him."

"What girl?" faltered Lucy.

"She at the Maze. She with the angel face."

Lucy slightly shivered. For a moment she made no comment. Her face turned ghastly.

"Oh, Lucy, my dear, forgive me!" cried Miss Blake. "Perhaps I have been wrong to tell you; but I cannot *bear* that you should be so deceived. I went up to London myself this morning after some embroidery silks that I could not get at Basham. Sir Karl and she were in the same train. I saw them get out together at the terminus."

It was cruel to hear and to have to bear; but Lucy said never a word. Her tell-tale face had betrayed her emotion, but she would not let anything else betray it.

"Perhaps both happened to have business in London," she quietly said, when she could trust her voice to be steady. "I am sure Karl went up to go to Plunkett and Plunkett's."

And not another allusion did she make to it. Ringing for Hewitt, she calmly told him his master would not be home: and after that talked cheerfully to Theresa until the evening was over. Miss Blake wondered at her.

Calm before *her* and the world. But when she got upstairs and was alone in her chamber, all the pent-up anguish broke forth. Her heart seemed breaking; her sense of wrong well-nigh overmastered her.

"And it was only on Saturday he vowed to me the sin was all of the past!" she cried. And she lay in torment through the live-long summer's night.

CHAPTER XX.

ONLY ONE FLY AT THE STATION.

THE railway station at Basham seemed to be never free from bustle. Besides pertaining to Basham proper, it was the junction for other places. Various lines crossed each other; empty carriages and trolleys of coal stood near; porters and guards were always running about.

Four o'clock on the Tuesday afternoon, and the train momentarily expected in from London. A few people had collected on the platform: waiting for friends who were coming by it, or else intending to go on by it themselves. Amidst them was a young and lovely lady, who attracted some attention. Strangers wondered who she was: one or two knew her for the lady of Foxwood Court, wife of Sir Karl Andinnian.

There had been a flower-show at Basham that day: and Lady Andinnian, as may be remembered, had promised to attend it with the family of General Lloyd, taking luncheon with them first. But when the morning came, she heartily wished she had not made the engagement. Sir Karl had not returned to accompany her. Miss Blake declared that she could not spare the time for it: for it happened to be a Saint's Day, and services prevailed at St. Jerome's. Another check arose: news was brought in from the coachman that one of the horses had been slightly hurt in shoeing, and the carriage could not be used that day. Upon that Lady Andinnian said she must go by train: for it would never have occurred to her to break her promise.

"I think, Theresa, you might manage to go with me," she said.

Miss Blake, calculating her hours, found she had two or three to spare in the middle of the day, and agreed to go: provided she might be allowed to leave Mrs. Lloyd's when luncheon was over and not be expected to go to the townhall. "You will only be alone in returning, for just the few minutes that you are in the train, Lucy," she said. "The Lloyds will see you into it, and your servants can have a fly waiting for you at Foxwood Station." This programme had been carried out: and here was Lucy waiting for the four o'clock train at Basham, surrounded by General Lloyd and part of his family.

It came steaming slowly in. Adieux were interchanged, and Lucy was put into what is called the ladies' carriage. Only one lady was in it besides herself; some one travelling from London. They looked at each other with some curiosity, sitting face to face. It was but natural; both were young, both were beautiful.

"What lovely hair! and what charming blue eyes! and what a bright, delicate complexion!" thought Lucy. "I wonder who she is."

"I have never in all my life seen so sweet a face!" thought the other traveller. "Her eyes are beautiful: and there's such a loving sadness in them! And what a handsome dress! —what style altogether!"

Lucy's dress was a rich silk, pearl grey in colour; her bonnet white; her small parasol was grey, covered with lace, its handle of carved ivory. She looked not unlike a bride. The other lady wore black silk, a straw bonnet, and black lace veil thickly studded with spots; which veil she had put back as if for air, just after quitting Basham; and she had with her several small parcels. Why or wherefore neither of them knew, but each felt instinctively attracted by the appearance of the other.

They were nearing Foxwood Station—it was but about eight

minutes' distance from Basham—when Lucy, in changing her position, happened to throw down a reticule bag which had lain beside her. Both of them stooped to pick it up.

"Oh, I beg your pardon! I ought to have moved it when you got in," said the stranger, placing it on her own side amidst her parcels. And Lucy, on her part, apologised for having thrown it down.

It served to break the ice of reserve: and for the next remaining minute or two they talked together. By the stranger beginning to gather together her parcels, Lucy saw she was preparing to get out at Foxwood.

"Are you about to make a stay in this neighbourhood?" she asked.

"For the present."

"It is a very charming spot. We hear the nightingales every evening."

"You are staying in it too, then?"

"Yes, it is my home."

The train came to a stand-still, and they got out. Foxwood station, after the manner of some other small rural stations, had its few buildings on one side only: the other was open to the high road, and to the fields beyond. In this road, drawn up close to the station, was a waiting fly, its door already open. The stranger, carrying some of her parcels, went straight up to it, supposing it was there for hire, and was about to get in.

"Beg pardon, ma'am," said the driver, "this here fly's engaged."

She seemed vexed, disappointed: and looked up at him. "Are you sure?" she asked. Lucy was standing close by and heard.

"It's brought here, ma'am, for the Lady Andinnian."

"For whom?" she cried, her voice turning to sharpness with his haste; her face, through her veil, changing to a ghastly white.

The driver stared at her: he thought it was all temper. Lucy looked too, unable to understand, and slightly coloured.

"For whom did you say the fly was brought?" the lady repeated.

"For Lady Andinnian of Foxwood Court," explained the man in full. "I shouldn't go to tell a untruth about it."

"Oh I—I misunderstood," she said, her voice dropping, her look becoming suddenly timid as a hare's: and in turning away with a sudden movement, she found herself face to face with Lucy. At that same moment, a tall footman with a powdered head—who had strayed away in search of amusement, and strayed a little too far—came bustling up to his mistress.

"This is your fly, my lady."

By which the stranger knew that the elegant girl she had travelled with, and whose sweet face was then close to her own, was the young Lady Andinnian. Her own white face flushed again.

"I—I beg your pardon," she said. "I did not know you were Sir Karl Andinnian's wife. The fly, I thought, was only there for hire."

Before Lucy could make any answer, she had disappeared from the spot, and was giving some of her parcels to a porter. Lucy followed.

"Can I offer to set you down anywhere? The fly is certainly waiting for me, but there is plenty of room."

"Oh, thank you, no. You are very kind: but—*no!* I can walk quite well. I am obliged to you all the same."

The refusal was spoken very emphatically; especially the last No. Without turning again, she rapidly walked from the station, the porter carrying her parcels.

"I wonder who she is?" murmured Lucy aloud, looking back as she was about to enter the fly, her powdered servant standing to bow her in. For she saw that there was no luggage, save those small parcels, and was feeling somewhat puzzled.

"It is Mrs. Grey, my lady; she who lives at the Maze."

Had the footman, Giles, said it was an inhabitant of the world of spirits, Lucy would not have felt more painfully and disagreeably startled. *She!* And she, Lucy, had sat with her in the same carriage and talked to her on pleasant terms of equality! She, Mrs. Grey! Well, Theresa was right: the face would do for an angel's.

"Why, my dear Lady Andinnian, how pale you look! It's the heat, I suppose."

Lucy, half bewildered, her senses seeming to have gone she knew not whither, found herself shaking hands with the speaker, Miss Patchett: an elderly and eccentric lady who lived midway between the station and the village of Foxwood. Lucy mechanically asked her if she had come in the train.

"Yes," answered Miss Patchett. "I've been to London

to engage a housemaid. And I am tired to death, my dear,
and the London streets were like fire. I wish I was at home
without having to walk there."

"Let the fly take you."

"It's hardly worth while, my dear: it's not far. And it
would be taking you out of the way."

"Not many yards out of it. Step in, Miss Patchett."

The old lady stepped in, Lucy following her: Giles took
his place by the driver. Miss Patchett was set down at her
house, and then the horse's head was turned round in the
direction of Foxwood Court. The old lady had talked incessantly; Lucy had comprehended nothing. St. Jerome's
absurd little bell was being swayed and tinkled by Tom Pepp,
but Lucy had not given it a second glance, although it was
the first time she had had the gratification of seeing and hearing it.

"I could almost have died, rather than it should have happened," she thought, her face burning now at the recollection
of the encounter with Mrs. Grey, so mortifying to every good
feeling within her. "How white she turned—how sharply
she spoke—when they told her the fly was there for Lady
Andinnian! And to think that I should have offered to set
her down! To think it! Perhaps those parcels contained
things that Karl bought for her in London!"

The fly, bowling on, was nearing the Maze gate. Lucy's
fascinated gaze was, in spite of herself, drawn to it. A middle-
aged woman servant had opened it, and was receiving the
parcels from the porter. Mrs. Grey had her purse out, paying
him. As she put the coin into his hand, she paused to look
at Lady Andinnian. It was not a rude look, but one that
seemed full of eager interest. Lucy turned her eyes the other
way, and caught a full view of Mr. Smith, the agent. He was
stretched out at one of his sitting-room windows, surveying
the scene with undisguised curiosity. Lucy sank into the
darkest corner of the fly, and flung her hands over her burning face.

"Was any position in the world ever so painful as mine?" she
cried with a rising sob. "How shall I live on, and bear it?"

The fly clattered in by the lodge gate and drew up at the
house. Hewitt appeared at the door, and Giles stood for his
mistress to alight.

"Has Sir Karl returned, Hewitt?" questioned Lucy.

"Not yet, my lady."

She stood for a moment in thought, then gave orders the fly to wait, and went indoors. An idea had arisen that if she could get no comfort whispered to her, she should almost go out of her mind. Her aching heart was yearning for it.

"Hewitt, I shall go and see poor Miss Sumnor. I should like to take her a little basket of strawberries and a few of Maclean's best flowers. Will you see to it for me, and put them in the fly?"

She ran up stairs. She put off her robes alone, and came down in one of her cool muslins and a straw bonnet as plain as Mrs. Grey's. Hewitt had placed the basket of strawberries —some of the large pine-apple beauties that the Court was famous for—in the fly, a sheet of tissue paper upon them, and some lovely hot-house flowers on the paper. Lucy got in; told the footman she should not require his attendance; and was driven away to the vicarage.

"Am I to wait for you, my lady?" asked the driver, as he set her down with her basket of fruit and flowers.

"No, thank you; I shall walk home."

Margaret was lying alone as usual, her face this afternoon a sad one. Lucy presented her little offering; and when the poor lonely invalid saw the tempting, luscious fruit, smelt the sweet perfume of the gorgeous flowers, the tears came into her eyes.

"You have brought all this to brighten me, Lucy. How good you are! I have had something to try me to-day, and was in one of my saddest moods."

The tears and the admission tried Lucy sorely. Just a moment she struggled with herself for composure, and then gave way. Bursting into a flood of grief, she knelt down and hid her face on Margaret's bosom.

"Oh Margaret, Margaret, you cannot have as much to try you as I have!" she cried out in her pain. "My life is one long path of sorrow; my heart is breaking. Can't you say a word to comfort me?"

Margaret Sumnor, forgetting as by magic all sense of her own trouble, tried to comfort her. She touched her with her gently caressing hand; she whispered soothing words, as one whispers to a child in sorrow: and Lucy's sobs exhausted themselves.

"My dear Lucy, before I attempt to say anything, I must ask you a question. Can you tell me the nature of your sorrow?"

But Lucy made no reply.

"I see. It is what you cannot speak of."

"It is what I can never speak of to you or to any one, Margaret. But oh, it is hard to bear."

"It seems so to you, I am sure, whatever it may be. But in the very darkest trial and sorrow there is comfort to be found."

"Not for me," impetuously answered Lucy. "I think God has forgotten me."

"Lucy, hush! You know better. The darkest cloud ever o'ershadowing the earth covers a bright sky. *We* see only the cloud, but the brightness is behind it; in time it will surely show itself, and the cloud will have rolled away. God is above all. Only put your trust in Him."

Lucy was silent. There are times when the heart is so depressed that it admits not of comfort; when even sympathy cannot touch it. She bent her face in her hands and *thought*. Look out where she would, there seemed no refuge for her in the wide world. Her duty and the ills of life laid upon her seemed to be clashing with each other. Margaret had preached to her of patiently bearing, of resignation to Heaven's will, of striving to live on, silently hoping and returning good for evil. But there were moments when the opposite course looked very sweet, and this moment was one. But one thought always held her back when this retaliation, this revenge appeared most tempting—should she not repent of it in the future?

"Lucy, my dear," broke in the invalid's voice, always so plaintive, "I do not pretend to fathom this trouble of yours. It is beyond me. I can only think it must be some difference between you and your husband——"

"And if it were?" interrupted Lucy, recklessly.

"If it were! Why, then, I should say to you, above all things, *bear*. You do not know, you cannot possess any idea of the bitter life of a woman at real issue with her husband. I know a lady—but she does not live in these parts, and you have never heard of her—who separated from her husband. She and my own mother were at school together, and she married young and, it was thought, happily. After a time she grew jealous of her husband; *she had cause for it;* he was altogether a gay, careless man, fond of show and pleasure. For some years she bore a great deal in silence, the world knowing nothing of things being wrong between them. Papa could tell you more about this than I: I was but a little

P

child: how he and my mother, the only friends who were in her confidence, urged her to go on bearing, with what patience she might, and trusting to God to set wrong things right. For a long while she listened to them; but there came a time when she allowed exasperation to get the better of her; and the world was astonished by hearing that she and her husband had agreed to separate. Ah, Lucy! it was then that her life of real anguish set in. Just at first, for a few weeks or so, perhaps months, she was borne up by the excitement of the thing, by the noise it made in the world, by the gratification of taking revenge on her husband—by I know not what. But as the long months and the years went on, and all excitement, I may almost say all interest in life, had faded, she then saw what she had done. She was a solitary woman, condemned to an unloved and solitary existence, and she repented her act with the whole force of her bitter and lonely heart. Better, Lucy, that she had exercised patience, and trusted in God; better for her own happiness."

"And what of her now?" cried Lucy, eagerly.

"Nothing. Nothing but what I tell you. She lives away her solitary years, not a day of them passing but she wishes to heaven that that one fatal act of hers could be recalled—the severing herself from her husband."

"And he, Margaret?"

"He? For aught I know to the contrary, he has been as happy since as he was before; perhaps, in his complete freedom, more so. She thought, poor woman, to work out her revenge upon him; instead of that, it was on herself she worked it out. Men and women are different. A separated man—say a divorced man, if you like—can go abroad; here, there, and everywhere; and enjoy life without hindrance, and take his pleasure at will: but a woman, if she be a right-minded woman, must stay in her home-shell, and eat her heart away."

Lucy Andinnian sighed. It was no doubt all too true.

"I have related this for your benefit, Lucy. My dear little friend, at all costs *stay with your husband.*"

"I should never think of leaving him for good as that other poor woman did," sobbed Lucy. "I should be dead of grief in a year."

"True. Whatever your cross may be, my dear—and I cannot doubt that it is a very sharp and heavy one—take it up as bravely as you can, and bear it. No cross, no crown."

Some of the school-children came in for a lesson in fine work—stitching and gathering—and Lady Andinnian took her departure. She had not gained much comfort; she was just as miserable as it was possible to be.

The church bell was going for the five o'clock evening service. Since the advent of St. Jerome's Mr. Sumnor had opened his church again for daily service, morning and evening. This, however, was a Saint's day. A feeling came over poor Lucy that she should like to sob out her heart in prayer to God; and she slipped in. Not going down the aisle to their own conspicuous pew, but into an old-fashioned, square, obscure thing near the door, that was filled on Sundays with the poor, and hidden behind a pillar. There, unseen, unsuspected, she knelt on the floor; she lifted up her heart on high, sobbing silent sobs of agony, bitter tears raining from her eyes; asking God to hear and help her; to help her to bear.

She sat out the service and grew composed enough to join in it. The pillar hid her from the clergyman's view; nobody noticed that she was there. So far as she could see, there were not above half-a-dozen people in the church. In going out, Mr. Sumnor and Mr. Moore's sister, Aunt Diana, came up to join her.

"I did not know you were in church, Lady Andinnian," said the clergyman.

"The bell was going when I left your house: I had been to see Margaret: so I stepped in," she replied. "But what a very small congregation!"

"People don't care to attend on week-days, and that's the truth," put in Miss Moore—a middle-aged, stout lady, with her brown hair cut short and a huge flapping hat on. "And the young folks are all off to that blessed St. Jerome's. My nieces are there; I know it. And so are your two daughters, Mr. Sumnor, more shame for them!"

"Ay," sighed Mr. Sumnor, whose hair and face were alike grey, and his look as sad as his tone. "Their running to St Jerome's, as they do, is nothing less, in my eyes, than a scandal. I don't know what is to be the end of it all."

"End of it all?" echoed Aunt Diana, in her strong-minded voice. "Why, the end will be nothing but a continuation of the folly; or perhaps worse—Rome, or a convent, or something of that kind. I truly believe, Mr. Sumnor, that heaven above was never so mocked before, since the world began, as

it is now, by this semblance of zeal in boys and girls for
religious services and worship. The true worship of a
Christian, awakened to his state of sin and to the need he has
of God's forgiveness and care, of Christ's love, is to be revered
—but that is totally different from this business at St. Jerome's.
This is hollow at the core; born of young men's and young
girls' vanity. Does all the flocking thither come of religion,
think you? Not it."

"Indeed no," said Mr. Sumnor.

"And, therefore, I say it is a mockery of true religion, and
must be a sin in the sight of heaven. They run after Mr. Cattacomb himself: nothing else. I went to St. Jerome's myself
this morning; not to say my prayers; just to watch my nieces,
and see what was going on. They had all sorts of ceremonies
and foolish folly: three of the girls had been there beforehand, confessing to the Reverend Guy: and there was he,
performing the service and turning up the tails of his eyes."

"O, Miss Diana," involuntarily exclaimed Lucy, hardly
knowing whether to laugh or reprove.

"It is true, Lady Andinnian. Mr. Sumnor here knows it is.
Why does Cattacomb go through his service with all that
affectation? Of course the girls like it: but they are little
fools, all of them; they'd think anything right that was done
by him. I fancy the young man has some good in him; I
acknowledge it; but he is eaten up with vanity, and lives in
the incense offered by these girls. Ah well, it's to be hoped
they will all, priest and children, come to their senses sometime."

She turned into her home as she spoke, after wishing
them good-bye. Lucy stayed to shake hands with the clergyman.

"Miss Diana is given to expressing herself strongly, but she
is right in the main," said Mr. Sumnor. "St. Jerome's is giving
me a great deal of trouble and sorrow just now, in more ways
than one. But we have all something to bear," he added, after
a pause. "All. Sometimes I think that the more painful it
is, the more God is caring for us. Fare you well, my dear
young lady. Give my kind regards to Sir Karl."

Lucy walked homewards, a feeling of peace insensibly
diffusing itself over her afflicted soul. The clergyman's words
had touched her.

Verses of Holy Writ, and thoughts connected with them,
kept rising in her mind like messages of consolation. In her

misery she felt how very weak and weary she was; that there was nothing for her but to resign herself to Heaven's protecting hand, as a helpless child. The cry for it broke out involuntarily from her lips.

"Lord, I am oppressed. Undertake for me!"

CHAPTER XXI.

HARD TO BEAR.

DINNER was waiting when Lady Andinnian entered, and the first person she saw was her husband. He met her in the hall with outstretched hands, his face clear and open, showing no signs of shame or guilt.

"Did you think I was lost, Lucy?"

She suffered her hand to touch his; for Hewitt and the tall footman, Giles, were standing in the hall, looking on. Sir Karl saw how red her eyes were.

"I meant to have returned by an earlier train; but as I had the day before me, I took the opportunity of seeing after a few things I wished to purchase—and the time slipped on," said Karl. "How have you been, Lucy?"

"Oh, quite well, thank you."

"Whom do you think I travelled down with, Lucy? My old friend, Lamprey. He had to come to Basham on some matter of business: so I have brought him here to dinner. Make haste," he added, as she turned to the staircase: "I think it must be ready."

"I will be down directly," she answered.

Aglaé was waiting; and in five minutes Lucy came down again, dressed. Captain Lamprey was introduced to her—for it happened that they had not been personally acquainted when at Winchester—and gave her his arm into the dining-room. Miss Blake fell to Karl.

But in Lucy's heart-sickness, she could scarcely be cheerful. Her tell-tale eyes were heavy; there arose ever and anon one of those rising sobs of the breath that speak most unmistakably of hidden grief: and altogether, Captain Lamprey felt somewhat disappointed in Lady Andinnian. He remembered how beautiful Lucy Cleeve used to be: he had heard of the renewed gaiety of heart her marriage with Karl brought her: but he saw only a sad woman, who was evidently not too happy, and whose beauty was marred by sadness and paleness. Karl was more cheerful than usual: and Miss Blake seemed not to tire of inquiring after Winchester and its people. But in the midst of all his observations, Captain Lamprey never suspected that there was anything but perfect cordiality between Sir Karl and his wife. And the dinner came to an end.

After coffee, Captain Lamprey set off to walk to Basham. Karl went out with him, to put him in the right road and accompany him part of it. Miss Blake had gone to Vespers. Lucy was alone.

It seemed to her to be dull everywhere; especially dull indoors, and she stepped out to the lawn: turning back almost immediately to get a shawl for her shoulders, in obedience to an injunction of her husband's. On the Sunday evening, when he found her sitting out of doors without one, he had fetched one at once, and begged her not to be imprudent or to forget her ague-fever of the previous year. She remembered this now, and went back for the shawl. Some wives, living in estrangement from their husbands, might have studiously set his commands at naught, and have risked ague, or what not, rather than obey them. Not so Lucy Andinnian. She was meek and gentle by nature. Moreover, in spite of the ill-feeling he had caused to rise up between them, in spite of her sense of wrong and insult, she loved Karl in her heart, and could not help it, as truly as ever. Visions would steal over her, in unguarded moments, of the present trouble being hushed to rest; of all that was amiss being done away with, and she and he reconciled and at peace again. Unhappily for the demands of pride, of self-assertion, Lucy was by no means one of your high-spirited and strong-minded heroines who rashly overlook all interests to indulge in reprisals and revenge.

She folded the shawl about her—one of substantial white silk crape—as carefully as Karl could have folded it; and she stayed, she knew not how long, in the open air. Pacing the lawn; sitting amidst the flowers; standing under the shade of the trees; always in deep thought. The nightingale sang, and the tears gathered in her eyes as she listened to the strain. "What a sweet place this would be to live in," thought Lucy, "if only we had but peace!"

But the nightingale's song and the oppressive thoughts, together with the falling dusk, brought back all her low spirits again. "There will never be any more happiness for me in this world, never, never," she sighed, and the tears were dropping as she went up to her own room.

By-and-by Sir Karl returned. Not seeing his wife downstairs, he went up and knocked at the door of her little sitting-room. He had not had an opportunity of speaking a private word to her since his return. There came no answer, and he entered. The room was empty: but as he stood for a moment in the deep silence of twilight, the sound of sobs in Lucy's bed-chamber smote his ear. He knocked at it.

"Lucy!"

She had, indeed, once more given way to all the abandonment of grief. Which was very foolish: but perhaps its indulgence brought a kind of relief, and indeed her spirit was very sore. The knock startled her: but she had not heard the call.

"Who's there?" she asked, stepping to the door and stifling her sobs as she best could.

"I want to speak to you, Lucy."

She dried her eyes and unlocked the door, and made believe to be calmly indifferent, as she stepped into the sitting-room.

"I beg your pardon, Sir Karl. I was busy, and did not hear you."

"You are looking very ill, Lucy," he said, with grieved concern. "I thought so when I first saw you this afternoon. Then, as now, your eyes were red with weeping."

She strove for calmness; she prayed for it. Her determination had been taken to bury in haughty silence all she had learnt of the London journey, its despicable deceit, and insult to her. She *could not* have spoken of it; no, not even to reproach him and to bring his shame home to him: it would have inflicted too much humiliation on her sensitive spirit. Besides, he must know what she suffered as well as she did.

"I have had rather a tiring day," she answered, leaning sideways against the open window. "There was the elaborate luncheon with General and Mrs. Lloyd, and the flower-show afterwards. The weather was very warm and oppressive."

"That may account for your being tired and not looking well: but not for the weeping, Lucy. As I stood here, waiting for you to answer my knock, I heard your sobs."

"Yes," she said, rather faintly, feeling how useless it would be to deny that there had been some weeping. "I get a little low-spirited sometimes in the evening."

"But why? Wherefore?"

"Is life so pleasant with us just now that I can always be gay, think you?" she retorted, after a pause, and her voice took a tone of resentment.

"But the unpleasantness is of your making; not mine. You *know* it, Lucy."

"Then—then it is right that I should be the one to suffer," was her impatient answer—for his words were trying her almost beyond endurance. "Let it go so: I do not wish to speak of it further."

Karl was standing at the opposite corner of the window, facing her, his arms folded. On his part he was beginning to be a little out of patience too, with what he deemed her unreasonable caprice. For a few moments there was silence.

"What I want to tell you is this, Lucy. My visits to London was connected with that wish which you seem to have so much at heart—though I cannot exactly understand why——"

"I have no wish at heart," she resentfully interrupted.

"Nay, but hear me. The wish you expressed to me I think you must have at heart, since on its fulfilment you say depends our reconciliation. I speak of the removal of—of the tenants of the Maze," he added, half breaking down, in his sensitive hesitation. "Since my conversation with you on Saturday, during which, if you remember, this stipulation of yours was made, there occurred, by what I should call a singular chance, only that I do not believe anything is chance that affects our vital interests in this life—there occurred to me a slight circumstance by which I thought I saw a possibility of carrying out your wish——"

"You said then that it was your wish also," again interrupted Lucy. "Or affected to say it."

"Your wish for it cannot be as hearty as mine," he impulsively answered. "I pray for it night and day."

And Lucy could not well mistake the emotional earnestness. She believed him there.

"Well, I thought I saw a chance of it," he resumed, "and I went to get some information, that I fancied might help me, from Plunkett and Plunkett——"

"Is it fitting that you should give these details to me?" she haughtily interposed.

"I wish you to understand that I am doing my best. Plunkett and Plunkett could not give me the information: but they directed me to some people where I might obtain it. To enable me to see one of these people, I had to stay in town all night; and that was the reason of my not getting home."

Lucy had taken a spray of jessamine from her waist-band, and stood pulling it to pieces, listening with an air of indifference.

"I do not really know more than I did before I went to town, as to whether or not the Maze can be left empty," he went on. "But I have a good hope of it. I think I may be able to accomplish it, though perhaps not immediately. It may take time."

"As you please, of course," answered Lucy coldly. "It is nothing to me."

Karl Andinnian had one of the sweetest tempers in the world, and circumstances had taught him patience and endurance. But he felt grieved to his very heart at her cutting indifference, and for once his spirit rebelled against it.

"Lucy, how dare you treat me so? What have I done to deserve it from you? You must know and see what a life of tempest and apprehension mine is. There are moments when I feel that I could welcome death, rather than continue to live it."

She was not ungenerous. And, as he so spoke, it struck her that, whatever her wrongs, she had been petty and ungracious to him now. And perhaps—Heaven knew—he was really striving to rid himself of Mrs. Grey as earnestly as she could wish it. Her countenance softened.

"I am as a man tied down in a net from which there is no extrication," he resumed, with increased emotion. "My days are so full of care that I envy the poor labourers at work by the road-side, and wish I was one of them—anything in the world, good or bad, but what that world calls me—Sir Karl Andinnian. And my wife, whom I have loved with my heart's best love, and whom I might have fondly hoped would pity my strait and comfort me—she turns against me. God forgive you for your harshness, Lucy."

The reproaches wrung her heart terribly. In the moment's repentance, she believed she had judged him more hardly than he deserved. Her tone was gentle, her eyes had tears in them.

"I have to bear on my side too, Karl. You forget that."

No, he did not forget it. But the temporary anger was pre-eminent just then. A hot retort was on his lips; when the sight of her face, sad with its utter sorrow, struck on every generous chord he possessed, and changed his mood to pity. He crossed over and took her unresisting hands in his.

"Forgive my words, Lucy: you tried me very much. We have both something to forgive each other."

She could not speak; sobs were rising in her throat. Karl bent forward and kissed her passionately.

"Need we make life worse for one another than it is?" he asked.

"I cannot help it," she sobbed. "Don't blame me, for I cannot help it."

"Suppose I take the matter into my own hands, Lucy, and say you shall help it."

"You will not do that," she said, the implied threat restoring her coldness and calmness, though her face turned as pale as the blossoms of the jessamine. "Things are bad enough as they are, but that would make them worse. I should leave your home for good and all—and should have to say why I do so."

She knew how to subdue him. This exposure, if she carried it out, might cost his brother's safety. Karl, feeling his helplessness most bitterly, dropped her hands, and went back to his post at the opposite side of the window.

"I have not said quite all I wish to say," he began, in a voice from which emotion had passed. "As I had the day in London before me, I thought I would look after a pony-chaise for you, Lucy, and I found a beauty. It will be home in a day or two."

"But you have not bought it?"

"Yes, I have."

"Oh, I'm sorry! I did not want one. But it was very kind of you to think of me, Karl," she added in her gratitude.

"And there's a pretty pony to match: a small, quiet, gentle creature. I hope you will like him. I cannot have you running about the place on foot, making yourself ill with the heat."

"Thank you; thank you. But I never drove in my life. I fear I should be a coward."

"I will drive you until you get used to him. That is, if you will permit me. Lucy, believe me, amidst all my care and trouble, your happiness lies next my heart."

On his way to leave the room, he stopped and shook hands with her: perhaps as an earnest of his friendliness. Theresa Blake, walking on the lawn beneath, had seen them conversing together at the window. She thought a taste of Jane Shore's pillory might not have been amiss for bringing Lady Andinnian to her senses.

Presently Lucy went down and had tea with Theresa, presiding herself at the cups and saucers by moonlight—for there was little light of day left. Sir Karl did not appear. He was in his room on the other side the house, holding some colloquy with Hewitt.

"I am going to have a pony-chaise, Theresa."

"Oh, indeed," returned Miss Blake, who seemed in rather a crusty humour. "I thought I heard you say that you did not require one."

"Perhaps I may be glad of it, for all that. At any rate, Sir Karl has bought it, pony, and chaise, and all; and they will be down this week."

Miss Blake's face was a scornful one just then, in her condemnation of wrong-doing. "He bribes her into blindness," was the thought that ran through her head.

"Why are your eyes so red and heavy, Lucy? They were so at dinner."

"My eyes red!" artfully responded Lucy. "Are they? Well, I have had rather a tiring day, Theresa; and it has been so very hot, you know. You ought to have waited for the flower-show. It was one of the best I ever saw."

"Yes, I should have liked it."

"I took home poor Miss Patchett in my fly, from the station," went on Lucy, who seemed to be running from one topic to another, perhaps to divert attention from herself. "She had been to London to engage a servant, and looked ready to drop with the heat. Did you ever know it so hot before, Theresa?"

"I think not. Not for a continuancy. Is Sir Karl going to take any tea? There's nothing else so refreshing these sultry evenings."

"He says tea only makes him hotter," returned Lucy with a smile. "Ring the bell, please, Theresa: you are nearer to it than I am."

Giles appeared, in answer, and was sent by Lucy to inquire whether his master would take tea or not. The message brought forth Karl. The moon was shining right on the table.

"I'll drink a cup of tea if you will put in plenty of milk to cool it," said he. "How romantic you look here, sitting in the moonlight! Thank you, Lucy."

"We are glad to do without lights so long as we can in this weather," observed Miss Blake. "They make the room warmer."

He drank the tea standing, and went back again. Lucy sent the tray away, and presently ordered the lights. She then ensconced herself in an easy chair with one of the romances Karl had brought her on the Saturday: and Miss Blake strolled out of doors.

At first Lucy held the book upside down. Then she read a page three times over, and could not comprehend it. Ah, it was of no use, this playing at light-hearted ease. She might keep up the farce tolerably well before people; but when alone with herself and her misery, it was a senseless mockery.

Leaving the book behind her, she went wandering about from room to room. The windows of all were put open, to catch what little air there might be. As she stood in one of the unlighted rooms, Sir Karl passed along the terrace. She drew back lest he should see her, and heard him go into the lighted drawing-room and call her.

"Lucy!"

Not a word would she answer. She just stood back against the wall in the dark beyond the curtain, and kept still. He went out again, and began pacing the opposite path in the shade cast by the overhanging trees. Lucy watched him. Suddenly he plunged in amidst the trees, and she heard one of the private gates open and close.

"He is gone *there*," she said, the pulses of her heart quickening and her face taking a ghastly tinge in the moonlight.

Miss Blake, who had been also lingering in the garden, in some of its shaded nooks and corners, her thoughts busy with Guy Cattacomb and with certain improvements that reverend man was contemplating to introduce at St. Jerome's, had also seen Sir Karl, and watched his stealthy exit. She immediately glided to another of the small private gates of egress, cautiously opened it, and looked out.

"Yes, I thought so: he is off to the Maze," she mentally cried, as she saw Sir Karl, who had crossed the road, walking towards that secluded spot, and keeping close against the opposite hedge. The moonlight was flung pretty broadly upon the road to-night, but the dark hedge served to screen him in a degree. Miss Blake's eyes were keen by moonlight or by daylight. She watched him pass under the trees at the entrance: she watched him open the gate, and enter. And Miss Blake, religious woman that she was, wondered that the skies did not drop down upon such a monster in human shape; she wondered that the same pure air from heaven could be permitted to be breathed by him and by that earthly saint, the Reverend Guy.

Some few of us, my readers, are judging others in exactly the same mistaken manner now: and have no more suspicion that we are wrong and they are right than Miss Theresa Blake had.

CHAPTER XXII.

WITH HIS BROTHER.

SIR KARL locked the gate safely, wound himself through the maze of trees, and soon reached the open space before the house. Part of the grass-plat was steeped in light, and he saw Mrs. Grey walking there. He crossed it to accost her.

"Did you get back yesterday, Rose?" he inquired, after shaking hands.

"No, not until this afternoon. Rennet kept me. I saw him when I drove there yesterday: but he was then preparing to go out of town for the rest of the day on business, and it was impossible for him to do what was wanted before this morning. So I had to wait in town."

"I wonder we did not chance to travel down together, then!" observed Karl. "I did not return until this afternoon. Would you like to take my arm, Rose, while you walk?"

"Thank you," she answered, and took it. She had on the black dress she had worn in London, and her golden hair gleamed with all its beauty in the moonlight. Karl noticed that she leaned upon him somewhat heavily.

"You are tired, Rose!"

"I felt very tired when I got home. But Ann Hopley preaches to me so much about the necessity of taking exercise, that I thought I would walk about here for half-an-hour. I have had scarcely any walking to-day; I was so fatigued with the journey and with the shopping yesterday that I had to keep as still as I could this morning. But there was a good deal to do; what with Rennet and some errands I had left to the last."

"Where's Adam?"

"In-doors. He is complaining of that sensation of pain again. I do not like it at all, Karl."

"And while he is lying concealed here he cannot have medical advice. At least I don't see how it would be possible."

"It would not be possible," said Rose, decisively. "Oh, but I forgot—I have to tell you something, Karl. Whom do you think I travelled with from Basham to Foxwood?"

"I don't know."

"Your wife."

"My wife!"

"It is true. I was in the ladies' carriage alone all the way from London. At Basham a young and elegant girl in pearl-grey silk and white bonnet, with the daintiest parasol I ever saw, was put in. An old gentleman—she called him 'General'—and some ladies were with her on the platform. We were alone in the carriage, she and I; and I think we looked at each other a good deal. What she thought of me I don't know; but I thought that she had one of the sweetest and gentlest faces my eyes ever rested on. She had a sweet voice, too, for we spoke a little just as we got to Foxwood?"

"But did you know her?—did she know you?" interrupted Karl.

"No, no. I should have had no idea who she was, but that there arose some question about the one fly waiting there, and some one said it had been brought for Lady Andinnian. Karl, if ever I felt startled in my life, it was then."

"Why were you startled?"

"Don't you see? 'Lady Andinnian!' I took it at the moment to mean myself, and I felt my face turn white at the danger. Fear is quick; and I am living in it always, Karl. What I thought was, that Adam had sent that fly for me, supposing I might come by that train; and that, in his incaution, or perhaps out of bravado, he had given my true name. Of course, nothing could have been more absurd than this fancy of mine—but it was what arose to me. Almost at once I recognized my mistake, and saw how it was—that *she* was the Lady Andinnian meant, Sir Karl's wife. I think I said something to her, but I was so confused I hardly know. I only have wondered since that I did not guess who she was at first, from her attire and her beauty."

"Lucy did not tell me of this."

"Oh dear no, she would not be likely to recall it, or to know me from any other stranger one may meet in travelling. Adam says you love her to excess: I am sure, Karl, I don't wonder at it."

He made no answer. Yes, he loved his wife with a wondrous love: but just now she was trying that love sharply.

"And about the matter you went up upon?' resumed Mrs. Grey. "Did you succeed in learning anything of Philip Salter?"

"Not much. I joined you on the grass here to tell you what I did learn, before going in to Adam. Salter has never been retaken: and the police have an idea that he is still in concealment in England. There's a reward of five hundred pounds out against him."

"Why do they think he is in England?" asked Rose, quickly.

"I don't know. They would not tell me."

"You communicated with the police, then, Karl. You were not afraid?"

"Not with the police as a body, but with one of their private detectives: a Mr. Burtenshaw. Plunkett and Plunkett gave me a note to him. It was he who said he believed Salter to be still in the country: but the reason for believing it he would not give me."

"And did you get him described?"

"Yes, by the very man who let him escape: a policeman named Grimley: Burtenshaw sent for him. In nearly every particular his description tallies with Smith."

"Oh, Karl! he is certainly Salter."

"Does Smith wear his own hair?"

"Yes. At least," she added, less decisively, "if it were false I think I should not have failed to notice it. It is very dark; his whiskers are nearly black and his hair is only a shade lighter."

"Just so. But—I should say Smith was forty."

"About that."

"Well, Salter, they say, would be now only five-and-thirty. I don't attach much importance to the disparity," added Karl: "Salter's trouble may have prematurely aged him."

"What shall you do in it?" she resumed, after a pause. "It seems to me that if we could get Smith removed so as to leave Adam, in that sense, free, the half of our dreadful trouble would be over."

"I don't know what I shall do," replied Karl. "It will not do to stir an inch, as to the bringing it home to Smith, unless I am sure and certain. At present, Rose, it seems to be for me only another care added to the rest."

"Karlo, old fellow, is that you?" interrupted a voice from the passage-window over the porch. "What on earth do you stay chattering to the wife for? I want you."

Karl looked up, nodded to his brother, and went in. Adam was in his customary evening attire, and just as gay as usual. He waited for Karl at the head of the stairs, and they went together into the sitting-room that was always used at night. This sitting-room had a second door; one in the panelling, not visible to a casual observer. It communicated with a passage that nothing else communicated with; the passage communicated with a spiral staircase, and that with nobody knew what or where. Had Adam Andinnian been surprised in his retreat by his enemies, it was by that private door he would have made his escape, or tried to do it.

"Rose says you are not very well, Adam: that you are feeling the pain again," began Karl. "What do you think it is?"

"Goodness knows: I don't," returned Adam. "My opinion is, that I must in some way have given my inside a deuce of a wrench. I don't tell Rose that: she'd set on and worry herself."

"I hope it is nothing serious—that it will soon pass off. You see, Adam, the cruel difficulty we should be in, if you were to require medical advice."

"Oh, bother!" cried Adam.

"Why do you say 'bother?'"

"Because it is bother, and nothing else. When did I ever want medical advice? In general health, I'm as strong as a horse."

"When we were young men at home, they used to say I had twice the constitution that you had, Adam, in spite of your strong looks."

"Home fallacy!" said Adam lightly. "It was the father used to say that I remember. For the most part, the preaching that people make over 'constitution' is worth no more than the breath wasted on it. The proof of a pudding is in the eating: and the proof of a sound constitution lies in a man's good strength. I am stronger than you, Karl."

"As regards muscular strength, you are."

"And what's muscular strength a proof of, pray, but constitutional strength? Come, old wise acre!"

To argue with Adam Andinnian had been always about as profitable as to tell a ship to sail against the wind. So Karl said no more about strength.

"The chance that such a necessity may arise, Adam, and the difficulty and danger that would attend it——"

"What necessity?" interrupted Adam.

"Of your requiring a medical man. Your wife will want one; but that's different; she is supposed to live here alone, and you will of course take care to keep out of the way at that time. But the other thought does cross my mind anxiously now and again."

"Karlo, old man, you were always one of the anxious ones. I am content to leave problems alone until they arise. It is the best way."

"Sometimes it may be: not always. Of course all these thoughts turn round to one point, Adam—the urgent expediency there exists for your quitting the Maze."

"And I am not going to quit it."

"The advance of those people on Saturday night: the studied tramp of policemen gave me a fright, Adam. Let us suppose such a thing for a moment as that they were coming after you! No earthly aid could have shielded you."

"But they were not coming after me, you see; they were but carrying some poor dead man to his home on my estate. The same fear may apply wherever I go."

"No, it could not. It could apply to nowhere as it does to here. In some place abroad, Adam, you would be comparatively secure and safe. I am convinced that this locality is, of all, the most dangerous."

"If I were already at the some place you mention, wherever that may be—an inaccessible island in the icy seas, say—I should undoubtedly be more out of the reach of English constables and warders than I am now: but as matters stand, Karl, I am safer here, because the danger to me would lie in getting away. I shall not attempt to do it."

Karl paused for a few minutes before he resumed. His brother, sitting near the shaded lamp, was turning over the pages of the "Art Journal," a copy of which Mrs. Grey had brought from London.

"How came you to know Smith, Adam?"

"How came I to know Smith!" repeated Sir Adam. "To

tell you the truth, Karl, Smith saved me. But for his sheltering me in the time you know of, I should not be at liberty now; probably not in life. Until then he was a stranger."

"And for saving you he exacts his black mail."

"Little blame to him for it," returned Sir Adam, with a half laugh.

"I believe that the man is keeping you here," continued Karl: "that you dare not go away unless he lifts his finger."

"Naturally he is anxious for my safety, Karl; for the sake of his own self-interest."

"Precisely so. He would rather keep you here in danger than suffer you to escape to freedom. Do you know anything of his antecedents?"

"Nothing. For all I can tell, as to who or what the man was before that night he rescued me, he might have dropped from the moon."

"And since then it has been the business of your life to conciliate him, Adam!"

"What would you? The man knows that I am Adam Andinnian: and, knowing it, he holds a sword over me. Is it worth my while, or not, to try to keep it from falling?"

Karl sighed deeply. He saw all the intricacies of the case; and, what was worse, he saw no outlet from them. If only he could but feel that his brother was passably safe at the Maze, he would have been less uneasy: but a secret instinct, that he surely believed was a prevision, warned him of danger.

"I wish, with my whole heart, Adam, that you had never come here!" broke from him, in his dire perplexity, the reiterated cry.

Sir Adam threw down the "Art Journal," and turned to confront his brother, leaning a little forward in his chair. His face was flushed, his voice took a tone of passion, even his beautiful teeth looked stern.

"Karl, did you ever try to realize to yourself all the horrors of my position at Portland?" he asked. "I, a gentleman, with a gentleman's habits—and a man to whom freedom of will and of limb was as the very essence of life—was condemned for ever to a manacled confinement; to mate with felons; to be pointed at as one of a herd of convict labourers. A felon myself, you will perhaps say; but I do not recognize it. Had I been guilty of aught disgraceful? No. What I did, in shooting that man Scott, I was perfectly justified in doing, after my solemn warning to him. Remember, it was my wife he insulted that evening; not simply, as the world was allowed to believe, my young neighbour, Miss Rose Turner. What would *you* feel if some low reprobate seized your wife, Lucy, before your eyes, and pressed his foul kisses on her innocent face? Your blood would be up, I take it."

"Adam, since I knew Rose was your wife, I have almost held you justified."

"To go on. Can you realize a *tithe* of what it was for me on Portland Island?"

"From the time you went there until I heard of your death, I never ceased to realize it in my own soul night or day."

"Karl, I believe it. I remember what your sensitively tender nature always used to be. And we did care for each other, old fellow."

"Ay, and *do*."

"Well, compare that life I escaped from with this that I lead now. Here I am, so to say, a free man, at perfect liberty within these small bounds, my wife for my companion, my table at my command, master on my own estate, the revenues of which I divide with you that you may be the baronet to the world, and keep up Foxwood. As fate has fallen, Karl, I could not be so happy anywhere as here."

"I know: I know. But it is the risk I fear."

"There must be some risk everywhere."

"Answer me truly—as you would to your own heart, Adam. If by some miracle you could be transported safely to a far-off land, would you not feel more secure there than here?"

"Yes. And for Rose's sake I would go if I could; she is just as apprehensive here as you. But I can't. When Smith says I must not attempt to get away, he is right. I feel that he is. The man's interest lies in my safety, and I believe he thinks my safety lies in my remaining here."

"Just so," said Karl. "Smith is the stumbling-block."

"Well, he holds the reins, you see. It is no use trying to fight against his opinion: besides, I think he is right. However that may be, I can't afford to come to a rupture with him. Good heavens, Karl! fancy his sending me back in irons to Portland! That will never be, however," added Sir Adam more calmly, "for I would not be taken alive. I or my capturers should fall."

He put his hand inside his white waistcoat, and showed the end of a pistol. One he kept close to him night and day, always loaded, always ready. Karl's arguments failed him, one by one. As he was helpless to combat the decisions of his wife, so was he helpless here.

And so the interview ended in nothing, just as others had ended.

A black cloud, threatening thunder, had come over the summer's night when Karl went out. It did not seem to him half so dark as the trouble at his own heart. He would have given his life freely, to purchase security for his brother.

CHAPTER XXIII.

THE MAZE INVADED.

THE previous night's black cloud had culminated in a thunderstorm, and the morning air felt fresh and cool; but the blue sky was clear, the sun as bright as ever.

Lucy came down with sad eyes and a pale face. Her night had been one of mental pain. She was wondering how much longer she could keep up this mask of cheerfulness—which she would especially have to wear that day; and she knew that she could not have done it at all, then or at any other time, but for the very present help of God. Karl, waiting in the breakfast-room, turned to shake hands with her. But for their being alone, he would not have ventured on this eminently suggestive action.

"How are you to-day, Lucy?"

"Oh, quite well, thank you. Did you hear the storm?"

"Yes. It has cleared away some of the sultry heat. We shall have a lovely day."

The Lloyds were expected from Basham. When at the flower-show the previous day, Lucy had remarked that some of the hot-house plants were not as fine as those at Foxwood: upon that, the General and one of his daughters had simultaneously expressed a wish to see those at Foxwood. Lucy at once gave the invitation; and it was arranged that they should spend the next day at the Court. She had told her husband of this while Captain Lamprey was present; but it had not been alluded to afterwards. She spoke again now, while she and Karl were waiting breakfast for Miss Blake, who was at Matins at St. Jerome's.

"I could not do less than ask them," she observed. "I hope you are not vexed."

"You did quite right, Lucy," he cheerfully answered. "I shall be glad to see them."

"I don't know how many will come. Perhaps all; except Mrs. Lloyd, who never goes out anywhere. I hope Theresa will give up St. Jerome's for the rest of the day, and stay at home to help me entertain them."

Karl smiled. "To make sure of that you should invite Mr. Cattacomb."

"But you would not like that, would you?"

"No. I was only joking, Lucy. Here she is."

The Lloyds had said they would come early, and Karl strolled out to meet the eleven o'clock train, leaving his wife decorating her drawing-room with flowers. Unhappy though Lucy was, she was proud of her home, and pleased that it should find admiration in the eyes of the world.

As Karl was passing Clematis Cottage, he saw Mr. Smith seated at the open window, leisurely enjoying the freshened air, and smoking a cigar. Karl had been wanting to take a close, observant view of him; and he turned in on the spur of the moment. The asking for something which he really required afforded an excuse. Mr. Smith rose up to receive him graciously, and threw his half-smoked cigar out at the window.

"I think you have the plan of the out-lying lands of the estate, Mr. Smith, where the new cottages are to be built? Will you spare it to me in the course of the day? I will send Hewitt for it."

"Certainly, Sir Karl; it is at your service. Won't you take a seat? The bit of a breeze at this open window is quite refreshing."

Karl sat down. Mr. Smith's green glasses lay on the table, and he could enjoy as clear a view of him as he pleased. The agent talked away, all unconscious, no doubt, that notes were being taken of his face and form.

"It is his own hair," mentally spoke Karl. "'Very dark brown,' they said: 'nearly black.' Just so. At the time of the escape Salter had neither whiskers nor beard nor moustache: the probability being, they thought, that he had now a full crop of all. Just so again. Eyebrows: thick and arched, Grimley said: these are not thick; nor, what I should call, arched: perhaps there may be some way of manipulating eyebrows, and these have undergone the process. Eyes brown: yes. Face fresh and pleasant: yes. Voice and manners free and genial: yes. Age?—there I can't make the two ends meet. I am sure this man's forty. Is it Salter, or is it not?" finally summed up Karl. "I don't know. I *think* it is: but I don't know."

"Truefit, the farmer, spoke to me yesterday, Sir Karl," broke in Mr. Smith on his musings. "He was asking whether you and Lady Andinnian viewed this new farce on his grounds with approbation. That's what he called it—farce. Meaning St. Jerome's."

"I suppose he does not like it," observed Karl.

"I fancy he does not really care about it himself, one way or the other, Sir Karl; in fact, he signified as much. But it seems his better-half, Mrs. Truefit, has taken a prejudice against it: calling the ceremonies 'goings-on,' and 'rubbish,' and 'scandal,' and all sorts of depreciating things. It is a pity Mr. Cattacomb can't confine himself to tolerable common-sense. The idea of their hanging that bell outside over the door, and pulling it perpetually!"

"Yes," said Karl. "So much nonsense takes all solemnity away."

"They are going to dress Tom Pepp in a white garment now, while he rings it, with a red cross down the back. It's that, I fancy, that has put up Mrs. Truefit. I told the farmer that I believed Sir Karl and Lady Andinnian did not favour the place: at least, that I had never seen them attend it."

"And you never will," returned Karl, as he rose.

There was nothing to stay for; his observations were taken, and he departed, having to walk quickly to be in time at the station. Had he been free in mind, the matters connected with St. Jerome's might have vexed him more than they did: but all minor annoyances were lost sight of in his one great care.

The train came in, and the party arrived by it; six of them. Captain Lloyd, who was at home on leave; two Miss Lloyds; a married sister and her husband, Mr. and Mrs. Panton, at present staying on a visit; and the General.

Karl had expressed pleasure at his wife's invitation; perhaps had felt it; but he could not foresee the unlucky contretemps that the visit was to bring forth. To his unbounded astonishment, his inward confusion, no sooner had his guests entered Foxwood Court, than they expressed a wish to see the place called the Maze, and requested Sir Karl to conduct them to it.

"I was telling Panton about the Maze last night—talking of the Court and its surroundings," observed the General.

"Panton does not believe it possible that one could lose oneself in any maze whatever: so I promised him he should have a try at it. You will afford us the opportunity of seeing it, Sir Karl."

"I—I am not sure," stammered Karl, utterly taken aback, while his wife's face flushed a burning red. "I hardly think it is in my power, General. The lady who inhabits it desires to keep herself so very quiet, that I should not feel justified in intruding upon her. She is not in strong health, I believe."

"But we would not think of disturbing the lady," called out all the voices together. "We only wish to see the maze of trees, Sir Karl: not the dwelling-house. What's her name?"

"Grey."

"Well, we shall not hurt her. Does she live by herself?"

"While her husband is abroad. I am sure she will not choose to be intruded upon."

Sir Karl might as well have talked to the winds. All opposed him. Of course there was no suspicion that *he* had any personal objection; only that he wished to respect the scruples of his lady-tenant. At length, the General declared he would go over to Mrs. Grey, ask to see her, and personally prefer the request. Poor Karl was at his wits' end. He saw that he should not be able to stem the storm—for he dared not be resolute in the denial, so fearful was he always of arousing any suspicion of there being a mystery in the place —and he was fain to yield. He would take them over, he said; but not before he had sent a note to say that they were coming. This he insisted on; it would be but common politeness, he urged; and they all agreed with him.

Hastily writing a few words to Mrs. Grey in his own room, he called Hewitt to take the note over, and gave him at the same time a private message to deliver to Ann Hopley. Of course Karl's object was to warn his brother to keep out of sight — and Mrs. Grey too. Hewitt looked more scared than his master.

"To think of their wanting to go over *there!*" he exclaimed in a low tone of covert fear.

"It can't be helped, Hewitt. Go."

A few minutes, and Hewitt came back with a message: which he delivered to his master in public. Mrs. Grey's compliments to Sir Karl Andinnian, and he was at liberty to bring his friends within her gates if he pleased. So they all started; Lucy with them.

Lucy with them!

The ladies had assumed it to be so much a matter of course that their hostess should accompany them, that Lucy, timid in her self-consciousness, saw not her way clear to make any plea of excuse. And it might be that, down deep in her woman's frail heart, there was a hankering longing to see the inside of that place which contained her rival. In the midst of her indecision she glanced at Karl and hesitated. But he saw not the look or the hesitation: for all the sign he gave out, she was as welcome to go to the place as these guests were. It is true that Miss Blake fixed her eyes upon her, and Lucy coloured under it: but perhaps the very fact only served to speed her on the way.

The party started, passing out at the grand gates of Foxwood. Between that spot and the Maze, short though it was, they encountered Mr. Cattacomb. Miss Blake took upon herself to introduce him, and to ask him to accompany them, saying they were going to see that renowned show-place, the Maze.

"I did not know we had a show-place in the neighbourhood," drawled Mr. Cattacomb in his affectation.

"Neither have we," curtly rejoined Sir Karl, who would willingly have pitched Mr. Cattacomb over a mile elsewhere, but did not see an excuse for doing it. "The Maze was never constituted a show-place yet, Miss Blake. I feel anything but comfortable at intruding there to-day, I assure you. Between my wish to gratify my friends, and my fear that it may be objectionable to the lady occupying the Maze, I am in a blissful state of uncertainty," he added in a laughing kind of way, for the general benefit, fearing he might have spoken too pointedly and shown that he was really ill at ease.

"Sir Karl is ultra-sensitive," remarked Miss Blake—and a keen observer might have fancied there was some sarcasm in her tone.

Karl rang the clanging bell—which might be heard far and wide; and Ann Hopley appeared, the key of the gate in her hand. She curtsied to the company as she admitted them.

"My mistress desires me to say, Sir Karl, that she hopes the gentlepeople will see all they wish to see," cried the woman aloud, addressing the rest as much as she did Sir Karl. "Mrs. Grey begs they will pardon her not appearing to welcome them, but she is not well to-day, and has to keep her room."

"Mrs. Grey is very kind," returned Sir Karl. "We shall be cautious not to disturb her."

They filed of their own accord into the maze. The old trees had not been so beset with gay tongues and laughter for many a day. One ran here, another there; they were like school boys and girls out for a holiday. Ann Hopley was about to follow them in when the clanging bell at the gate once more sounded, and she turned back to open it. Karl, never at rest—as who could be, knowing what he knew— looked after her while he talked with his friends; and he saw that the visitor was a policeman.

His heart leaped into his mouth. Careless, in the moment's terror, of what might be thought of him, he broke off in the middle of a sentence to the General, and returned to the gate. His face was never very rosy, but every vestige of colour had forsaken it now. At a collected moment, he would have remembered that it was not in *that* way his brother would be sought out—in the person of one solitary, unarmed policeman—but fear scares probability away: as Rose had observed to him only the previous evening. Worse than all, the rest came flocking to the gate after him.

"Grey, ain't it?" the policeman was saying to Ann Hopley. He had a paper in his hand and a pencil.

"Mrs. Grey," replied the servant.

"Mrs. Grey. There ain't no husband, I think?"

"No."

"What's her Chris'en name?"

A warning glance shot from Sir Karl's eyes, cautioning Ann Hopley to be on her guard. In truth it was not needed: the woman was caution itself, and had her ready wits at hand always. Karl saw what it was—some parish paper about to be left—and was recovering his inward equanimity.

"My mistress's Christian name? Mary."

"Mrs. Mary Grey," repeated the policeman, writing down the name on the paper. "You'll please to give it her," he added, handing the paper in. "It have got to be attended to."

"All tax-papers for Mrs. Grey must come to Foxwood Court," interposed Sir Karl. "Mrs. Grey takes the house furnished, and has nothing to do with the taxes."

"Beg pardon, Sir Karl, but that there's a voting paper for a poor-law guardian," said the man, touching his hat.

"Oh, a voting paper. Let it go in, then," concluded Sir

Karl. Mrs. Grey had no more to do with voting than she had with taxes; but Sir Karl let it pass.

They were in the maze again: Ann Hopley having wound herself out of sight with the paper. Mr. Panton, the disbeliever, wound *himself* in and out of the trees and about the paths: but the voices always guided him back again.

"What a delightful place, Sir Karl!" cried Mrs. Panton. "Quite like a Fair Rosamond's Bower."

Sir Karl laughed in reply. And—as Miss Blake noticed—there was not a trace of shame in his face. Lucy's colour, though, rose painfully.

"Let me see! it was a silken thread, was it not, that guided Queen Eleanor to her rival?" continued Mrs. Panton. "A cruel woman! I wonder whether she carried the bowl of poison in her hand?"

"I wonder if the woman who destroyed the Queen's happiness, had any forewarning in her dreams of the fate in store for her?" retorted Miss Blake, sharply—for she was thinking of another case, very near to her, that she judged to be analogous. "For her punishment it is to be hoped she had."

"Oh, but you know she was so lovely, poor thing! One can but pity her; can we, Lady Andinnian?"

"I know nothing of it," spoke Lucy, in so chafed a tone that Karl turned to look at her.

"My opinion is, that the King should have taken half the bowl," said Miss Blake. "That would have been even justice, Mrs. Panton."

"Well, well, judge it as you will, Fair Rosamond was very beautiful; and her fate was shocking. Of course the Queen was incensed; naturally: and the crime of poisoning in those days was, I suppose, looked upon as no crime at all. I have always wished the Queen had been lost in the maze and the poison spilt."

"Suppose we get lost in this one!"

It was Miss Lloyd who spoke, hurriedly and somewhat anxiously. It brought most of them around her.

"There is no danger here, is there? Sir Karl, you know the way out, I suppose?"

Karl evaded the question. "If the worst come to the worst, we can set on and shout," he observed.

"But *don't* you know the clue? Is there not a clue? There must be."

"I see nothing of the kind," returned Karl. "You forget that I am almost a stranger in the neighbourhood. We shall be all right. Don't fear."

How Lucy despised him for his deceit! She felt that he must have the clue; why else need he let himself within the gate with his key—at least, with any purpose of finding his way further in after it? Miss Blake caught her eye; and Lucy turned away, sick at heart, from the compassion Miss Blake's glance wore.

Sir Karl's "Don't fear" had been reassuring, and they dispersed about the Maze and lost themselves in it, very much as Miss Blake had once done. Mr. Cattacomb kept asking questions about the mistress of the Maze: why she lived there alone? where her husband was? for all of which Sir Karl could have struck him. He, Karl, would have contrived to keep them from the boundaries near the house: but they were as nine to one, and went whither they would: and, as had been Miss Blake's case, they got within view of it at last.

"What a pretty place!" was the involuntary exclamation from more than one.

It did look pretty: pretty and very cheerful. The windows of the house were open; the door of the porch was fastened back, as if to invite entrance. Not a sign or symptom existed of there being any cause for concealment.

So far good, and Karl felt satisfied. But, as his eyes went ranging far and wide in their longed-for security, there was no doubt that he somewhere or other caught sight of his imprudent brother; for his face turned to an ashy paleness, and he groaned in spirit.

"Adam is surely mad," was his mental cry.

Ann Hopley, who had probably been waiting about, stepped up at this moment, and asked with much civility if they would like to walk indoors and rest. Sir Karl, looking at his friends, as if for acquiescence in his denial, declined. "We have *no right* to intrude," he whispered: and the General said so too.

"This might really do for a Rosamond's Bower!" cried Mrs. Panton. "It is a sweetly pretty place."

The lawn was level as a bowling-green; the flowers and shrubs surrounding it were well kept, fragrant and blooming. Mounted on a ladder, nailing some branches against a wall that probably belonged to a tool-house, was the toothless old gardener, his knees swollen and bent, his white smock frock rolled up around him.

"That's the gardener at his work, I suppose?" observed the General, whose eyes were dim.

"Yes, that's Hopley," said Karl.

"What d'ye call his name, Sir Karl?"

"Hopley. He is the woman's husband."

"I had a servant once of that name when I was quartered at Malta. A good servant he was, too."

"That man yonder looks ill," remarked Mrs. Panton.

"I fancy he's subject to rheumatism," said Sir Karl. "How is your husband?" he enquired of Ann Hopley.

"Pretty middling, sir, thank you," she answered. "He is getting in years, you see, gentlefolks, and is not as strong as he was."

"Will you be so good as precede us through the maze and let us out," said Karl to her. "I think it is time we went," he added to the others: "we have seen all there is to see."

Ann Hopley, key in hand, went winding through the maze, in and out of the numberless paths. It seemed to those following her that they only went round and round—just as it had seemed to Miss Blake that former day; and it took some time to get through it. The Reverend Mr. Cattacomb called it "a pilgrimage."

She was crafty, that faithful woman. Just as she had led Miss Blake a needlessly roundabout way, so she led them now. Had she taken them direct through, who knew but they might have caught some inkling of the clue? While opening the gate, General Lloyd would have put half-a-crown into her hand. She would not take it.

"I'd rather not, sir; I've done nothing to merit it. Our mistress pays us both well. Thank you, sir, all the same."

"A good, respectable, honest servant, that," remarked the General, slipping the money into his pocket again.

Crossing the road from the Maze, the party came right in view of Clematis Cottage and Mr. Smith, who was leaning over the gate of it, and staring with all his might. He raised his hat to the ladies generally, and then accosted Sir Karl, saying he had taken the plan asked for, to the Court.

"Thank you," replied Karl.

"Who *is* that man?" cried Captain Lloyd with some energy as they went on. "I am sure I know him."

"His name's Smith," replied Karl. "He is a sort of agent on my estate."

"Smith—Smith! I don't recollect the name. His face is quite familiar to me, though. Where can I have seen it?"

Karl longed in his heart to ask whether the face had ever belonged to the name of Salter; but he did not dare. There had been a peculiar expression in Mr. Smith's eyes as he spoke to him just now, which Karl had read rightly—he was sure Smith wanted to speak to him privately. So, after the rest had entered the home gates, he turned back. The agent had not stirred from his place.

"What have those people been doing there, Sir Karl?" he asked, with a peremptory action of his hand towards the Maze.

Karl explained. He did not dare do otherwise. Explained in full.

"Curious fools!" cried the man angrily. "Well, no harm seems to have been done, sir. Seeing you all come out of the gate, I could not believe my eyes, or imagine what was up."

"I fancied you wished to speak to me, Mr. Smith."

"And so I do, Sir Karl. The letters were late this morning—did you know it? They've only just been delivered. Some accident, I suppose."

"I only know that none came to Foxwood Court this morning."

"Just so. Well, Sir Karl, I've had one; ten minutes ago. I wrote to make inquiries about that paragraph in the newspaper, and this letter was the answer to mine. It is as I thought. There's nothing known or suspected at all at head-quarters; neither at Scotland Yard nor Portland Island. It was the work of a penny-a-liner, hang him!——just an invention, and nothing else."

"To whom did you write?"

"Well, that's my business, and I cannot tell you. But you may rely upon what I say, Sir Karl, and set your mind at rest. I thought you'd like to know this, sir, as soon as possible."

"Thank you," replied Karl.

He went back to his guests, his brain busy. Was this true, that Smith said? Who then was Smith that he could get this information? Or, was it that Smith was saying it for a purpose?

CHAPTER XXIV.

RECOGNISED.

The buff-coloured blinds were down before Mr. Burtenshaw's windows in the Euston Road, shutting out the glare of the afternoon sun, and throwing an unwholesome kind of tint over the rooms. In one of them, the front room on the first floor, sat the detective himself. It was indeed a kind of office as well as a sitting-room: papers strewed the table; pigeon-holes and shelves, all filled, were ranged along the walls.

Mr. Burtenshaw had a complicated case in hand at that period. Some fresh information had just come in by a private letter, and he was giving the best attention of his clear mind to it: his head bent over the table; his hands resting on the papers immediately before him. Apparently he arrived at some conclusion: for he nodded twice and then began to fold the papers together.

The servant-maid, with the flaunty cap tilted on her head, entered the room, and said to her master that a gentleman had called and was requesting to see him.

"Who is it?" asked Mr. Burtenshaw.

"He gave no name, sir. It's the same gentleman who called twice or thrice in one day somewhile ago: the last time late at night. He's very nice-looking, sir; might be known for a gentleman a mile off."

The detective carried his thoughts back, and remembered. "You can show him up," he said. "Or,——stay, Harriet," he suddenly added, as the girl was leaving the room. "Go down first of all and ask the gentleman his name."

She went as desired; and came up again fixing her absurd cap on its tottering pinnacle.

"The gentleman says, sir, that you don't know him by name, but his solicitors are Messrs. Plunkett and Plunkett."

"Ay. Show him up," said Mr. Burtenshaw. "He has a motive for withholding his name," mentally added the detective.

The reader need not be told that it was Karl Andinnian who entered. The object of his visit was to get, if possible, some further information respecting Philip Salter.

Day by day and week by week, as the days and weeks went

on, had served to show Karl Andinnian that his brother's stay at the Maze was growing more full of risk. Karl and Mrs. Grey, conversing on the matter as opportunity occurred, had nearly set it down as a certainty that Smith was no other than Salter. She felt sure of it. Karl nearly so. And he was persuaded that, once Smith's influence could be removed, Adam might get safely away.

The question ever agitating Karl's brain, in the midnight watches, in the garish day, was—what could he do in the matter?—how proceed in it at all with perfect security? The first thing of course was to ascertain that the man was Salter; the next to make a bargain with him: "You leave my brother free, and I will leave you free." For it was by no means his intention to deliver Salter up to justice. Karl had realized too keenly the distress and horror that must be the portion of a poor fugitive, hiding from the law, to denounce the worst criminal living.

The difficulty lay entirely in the first step—the identification of Smith with Salter. How could he ascertain it? He did not know. He could not see any means by which it might be accomplished with safety. Grimley knew Salter—as in fact did several of Grimley's brotherhood—but, if he once brought Grimley within a bird's-eye view of Smith (Smith being Salter) Grimley would at once lay his grasping hands upon him. All would probably be over then: for the chances were that Salter in revenge would point his finger to the Maze, and say, "There lives a greater criminal than I; your supposed dead convict, Adam Andinnian."

The reader must see the difficulty and the danger. Karl dared not bring Grimley or any other of the police in contact with Smith; he dared not give them a clue as to where he might be found: and he had to fall back upon the uncertain and unsatisfactory step of endeavouring to track out the identity himself.

"If I could but get to know Burtenshaw's reason for thinking Salter was in England," he exclaimed to himself over and over again, "perhaps it might help me. Suppose I were to ask Burtenshaw again—and press it on him? Something might come of it. After all, he could but refuse me."

Just as Karl, after much painful deliberation, had determined to do this, there arrived at Foxwood a summons for his wife. Colonel Cleeve was attacked with sudden illness. In the first shock of it, Mrs. Cleeve feared it might prove fatal, and she sent for Lucy. Karl took her to Winchester and left her, and at once took up his own abode in London. The Court had none too much attraction for him as matters stood, and he did not care to be left to entertain Miss Blake. So long as his wife stayed away from it, he meant to stay away.

The following afternoon saw him at the detective's. Mr. Burtenshaw had thought his unknown visitor looking ill before: he looked worse now. "A delicate man with some great care upon him," summed up the officer to himself.

Karl, opening his business, led up to the question he had come to ask. Would Mr. Burtenshaw confide to him the reason for his supposing Philip Salter to be still in England? At first Mr. Burtenshaw said No; that it could not, he imagined, concern him or any one else to hear it. Karl pleaded, and pleaded earnestly.

"Whatever you say shall be kept strictly sacred," he urged. "It cannot do harm to any one. I have a powerful motive for asking it."

"And a painful one, too," thought the detective. Karl was leaning forward in his chair, his pale face slightly flushed with inward emotion, his beautiful grey eyes full of eager entreaty, and a strange sadness in their depths.

"Will you impart to me, sir, your motive for wishing to know this?"

"No, I cannot," said Karl. "I wish I could, but I cannot."

"I fancy that you must know Salter's retreat, sir—or think you know it: and you want to be assured it is he before you denounce him," spoke the detective, hazarding a shrewd guess.

Karl raised his hand to enforce what he said, speaking solemnly. "Were I able to put my finger this moment upon Salter, I would not denounce him. Nothing would induce me. You may believe me when I say that, in asking for this information, I intend no harm to him."

The detective saw how true were the words. There was something in Karl Andinnian strangely attractive, and he began to waver.

"It is not of much consequence whether I give you the information or whether I withhold it," he acknowledged, giving way. "The fact is this: one of our men who knew Salter, thought he saw him some three or four months ago. He, our man, was on the Great Western line, going to Bath; in passing a station where they did not stop, he saw (or thought he saw) Salter, standing there. He is a cool-judging, keen-sighted officer, and I do not myself think he could have been mistaken. We followed up the scent at once, but nothing has come of it. Salter, if it was he, had made good his escape."

Karl made no answer: he was considering. Three or four months ago? That was about the time, he fancied, that Smith took up his abode at Foxwood. Previous to that, he might have been all over England, for aught Karl could tell.

"Just before that," resumed the detective, "another of the men struck up a cock-and-bull story that Salter was living in Aberdeen. I forgot the precise reason he had for asserting it. We instituted inquiries: but, like the latter tale, they resulted in nothing. As yet, we have no sure clue to Salter."

"That is all you know?" asked Karl.

"Every word. Has the information helped you?"

"Not in the least degree."

There was nothing else for Karl to wait for. His visit had been a fruitless one. "I should have liked to see Grimley once again," he said as he rose. "Is he in town?"

"Grimley is in the house now. At least, he ought to be. He is engaged in a case under me, and was to be here at three o'clock for instructions. Will you see him?"

"If you please."

It had occurred to Karl more than once that he should like to describe Smith accurately to Grimley, and ask whether the description tallied with Salter's. He could do it without affording any clue to Smith or his locality.

Mr. Burtenshaw rang, and told the maid to send up Grimley, if he had come. In obedience to this, Grimley, in his official clothes, appeared, and another officer with him.

"Oh, I don't want you just yet, Watts," said Mr. Burtenshaw. "Wait down stairs."

"Very well, sir," replied the man. "I may as well give you this, though," he added, crossing the room and placing a small box, the size of a five-shilling piece, on the table. Mr. Burtenshaw looked at it curiously, and then slipped it into the drawer at his left hand.

"From Jacob, I suppose?"

"Yes, sir."

The man left the room. Karl, after a few preliminary words with Grimley, gave an elaborate and close description of Smith's figure and features. "Is it like Salter?" he asked.

"If it isn't him, sir, it's his twin brother," was Grimley's emphatic answer. "As to his looking forty, it is only to be expected. Nothing ages a man like living a life of fear."

Karl remembered how Adam had aged and was ageing, and silently acquiesced. He began to think he saw his way somewhat more clearly; that the man at Foxwood was certainly Salter. Handing over a gratuity to Grimley, and taking leave of Mr. Burtenshaw, he departed, leaving the other two talking of him.

"He has dropped upon Salter," remarked Grimley.

"Yes," said Mr. Burtenshaw. "But he does not intend to deliver him up."

"No!" cried the other in amazement. "Why not, sir?"

"I don't know," said Mr. Burtenshaw. "He said he had no intention of the kind—and I am sure he has not. It seemed to me to be rather the contrary—that he wants to screen him."

"Then he told you, sir, that he *had* found Salter?"

"No, he did not. We were speaking on supposition."

"Who is this gentleman, sir?"

"I don't know who he is. He keeps his name from me."

Mr. Grimley felt anything but satisfied with the present aspect of the affair. What right had this stranger, who wanted to know all about Salter, to refuse to denounce him? Once more he asked Mr. Burtenshaw if he did not know who he was, but the latter repeated his denial. During the discussion, the man Watts entered the room again, and heard what passed. He looked at Mr. Burtenshaw.

"Are you speaking of the gentleman just gone out, sir? I know him."

"Why, who is he?" asked Mr. Burtenshaw, who had taken out the little box again, and was opening it.

"Sir Karl Andinnian."

"Nonsense!" exclaimed the detective, aroused to interest. For Sir Karl Andinnian, brother to the criminal who had made so much stir in the world, was a noted name amongst the force.

"It is," said Watts. "I knew him the minute I came in. I was present at the trial in Northampton, sir, when his brother was condemned to death; this gentleman sat all day at the solicitors' table. I had gone down there on that business of Patteson's."

"No wonder he has a sad look," thought the detective. "Adam Andinnian's was a mournful case, and his death was mournful. But what interest can Sir Karl have in Salter?"

There was one, at least, who determined to ascertain, if possible, what that interest was—and that was Mr. Policeman Grimley. A shrewd man by nature, a very shrewd one by experience, he drew his own deductions—and they were anything but favourable to the future security of some of the inhabitants of Foxwood. Could Karl Andinnian have seen what his morning's work had done for him, he would have been ready to sit in sackcloth and ashes, after the manner of the mourners of old.

"Sir Karl's living at Foxwood Court with his young wife," ran Mr. Grimley's thoughts: "I know that much. Wherever this Salter is, it's not far from him, I'll lay. Hid in Foxwood, and no mistake! I'll get him unearthed if it costs me my place. Let's see; how shall I set about it?"

As a preliminary step, he gently sounded Mr. Burtenshaw; but found he could get no help from him: it was not the detective's custom to stir in any matter without orders. Mr. Grimley then slept a night upon it, and in the morning had resolved to strike a bold stroke. Obtaining a private interview with one who was high in the force at Scotland Yard, he denounced Salter, telling of Sir Karl Andinnian's visits to Burtenshaw, and their purport.

"Salter is in hiding at Foxwood, or somewhere in its neighbourhood, sir, as sure as that my name's Dick Grimley," he said. "I want him took. I don't care about the reward—and perhaps it would not be given to me in any case, seeing it was me that let the fellow go—but I want him took. He's a crafty fox, sir, mark you, though; and it will have to be gone about cautiously."

"If Salter be retaken through this declaration of yours, Grimley, I daresay you'll get some of the reward," was the consoling answer. "Who knows the man? It will not do for you to go down."

"No, it wouldn't," acquiesced Grimley. "He knows me; and, once he caught sight of me, he'd make off like a rat sneaking out of a sinking ship. Besides, sir, I couldn't leave that other thing Mr. Burtenshaw has in hand."

"Well, who knows Salter, I ask?"

"Tatton does, sir; knows him as well as I do; but Salter does not know Tatton. Tatton would be the best man for it, too. Burtenshaw himself can't manage a case as Tatton does when it comes to personal acting."

There was a little more conversation, and then Grimley

withdrew, and Tatton was sent for. The grass could not be let grow under their feet in the attempt to re-take that coveted prize, Philip Salter.

This Tatton had begun life as an ordinary policeman: but his talents raised him. He was smart in appearance and manner, had received a fairly good education, conversed well on the topics of the day, could adapt himself to any society he might happen to be in, from that of a gentleman to a shoe-black, and was found to possess the rare prudence, the certain tact, necessary to undertake the conduct of delicate cases, and bring them to a successful conclusion. Grimley was correct, in judging that Tatton would be the right man to put on the track of Philip Salter.

CHAPTER XXV.

A NEW LODGER IN PARADISE ROW.

THE sun was drawing towards the west, and the summer's afternoon was waning, for the days were not so long as they had been a month or two ago, when a gentleman, slight and rather short, with light eyes, fair curly hair, and about thirty years of age, alighted from the London train at Foxwood station. He had a black bag in his hand and a portmanteau in the van, and enquired of the porter the way to Foxwood.

"Do you mean Foxwood proper, sir; or Foxwood, Sir Karl Andinnian's place?" returned the porter.

"Foxwood proper, I suppose. It is a village, is it not?"

"Yes, sir. Go down the road to the left, sir, then take the first turning on your right, and it will bring you into Foxwood."

"Thank you," said the gentleman, and slipped a small silver coin into the porter's hand. He knew, nobody better, the value of a silver key: and the chances were that he might shortly get gossiping with this station-porter about the neighbourhood and its politics.

Bag in hand, and leaving his portmanteau at the station, he speedily found himself in the heart of Foxwood. Casting about his eyes on this side and that, they settled on Paradise Row, on which the sun was shining, and on a white embossed card hanging in the first-floor window of the middle house, which card had on it, in large letters, "Apartments furnished."

A New Lodger in Paradise Row.   245

At the open entrance-door of the same house stood a widow woman, in a clean cap and smart black silk apron. Mrs. Jinks was en grande toilette that afternoon.

"It looks likely," said the stranger to himself. "Madam there will talk her tongue sore, I see, once prompted." And going up to the door, he politely took off his hat as he might to a duchess.

"You have apartments to let, I think, madam?"

"Good gracious!" cried the Widow Jinks, taken by surprise—for she was only looking out for the muffin-boy, and the slanting rays of the sun were dazzling her eyes, so that she had not observed the traveller. "I beg pardon, sir; apartments, did you say? Yes, sir, I've got my drawing-room just emptied."

It happened that an elderly lady from Basham and her grand-daughters had been lodging there for a month, the young ladies being ardent disciples of Mr. Cattacomb; but they had now left, and the drawing-room was ready to be let again. Mrs. Jinks went on to explain this, rather volubly.

"I will go up and look at it, if you please," said the stranger.

The widow ushered him along the passage towards the stairs, treading softly as she passed the parlour door.

"I've got a Reverend gent lodging in there," she said "minister of the new church, St. Jerome's. He has a meeting every Thursday evening, for Scripture reading, or something of that—exercises, I think they call it. This is Thursday, and they be all expected. But he wants his tea first, and that there dratted muffin-boy's not round yet. The Reverend gent have dropped asleep on three chairs in his shirt sleeves, while he waits for it.——This is the drawing-room, sir."

The stranger liked the drawing-room very much; the sun made it cheerful, he said; and he liked the bed-room behind it. Mrs. Jinks rather hesitated at letting the two rooms alone. She generally let the bed-rooms at the top of the house with them.

"How long shall you be likely to stay, sir?" questioned she.

"I do not know. It may be a week, it may be a month, it may be more. I am seeking country air and rest to re-establish my health, ma'am, and want a quiet place to read in. I shall not give you much trouble."

Mrs. Jinks agreed to let him have the rooms at last, demanding a few shillings over the usual terms for the two: a bird in the hand, she thought, was worth two in the bush. Next she asked for references.

"I cannot refer you to any one here," he said, "for I don't know a soul in the place, and not a soul in it knows me. I will pay you every week in advance; and that I presume will do as well as references."

He laid down the sum agreed upon and a sovereign beside it. "You will be so good as to get in for me a few things to eat and drink, Mrs. Jinks. I should like to have some tea first of all, if convenient, and one of those muffins you spoke of. Well buttered, if you please."

"Yes, sir; certainly, sir. We get muffins at Foxwood all the year round, sir, on account of there being company in the place at summer time: in other towns, Basham, for instance, they are only made in winter. Buttered muffins and cress, sir, is uncommonly good together."

"Are they? I'll have some cress too."

Telling her, as well as he could remember, what articles he should want besides butter and muffins, and bidding her to add anything else that she thought he might require, he picked up his black bag to take it into the bed-room. Mrs. Jinks in her politeness begged him to let her take it, but he said certainly not.

"Is it all the luggage you've got, sir, this?"

"My portmanteau is at the station. I could not order it on until I knew where I should be; or, in fact, whether I should stay at Foxwood at all. Had I not found lodgings to my mind, ma'am, I might have gone on somewhere else."

"Foxwood's the loveliest, healthiest spot you can find, sir," cried the widow, eagerly. "Sweet walks about it, there is."

"So I was told by my medical man. One wants nice rural walks, Mrs. Jinks, after reading hard."

"So one does, sir. You are reading up for college, I suppose? I had a young gent here once from Oxford. He got plucked, too, afterwards. There's the muffin-boy!" added Mrs. Jinks, in delight, as the fierce ring of a bell and the muffin call was heard beneath. "Oh, I beg pardon, sir, what name?"

The gentleman, who had his head and hands just then in his bag, merely responded that he was a stranger. Mrs. Jinks, in the hurry to be gone, and confused with the ringing and the calling below, caught up the answer as "Strange."

"A Mr. Strange," she said to herself, going down with the money in her hand. "And one of the nicest gents I've ever come across. 'Put plenty o' butter,' says he. *He* ain't one as'll look sharp after every crumb and odd and end, as too many of 'em does, and say where's the rest of this, that it don't come up, and where's the remainder of that."

Mrs. Jinks had a young help-mate when she was what she considered in "full let;" a young damsel of fourteen, who wore her hair in a pink net. Sending the girl flying to the general shop for various things, she set on to toast the muffins; and tea was speedily served in both rooms. She took in the clergyman's first. Mr. Cattacomb was asleep on the three chairs, in his shirt sleeves. He was beginning to find his work somewhat hard. What with the duties in the church, the services, and sermons, and confessions, and the duties out of church connected with little boys and girls, and with those anxious Christians who never left him alone, the young ladies, Mr. Cattacomb was often considerably fatigued; and it was under consideration whether his former coadjutor, the Reverend Damon Puff, should not be summoned to assist him.

"Here's your tea, sir," said Mrs. Jinks, "and a beautiful hot muffin. I couldn't get it up afore, for the muffin-boy was late."

"My tea, is it, Mrs. Jinks?" replied Mr. Cattacomb, slowly rising. "Thank you, I am dead tired."

And, perhaps in consequence of the fatigue, or that Mrs. Jinks was not worth any display, it might have been observed that the affectation, so characteristic of the reverend gentleman when in society, had entirely disappeared now. Indeed, it seemed at this undress moment that Mr. Cattacomb was a simple-mannered, pleasant man.

"I've been in luck, this afternoon, sir, and have let my drawing-room floor," continued the widow, as she settled the tea-tray before him. "It's a Mr. Strange, sir, that's took it; a gent reading for Oxford, and out of health. His doctor have ordered him into the country for change, and told him he'd find quiet air and nice walks at Foxwood. You may hear his boots walking about overhead, sir. He seems to be as nice and liberal a gent as ever I had to do with."

"Glad to hear it," said Mr. Cattacomb, beginning upon his muffin vigorously. "We shall want more chairs here presently, you know, Mrs. Jinks."

The tea-tray had scarcely disappeared, and Mr. Cattacomb

put on his coat and his fascinating company manners, before
the company began to arrive. On these Thursday evenings
Mr. Cattacomb gave at his own home a private lecture, de-
scriptive of some of the places mentioned in holy Scripture.
The lectures were attended by all his flock at St. Jerome's and
by several young ladies from Basham. Of course it necessi-
tated a great many seats; and the new lodger above was yet
at his tea, when Mrs. Jinks appeared, her face redder than
usual with running about, and begged the loan of "Mr.
Strange's" chairs, explaining what they were wanted for.

"Oh, certainly: take them all, Mrs. Jinks," replied he, in
the most accommodating manner possible. "I can sit upon
the table."

Mrs. Jinks considerately left him one, however, and went
down with the rest. He found out she had taken up the notion
that his name was "Strange," and laughed a little.

"Some misunderstanding, I suppose, on her part, when I
said I was a stranger," thought he. "All right; I'll not con-
tradict it."

While the bumping and thumping went on, caused by the
progress of chairs down from the chambers and up from the
kitchen, and the knocker and the bell kept up a perpetual
duet, Mr. Strange (we will call him so at present ourselves)
put on his hat to go round and order his portmanteau to be
sent from the station. As he passed the parlour door it stood
open; no one was looking his way; he had a good view of the
interior, and took in the scene and the details with his observant eyes. A comfortable room, containing a dozen or two
charming and chattering ladies, surrounded by a perfect epitome of tasty and luxurious objects that had been worked by
fair fingers. Cushions, anti-macassars, slippers, scrolls, draw-
ings enshrined in leather frames, ornamental mats by the
dozen, cosies for tea-pots, lamp tops and stands, flowers in wax
under shades, sweet flowers from hot-houses in water, and
other things too numerous to mention.

"A man beset, that clergyman," thought Mr. Strange,
with a silent laugh, as he bent his steps towards the railway.
"He should get married and stop it. Perhaps he likes it,
though: some of them do who have more vanity than brains."

So he ordered his portmanteau to No. 5, Paradise Row,
contriving to leave the same impression at the station that
he had given Mrs. Jinks—a reading man in search of quiet
and health.

Mrs. Jinks presided at the arrival of the portmanteau, and saw some books taken out of it in the drawing-room. While her lodger's back was turned, she took the liberty of peeping into one or two of them; and finding their language was what she could not read, supposed it to be Greek or Latin. Before the night was over, all Paradise Row, upwards and downwards, had been regaled with the news of her new lodger, and the particulars concerning his affairs.

"A scholar-gent by name of Strange, who had come down to read and get up his health, and had brought his Greek and Latin books with him."

CHAPTER XXVI.

NURSE CHAFFEN ON DUTY.

How short a period of time may serve to bring forth vital chances and changes! Sir Karl and Lady Andinnian were absent only a week, yet before they returned a stranger had taken up his abode at Foxwood, indirectly brought to it by Karl himself; and something had happened at the Maze.

Lucy was out amidst her plants and shrubs and flowers the evening of her return, when the shadows were lengthening on the grass. Karl was writing letters indoors; Miss Blake had hurried up from dinner to attend vespers. In spite of the estrangement and misery that pervaded the home atmosphere, Lucy felt glad to be there again. The meeting with her husband, after the week's entire separation, had caused her pulses to quicken and her heart to bound with something that was very like joy. Colonel Cleeve was out of all danger; was nearly well again. It had been a sharp but temporary attack of sickness. The Colonel and his wife had pressed Lucy to prolong her stay, had asked Sir Karl to come and join her; and they both considered it somewhat unaccountable that Lucy should have persisted in declining. Theresa was alone at Foxwood, was the chief plea of excuse she urged: the real impediment being that she and Karl could not stay at her mother's home together without risk of the terms on which they lived becoming known. So Karl, on the day appointed, went from London to Winchester, and brought Lucy home.

For the forbearance she had exercised, the patient silence she had maintained, Lucy had in a degree received the reward during this sojourn with her father and mother. More than ever was it brought home to her conviction then, that she would almost rather have died than betray it. It would have inflicted on them so much pain and shame. It would have lowered herself so in their sight, and in the sight of those old and young friends who had known her in her girlhood, and who whispered their sense of what her happiness must now be, and their admiration of her attractive husband. "Martyrdom rather than that!" said Lucy, clasping her hands with fixed resolution, as she paced the grass, on this, the evening of her return.

Karl came up to her with two letters in his hand. She was then sitting under the acacia tree. The sun had set, but in the west shone a flood of golden light. The weather in the daytime was still hot as in the middle of that hot summer, but the evenings and nights were cool. Lucy's shawl lay beside her.

"It is time to put it on," said Karl—and he wrapped it round her himself carefully. It caused her to see the address of the two letters in his hand. One was to Plunkett and Plunkett; the other to Mrs. Cleeve.

"You have been writing to mamma!" she exclaimed.

"She asked me to be sure and let her have one line to say you got home safely. I have given your love, Lucy."

"Thank you, Karl. And now you are going to the post."

"And now I am going to the post. And I must make haste, or I shall find the box shut."

He took his hand from her shoulder, where it had momentarily rested, and crossed the grass, Lucy looking after him.

"How thoughtful and kind he is!" she soliloquised. "It is just as though he loved me." And her imagination went off wandering at random, as imagination will. Once more she reverted to that former possibility—of condoning the past and becoming reconciled again. It was *very* good of him, and she felt it so, to have stayed that week in London. She fancied he had done it that she might know he did not spend his time at the Maze in her absence. And so, the evening shadows came on, and still Lucy sat there, lost in her dreams.

Miss Blake, it has been said, had hurried from dinner, to go to vespers. As she turned into the road from the Court, she saw a boy a little in advance of her on the other side, his basket on his arm. It was the doctor's boy, Cris Lumley, against whom Miss Blake had a grievance. She crossed over and caught him up just as he rang at the Maze gate.

"Now, Cris Lumley, what have you to say for yourself? For three days you have not appeared at class."

"'Tain't my fault," said Cris Lumley, who was just as impudent as he looked; a very different boy indeed from civil-natured Tom Pepp. "It be master's."

"How is it your master's?"

"What master says is this here: 'I be to attend to him and my place, or to give it up if I wants to kick up my heels all day at school.'"

"I don't believe you," said Miss Blake. "I shall speak to Mr. Moore."

"Just do, then," said the independent boy.

"The fact of the case is no doubt this, Cris Lumley—that you play truant for half the day sometimes, on the plea of being all that while at school."

"Master said another thing, he did," resumed the young gentleman, ignoring the last accusation. "He said as if Parson Sumnor warn't no longer good enough for me to learn religion from, he'd get another boy in my place, that he was good enough for. There! you may ask him whether he said it or not."

Declining to bandy further words with him until she should have seen the surgeon, Miss Blake was hastening on, when the fringe of her mantle caught against his medicine basket. It reminded her that some one must be ill. Battling for a moment with her curiosity, but not for long, she condescended to inquire who was ill at the Maze.

"It be the missis," replied Cris.

"The mistress! Do you mean Mrs. Grey?"

Mr. Lumley nodded.

"What is the matter with *her?*"

"Got a baby," said the boy shortly.

For the instant Miss Blake felt struck into herself, and was dumb. She did not believe it.

"He was born yesterday," added the boy. "This be some physic for him: and this be the missis's."

Throwing back the lid of one end of his basket, Miss Blake saw two bottles, done up in white paper. The larger one was addressed "Mrs. Grey," the smaller one "Mrs. Grey's infant."

She turned away without another word, feeling ready to

sink with the weight of the world's iniquity. It pressed upon her most unpleasantly throughout the evening service at St. Jerome's, and for once Miss Blake was inattentive to the exhortations of the Rev. Guy. Looking at the matter as Miss Blake looked at it, it must be confessed that she had just cause for condemnation.

To return to Lucy. It grew dusk and more dusk: and she at length went in-doors. Karl came in, bringing Mr. Moore, whom he had overtaken near the gate: and almost close upon that, Miss Blake returned. The sight of the doctor, sitting there with Karl and Lucy, brought back all Miss Blake's vexation. It had been at boiling point for the last hour, and now it bubbled over. The wisest course no doubt would have been to hold her tongue: but her indignation—a perfectly righteous and proper indignation, as she deemed it—forbade that. The ill-doing of the boy, respecting which she had been about to appeal to Mr. Moore, was quite lost sight of in this ill-doing. There could be no fear of risking Jane Shore's sheet of penance in repeating what she had heard. It was her duty to speak: she fully believed that: her duty to open Lucy's obtuse eyes—and who knew but Sir Karl might be brought to his senses through the speaking? The surgeon and Lucy were sitting near the window in the sweet still twilight: Karl stood back by the mantel-piece: and they were deep in some discussion about flowers. Miss Blake sat in silence, gathering her mental forces for the combat, when the present topic should have died away.

"I—I have heard some curious news," she began then in a low, reluctant tone: and in good truth she was reluctant to enter on it. "I heard it from that boy of yours, Mr. Moore. He says there's a baby at the Maze."

"Yes," readily acquiesced Mr. Moore. "A baby-boy, born yesterday."

And Miss Blake, rising and standing at angles between the two, saw a motion of startled surprise on the part of Karl Andinnian. Lucy looked up, simply not understanding. After a pause, during which no one spoke, Miss Blake, in language softened to ambiguousness, took upon herself to intimate that, in her opinion, the Maze had no business with a baby.

Mr. Moore laughed pleasantly. "That, I imagine, is Mrs. Grey's concern," he said.

Lucy understood now: she felt startled almost to sickness.

"Is it Mrs. Grey who has the baby?" was on the point of her tongue: but she did not speak it.

"Where is Mrs. Grey's husband?" demanded Miss Blake, in her most uncompromising tone.

"In London, I fancy, just now," said the doctor.

"*Has she one at all*, Mr. Moore?"

"Good gracious, yes," cried the hearty-natured surgeon, utterly unconscious that it could be of particular moment to anybody present whether she had or not. "I'd answer for it with my life, nearly. She's as nice a young lady as I'd ever wish to attend; and good too."

"For Lucy's sake, I'll go on; for his sake, standing there in his shame," thought Miss Blake, in her rectitude. "Better things may come of it: otherwise I'd drop the hateful subject for ever."

"Mr. Moore," she continued aloud, "why do you say the husband is in London?"

"Because Mrs. Grey said something to that effect," he answered. "At least, I understood her words to imply as much; but she was very ill at the moment, and I did not question further. It was when I was first called in."

"It has hitherto been represented that Mr. Grey was travelling abroad," pursued Miss Blake, with a tone and a stress on the "Mr. Grey."

"I know it has. But he may have returned. I am sure she said she had been up to London two or three weeks ago—and I thought she meant to imply that she went to meet her husband. It may have been a false conclusion I drew; but I certainly thought it."

Sir Karl took a step forward. "I can answer for it that Mrs. Grey did go up," he said, "for I chanced to travel in the same carriage with her. Getting into the up-train at the station one day, I found Mrs. Grey seated there."

Lucy glanced towards him as he spoke. There was no embarrassment in his countenance; his voice was easy and open as though he had spoken of a stranger. Her own face looked white as death.

"You did!" cried the doctor. "Did she tell you she was going up to meet Mr. Grey?"

"No, she did not. I put her into a cab at the terminus, and that's all I know about it. It was broiling hot, I remember."

"Well," resumed the doctor, "whether it was to meet her

husband or whether not, to London she went for a day or two in the broiling heat—as Sir Karl aptly terms it—and she managed to fatigue herself so much that she had not been able to recover it, and has been very unwell ever since. This young gentleman, who chose to take upon himself to make his appearance in the world yesterday, was not due for a good couple of months to come."

Lucy rose and left the room, she and her white face. Karl followed her with his eyes; he had seen the whiteness.

"Is it a healthy child?" he asked.

"Quite so," replied the surgeon; "but very small. The worst of these little monkeys is, you can't send them back again with a whipping when they make too much haste, and tell them to come again at proper time. Mrs. Grey's very ill."

"Is she?" breathed Karl.

"Yes. And there's no nurse and no anything; matters are all at sixes and sevens."

"I hope she'll do well!" said Karl.

"So do I."

Miss Blake looked at the two speakers. The one seemed just as open as the other. She thought what a finished adept Karl Andinnian was getting to be in deception.

"I am going to the Maze now," said the doctor: "was on my way to it when you seduced me in here, Sir Karl. Good evening, Miss Blake."

He took his departure hastily as he spoke. He was, as he told them, on his way to the Maze then. Karl went with him to the outer gate, and then paced the lawn in the evening twilight.

"After all, it is well it's over," ran his thoughts. "This expected future illness was always putting itself in view when I was planning to get away Adam. Once Rose is well again, the ground will be, so far, clear. But good heavens! how it increases the risk! Here's Moore going in at any hour of the day or night, I suppose—and Adam so incautious! Well, I think he will take care of himself, and keep in seclusion for his own sake. And for myself—it brings more complication," he added with a sigh. "The child is heir now instead of me: and the whole property must eventually come to him. Poor Lucy! I saw she felt it. Oh, she may well be vexed! Does she quite comprehend, I wonder, who this baby is, and what it will take from us?—Foxwood amidst the rest? I wish I had never married! I wish a merciful heaven had interposed to prevent it."

When Mr. Moore, some eight-and-forty hours previously, received a hurried visit from Mrs. Grey's servant, Ann Hopley, at the dusk of evening, and heard what she had to say about her mistress, he was excessively astonished, not having had the slightest idea that his services were likely to be wanted in any such way at the Maze. It s possible that some doubts of Mrs. Grey's position crossed his mind at the moment: but he was a good man, and he made it a rule never to think ill if he could by possibility think good; and when he came to see and converse with Mrs. Grey, he felt sure she was all she should be. The baby was born on the following morning. Since then the doctor, as Karl expressed it, had been going in at all hours: Ann Hopley invariably preceding him through the Maze, and conducting him out of it again at his departure. As he marched on to the Maze to-night after the above conversation at the Court, he wondered what Miss Blake had got in her head, and why she should betray so much anger over it.

Three or four days went on. The doctor passed in and out in the care of his patient, and never a notion entered his head that the Maze was tenanted by any save its ordinary inmates, or that one under a ban was lying there in concealment. Ann Hopley, letting her work go how it would, attended on her mistress and the baby: the old gardener was mostly busy in his garden as usual. On the fifth or sixth day from the commencement of the illness, Mr. Moore, upon paying his usual morning visit, found Mrs. Grey worse. There were rather dangerous symptoms of fever.

"Has she been exciting herself?" he privately asked of Ann Hopley.

"She did a little last night, sir," was the incautious admission.

"What about?"

"Well, sir—chiefly talking."

"Chiefly talking!" repeated the doctor. "But what were you about to let her talk?" he demanded, supposing Ann Hopley to be the only other inmate of the house. "What possessed you to talk to her?"

Ann was silent. She could have said that it was not with her Mrs. Grey had talked, but with her husband.

"I must send a nurse in," he resumed. "Not only to see

that she is kept quiet, but to attend to her constantly. It is not possible that you can be with her always with your house-work to do."

But all of this Ann Hopley most strongly combated. She could attend to her mistress, and would, and did attend to her, she urged, and a nurse she would not have in the house. From the first, this question of a nurse had been a bone of contention : the doctor wanting to send one in; Ann Hopley and also Mrs. Grey strenuously objecting. So once more the doctor yielded, and let the matter drop, inwardly resolving that if his patient did not get better during the day, he should take French leave to pursue his own course.

Late in the afternoon he went in again. Mrs. Grey was worse: flushed, restless, and slightly delirious. The doctor said nothing; but when he got home, he sent a summons for Mrs. Chaffen. A skilled nurse, she; and first cousin to the Widow Jinks, both in respect of kin and of love of gossip.

That same evening, after dark, when Adam Andinnian was sitting in his wife's room, and Ann Hopley was concocting something in a saucepan over the kitchen fire, the gate bell clanged out. It had been nothing unusual to hear it these last few days at any hour; and the woman, putting the saucepan on the hob for safety, went forth, key in hand.

No sooner had she unlocked the gate than Mr. Moore brushed past her, followed by a little thin woman with a bundle. Ann Hopley stared: but never a word said he.

"Keep close to me, and you won't lose yourself," cried he to the little woman; and went tearing off at a double-quick pace through the intricacies of the maze.

Ann Hopley stood like one bewildered. For one thing, she had not possessed the slightest notion that the surgeon knew his way through, for he had given no special indication of it, always having followed her. He could have told her that he had learnt the secret of the maze long before she came to Foxwood. It had been shown to him in old Mr. Throckton's time, whom he had attended for years. And, to see a second person pass in, startled her. All she could do was to lock the gate, and follow them.

On went the doctor; the little woman keeping close to his coat tails: and they were beyond the maze in no time. Mr. Moore had no private motive for this unusual haste, except that he had another patient waiting for him, and was in a hurry. In, at the open portico, passed he, and made direct for the stairs, the woman after him. Ann Hopley, miles behind, could only pray in agony that her master might escape their view.

But he did not. The doctor had nearly reached the top of the staircase, when a gentleman, tall, and in evening dress, suddenly presented himself in front, apparently looking who it might be, coming up. He drew back instantly, strode noiselessly along the corridor, and disappeared within a door at its extreme end. It all passed in a moment of time. What with the speed, and what with the obscurity of the stairs and passages, any one, less practical than the doctor, might have questioned whether or not it had happened at all.

"That's Mr. Grey, come down," thought he. "But he seems to wish not to be noticed. Be it so."

Had he cared to make any remark upon it to Mrs. Grey, he could not have done so, for she was quite delirious that night. And, as he saw no further sign of the gentleman at any subsequent visit, he merely supposed that Mr. Grey had come down for a few hours and had gone again. And the matter passed from his mind.

It did not so pass from the nurse's. Mrs. Chaffen had distinctly seen the gentleman in evening attire looking down the stairs at her and the doctor; she saw him whisk away, as she phrased it, and go into the further room. In the obscure light, Mrs. Chaffen made him out to be a very fine-looking gentleman with beautiful white teeth. She had keen eyesight, and she saw that much: she had also a weakness for fine-looking men, and felt glad that one so fine as this should be in the house. It could not make much difference to her; but she liked gentlemen to be in a dwelling where she might be located: they made it lively, were pleasant to talk to; and were generally to be found more liberal in the offers of glasses of wine and what not than the mistresses. Like the doctor, she supposed this was Mrs. Grey's husband come down at last.

She neither saw nor heard more of the gentleman that night, though she sat up with her patient. Neither did she on the following day—and then she began to think it somewhat odd. At dusk, when Mrs. Grey and the baby were both sleeping, she went down stairs.

When Ann Hopley found the nurse installed there, and that she was powerless to prevent it, she had to make the best of the unfortunate occurrence—and most unfortunate it was destined to turn out in the end. She gave the nurse certain directions. One of them was, "Ring for everything you want, and I will bring it up." The woman's meals also were brought up to her punctually: Ann's object of course being to prevent her going about the house. But nurses are but human. Mrs. Chaffen was longing for a word of social gossip, and downstairs she went this night, and made her way to the kitchen. Ann Hopley was in it, ironing at a table under the window.

"What do you want?" cried she, in a quick, startled tone, as the nurse appeared.

"I thought I'd get you to give me a sup o' beer, Mrs. Hopley," was the answer. "I'm a'most faint, stopping so long in that there room with its smell of ether about."

"Why could you not have rung? I'll bring it up to you."

In the very teeth of this plain intimation, Mrs. Chaffen sat herself down on a chair by the ironing board, and began fanning her face with the corner of her white apron. "The missis is asleep," she said: "she's a sight better to-night; and I shall stop here while I drink the beer, for a bit of relief and change."

Ann took a small jug that was hanging on the dresser shelves, went down in the cellar, brought up the beer, and poured it into a tumbler. Mrs. Chaffen took a good draught and smacked her lips.

"That ain't bad beer, is it, Mrs. Hopley?"

"Not at all," said Ann Hopley. "Drink it up."

She would not go on with her ironing, lest it might seem an excuse for the nurse to linger: she stood by the fire, waiting, and evidently wanting the nurse gone.

"Your husband's a-taking of it easy, out there!"

Ann glanced from the window, and saw the gardener seated amongst a heap of drying weeds, his back against the tool house, and a pipe in his mouth.

"He has done his work, I suppose, for the day," she said.

"And he knows his missis's eyes can't be upon him just now," added the nurse, taking another draught. "He don't hardly look strong enough to do all this here big garden."

"You couldn't offend Hopley worse than by telling him that. His mistress says nothing about it now, it puts him up so. Last May, when he was laid up in bed with the rheumatis, she ordered a gardener in for two or three days to clear up some of the rough work. Hopley was not at all grateful: he only grumbled at it when he got about again."

"It's just like them good old-fashioned servants that takes pride in their work," said the nurse. "There's not many of the young uns like 'em. The less work they have to do the better it pleases *them*. Is that a hump now, or only a stoop of the shoulders?" continued she, ignoring good manners in her sociability.

"It used to be only a stoop, Mrs. Chaffen. But those things, you know, always get worse with years."

Mrs. Chaffen nodded. "And gardening work, when one has a natural stoop, is the worst sort of work a man can take to."

"True," assented Ann. She had spoken absently all along, and kept glancing round and listening, as though ill at ease. One might have fancied she feared a ghost was coming down the staircase.

"What be you a-harkening at?" asked Mrs. Chaffen.

"For fear the baby should cry."

"The baby's in a sweet sleep, he is. I wonder whether he'll get reared, that baby?—he's very little. Where's the gentleman?" abruptly inquired Mrs. Chaffen, after a pause.

"What gentleman?"

"Mrs. Grey's husband. Him we saw here last night."

If Ann Hopley had been apathetic before, she was fully aroused to interest now, and turned her eyes upon the nurse with a long stare.

"Why, what is it that you are talking of?" she asked. "There has been no gentleman here. Mrs. Grey's husband is abroad."

"But I saw him," persisted the nurse. "He stood right at the head of the staircase when me and Dr. Moore was agoing up it. I saw him."

"I'm sure you didn't."

"I'm sure I did."

Then they went on, asserting and reasserting. Nurse Chaffen protesting, by all that was truthful, that she did see the gentleman: Ann Hopley denying in the most emphatic language that any gentleman had been there, or could have been. Poor woman! in her faithful zeal for her master's safety; in her terrible inward fear lest this might bring danger upon him, she went so far as to vow by heaven that no living soul had been in the house or about it, save her mistress and the infant, herself and Hopley.

The assertion had its effect. Nurse Chaffen was not an

irreligious woman, though she did indulge in unlimited gossip, and love a glass of beer when she could get it; and she could not believe that a thing so solemnly asserted was a lie. She felt puzzled to death: her eyes were good and had never played her false yet.

"Have ye got a ghost in the house?" she asked at length, edging a little nearer to the ironing board and to Ann Hopley.

"I have never seen or heard of one."

"It's a rare old place, this house. Folks said all kinds of queer things about it in Miser Throckton's time."

"He left no ghost in it, that I know of," repeated Ann.

"Well, I never! I can't make it out. You might a'most as soon tell me to believe there's no truth in the Bible. He stood atop o' the stairs, looking down at me and the doctor. It was dusk, I grant; a'most dark; but I saw him as plain as plain could be. He had got white teeth and a suit of black on; and he went off into that door that's at the fur end of the passage."

A keen observer might have detected a sleeping terror in Ann Hopley's eyes; but she was habitually of calm manner and she showed perfect calmness now, knowing how much was at stake. A great deal had all along depended upon her ready presence of mind, her easy equanimity in warding off suspicion: it depended more than ever on her at this trying time, and she had her wits at hand.

"Your eyes and the dusk must have misled you, Mrs. Chaffen," she quietly rejoined. "Is it possible—I put it to yourself—that any gentleman could be in this house, and me and Hopley not know it? That night I had run down from my mistress's room, where she was lying off her head with the fever, and the baby asleep in its little bed by the fire, and was making a drop of gruel in the kitchen here, when the ring at the gate came. I had a great mind to send Hopley to open it: I heard him out yonder putting up his tools for the night: but I should have had to go close up to make him understand, for he's as deaf as a post; and his knees would have been a long while making their way through the maze. So I went myself: it seemed less trouble; and I let in you and the doctor. As to any soul's having been in the place, save me and Hopley and the missis and baby, it's a moral impossibility; and if necessary I could swear to it."

"Where do that there end door lead to?" questioned Mrs. Chaffen, only half-convinced; and that half against her will.

"It leads to nowhere. It's a sitting-room. Mrs. Grey does not often use it."

"Well, this beats everything, this do. I'm sure I could have swore that a gentleman was there."

"It was quite a mistake. Hark! there *is* the baby."

Nurse Chaffen flew up the stairs. Ann Hopley went on with her ironing; her face, now that she was alone, allowing its terror scope.

"It is so foolish of my master to run risks just at this time, when the house is liable to be invaded by strangers!" she ejaculated wearily. "But who was to foresee the doctor would come bursting in like that? Pray Heaven master doesn't show himself again like that while the woman's here!"

Mrs. Chaffen sat in the sick-room, the awakened baby occupying her lap, and the problem her mind. Never in her life had she felt to be in so entire a mist. Ann Hopley she could not and would not disbelieve: and yet, in her reasoning moments, she was as fully persuaded that a gentleman had been there, and that she had seen him, as that the sun shone in the sky.

A day or two went on; and the subject was never out of the woman's mind. Now leaning to this side of the question, now wavering to that, she could not arrive at any positive conclusion. But, taking one thing with another, she thought the house was rather a strange house. Why did Ann Hopley want to keep her for ever in that one room?—as she evidently did want to—and prevent her from moving freely about the house? An unfortunate doubt got possession of her—was there a gentleman in the house after all; and, for some reason or other, keeping himself concealed? Unfortunate, because it was to bear unpleasant fruit.

"Be whipped if it is not the most likely solution o' the matter I've thought of yet!" cried she, striking her hand on the tall fender. "But how do he manage to hide himself from Ann Hopley?—and how do he get his victuals? Sure-*ly* she can't have been deceiving me—and as good as taking oaths to an untruth! She'd not be so wicked."

From that time Mrs. Chaffen looked curiously about her, poking and peering around whenever she had the opportunity. One morning in particular, when Mrs. Grey was asleep, and she saw Ann go out to answer the bell, and Hopley was safe at the end of the garden, for she could hear him rolling the path there, Mrs. Chaffen made use of the occasion. She went along the passage to the door where the gentleman had disappeared, and found herself in a dull sitting-room wainscoted with mahogany, its wide, modern window looking to the maze. Keenly Mrs. Chaffen's eyes darted about the room: but there was no other outlet that she could see. The dark panelling went from the door to the window, and from the window round to the door again. After that, she made her way into the small angular passages that the house seemed to abound in: two of them were bedrooms with the beds made up, the others seemed to be out of use. None of them were locked; the doors of most of them stood open; but certainly in not one of them was there any trace of a hidden gentleman.

That same day, when she had finished her dinner, brought up to her as usual, she hastily put the things together on the tray and darted off with it down stairs. Mrs. Grey feebly called to her: but the nurse, conveniently deaf, went on without hearing. The staircase was angular, the turnings were short, and Mrs. Chaffen, as she went through the last one, gave the tray an inadvertent knock against the wall. Its plates rattled, its glasses jingled, betraying their approach: and—if ever she had heard a bolt slipped in her life, she felt sure she heard one slipped inside the kitchen-door.

"It's me, Mrs. Hopley, with the tray," she called out, going boldly on. "Open the door."

No answer. No signs of being heard. Everything seemed perfectly still. Mrs. Chaffen managed to lodge the tray against the door-post and hold it steady with one hand, while she tried the door with the other. But she could not open it.

"Mrs. Hopley, it's me with the tray. Please open."

It was opened then. Ann Hopley flung it wide, and stood there staring, a saucepan in her hand. "What! have you brought the things down!" she exclaimed in a voice of surprise. "Why on earth couldn't you have let them be till I came up?"

The nurse carried her tray onwards, and put it on the board under the window. At the table, not having been polite enough to his wife to take off his flapping straw hat in her presence, sat the gardener, munching his dinner as toothless people best can, his back to the light.

"Why did you keep me waiting at the door?" asked the nurse, not pleased.

"Did you wait?" returned Ann Hopley. "I was in the back place there, washing out the saucepans. You might have come in without knocking."

"The door was bolted."

"The door bolted!—not it," disputed Ann. "The latch has got a nasty trick of catching, though."

"This is fine weather, Mr. Hopley!" said the nurse, leaving the point uncontested, and raising her voice.

He seemed to be, as Ann had formerly expressed it, as deaf as a post. Neither turning his head nor answering, but keeping on at his dinner. Ann bent her head to his ear.

"The nurse, Mrs. Chaffen, spoke to you, Hopley. She says what fine weather it is."

"Ay, ay, ma'am," said he; "fine and bright."

What more might have passed was stopped by the ringing of Mrs. Grey's bell; a loud, long, impatient peal. The nurse turned to run.

"For pity's sake don't leave her again, Mrs. Chaffen!" called out Ann Hopley with some irritation. "If you do, I shall complain to Mr. Moore. You'll cause the fever to return."

"I could be upon my oath that she slipped the bolt to keep me out," thought the nurse, hurrying along. "Drat the cross-grained woman! Does she fear I shall poison her kitchen?"

CHAPTER XVII.

WATCHING THE HOUSE.

MRS. JINKS's new lodger, Mr. Strange, was making himself at home, not only at Mrs. Jinks's, but in the village generally, and gradually getting familiar with its stories and its politics. Talking with the men at the station one hour, chatting to the field labourers the next; stepping into the shops to buy tobacco, or paper, or lozenges, or what not, and staying a good twenty minutes before he came out again: Mr. Strange was ingratiating himself with the local world.

But, though he gossiped freely enough without doors and with Mrs. Jinks within, he did not appear anxious to cultivate intimacy with the social sphere; but rather avoided it. The Rev. Mr. Cattacomb, relying on the information that the new lodger was a gentleman reading for Oxford, had taken the initiative and made an advance to acquaintanceship. Mr. Strange, while receiving it with perfect civility, intimated that he was obliged to decline it. His health, he said, left him no alternative, and he had come to the country for entire quiet. As to his reading for Oxford, it was a mistake, he hinted. He was reading; but not with a view of going to any college. After that, the gentlemen bowed when they chanced to meet in the passages or out of doors, exchanged perhaps a remark on the fine weather; and there it ended.

The reader has not failed to detect that this "Mr. Strange," the name caught up so erroneously by Mrs. Jinks, was in reality the shrewd detective officer sent down by Scotland Yard in search of Philip Salter. His instructions were, not to hurry matters to an abrupt conclusion and so miss his game, but to track out Salter patiently and prudently. A case on which he had been recently engaged *had* been hurried and lost. Circumstances connected with it had caused him to lose sight of his usual prudence: he thought he was justified in doing what he did, and acted for the best: but the result proved him to have been wrong. No fear, with this failure on his mind, and the caution of his masters in his ears, that he would be in over much hurry now. In point of fact he could not if he would, for there was nothing to make hurry over.

For some time not a trace of any kind could Mr. Strange find of Philip Salter. People with whom he gossiped talked to him without any reserve; he was sure of that; and he would artfully lead the conversation and twist it the way he pleased; but he could hear nothing of any one likely to be Salter. The man might as well never have been within a hundred miles of Foxwood; for the matter of that, he might as well never have had existence, for all the trace there was left of him. Scotland Yard, however, was sure that Salter was to be found not far off, and that was enough: Mr. Strange, individually, felt sure of it also.

Knowing what he had been told of the visits of Sir Karl Andinnian to Detective Burtenshaw, and their object, Mr. Strange's attention was especially directed to Foxwood Court. Before he had been three days in the village, he had won the heart of Giles the footman (much at liberty just then, through the temporary absence of his master and mistress) and treated him to five glasses of best ale at different times in different public-houses. Giles, knowing no reason for reticence, freely described all he knew about Foxwood Court: the number of inmates, their names, their duties, their persons, and all the rest of it. Not the least idea penetrated his brain that his gentleman friend had any motive for listening to the details, save the whiling away of some of the day's idle hours. There was certainly no one at the Court that could be at all identified with the missing man; and, so far, Mr. Strange had lost his time, and his money paid for ale. Of course he put questions as to Sir Karl's movements—where he went to in the day, what calls he made, and what he did. But Giles could give no information that was available. Happily, he was ignorant of his master's visits to the Maze.

In short—from what Mr. Strange could gather from Giles and others, there was no one whatever in or about Foxwood, then or in time past, that at all answered to Philip Salter. He heard Mr. Smith spoken of—"Smith, the agent, an old friend of the Andinnian family"—but it did not once occur to him to attempt to identify him with the criminal. Smith the agent (whom, by the way, Mr. Strange had not chanced yet to see) was living openly in the place, going about amid the tenants on the estate, appearing at church, altogether transacting his business and pursuing his course without concealment: that is not how Salter would have dared to live, and the detective did not give Smith a suspicious thought. No: wherever Salter might be, he was evidently in strict concealment: and it must be Mr. Strange's business to hunt him out of it.

In the meantime, no speculation whatever had been aroused in the village as to Mr. Strange himself. He had taken care to account for his stay there at the first onset, and so people's minds were at rest. The gentleman in delicate health was free to come and go; his appearance in the street, or roads, or fields, excited no more conjecture or observation than did that of the oldest inhabitant. The Reverend Mr. Cattacomb was stared at whenever he appeared, in consequence of the proceedings of St. Jerome's: Mr. Strange passed along in peace.

Still, he learnt nothing. Sir Karl and Lady Andinnian had returned home long and long ago; he often saw them out (though he took care they should not see him), together or separately as might be, Sir Karl sometimes driving her in a beautiful little pony-chaise: but he could learn no trace of the man he was sent after. Sir Karl heard that some young student was in the village, out of health and reading for Oxford; he somehow caught up the notion that it was only a lad, and as he never chanced to see him, thought no more of him. And whether Mr. Strange might not have thrown up the game in a short time for utter lack of scent, cannot be told. A clue—or what he thought a clue—arose at last.

It arose, too, out of a slight misfortune that happened to himself. Entering the house one evening at dusk, before the passage lamp was lighted, he chanced to put his foot into a tray of wine-glasses, that the young maid had incautiously placed on the floor outside the parlour-door. In trying to start back and save the glasses, Mr. Strange slipped, went down with his right hand upon the tray, broke a glass or two, and cut his hand in three or four places. Miss Blake was there at the time, helping to catechise some young children: she felt really sorry for the mishap, and kindly went upstairs to the drawing-room to see its extent. The hand was in a bowl of warm water, and Mrs. Jinks was searching for linen to bind it up.

"Why do you put it into warm water, Mr. Strange?" Miss Blake asked; "it will make it bleed all the more."

"Some bits of glass may have got in," he replied.

"Will you have Mr. Moore?"

But he laughed at the notion of sending for a doctor to cut fingers, and he bound up the hand himself, saying it would be all right. The next day, in the afternoon, Miss Blake made her appearance in his room to inquire how the damage was progressing, and found Mrs. Jinks in the act of assisting him to dress it with some precious ointment that she vowed was better than gold, and would not fail to heal the cuts in a day or two.

Miss Blake had previously a speaking acquaintanceship with Mr. Strange, having often met him going in and out. She sat down; and the three were chatting amicably, when they were pounced in upon by little Mrs. Chaffen. Happening to call in to see her cousin, and hearing from the maid downstairs what Mrs. Jinks was then engaged upon—dressing the gentleman's hand—the nurse ran up to offer her more experienced services.

She took the hand out of Mrs. Jinks's into her own, and dressed it and bound it up as well as Mr. Moore himself could have done. It was nearly over when, by a curious coincidence—curious, considering what was to come of it—the conversation turned upon *ghosts*. Upon ghosts, of all things in the world! Some noise had been heard in the house the previous night by all the inmates—which noise had not been in any way accounted for. It was like the falling down of a piece of heavy furniture. It had awakened Mr. Cattacomb; it had awakened Mrs. Jinks; it had startled Mr. Strange, who was not asleep. The history of this was being given to Miss Blake, Mr. Strange gravely asserting it could have been nothing but a ghost—and that set Mrs. Chaffen on. She proceeded to tell them with real gravity, not assumed, that she did believe a ghost in the shape of a gentleman in dinner dress, haunted the Maze: or else that her eyes were taking to see visions.

It should be mentioned that after a week's attendance on Mrs. Grey, Nurse Chaffen had been discharged. The patient was then going on quite well: and, as Mr. Moore saw that it worried her to have the nurse there—for whom she seemed to have conceived an insurmountable dislike—he took her away. The summary dismissal did not please the nurse: and she revenged herself by reporting that the Maze had a ghost in it. As a rule, people laughed at her and thought no more about it: this afternoon her tale was to bear different fruit.

She told it consecutively. How she had been quite flurried by being called out by Dr. Moore all on a sudden; how he had taken her straight off to the Maze without saying where it was she was going till she got to the gate; how she and the doctor had seen the gentleman at the top of the stairs (which she took it to be the sick lady's husband), and watched him vanish into an end room, and had never seen the least sign of him afterwards; how the servant, Mrs. Hopley, had vowed through thick and thin that no gentleman was, or had been, or could have been in the house, unbeknown to her and Hopley.

Nurse Chaffen talked away to her heart's content, enlarging upon points of her story. Not one of them interrupted her: not one but would have listened with interest had she run on until midnight. Mrs. Jinks from her love of marvellous tales; the detective because he believed this might be the clue he wanted to Philip Salter; and Miss Blake in her resentful condemnation of Sir Karl Andinnian. For, that the "gentleman in dinner dress" was no other than Sir Karl, who had stolen in on one of his secret visits, she could have staked her life upon.

"A tall gentleman with dark hair, you say it looked like?" questioned Mr. Strange, indifferently.

"Tall, for certain, sir. As to his hair, I don't know; it might have been darkish. I see he had nice white teeth."

"Salter had good teeth," was the mental comment of the detective. "*I have found him.*"

"And in dinner dress?" added Miss Blake with a cough.

"So it looked like, ma'am. The sort of coat that gentlefolks wears in an evening."

"And you mean to say you never see him after; never but that there one time?" tartly interposed the Widow Jinks.

"Never at all. The rooms was all open to daylight while I was there, but he wasn't in never a one of 'em."

"Then I tell you what, Betsey Chaffen; it was a ghost, and you need not hesitate to stand to it."

"Well, you see, he didn't look like a ghost, but like an ordinary gentleman," confessed Mrs. Chaffen. "What came over me, and what I can't make out, was Ann Hopley's standing it out that neither ghost nor gentleman was there: she said she'd take her oath to it."

"Thank you, you've done my hand up beautifully, Mrs. Chaffen," said the patient. "I should give my credence to the spirit theory. Did Mr. Moore see the appearance of this ghostly gentleman?"

"Yes he did, sir. I'm sure he did. For he lifted his head, like, at the gentleman, and stood still when he got to the top of the stairs, staring at the room he had vanished into. I told him a day or two afterwards that Mrs. Hopley denied that any one had been there, and the doctor quietly said, 'Then we must have been mistaken.' I did not like to ask whether he thought it was a ghost."

"Oh, I think you may depend upon the ghost," returned Mr. Strange, biting his lips to prevent a laugh.

"Well, sir, queer stories was told of that Maze house in the late tenant's time. My cousin Jinks here knows that well enough."

"It was haunted by more than one ghost then, if all folks told true," assented Mrs. Jinks. "Mr. Throckton's son—a wild young blade he was—hung hisself there. I was but a girl at the time."

"Ah, one of the old ghosts come back again; not been laid yet," solemnly remarked the detective, staring at Mrs. Chaffen. "Did the lady herself seem alarmed?"

"Well, sir, I can't say she did then, because she couldn't have seen it, and was too ill besides. But she had got a curious manner with her."

"Curious?" questioned Mr. Strange.

"Yes, sir, curious. As if she was always frightened. When everything was as still as still could be, she'd seem to be listening like, as though expecting to hear something. Now and then she'd start up in bed in a fright, and cry out What was that?—when there had been no noise at all."

"Feverish fancies," quietly remarked Mr. Strange, with a cough.

By-and-by, the party separated. As Nurse Chaffen was descending to the kitchen, leaving Mrs. Jinks putting the room straight, Miss Blake, who had gone down first, put forth her hand and drew the nurse into Mr. Cattacomb's parlour; that reverend man being absent on some of his pastoral calls.

"I have been *so much* interested in this that you have been telling us, nurse," she breathed. "It seems quite to have taken hold of me. What was the gentleman like? Did he resemble any one you know—Sir Karl Andinnian, for instance?"

"Why, ma'am, how can I tell who he resembled?—I didn't get enough look at him for that," was the answer. "I saw his head and the tails of his coat when he turned—and that was all. Except his teeth: I did see them."

"And they were white teeth—good teeth?"

"Oh, beauties. White and even as a die."

"Sir Karl's teeth are white and even," nodded Miss Blake to herself. "Had Mrs. Grey any visitors while you were there, nurse?"

"Never a one. Never a soul came inside the gates, good or bad, but the doctor. I don't fancy the lady has made friends in the place at all, ma'am. She likes to keep herself to herself, Ann Hopley thinks, while Mr. Grey's away."

"Oh, naturally," said Miss Blake. And she dismissed the woman.

The Widow Jinks had a surprise that night. Mr. Strange, hitherto so quiet and well conducted asked for the latch-key! She could not forbear a caution as she gave it him: not to stay out too late on account of his health. He laughed pleasantly in answer; saying he expected a friend down by the last train from London, and might stay out late with him.

But he never went near the station, and he met no friend. Keeping as much in the shades of night as the very bright moon allowed him to do, Mr. Strange arrived by a circuitous way at the gate of the Maze, and let himself in with a master-key.

"The dolt I was, never to have suspected this shut-in

place before!" he exclaimed. "Salter is lying here in concealment: there can be no doubt of it: and, if his career's at an end, he may thank his own folly in having allowed himself to be seen by the woman, Chaffen. Wonder who the sick lady is? Perhaps his wife: perhaps not. And now—how to get through this maze that they talk of? Knowing something of mazes, I daresay I shall accomplish it without trouble."

And he did. His keen intelligence, sharpened no doubt by experience, enabled him, if not to hit upon the clue, at least to get through the maze. A small compass was hanging to his watch-guard, and he lighted a match frequently to consult it. So he got through. He regarded the house from all points; he penetrated to the outer path or circle, and went round and round it: he made, so to say, the outer premises his own. Then he went through the maze to reconnoitre the house again.

It lay quiet, steeped in the moonlight. He stood at the back of the lawn, against the laurel trees that skirted the flower-beds, and gazed at it. In one of the rooms a night-light was burning faintly, and he fancied he could hear the continuous wail of an infant. To make sure whether it was so, or not—though in truth it mattered not to him, and was a very probable thing to happen—he stood forward a little on the lawn: but as that brought him into the moonlight, he retreated into the shade again. Most of the windows had blinds or curtains drawn before them: the only one that had none was the casement over the portico. Mr. Strange stood there as if rooted to the spot, making his silent observations.

"Yes; this is where my gentleman is lying concealed, safe enough—safe enough as *he* thinks. There may be some difficulty in as safely unearthing him. He'd not dare to be here without facilities for guarding against surprise and for getting away on the first sound of the alarm bugle. This is a queer old house: there may be all kinds of hiding-places in it. I must go to work cautiously, and it may be a long job. Suppose I look again to the door fastenings?"

The moon was beginning to wane when the detective officer with his false key got out again; and he thought he had his work tolerably well cut out to his hand.

The faint wailing had not been fancy. For the first week or two of the child's life it had seemed to thrive well, small though it was; but, after that, it began to be a little delicate, and would sometimes wail as though in pain. On this night the child—who slept with its mother—woke up and began its wail. Ann Hopley, whom the slightest noise awoke, hearing that her mistress did not seem able to soothe it, left her own bed to try and do so. Presently, in going to fetch some medicine-cordial for the child, she had to pass the casement window in the passage; the one that was uncurtained. The exceeding beauty of the night struck her, and she paused to look out upon it, the old black shawl she had thrown on being drawn closely round her. The grass shone in the moonlight; the leaves of the laurels flickered white in its rays. At that self-same moment, as the woman looked, some movement directed her attention to these very laurels: and to her utter horror she thought she saw a man standing there, apparently watching the house.

The sickness of intense fear seized upon her as she drew aside—but the black shawl and the small diamond panes of the casement window had prevented her from being observed. Yes: she was not mistaken. The man came forth for an instant into the moonlight, and then went back again. Ann Hopley's fear turned her heart to sickness. Her first impulse was to rush on through the passages and arouse Sir Adam Andinnian. Her second impulse was to wait and watch. She remembered her master's most dangerous fiery temperament, and the pistols he kept always loaded. This intruding man might be but some wretched night marauder, who had stolen in after the fruit. Watching there, she saw him presently go round in the direction of the fruit-trees, and concluded that her surmise was correct.

So she held her tongue to her master and mistress. The latter she would not alarm; the former she dared not, lest another night Sir Adam should take up his stand at the window, pistol in hand. Two things puzzled her the next morning: the one was, how the man could have got in; the other, that neither fruit nor flowers seemed to have been taken.

That same day, upon going to the gate to answer a ring, she found herself confronted by a strange gentleman, who said he had called from hearing the house was to let, and he wished to look at it. Ann Hopley thought this rather strange. She assured him it was a mistake: that the house was not to let: that Mrs. Grey had no intention of leaving. When he pressed to go in and just look at the house, " in case it should be to let later," she persisted in denying him admittance, urging her mistress's present sick state as a reason for keeping out all visitors.

"Is Mr. Grey still at home?" then asked the applicant.

"Mr. Grey has not been at home," replied Ann Hopley. "My mistress is alone."

"Oh, indeed! Not been here at all?"

"No, sir. I don't know how soon he may be coming. He is abroad on his travels."

"What gentleman is it, then, who has been staying here lately?"

Ann Hopley felt inwardly all of a twitter. Outwardly she was quietly self-possessed.

"No gentleman has been here at all, sir. You must be mistaking the house for some other one, I think. This is the Maze."

"A lady and gentleman and two servants, I understand, are living here."

"It is quite a mistake, sir. My mistress and us two servants live here—me and my husband—but that's all. Mr. Grey has not been here since we came to the place."

"Now that's a disappointment to me," cried the stranger. "I have lost sight of a friend of mine, named Grey, for the past year or two, and was hoping I might find him here. You are sure you don't know when Mr. Grey may be expected?"

"Quite sure, sir. My mistress does not know, herself."

The stranger stepped back from the gate to take his departure. In manner he was a very pleasant man, and his questions had been put with easy courtesy.

"And you are equally sure the house is not about to be vacated?"

"I feel sure of this much—that if Mrs. Grey had thoughts of vacating it, she would have informed me. But, in regard to any point connected with the house, sir, you had better apply to the landlord, Sir Karl Andinnian."

"Thank you; yes, that may be the best plan. Good morning," he added, taking off his hat with something of French civility.

"Don't think she is to be bribed," thought he as he walked away. "At least not easily. Perhaps I may in time work my way on to it."

Ann Hopley, locking the gate with double strength—at least, in imagination—pushed through the maze without well knowing whether she was on her head or her heels, so entirely had terror overtaken her. In the height and shape of this man, who had been thus questioning her, she fancied she traced a resemblance to the one who was watching the house in the night. What if they were the same?

"The end is coming!" she murmured, clasping her faithful hands. "As sure as my poor master is alive, the end is coming."

Not to her master or to his wife, but to Karl Andinnian, did she impart all this. It happened that Karl went over to the Maze that evening. Ann Hopley followed him out when he departed, and told him of it amidst the trees.

It startled him in a more painful degree even than it had startled her: for, oh, what were her interests in the matter as compared with his?

"Inside the grounds!—watching the house at night!" he repeated.

"Indeed he was, sir!"

"But who is it?"

"I don't know," said Ann. "I hoped it was only some thief who had come after the fruit: I thought he might have got over from the fields by means of a high ladder. That would have been nothing. But if the man who came to the gate to-day is the same man, it must mean mischief."

"You have not told my brother?"

"How could I dare to tell him, sir He might watch for the man; and, if he came another night, shoot him. That would make things worse."

"With a vengeance," thought Karl. What was there to do? What could he do? Karl Andinnian went out, the question beating itself into his brain. Why, there seemed nothing for it but to wait and watch. He took off his hat and raised his bared head to the summer sky, in which some stars were twinkling, wishing he was there, in that blessed heaven above, where no pain can come. What with one tribulation and another, earth was growing for him a hard resting-place.

CHAPTER XXVIII.

AT AFTERNOON SERVICE.

THE still quietness of the Sabbath morning shed its peace over Foxwood. Within the Court of that name—where the lawns were green and level, and the sweet flowers exhaled their perfume, and a tree here and there was already putting on its autumn tints—the aspect of peace seemed to be more especially exhaled.

The windows of the rooms stood open. Inside one of them the breakfast was on the table yet, Miss Blake seated at it. Matins at St. Jerome's had been unusually prolonged; and Sir Karl and Lady Andinnian had taken breakfast when she got home. The Reverend Damon Puff had now come to help Mr. Cattacomb; imparting to St. Jerome's an additional attraction.

While Miss Blake took her breakfast, Lucy went out amidst her flowers. The scent of the mignonette filled the air, the scarlet of the geraniums made the beds brilliant. Lucy wore one of her simple muslin dresses; it had sprigs of green upon it—for the weather was still that of summer, though the season was not, and the nightingales were no longer heard of an evening. Trinity Church boasted a set of sweet-toned bells, and they were ringing on the air. When the Sacrament was administered—the first Sunday in each month—they generally did ring before service. This was the first Sunday in September. Lucy stooped to pick some mignonette as she listened to the bells. She was getting to look what she was—worn and unhappy. Nothing could be much less satisfactory than her life: it seemed to herself sometimes that she was like a poor flower withering for lack of sunshine. For the first time for several weeks she meant, that day, to stay for the after-service: her mind had really been in too great a chaos before: but this week she had been schooling herself in preparation for it, and praying and striving to feel tranquil.

Karl came round the terrace from his room and crossed the lawn. In his hand he held a most exquisite rose, and offered it to her. She thanked him as she took it. In manner they were always courteous to one another.

"What a lovely day it is!" she said. "So calm and still."

"And not quite so hot as it was a few weeks ago," he replied. "Those must be Mr. Sumnor's bells."

"Yes. I wish they rang every Sunday. I think—it may be all fancy, but I can't help thinking it—that people would go to church more heartily if the bells rang for them as they are ringing now, instead of calling them with the usual ding-dong."

"There is something melancholy in the ringing of bells," observed Karl, in abstraction.

"But, when the heart is in itself melancholy, the melancholy of the bells brings to it a feeling of soothing consolation," was Lucy's hasty answer. And the next moment she felt sorry that she had said it. Never, willingly, did she allude to aught that could touch on their estrangement.

"Talking of church, Lucy," resumed Karl, in a different and almost confidential tone, "I am beginning to feel really annoyed about that place, St. Jerome's. They are going too far. I wish you would speak a word of caution to Theresa."

"I—I scarcely like to," answered Lucy, after a pause, her delicate cheek faintly flushing, for she was conscious that she had not dared to talk much on any score with Theresa lately, lest Theresa might allude to the subject of the Maze. Fearing that, she avoided her when she could, so as to give no opportunity for private conversation. "She is so much older and wiser than I am——"

"Wiser?" interrupted Karl. "I think not. In all things, save one, you have ten times the good plain sense that she has. That one thing, Lucy, I shall never be able to understand, or account for, to my dying day."

"And, moreover, I was going to add," continued Lucy, flushing deeper at the allusion, "I am quite sure that Theresa would not heed me, whatever I might say."

"Well, I don't know what is to be done. People are mocking at St. Jerome's and its frequenters' folly more than I care to hear, and blame me for allowing it to go on. I should not like to be written to by the Bishop of the Diocese."

"*You* written to!" cried Lucy in surprise.

"It is within the range of possibility. The place is on the Andinnian land."

"I think, were I you, I would speak to Mr. Cattacomb."

Karl made a wry face. He did not like the man. Moreover he fancied—as did Lucy in regard to Miss Blake—that whatever he might say would make no impression. But for this, he had spoken to him before. But now that another was come and the folly was being doubled, it ay in his duty to remonstrate. The whole village gossiped and laughed; Sir Adam was furious. Ann Hopley carried the gossip home to her master—which, of course, lost nothing in the transit—and he abused Karl for not interfering.

They went to church together, Karl and his wife. It was a thinner congregation than ordinary. Being a grand field-day at St. Jerome's, with procession and banners, some of them had gone off thither as to a show. Kneeling by her husband's side in their pew, Lucy felt the influence of the holy place, and peace seemed to steal down upon her. Margaret Sumnor was opposite, looking at her: and in Margaret's face there was a strange, pitying compassion, for she saw that that other face was becoming sadder day by day.

It was a plain, good sermon: Mr. Sumnor's sermons always were: its subject the blessings promised for the next world; its text, "And God shall wipe away all tears from their eyes." The tears rose to Lucy's eyes as she listened. Karl listened too, wrapt in the words. Just for the quarter of an hour it lasted—the sermons were always short the first Sunday in the month—both of them seemed to have passed beyond their cares into Heaven. It almost seemed to matter little what the trouble of this short span on earth might be, with that glorious fruition to come hereafter.

"I am going to stay," whispered Lucy, as the service ended. A hint to her husband that he might depart without her.

Karl nodded, but made no other answer. The congregation filed out, and still he sat on. Lucy wondered. All in a moment it flashed upon her that he also must be going to stay. Her face turned crimson: the question, was he fit for it, involuntarily suggested itself.

He did stay. They knelt side by side together and received the elements of Christ's holy Ordinance. After that Karl was on his knees in his pew until the end, buried, as it seemed, in beseeching prayer. It was impossible for Lucy to believe that he could be living an ill life of any kind at that present time —whatever he might have done.

He held out his arm as they quitted the church, and she took it. It was not often that she did. Thus they walked home together, exchanging a sentence or two between whiles. Karl went at once to his room, saying he should not take anything to eat: he had a headache. Miss Blake had "snatched a morsel," and had gone out again to hear the children's catechism, Hewitt said. One thing must be conceded—that she was zealous in her duties.

And so, Lucy was alone. She took a "morsel" too, and went to sit under the acacia tree. When an hour or so had passed, Karl came up, and surprised her with tears on her cheeks.

"Is it any new grief?" he asked.

"No," she answered, half lost in the sorrow her thoughts had been abandoned to, and neglecting her usual reticence. "I was but thinking that I am full young to have so much unhappiness."

"We both have enough of that, I expect. I know I have. But yours is partly of your own making, Lucy: mine is not."

"Not of his own making!" ran her thoughts. "Of his own planning, at any rate." But she would not say a word to mar the semi-peace which pervaded, or ought to pervade their hearts that day.

"That was a nice sermon this morning," he resumed, sitting down by her on the bench.

"Very. I almost forgot that we were not close to Heaven: I forgot that we had, speaking according to earth's probabilities, years and years and years to live out here first."

"We shall have to live them out, Lucy, I suppose—by Heaven's will. The prospect of it looks anything but consolatory."

"I thought you seemed very sad," she remarked in a low tone. "I had no idea you were going to stay."

"*Sad?*"

He laid his hand upon her knee, not in any particular affection, but to give emphasis to his word. "Sad is not the term for it, Lucy. Misery, rather; dread; despair—the worst word you will. I wished, with a yearning wish, that I was in Mr. Sumnor's heaven—the heaven he described—if only some others could go before me, so that I did not leave them here."

Lucy wondered of whom he spoke. She thought it must lie between herself and Mrs. Grey. Karl had been thinking of his poor proscribed brother, for whom the glad earth could never open her arms freely again.

"I think what Mr. Sumnor said must be true," resumed Lucy. "That the more sorrow we have to endure in this world, the brighter will be our entrance to the next. I am sure he has a great deal of sorrow himself: whenever he preaches of it he seems to feel it so deeply."

Karl appeared not to hear. He was gazing upwards, a look of patient pain on his pale face. There were moments—and this was one—when Lucy's arms and heart alike yearned to encircle him and ask for his love to be hers again. She cared for him still—oh, how much!—and wished she could awake to find the Maze, and all the trouble connected with it, a hideous dream.

They sat on, saying nothing. The birds sang as in spring, the trees waved gently beneath the blue sky, and the green grass was grateful for the eye to rest upon. On the handsome house lay the glad sun: not a sound of every-day labour, indoors or out, broke the stillness. All was essentially peace. Except—except within their own wearied breasts.

The bell of Trinity Church rang out for service, arousing Lucy from her reverie. She said she should like to attend it.

"What! this afternoon?" exclaimed Karl. "You are not accustomed to go in the afternoon."

That was true. The heat of the summer weather had been almost unbearable, and Lucy had not ventured to church in it more than once a day.

"It is cooler now," she answered. "And I always like to go, if I can, when I have stayed for the communion."

But Karl held back from it: rather, Lucy thought, in an unaccountable manner, for he was ever ready to second any wish of hers. He did not seem inclined to go forth again, and said, as a plea of excuse, that he preferred to retain the impression of the morning's sermon on his mind, rather than let it give place to an inferior one. His head was aching badly.

"I do not ask you to come," said Lucy, gently. "I should like to go myself, but I can go quite well alone."

"When she came down with her things on, however, she found him ready also; and they set off together.

It may be questioned, though, whether Lucy would have gone, had she foreseen what was to happen. In the middle of the service, while the "Magnificat" was being sung, a respectable, staid woman entered the church with an infant in her arms. A beautifully dressed infant. Its long white robe was elaborately embroidered, its delicate blue cloak was of surpassing richness, its veil of lace was fine and dainty as a gossamer thread. The attire, not often seen at Foxwood, caught Lucy's eye, and she wondered who the infant was. It seemed to her that she had seen the nurse's face before, and began to ransack her memory. In an instant it flashed on her with a shock—it was the servant at the Maze.

She turned her eyes on her husband: not intentionally, but in an uncontrollable impulse. Karl was looking furtively at the woman and child—a red flush dyeing his face. Poor Lucy's benefit in the afternoon service was over.

The baby had come to be baptised. Ann Hopley sat down on a bench to which she was shown, just underneath the Andinnian pew. Towards the close of the second lesson, the clerk advanced to her, and entered on a whispered colloquy. Every word of which was distinct to Karl and Lucy.

"Have you brought this infant to be christened?"

"To be baptised," replied Ann Hopley. "Not christened."

The clerk paused. "It's not usual with us to baptise children unless they are so delicate as to render it necessary," said he. "We prefer to christen at once."

"But this child is delicate," she answered. "My mistress, who is herself still very ill, has got nervous about it and wishes it to be done. The christening must be left until she is better."

"It's the baby at the Maze, I think?"

"Yes. Mrs. Grey's."

The second lesson came to an end. Mr. Sumnor's voice ceased, and he stepped out of the reading-desk to perform the baptism. Ann Hopley had drawn away the veil, and Lucy saw the child face; a fair, sweet, delicate little face, calm and placid in its sleep.

The congregation, a very small one always in the afternoon, rose up and stood on tiptoe to see and hear. Mr. Sumnor, standing at the font, took the child in his arms.

"Name this child."

"Charles," was the audible and distinct reply of Ann Hopley. And Lucy Andinnian turned red and white; she thought it was, so to say, named after her husband. As indeed was the case.

The child was brought back to the bench again; and the afternoon service went on to its close. There was no sermon. When Lucy rose from her knees, the woman and baby had gone. Karl offered her his arm as they quitted the church, but she would not take it. They walked home side by side, saying never a word to each other.

"*That* was the reason why he wanted to keep me away from church this afternoon!" was Lucy's indignant thought. "And to dress it up like that! How, how, shall I go on, and bear?"

But Lucy was mistaken. Karl had known no more about it than she, and was struck with astonishment to see Ann Hopley come in. It arose exactly as the woman had stated. During the night the child had seemed so ill that its mother had become nervously uneasy because it was not baptised, and insisted upon its being brought to church that afternoon.

Meanwhile Ann Hopley had hurried homewards. Partly to get out before the rest and avoid observation, partly because she wanted to be back with her mistress. After passing the Court gates, in traversing the short space of road between them and the Maze, she encountered Miss Blake coming home from St. Jerome's. Miss Blake, seeing a baby sumptuously attired, and not at the moment recognizing Ann Hopley in her bonnet, crossed the road to inquire whose child it was. Then she saw it was the servant at the Maze: but she stopped all the same.

"I should like to take a peep at the baby, nurse."

"It's asleep, ma'am, and I am in a hurry," was the answer, given in all truthfulness, not in discourtesy; for it must be remembered that Ann Hopley had no grounds to suspect that this lady took any special interest in affairs at the Maze. "It slept all through its baptism."

"Oh, it has been baptised, has it! At Mr. Sumnor's church?"

"Yes, at Mr. Sumnor's. There is no other church in the place but that," added the woman, totally ignoring St. Jerome's, but not thinking to give offence thereby.

Miss Blake put aside the lace and looked at the sleeping baby. "What is its name, nurse?"

"Charles."

"Oh," said Miss Blake, the same notion striking her, as to the name, that had struck Lucy. "It is Mr. Grey's name, I suppose—or something like it."

"No, it is not Mr. Grey's name," replied the woman.

"Who is the baby considered like?" went on Miss Blake, still regarding it. "Its father or its mother?"

"It's not much like anybody that I see, ma'am. The child's too young to show any likeness yet."

"I declare that I see a likeness to Sir Karl Andinnian," cried Miss Blake, speaking partly upon impulse. For, in looking whether she could trace this likeness, her fancy seemed to show her that it was there. "What a strange thing, nurse!"

With one startled gaze into Miss Blake's eyes, Ann Hopley went off in a huff. The suggestion had not been palatable.

"If he's like Sir Karl, I must never bring him abroad again, lest by that means suspicion should come to my master," she thought, as she took the gate key from her pocket and let herself in. "But I don't believe it can be: for I'm sure there's not a bit of resemblance between the two brothers."

"How plain it all is!" sighed Miss Blake, meekly regarding the cross upon her ivory prayer-book as she went over to the Court. "And that ridiculously simple Lucy does not see it! Bartimeus was blind, and so is she. He could see nothing until his eyes were opened: her eyes have been opened and yet she will not see!"

No, Miss Blake, neither could the self-righteous Pharisee see, when he went into the Temple to thank God that he was better than other men, and especially than the poor publican.

St. Jerome's was prospering. It had taken—as Tom Pepp the bell-ringer phrased it—a spurt. A rich maiden lady of uncertain age, fascinated by the Rev. Guy Cattacomb's oratory and spectacles, came over once a day in her brougham from Basham, and always put a substantial coin into the offertory-bag during the service.

The Reverend Damon Puff found favour too. He had a beautiful black moustache, which he was given to stroke lovingly at all kinds of unseasonable times, his hair was parted down the middle carefully, back and front, and he had an interesting lisp: otherwise he was a harmless kind of young man, devotedly attentive to the ladies, and not over-burdened with brains. Mr. Puff had taken up his abode for the present at Basham, and came over in the omnibus. Two omnibus-loads of fair worshippers arrived now daily: there was frightful scuffling among them to get into the one that contained the parson.

But, flourishing though St. Jerome's was, people were talking about it in anything but a reverend manner. Sir Karl Andinnian was blamed for allowing it to go on unchecked —as he told his wife. Had Karl been a perfectly free man, unswayed by that inward and ever-present dread, he had certainly put a stop to it long ago, or obliged Farmer Truefit to do so; but as it was, he had done nothing. Not a single male person attended the services; and most of the ladies who did so were in their teens, or not much beyond them. Karl felt that this was not as it should be: but he had made no move to alter it. The sensitive fear of making enemies swayed him. Not fear for his own sake, but lest it should in some way draw observation on the Maze and on him whom it contained. When the mind is weighed down with an awful secret, danger seems to lie in every approach, reasonable and unreasonable. But Karl found he must do something.

A comic incident happened one day. There came a lady to Foxwood Court, sending in her card as "Mrs. Brown" and asking to see Sir Karl Andinnian. Sir Karl found she was from Basham. She had come over to pray him, she said with tears in her eyes, that he would put a stop to the goings-on at St. Jerome's and shut up the place. She had two daughters who had been drawn into its vortex and she could not draw them out again. Twice and three times every day of their lives did they come over to Foxwood, by rail, omnibus, or on foot; their whole thoughts and days were absorbed by St. Jerome's: by the services, by cleaning the church, by Mr. Cattacomb's lectures at home, or in helping Mr. Puff teach the children. Sir Karl replied that he did not know what he could do in the matter, and intimated very courteously that the more effectual remedy in regard to the Miss Browns would be for Mrs. Brown to keep the young ladies at home. They would not be kept at home, Mrs. Brown said, with a burst of sobs; they had learnt to set her at defiance: and—she begged to hint to Sir Karl—that in her opinion it was not quite the right thing for a young girl to be closeted with a young man for half an hour at a time, under plea of confession, though the man did write himself priest. What on earth had they got to confess, Mrs. Brown wanted to know, becoming a little heated with the argument: if they'd confess how undutiful they were to her, their mother, perhaps some good might come of it.

Well, this occurred. Sir Karl got rid of Mrs. Brown; but he could not shut his ears to the public chatter; and he was conscious that something or other ought to be done, or attempted. He could not see why people should expect that it lay in his hands, and he certainly did not know whether he could effect anything, even with all the good will in the world

Mr. Cattacomb might civilly laugh at him. Not knowing whether any power lay with him, or not, he felt inclined to put the question to the only lawyer Foxwood contained—Mr. St. Henry.

But oh, what was this petty grievance to the great trouble ever lying upon him? As nothing. The communication made to him by Ann Hopley, of the night watches she had seen, of the stranger who afterwards presented himself at the Maze gate with his questions, was so much addition to his tormenting dread. Just about this time, too, it came to his knowledge through Hewitt, that inquiries were being made as to the Maze. Private, whispered inquiries, not apparently with any particular object; more in the way of idle gossip. Who was putting them? Karl could not learn. Hewitt did not know who, but was sure of the fact. The story told by Mrs. Chaffen, of the gentleman she had seen at the Maze the night she entered it, and "which it was at her wits' end to know whether he were a ghost, or not," was circulating round the village and reached Karl's ears, to his intense annoyance and dismay. Added to all this, was the doubt that lay within himself, as to whether Smith the agent was Philip Salter, and what his course in the matter should be. In his own mind he felt persuaded that it was Salter, and no other; but the persuasion was scarcely sufficiently assured to induce him to act. He felt the danger of speaking a word of accusation to Smith wrongfully—the danger it might bring on his brother—and therefore he, in this, vacillated and hesitated, and did nothing.

Do not reproach Karl Andinnian with being an unstable or vacillating man. He was nothing of the kind. But he was living under exceptional circumstances, and there seemed to be risk to his unfortunate brother on the left hand and on the right. If discovery should chance to supervene through any rash step of his, Karl's, remorse would never cease from racking him to the end of his bitter life.

CHAPTER XXIX.

AT LAWYER ST. HENRY'S.

LAWYER ST. HENRY sat at his well-spread breakfast-table. He was a little man with a bald head and good-natured face, who enjoyed his breakfast as well as all his other meals. Since his nieces had considered it necessary to their spiritual welfare to attend matins at St. Jerome's the lawyer had been condemned to breakfast alone. The sun shone on the street, and Mr. St. Henry sat in a room that faced it. Through the wire blinds he could see all the passings and repassings of his neighbours; which he very well liked to do; as well as the doings of Paradise Row opposite.

"Hallo!" he cried, catching sight of a face at Mrs. Jinks's parlour window, "Cattacomb's not gone out this morning! Puff must have come over early to officiate. Thinks he'll take it easy, I suppose, now he's got an underling: no blame to him, either. The girls will be dished for once. Nobody goes down with 'em like Cattacomb."

Laughing a little at the thought, he helped himself to a portion of a tempting-looking cutlet surrounded with mushrooms. This being nearly despatched, he had leisure to look abroad again and make his mental comments.

"There goes the doctor: he's out early this morning. Going to see old Etheridge, perhaps: wonder how the old fellow is. And there's Mother Jinks taking in a sweetbread. Must be for the parson's breakfast. Sweetbreads are uncommonly good, too: I'll have one myself to-morrow morning if it can be got. Why, here comes Sir Karl Andinnian! *He* is out early, too. That young man looks to me as though he had some care upon him. It's a nice countenance; very: and if —I declare he is coming here! What on earth can he want?"

Sir Karl Andinnian was ringing the door-bell. It has been already said that the lawyer's offices were in Basham, for which place he generally started as soon as his breakfast was over. Therefore, if any client wished to see him at Foxwood, it had to be early in the morning or late in the evening. This was known and understood.

Sir Karl was shown in, Mr. St. Henry glancing at his breakfast-table and the three or four dirty plates upon it. He had finished now, and they sat down together at the window. Sir Karl, not to detain him unnecessarily, entered at once upon the question he had come to ask—Had he, or had he not, power to do anything with St. Jerome's? And the lawyer laughed a little; for St. Jerome's afforded him fun rather than otherwise.

"Of course, Sir Karl, if Truefit chose to warn them off the land, he could do it," was the lawyer's reply. "Not without notice, though, I think: I don't know what the agreement was. As to yourself—well, I am not clear whether you could do anything: I should like to see Truefit's lease before giving an opinion. But, if they were shut out of St. Jerome's to-day, they'd contrive to start another place to-morrow."

"That is quite likely," said Karl.

"My advice to you is this, Sir Karl: don't bother yourself about it," said the easy-going lawyer. "People expect you to interfere? Never mind that: let them expect. The thing will die away of itself when winter comes. Once the frost and snow set in, the girls, silly monkeys, won't go trapesing to St. Jerome's; neither will they come jinketing over by omnibusfuls from Basham. Wait and shut it up then. If you attempt to do it now, you will meet with wide opposition: by waiting, you may do it almost without any."

"You really think so!"

"I am nearly sure so," said the hearty lawyer. "There's nothing like bad weather for stopping expeditions of chivalry. But for having had the continuous sunshine the summer has given us, St. Jerome's would not have been the success it is."

"They have dressed Tom Pepp in a conical cap, and put a red cross all down his back outside," said Sir Karl.

The lawyer burst into a laugh. "*I* know," he said. "I hear of the vagaries from my nieces. It's fun for me. They go in for them wholesale, and come home with their heads full."

"But it's not religion, Mr. St. Henry."

"Bless me, no. Religion? The girls may give it that name; and perhaps one or two among them may be earnest enough in thinking it so; the rest are only after Cattacomb."

"There's another one now, I hear. One Puff."

"And a fine puff of wind *he* is. Got no more brains than a gander. I'll see Truefit and inquire what agreement it was he made with them, if you like, Sir Karl; but I should certainly recommend you to leave the matter alone a little longer."

Sir Karl thought he would accept the advice; and got up to leave. He often met Truefit on the land, and could take an opportunity of questioning him himself. As he stood for a moment at the window, there passed down the middle of the street a stranger, walking slowly; that is, a stranger to Karl. It was Mr. Strange.

Now it happened that Karl had never yet seen this man—at

least, he had never noticed him. For the detective, being warned by Grimley that Sir Karl had, or seemed to have, some reason for screening Salter—had kept himself out of Sir Karl's way. He thought it would not conduce at all to his success to let Sir Karl know he was down there on the scent. Therefore, whenever he had observed Sir Karl coming along —and he had kept his eyes sharply open—he had popped into a shop, or drawn behind a hedge, or got over a stile into another field. And Karl, in his mind's abstraction—for it nearly always was abstracted, lost in its own fear and pain— had not thought of looking out gratuitously for strangers. But, standing up at the lawyer's window, the street close before him, he could not fail to observe those who passed up and down: and his attention was at once drawn to this man.

"Who is that?" he asked.

"That! oh, that's a Mr. Strange," said the lawyer, laughing again—and in his laugh this time there was something significant. "At least, that's his name *here*."

"And not elsewhere?"

"I fancy not."

"Is he staying at Foxwood? What is he doing here?"

"He is certainly staying at Foxwood. As to his business, I conclude it is something in the private detective line, Sir Karl."

Mr. Strange, whose attention in passing had been directed to some matter on the other side of the way, and not to the lawyer's window, consequently he did not know that he was being watched, had halted a little lower down to speak to the landlord of the Red Lion. All in a moment, as Karl looked at him, the notion flashed into his mind that this man bore a strong resemblance to the description given by Ann Hopley of the man who had invaded the Maze. The notion came to him in the self-same moment that the words of the lawyer fell on his ears—"His business, I conclude, is something in the private detective line." What with the notion, and what with the words, Karl Andinnian fell into a confused inward tumult that caused his heart's blood to stop and then course wildly on. Business at Foxwood, connected with detectives, must have reference to his brother, and to him alone.

"A slight-made gentleman with a fair face and light curly hair, looking about thirty," had been Ann Hopley's description; it answered in every particular to the man Karl was gazing at; gazing till he watched him out of sight. Lawyer St. Henry, naturally observant, thought his guest stared after the man as though he held some peculiar interest in him.

"Do you know who that man really is, Mr. St. Henry?"

"Well, I'll tell you, Sir Karl. No reason why I should not, for I have not been told to keep it a secret. Some little time back, my nieces grew full of the new lodger at Mrs. Jinks's; they were talking of him incessantly. A gentleman reading divinity——"

"Why, that's Mr. Cattacomb," interrupted Sir Karl. "He lodges at Mrs. Jinks's."

"Not *that* ladies' idiot," cried the lawyer, rather roughly. "I beg your pardon, Sir Karl, but the Reverend Guy sometimes puts me out of patience. This man has the upper rooms, Cattacomb the lower——"

"But I—I thought that was a boy: a lad at his studies," reiterated Karl, in some perplexity. "I assumed him to be a pupil of Cattacomb's."

"It is the man you have just watched down the street, Sir Karl. Well, to go on. My nieces were always talking of this new gentleman, a Mr. Strange, who had come to Foxwood to get up his health, and to read up for some divinity examination. That was *their* account. They said so much about him that I got curious myself: it was a new face, you see, Sir Karl, and girls go wild over that. One morning when I was starting for the office, the gig at the door, Jane ran out to me. 'Uncle,' she said, 'that's Mr. Strange coming down Mrs. Jinks's steps now: you can see him if you look.' I did look, Sir Karl, and saw the gentleman you have just seen pass. His face struck me at once as one that I was familiar with, though at the moment I could not tell where I had seen him. Remembrance came to me while I looked—and I knew him for an officer connected with the detective force at Scotland Yard."

Karl drew a long breath. He was listening greedily.

"About a year ago," resumed the lawyer, "my agent in London, Mr. Blair, had occasion to employ a detective upon some matter he was engaged in. I was in London for a few days at that time, and saw the man twice at Blair's—and knew him again now. It was this same Mr. Strange."

"And you say Strange is not his right name?"

"No, it's not."

"What is the right one?"

"Well, I can't tell you the right one, Sir Karl, for I cannot remember it. I am sure of one thing—that it was not Strange. It was a longer name, and I think rather a peculiar name; but I can't hit upon it. He must be down here on some private business, and has no doubt his own reasons for keeping incog. I recollect Blair told me he was one of the most astute officers in the detective force."

"Has he recognized you?"

"He could not recognize me," said Mr. St. Henry. "I don't suppose he ever saw me to notice me. Each time that he called on Blair, it happened that I was in the front office with the clerks when he passed through it. He was not likely to have observed me."

"You have not spoken to him, then?"

"Not I."

"And—you don't know what his business here may be."

"Not at all. Can't guess at it. It concerns neither you nor me, Sir Karl, and therefore I have not scrupled to tell you so much. Of course you will not repeat it again. If he chooses to remain unknown here, and pass himself off for a student of divinity—doubtless for sufficient reasons—I should not be justified in proclaiming that he is a London detective, and so possibly ruin his game."

Sir Karl made a motion of acquiescence. His brain was whirling in no measured degree. He connected the presence of this detective at Foxwood with the paragraph that had appeared in the newspaper touching the escaped convict from Portland Island.

"Would there—would there be any possibility of getting to know his business?" he dreamily asked.

"Not the slightest, I should say, unless he chooses directly to disclose it. Why? You cannot have any interest in it, I presume, Sir Karl, whatever it may be."

"No, no; certainly not," replied Sir Karl, awaking to the fact that he was on dangerous ground. "One is apt to get curious on hearing of business connected with detectives," he added, laughing; "as interested as one does in a good novel."

"Ay, true," said the lawyer, unsuspiciously.

"At Mrs. Jinks's he is lodging, is he?" absently remarked Karl, turning to depart; and inwardly marvelling how he could have caught up the notion that the person there was only a lad, a pupil of Cattacomb's.

"At Mrs. Jinks's, Sir Karl: got her drawing-room. Wonder how the Rev. Guy would feel if he knew the man over his head was a 'cute detective officer?"

"I suppose the officer cannot be looking after *him*," jested Sir Karl. "St. Jerome's is the least sound thing we know of at Foxwood."

The lawyer laughed a hearty laugh as he attended Sir Karl to the door; at which Mr. St. Henry's gig was now waiting to take him into Basham.

It was not a hot morning, but Karl Andinnian took off his hat repeatedly on the way home to wipe his brow. The dreadful catastrophe he had been fearing for his unfortunate brother seemed to be drawing ominously near.

"But for that confounded Smith, Adam might have been away before," he groaned. "I know he might. Smith——"

And there Karl stopped; stopped as though his speech had been suddenly cut off. For a new idea had darted into his mind, and he stayed to ponder it.

Was the detective officer down here to look after Philip Salter?—and not after Adam at all?

A conviction that it must be so took possession of him; and in the first flush of it the relief was inexpressibly great. But he remembered again the midnight watcher of the Maze and the morning visit following it: and his hope fell back to zero. That this was the same man who had watched there could remain no doubt whatever.

Passing into his own room, Karl sat down and strove to think the matter out. He could arrive at no certain conclusion. One minute he felt sure the object was his brother the next, that it was only Salter.

But, in any case, allowing that it was Salter, there must be danger to Adam. If this cunning London detective were to get into the Maze premises again and *see* the prisoner there, all would be over. The probability was, that he was personally acquainted with the noted criminal Adam Andinnian: and it might be, that he had gained a suspicion that Adam Andinnian was alive.

One thing Karl could not conceal from himself—and it brought to him a rush of remorse. If the detective had come down after Salter, he—he, Karl—must have been the means of bringing him there.

But for that unpleasant consciousness, he would have gone straight off to Smith the agent, and told him of the trouble that was threatening Adam, and said, "What shall we do in it; how screen him?" But he did not dare. He did not dare to make a move or stir a step that might bring Smith and the detective in contact. He could not quite understand why, if Smith were really Salter, the detective had not already pounced upon him: but he thought it quite likely that Smith might be keeping himself out of sight. In short, the thoughts and surmises that crossed and recrossed Karl's brain, some probable enough, others quite improbable, were legion. Not for the world, if he could help it, would he aid—further than he had perhaps unhappily aided—in denouncing Salter; and knowing what he had done, he could not face the man. He had never intended to harm him.

So there Karl was, overwhelmed with this new perplexity, and not able to stir in it. He saw not what he could do. To address the detective himself, and say Whom are you after, would be worse than folly; of all people he, Karl Andinnian, must keep aloof from him. It might be that there was only a *suspicion* about Adam's being alive, that they were trying to find out whether it was so or not. For Karl to interfere or show interest would help it on.

But this suspense was well nigh intolerable. Karl could not live under it. Something he must do. If only he could set the question at rest, as to which of the two criminals the detective was after, it would be a good deal gained. And he could only do that by applying to Mr. Burtenshaw. It was not sure that he would, but there was a chance that he might.

Lady Andinnian was in her little sitting-room upstairs, when she heard Sir Karl's footstep. He entered without knocking: which was very unusual. For they had grown ceremonious one with another since the estrangement, and knocked at doors and asked permission to enter, as strangers. Lucy was adding up her housekeeping bills.

"I am going to London, Lucy. Some business has arisen that I am very anxious about, and I must go up at once."

"Business with Plunkett and Plunkett?" she asked, a slight sarcasm in her tone, though Karl detected it not, as she remembered the plea he had urged for the journey once before.

"No, not with Plunkett and Plunkett. The business, though, is the same that has been troubling my peace all the summer. I think I shall be home to-night. Lucy: but if I cannot see the person I am going up to see, I may have to wait in town until to-morrow. Should the last train not bring me down, you will know the reason."

"Of course your movements are your own, Sir Karl."

He sighed a little, and stood looking from the window. The first train he could catch would not go by for nearly an hour, so he had ample time to spare. Lucy spoke.

"I was going to ask you for some money. I have scarcely enough, I think, for these bills."

"Can you wait until I return, Lucy? I have not much more in the house than I shall want. Or shall I give you a cheque? Hewitt can go to the bank at Basham and cash it."

"Oh, I can wait quite well. There's no hurry for a day or two."

"You shall have it to-morrow, in any case. If I stay away as long as that I shall be sure to return during banking hours, and will get out at Basham and draw some money."

"Thank you."

"Good-bye, Lucy."

She held out her hand in answer to his, and wished him good-bye in return. He kept it for a minute in his, stooped, and kissed her cheek.

It brought a rush of colour to her face, but she said nothing. Only drew away her hand, bent over her figures again, and began adding them up steadily. He passed round to his chamber to put a few things into a hand-bag in case he had to stay away for the night.

Then he went down to his room and penned a few lines to Adam, entreating him to be unusually cautious. The note was enclosed in an outer envelope, addressed to Mrs. Grey. He rang the bell for Hewitt, and proceeded to lock his desk.

"I want you to go over to the Maze, Hewitt," he said in a low tone—and had got so far when, happening to raise his eyes, he saw it was Giles and not Hewitt who had entered. Karl had his wits about him, and Hewitt came in at the moment.

"Hewitt, I want you to step over to the Maze and inquire whether the plumbers have been there yet. There's something wrong with a drain. Ask the servants at the same time how their mistress is getting on. And——"

Giles had stood gaping and listening. Karl broke off to bid him look for his umbrella.

"No message, Hewitt, and no answer," breathed his master, as he handed him the note. "Put it in your pocket."

"All right, sir," nodded Hewitt, and was away before Giles came back with the umbrella. And Karl got off at last.

Perhaps Mr. Burtenshaw was astonished, perhaps not, to see Sir Karl Andinnian enter that same afternoon. He, the detective, was poring over his papers, as usual, but he turned from them to salute his visitor.

"Will you take a seat, Sir Karl, for two minutes. After that, I am at your service."

"You know me, then, Mr. Burtenshaw!" exclaimed Karl.

"The man who happened to come into the room with Grimley, the last time you were here, sir, said you were Sir Karl Andinnian," replied the officer without scruple. "Take a seat, sir, pray."

Mr. Burtenshaw placed four or five letters, already written, within their envelopes, directed, and stamped them. Then he quitted the room, probably to send them to the post, came in again, and drew a chair in front of Karl. "He is looking worse than ever," was the mental summary of the detective—"but what a nice face it is!"

Ay, it was. The pale, beautiful features, their refined expression, the thoughtfulness in the sweet grey eyes, and the strange sadness that pervaded every lineament, made a picture that was singularly attractive. Karl had one glove off; and the diamond and opal ring, that he always wore in remembrance of his father, flashed in the sunlight. For the buff blinds were not down to-day. He had wished to give the ring back to his brother, when he found he had no right to it himself, but Adam had insisted upon his keeping it and wearing it, lest "the world might inquire where the ring was gone." Another little deceit, as it always seemed to Karl.

"I have called here, Mr. Burtenshaw, to ask you to answer me a question honestly. Have you—stay though," he broke off. "As you know me, I presume you know where I live?"

"Quite well, Sir Karl. I was at the Court once in Sir Joseph Andinnian's time."

"Aye; of course you would know it. Now for my question. Have you sent a detective officer down to Foxwood after Philip Salter?"

"I have not," replied Mr. Burtenshaw, with, Karl thought, a stress upon the "I."

"But you know that one is there?"

"Why do you ask me this?" cried Mr. Burtenshaw, making no immediate reply.

"Because I have reason to believe, in fact to know, that a detective officer is at Foxwood, and I wish to ascertain what he is there for. I presume it can only be to search after Philip Salter."

"And what if it were?" asked Mr. Burtenshaw.

"Nothing. Nothing that could in any way affect you. I want to ascertain it, yes or no, for my own private and individual satisfaction."

"Well, you are right, Sir Karl. One of our men has gone down there with that object."

Karl paused. "I suppose *I* have led to it," he said. "That is, that it has been done in consequence of the inquiries I made of you."

"Of those you made of Grimley, sir, not of me. I had nothing to do with sending Tatton down——"

Karl caught at the name. "Tatton, do you call him?" he interrupted. And Mr. Burtenshaw nodded.

"He calls himself 'Strange' down there," said Karl.

"Oh, does he? He knows what he is about, Sir Karl, rely upon it."

"Who did send him down?"

"Scotland Yard. It appears that Grimley, taking up the notion, through you, that he had found a clue to the retreat of Salter, went to Scotland Yard, announced that Salter was in hiding somewhere in the neighbourhood of Foxwood, and asked that a search should be set on foot for him."

Karl sat thinking. If the man Tatton went down after Philip Salter, what brought him within the grounds of the Maze, watching the house at night? Whence also that endeavour to get in by day, and his questions to Ann Hopley? Was it Tatton who did this?—or were there two men, Strange and Tatton?

"What sort of a man is Tatton?" he asked aloud. "Slight and fair?'

"Slight and fair; about thirty years of age, Sir Karl. Curly hair."

"They must be the same," mentally decided Karl. "I presume," he said, lifting his head, "that Tatton must have started on this expedition soon after I was here last?"

"The following day, I think."

"Then he has been at Foxwood over long. More than

long enough to have found Salter if Salter's there, Mr. Burtenshaw."

"That depends upon circumstances, Sir Karl," replied the detective, with a wary smile. "I could tell you of a case where an escaped man was being looked after for twelve months before he was unearthed—and he had been close at hand all the while. They have as many ruses as a fox, these fugitives."

"Nevertheless, as Tatton has not yet found Salter, I should consider it a tolerably sure proof that Salter is not at Foxwood."

Mr. Burtenshaw threw a penetrating gaze at his visitor. "Will you undertake to give me your word, Sir Karl, that you do not *know* Philip Salter to be at Foxwood?"

"On my word and honour I do not know him to be there," said Karl, decisively. "I should think he is not there."

He spoke but in accordance with his opinion. The conviction had been gaining upon him the last few minutes that he must have been in error in suspecting Smith to be the man. How else was it, if he was the man, that Tatton had not found him?

"Salter *is* there," said the detective—and Karl pricked up his ears to hear the decisive assertion. "We have positive information from Tatton that he is on his trail:—I am not sure but he has seen him. For the first week or two of Tatton's sojourn there, he could discover no trace whatever of the man or his hiding-place; but accident gave him a clue, and he has found both: found his hiding-place and found him."

"Then, why does he not lay his hands upon him?" returned Karl, veering round again to the impression that it must be Smith.

"It is only a question of time, Sir Karl. No doubt he has good reasons for his delay. To *know* where a man is hiding may be one thing; to capture him quite another. Too much haste sometimes mars the game."

"Tatton is going to remain at Foxwood, then?"

"Until the capture is accomplished. Certainly."

Karl's heart sunk within him at the answer. While Tatton was delaying his capture of Smith, he might be getting a clue to another escaped fugitive down there—Adam Andinnian. Nay, had he not already the clue? Might not this very delay be caused by some crafty scheme to take both criminals at once—to kill two birds with one stone? He asked one more question.

"Mr. Burtenshaw, how was it that suspicion was directed at all to Foxwood?"

"Grimley took up the notion after your second visit here, Sir Karl, that you had a suspicion of Salter yourself. I thought you understood this. Grimley fancied you were in the habit of seeing some one whom you believed, but did not feel quite sure, might be Salter. And he judged that the individual, whether it was Salter or not, must be in hiding near your dwelling-place—Foxwood."

Ay; Karl saw how it was. *He* had done this. He and no other had brought this additional danger upon his ill-fated brother, whom he would willingly have given his own life to shield.

There was nothing more to be asked of Mr. Burtenshaw: he had learnt all he came to hear. And Sir Karl, with his load of care, returned to Foxwood by the evening train.

CHAPTER XXX.

ANOTHER KETTLE-DRUM.

COMMOTION at Mrs. Jinks's. Another afternoon kettle-drum on a grand scale. The two pastors, and more guests than could squeeze into the parlour. All the Foxwood ladies and an omnibus-load or two from Basham.

Mr. Strange sat in his drawing-room on a three-legged stool: the one that supported Mrs. Jinks's tub on washing days. His chairs had been borrowed. He had good-naturedly given up every one: so Mrs. Jinks introduced the wooden stool. These crowded meetings below had amused him at first; but he was getting a little tired of the bustle and the noise. Every time the street door was knocked at, it shook his room; the talking below could be heard nearly as plainly as though he were taking part in it. Still it made a little diversion in Mr. Strange's solitary existence, if only to watch the arrival of the articles needed for the feast, and to smell the aroma of the coffee, made in the huge kitchen kettle. The supplies did not concern Mr. Cattacomb: his gentle flock took that on themselves, cost and all. There was no lack of good things, but rather a superabundance: since the Rev. Mr. Puff had come to augment the clerical force, the contributions had been too profuse. So that everyone connected with the entertainment was in the seventh heaven of enjoyment and good humour: except Mrs. Jinks.

Perched on the hard stool, Mr. Strange, for lack of other employment, had noted the dainties as they came in. The wisest of us must unbend sometimes. A basket of muffins, full to the brim; eleven sorts of jam—since it was discovered that the Reverend Guy loved preserves to satiety, the assortments had never failed; thirteen kinds of biscuits, trays of cake, glass pots of marmalade and honey, ripe, rich fruits of all tempting colours, chocolate creams, candied oranges, lovely flowers.

Mr. Strange grew tired of looking; his head ached with the noise, his eyes with the splendour of the ladies' dresses. For the company was arriving now, thick and threefold.

There had arisen a slight, a very slight, modicum of displeasure connected with Mr. Cattacomb. That zealous divine had been met four or five times walking with Mr. Moore's third daughter, Jemima: at the last lecture he had distinctly been seen manœuvring to get the young lady next to him. It gave offence. While he belonged to them all, all adored him; but let him once single out one of the flock for favour more than the rest, and woe betide his popularity. "And that little idiot of a Jemima Moore, too, who had not two ideas in her vain head!" as Jane St. Henry confidentially remarked. However, the Reverend Guy, upon receiving a hint from Miss Blake that he was giving umbrage, vowed and protested that it was all accident and imagination—that he hardly knew Miss Jemima from her sisters. So peace was restored, and the kettle-drum grew out of it.

"I must have my chop all the same, Mrs. Jinks," said Mr. Strange to the widow; who had come upstairs to ask for the loan of his sugar-tongs, and looked very red and excited over it.

"In course, sir, you shall have it. It might be ten minutes later, sir, than ord'nary, but I do hope you'll excuse it, sir, if it is. You see how I'm drove with 'em."

"I see that there seems to be a large company arriving."

"Company!" returned Mrs. Jinks, the word causing her temper to explode; "I don't know how they'll ever get inside the room. I shall have to borrow a form from the school next door but one, and put it in the passage for some of 'em; and when that and the chairs is filled, the rest must stand. Never as long as I live will I take in a unmarried parson-gent again, if he's one of this ere new sort that gets the ladies about him all day in church and gives drums out of it. Hark at the laughing! Them two parsons be in their glory."

"The ladies must be fond of drums, I should think, by their getting them up so frequently," remarked Mr. Strange.

"Drat the huzzies!—they'd be fond of fifes too, if it brought 'em round Cattakin," was the widow's uncomplimentary rejoinder. "Better for 'em if they'd let the man alone to drink his tea in quiet and write his sermons—which I don't believe ever does get writ, seeing he never has a minute to himself. Hark at that blessed door!" she continued; and indeed the knocking was keeping up a perpetual chorus. "If they'd only turn the handle they could come in of theirselves. I said so to the Miss St. Henrys one cleaning day, that I had been called to it six times while scrubbing down the kitchen stairs, and the young ladies answered me that they'd not come in to Mr. Cattakin's without knocking, for the world."

"I suppose not," said Mr. Strange, slightly laughing.

"Hang that knocker again. There it goes! And me with all the drum on my shoulders. You should see the muffins we've got to toast and to butter downstairs, sir; your conscience 'ud fail you. Betsey Chaffen has come in to help me, and she and the girl is at it like steam. I'm afear'd that there stool's terrible hard for you, Mr. Strange, sir!" broke off the widow, in condolence.

"It's not as soft as velvet," was the reply. "But I'm glad to oblige: and I am going out presently. Get my chop and tea up when you can."

Mrs. Jinks disappeared; the hum continued. Whether the two parsons, as Mrs. Jinks surmised, felt "in their glory," cannot be told: the ladies were certainly in theirs. These kettle-drums at Mr. Cattacomb's were charmingly attractive.

When Mr. Strange did not return home for his chop at midday, he took it with his tea. His tray was yet before him this evening when the kettle-drum trooped out to attend vespers. At least, the company who had formed the drum. The two reverend gentlemen hastened on together a little in advance; Miss Blake led the van behind; and curious Foxwood ran to its windows to see.

Mr. Strange, who had nothing particular on his hands or mind that evening, looked after them. Example is infectious. He felt an inclination to follow in their wake—for it had not

been his good fortune yet to make one of the worshippers at
St. Jerome's; he had never indulged himself with as much as
a peep inside the place. Accordingly, Mr. Strange started
after some short delay, and gained the edifice.

The first object his eyes rested on, struck him as being as
ludicrous as an imp at the play. It was Tom Pepp in a
conical hat tipped with red, and a red cross extending down
his white garmented back. Tom Pepp stood near the bell,
ready to tinkle it at parts of the service. It may as well be
stated—lest earnest disciples of new movements should feel,
or take, offence—that the form and modeling of the services
at St. Jerome's were entirely Mr. Cattacomb's own; invented
by himself exclusively, and not copied from any other standard,
orthodox or unorthodox. The description of it here is taken
from facts. Mr. Strange, standing at the back near to Tom
Pepp, enjoyed full view of all: the ladies prostrate on the
floor, *actually prostrate*, some of them, the Reverend Guy
facing them with the whites of his eyes turned up; Damon
Puff on his knees, presenting his back to the room and giving
every now and then a surreptitious stroke to his moustache.
The detective had never seen so complete a farce in his life,
as connected with religion. He thought the two reverend
gentlemen might be shut up for a short term as mutinous
lunatics, by way of receiving a little wholesome correction:
he knew that if he had a daughter, he would shut *her* up as
one, rather than she should make a spectacle of herself as
these girls were doing.

The services over, Tom Pepp set on at the bell to ring them
out with all his might—for that was the custom. Most of
them filed out; as did Mr. Damon Puff; and they went on
their way. A few of them stopped in, for confession to Mr.
Cattacomb.

It was growing dusk then. A train was just in, and had
deposited some passengers at the station. One of them came
along, walking quickly, as if in haste to get home. Happening
to turn his head towards St. Jerome's entrance as he passed
it, attracted by the bell, he saw there, rather to his surprise,
Mr. Moore's strong-minded sister. She peered at him in the
twilight; she was no longer so quick of sight as she had been;
and recognized Sir Karl Andinnian.

"What, is it you, Miss Diana!" he cried, stopping to hold
out his hand. "Have you gone over to St. Jerome's?"

"I'd rather go over to Rome, Sir Karl," was the candid

answer. "I may lapse to St. Jerome's when I get childish perhaps, if it lasts so long. There's no answering for any of us when the mind fails."

Sir Karl laughed slightly. He saw before him the receding crowd turning down towards Foxwood village, and knew that vespers must be just over. The ringing of Tom Pepp's bell would have told him that. It was clanging away just above Miss Diana's head.

"You have been to vespers, then," remarked Sir Karl again, almost at a loss what to say, and unable to get away until Miss Diana chose to release his hand.

"Yes, I have been to what they call vespers," she rejoined tartly; "more shame for a woman of my sober years to say it, as connected with this place. Look at them, trooping on there, that Puff in the midst, who is softer than any apple-puff ever made yet!" continued Miss Diana, pointing her hand in the direction of the vanishing congregation. "*They* have gone; but there are five staying in for confession. Hark! Hark, Sir Karl! the folly is going to begin."

A sweet, silvery-toned bell rang gently within the room, and the clanging bell of Mr. Pepp stopped at the signal. The Reverend Guy had gone into the confessional box, and all other sounds must cease.

"I should think they can hardly see to confess at this hour," said Sir Karl jestingly.

"They light a tallow candle, I believe, and stick it in the vestry," said Miss Diana. "Five of them are staying to-night, as I told you: I always count. They go in one at a time and the others wait their turn outside the vestry. Do you think I am going to let my nieces stay here alone to play at that fun, Sir Karl? No: and so I drag myself here every confessional night. One of them, Jemima, is always staying. She is a little fool."

"It does not seem right," mused Sir Karl.

"Right!" ejaculated Miss Diana in an angry tone, as if she could have boxed his ears for the mild word. "It is wrong, Sir Karl, and doubly wrong. I do not care to draw the curb-rein too tightly; they are not my own children, and might rebel; but as sure as they are living, if this folly of stopping behind to confess is to go on, I shall tell the doctor of it. I think, Sir Karl—and you must excuse me for saying so to your face—that you might have done something before now, to put down the pantomime of this St. Jerome's."

"Only this very morning I was with St. Henry, asking him what I could do," was the reply. "His opinion is, that it will cease of itself when the cold weather comes on."

"*Will* it!" was the sarcastically emphatic retort. "Not if Cattacomb and the girls can help it. It's neither cold nor heat that will stop them!"

"Well, I am not sure about the law, Miss Diana. I don't know that St. Henry is, either."

"Look here, Sir Karl. If the law is not strong enough to put down these places, there's another remedy. Let all the clergy who officiate at them be elderly married men. It would soon be proved whether, or not, the girls go for the benefit of their souls."

Sir Karl burst into a laugh.

"It is these off-shoots of semi-religious places, started up here and there by men of vanity, some of whom, I venture to say it, are not licensed clergymen, that bring the shame and the scandal upon the true church," concluded Miss Diana. "There: don't let us talk of it further. Have you come from the train?"

"Yes. I had to run up to London for an hour or two to-day."

"Then I daresay you are tired. Give my love to your wife," added Miss Diana, as she wished Sir Karl good evening, and turned into St. Jerome's again to watch over her niece Jemima.

Sir Karl strode onwards. He had just come home from his interview with Mr. Burtenshaw. Miss Diana Moore and her sentiments had served to divert his mind for a moment from his own troubles, but they were soon all too present again. The hum of the voices and sound of the footsteps came back to him from the crowd, pursuing its busy way to the village: he was glad to keep on his own solitary course and lose its echo.

Some one else, who had come out of St. Jerome's, but who could not be said properly to pertain to the crowd, had kept on the solitary road—and that was Mr. Strange. He knew the others would take the direct way to the village and Mrs. Jinks's, and perhaps that was the reason why he did not. But there was no accounting for what Mr. Strange did: and one thing was certain—he had been in the habit lately of loitering in that solitary road a good deal after dusk had fallen, smoking his cigar there between whiles.

Sir Karl went on. He had nearly reached the Maze, though he was on the opposite side; when, at a bend of the road, there suddenly turned upon him a man with a cigar in his mouth, the end of it glowing like an ember. The smoker would have turned his head away again, and passed on, but Sir Karl stopped. He had recognized him: and his mind had been made up on the way from London, to speak to this man.

"I beg your pardon. Mr. Tatton, I think."

Mr. Tatton might possibly have been slightly taken to at hearing himself addressed by his own name: but there was no symptom of it in his voice or manner.

"The same, sir," he readily answered, taking the cigar from his mouth.

"I wish to say a few words to you," pursued Sir Karl. "As well, perhaps, say them now as later."

"Better, sir. No time like the present: it's all we can make sure of."

"Perhaps you know me, Mr. Tatton?"

"Sir Karl Andinnian—unless I am mistaken," replied the detective, throwing away his cigar.

Sir Karl nodded, but made no assent in words. He would have given a portion of his remaining life to discern whether this man of law, whom he so dreaded, knew, or suspected, that he had not a right to the title.

"I have just come from London," pursued Sir Karl. "I saw Mr. Burtenshaw there to-day. Finding previously that you were down here, I wished to learn whether or not you had come here in search of one Philip Salter, and went up to ascertain. And I hear that it is so."

The officer made no remark to this. It might be, that he was uncertain how far he might trust Sir Karl. The latter observed the reticence: guessed at the doubt.

"We may speak together in perfect confidence, Mr. Tatton. But for me, you would not have been sent here at all. It was in consequence of a communication I made myself, that the suspicion as to Salter reached Scotland Yard."

"I know all about that, Sir Karl," was the reply. "To tell you the truth, I should have made my presence here at Foxwood known to you at once, and asked you to aid me in my search, but I was warned at Scotland Yard that you might possibly obstruct my work, instead of aiding it, for that you wished to screen Salter."

"Scotland Yard warned you of that!" exclaimed Sir Karl.

"Yes. They had it from Grimley."

"The case is this," said Sir Karl, wishing with his whole heart he could undo what he had done. "Some short while back, I had a reason for making some inquiries respecting Philip Salter, and I went to my solicitors, Plunkett and Plunkett. They could not give me any information, and referred me to Mr. Burtenshaw. Burtenshaw introduced Grimley to me, and I saw them both twice. But I most certainly never intended to imply that Salter was in this neighbourhood, or to afford just grounds for sending down to institute a search after him."

"But I presume that you do know Salter is here, Sir Karl."

"Indeed I do not."

The officer was silent. He thought Sir Karl was intending to deceive him.

"I can tell you that he is here, Sir Karl—to the best of my belief. I could put out my hand at this minute and almost touch the dwelling that contains him."

They were nearly opposite the Maze gates, close upon the gate of Clematis Cottage. Karl wondered, with an anxiety amounting to agony, *which* of the two dwellings was meant. It would be almost as bad for this man to take Salter as to take Adam Andinnian; since the capture of the former might lead to that of the latter.

"You say 'to the best of your belief,' Mr. Tatton. You are not sure, then?"

"I am as sure as I can be, Sir Karl, short of actual sight."

"Good-night, Sir Karl."

The interruption came from Mr. Smith, who was leaning over his gate, smoking a pipe. Karl returned the salutation and passed on.

"He seems to have a jolly kind of easy life of it, that agent of yours, Sir Karl?" remarked the officer.

"Do you know him?" questioned Karl.

"Only by sight. I have seen Mr. Smith about on the land; and I took the liberty this afternoon, meeting him by chance near the Brook field, of asking him what the time was. The spring of my watch broke last night as I was winding it."

Karl's heart was beating. Had he been mistaken in supposing Philip Smith to be Philip Salter? Had he been nursing a foolish chimera; and running his head—or, rather, his poor brother's head—into a noose for nothing? God help him, then!

"You seem to know my agent well by sight." he breathed, in a tone kept low, lest its agitation should be heard.

"Quite well," assented the officer.

"Is he—does he bear any resemblance to Salter?"

"Not the slightest."

Karl paused. "You are sure of that?"

Tatton took a look at Sir Karl in the evening dusk, as if not able to understand him. "He is about the height of Salter, and in complexion is somewhat similar, if you can call that a resemblance," said he. "There is no other."

Karl spoke not for a few moments: the way before him was darkening. "You know Salter's person well, I conclude?" he said presently.

"As well as I know my own brother's."

Another pause; and then Karl laid his hand upon the officer's arm, bespeaking his best attention.

"I am sorry for all this," he said; "I am vexed to have been the cause of so much trouble. Your mission here may terminate as soon as you will, Mr. Tatton, for it is Smith that I was suspecting of being Salter!"

"No!" cried Tatton, in surprised disbelief.

"On my solemn word, I assert it. I suspected my agent, Smith, to be Salter."

"Why, Sir Karl, I can hardly understand that. You surely could not suppose it to be within the bounds of probability that Philip Salter, the fugitive criminal, would go about in the light of day in England as your agent goes—no matter how secluded the spot might be! And with five hundred pounds on his head!"

How a word of ridicule, of reason, even, will serve to change our cherished notions! Put as the cool and experienced police officer put it, Karl seemed to see how poor and foundationless his judgment had been.

"The whole cause of the affair was this," he said, hoping by a candid explanation to disarm the suspicions he had raised. "A circumstance—I own it was but a slight one—put it into my head that Philip Smith, of whom I had known nothing until he came here a few months ago as my agent, might be the escaped prisoner, Philip Salter. The idea grew with me, and I became anxious—naturally, you will say—to ascertain whether there were any real grounds for the suspicion. With this view I went up to see if Plunkett's people could give me any information about Salter or describe his person; and they referred me to Mr. Burtenshaw."

"Well, sir?" interposed Tatton, who was listening attentively.

"I am bound to say that I obtained no corroboration of my suspicions, except in regard to the resemblance," continued Sir Karl. "Burtenshaw did not know him; but he summoned the man who had let him escape, Grimley. As Grimley described Salter, it seemed to me that it was the precise description of Smith."

"There is a kind of general resemblance, I admit, Sir Karl, and the description of one might perhaps sound like that of the other. But if you knew the two, you would see how unlike they are."

"Grimley's description seemed to me to be that of Smith," went on Karl. "I came back here, strengthened in my opinion: but not fully confirmed. It was not a satisfactory state of things, and the matter continued to worry me. I longed to set it at rest, one way or the other; and I went up again to town and saw Grimley and Mr. Burtenshaw. When I came back once more, I felt nearly as sure as a man can feel that it was Salter."

"And yet you did not denounce him, Sir Karl. You would never have done it, I suppose?"

"I should not," admitted Karl. "My intention was to tax Smith with it privately, and—and send him about his business. Very wrong and illegal of me, no doubt: but I have suffered too severely in my own family by the criminal law of the land, to give up another man gratuitously to it."

At this reference to Sir Adam Andinnian, Mr. Tatton remained silent from motives of delicacy. He could understand the objection; especially as coming from a refined, sensitive, and merciful-natured man, as Sir Karl appeared to be.

"Well, sir, I can only say for myself that I wish your agent had been Salter," he resumed: "my hands would have been upon him before to-night. But is it true that you have no other suspicion, Sir Karl."

"What suspicion?"

"That the real Salter is in hiding at Foxwood."

Karl's heart beat a shade faster. "So far from having any

suspicion of that kind, I am perfectly certain, now that you have proved to me Smith is not Salter, that he is not at Foxwood. I know every soul in the place and around it."

"Were you acquainted with the real Salter, Sir Karl?"

"No."

"You take no interest in him, I presume?"

"None whatever."

During the conversation, they had been slowly pacing onwards, had passed the Court gates, and were now fairly on the road to Foxwood. It seemed as if Sir Karl had a mind to escort Mr. Tatton to his home.

"By the way," he said, "why did you call yourself Strange down here?"

"I never did," answered Tatton, laughing slightly. "The Widow Jinks gave me that name: I never gave it myself. I said to her I was a stranger, and she must have misunderstood me; for I found afterwards that she was calling me Mr. Strange. It was rather convenient than otherwise, and I did not set it right."

Karl strolled on in silence, wondering how all this would end, and whether this dangerous man—dangerous to him and his interests—was satisfied, and would betake himself to town again. A question interrupted him.

"Do you know much of a place here called the Maze, Sir Karl?"

"The Maze is my property. Why?"

"Yes, I am aware of that. What I meant to ask was, whether you knew much of its inmates."

"It is let to a lady named Grey. Her husband is abroad."

"That's what she tells you, is it? Her husband is there, Sir Karl, if he be her husband. *That* is where we must look for Philip Salter."

Something born of emotion, of sudden fear, seemed to flash across Karl's eyes and momentarily blind him. A wild prayer went up for guidance, for help to confront this evil.

"Why do you say this?" he asked, his voice controlled to a calm indifference.

"I have information that some gentleman is living at the Maze in concealment, and I make no doubt it is Salter. The description of his person, so far as I have it, answers to him. Until to-night, Sir Karl, I have believed that it was to the Maze your own suspicions of Salter were directed."

"Certainly not—on my word of honour as a gentleman,"

x

was the reply. "I feel sure you are mistaken; I know you
are. Mrs. Grey lives alone at the Maze, save for her servants:
two old people who are man and wife."

"I am aware the general belief is that she lives alone.
It's not true, though, for all that, Sir Karl."

"Indeed it is true," returned Karl, calmly as before, for
he did not dare to show too much zeal in Mrs. Grey's cause.
"I have been over there pretty often on one matter or
another—the house is an old one, and no end of repairs seem
to be wanted to it—and I am absolutely sure that no inmate
whatever is there, save the three I have mentioned: the lady,
and the man and woman. I do not count the infant."

"Ay; there; the infant. What does that prove?"

"Nothing as to your argument. Mrs. Grey only came to
the place some five or six months ago. Not yet six, I think."

"Rely upon it, Sir Karl, the lady has contrived to blind
you, in spite of your visits, just as she has blinded the outside world. Some one is there, concealed; and I shall be
very much surprised if it does not turn out to be Salter. As
to the two old servants, they are bound to her interests;
are of course as much in the plot as she is."

"I know you are mistaken. I could stake my life that no
one else is there. Surely you are not going to act in any
way on this idea!"

"I don't know," replied Mr. Tatton, with inward craft.
"Time enough. Perhaps I may get some other information
before long. Should I require a search-warrant to examine
the house, I shall apply to you, Sir Karl. You are in the
commission of peace, I believe."

Sir Karl nodded. "If you must have one, I shall be happy
to afford it," he said, remembering that if it came to this
pass, his being able to apprize the Maze privately beforehand,
would be a boon. And, with that, they separated: the detective continuing to pace onwards towards Paradise Row,
Sir Karl turning back to his own house.

But the events of the evening, as concerning the Maze
interests, were not altogether at an end. Miss Blake was
the last to come out of the confessional, for the rest had taken
their turn before her. It was tolerably late then; quite
dark; and both Aunt Diana and Tom Pepp were rampant
at being kept so long. They all turned out of St. Jerome's
together, including Mr. Cattacomb; and all, save Miss Blake
and the boy, went in the direction of the village. Tom Pepp,

having doffed his bell-ringing garments and locked up, proceeded the other way, accompanied by Miss Blake.

She was going to visit a sick woman who lived next door to Tom's mother. Miss Blake had her good points, though she was harsh of judgment. This poor woman, Dame Bell, was dying of consumption; the end was drawing near, and Miss Blake often went to sit by and read to her. The boy had told her at vespers that night that it was thought she could hardly live till morning: hence the late visit. She found the woman very ill, and stayed to do what she could.

It was striking ten when Miss Blake quitted the cottage: she heard the quarters and strokes told out from the distant church at Foxwood. The night was a still one. Tom Pepp, waiting outside, gallantly offered to attend her home. She accepted the escort readily, not caring to go alone, as it was so late.

"But I fear it will be keeping your mother up, Tom," she said, in hesitation. "I know you go to bed early."

"That's nothing, 'um," said Tom. "Mother have got her clothes from the wash to fold to-night. She telled me I was not to let you go back alone. It have been a rare good day for drying."

So they set off together, talking all the way; for Tom was an intelligent companion, and often had items of news to regale the public with. When they came within view of the Maze gates and Clematis Cottage, the loneliness of the road was over, and Miss Blake sent the lad back again, giving him a threepenny-bit.

She was on the Maze side of the way, not having crossed since leaving Mrs. Bell's cottage. And she had all but reached the gates, when the sound of advancing footsteps grew upon her ear. Drawing back amidst the trees—not to watch for Sir Karl Andinnian as she had watched at other times, for she believed him to be in London, but simply to shield herself from observation, as the hour was so late—Miss Blake waited until the footsteps should have gone by.

The footsteps did not go by. They halted at the gate: and she, peeping through the leaves, saw it was Sir Karl. He took the key from his pocket as usual, opened the gate, locked it after him, and plunged into the maze. Miss Blake heaved a sigh at man's inventions, and kept still until there was no fear that her rustling away would be heard. Then she moved.

She had never been in all her life so near screaming. Taking one step forward to depart, she found herself right in the arms of somebody who had coat-sleeves on; another watcher like herself.

"I beg your pardon, ma'am."

"Good gracious, Mr. Strange, how you frightened me!" she whispered. "Whatever are you doing here?"

"Nay, I may ask what you were doing," was the smiling retort. "On your way home, I take it. As for me, I was smoking my cigar, and it has gone out. That was our friend, Sir Karl Andinnian, I fancy, who let himself in there."

"Oh yes, it was Sir Karl," was the contemptuous answer, given as they walked on together. "It is not the first night by a good many he has been seen stealing in at those gates."

"Paying his court to Mrs. Grey!" returned Mr. Strange, really speaking without any sinister motive, and his mind full of Salter.

Miss Blake, in the honest indignation of her heart, and lately come from the upright exhortations of the Reverend Guy, allowed her sentiments their play. Mr. Strange's remark, made in all innocence, had seemed to show her that he too knew of the scandal.

"It is shameful!" she said. "Doubly shameful in Sir Karl, a married man."

Mr. Strange pricked up his ears. He caught her meaning instantly.

"Nonsense!" he said.

"I wish it was nonsense," said Miss Blake. "When the woman, Betsy Chaffen, was telling the tale in your rooms that day, of the gentleman she saw, and whom she could never see afterwards, I could hardly contain myself, dear sir, knowing it was Sir Karl."

"And—and—do you mean—do you think that there's no Mr. Grey there—no gentleman inmate, I would say?" cried the detective, surprised for once.

"Mr. Grey!" she repeated scoffingly. "The only 'Mr. Grey' that exists is Sir Karl Andinnian; I have known it a long while. One or two others here know it also. It is a scandal."

She wished him good-night with the last words, crossed the road, and let herself into the grounds of the Court by one of the small gates. Leaving Mr. Strange looking after her like a man in a dream, as he tried to solve the problems set a-working in his brain.

CHAPTER XXXI.

ONLY A NIGHT OWL.

The wide window of the upper sitting-room at the Maze was thrown open to the night air. Gazing forth from it, stood Sir Adam Andinnian and his wife. He was in his usual evening dress, that he so obstinately continued to persist in assuming in the teeth of remonstrance: she wore a loose white robe and a blue cashmere shawl over it. She looked delicately fragile, very weak and ill still; and this was the first day that she had left her chamber for any length of time. There was no light in the sombre room: before light was allowed to come in, the window would be closed and the shutters shut for the night.

Not a word was being spoken between them. She had not long come into the room. A great terror lay on both their hearts. At least, it did on hers: and Sir Adam had grown to feel anything but easy. The suspicions, that appeared to be attaching themselves to the Maze outside the walls, were producing their effects on the comfort of the inmates within: and perhaps these suspicions were feared all the more because they did not as yet take any tangible or distinct form. That a detective officer was in the neighbourhood looking about, Adam had heard from his brother; and that it was the same man who had been seen by Ann Hopley watching the house in the moonlight and who had boldly presented himself at the gate the next day demanding permission to enter, Sir Adam had no doubt whatever of. Karl, too, was taking to write him notes of caution.

Brave though he was, he could not feel safe. There was not a moment of the day or night but he might see the officers of justice coming in to look for him. His own opinion was, that he should be able to evade them if they did come; to baffle their scrutiny; but he could not feel quite as easy as though he were on a bed of rose-leaves. In consequence of this apprehension, the ears of himself and his wife were ever on the alert: their eyes rarely went off the watch, their conscious hearts never lost the quick beat of fear. It was enough to wear them both out.

Can the reader fully realize, I wonder, what the situation was? Can he only imagine one single hour of its terrors, or picture its never-ceasing, prolonged doubt and agony? I think not. It cannot be adequately told of. Behind and before there was the awful vista of that dreadful Portland Island: look which way they would, nothing else presented itself.

A gentle breeze suddenly arose, stirring the trees outside. Never an unexpected sound, however faint, was heard, but it stirred their beating hearts; stirred them to a fast, fluttering, ugly throbbing. It was but the wind; they knew it was only that: and yet the emotion did not subside quickly. Rose had another great anxiety, separate and apart: perhaps he had it also in a degree, but he did not admit it. It was on the score of her husband's health. There could be no doubt that something or other was amiss, for he had occasional attacks of pain that seemed to arise without any explainable cause. Ann Hopley, who considered herself wise in ailments, declared that he ought to see a doctor. She had said it to her master ineffectually; she now began to say it to her mistress. Sir Adam laughed at her when his wife was present, and ridiculed her advice with mocking words of pleasantry; but Ann Hopley gave nothing but grave looks in return.

The fact was, she knew more than Rose did: more than Sir Adam intended or would allow his wife to know. One day, going to a part of the grounds where she knew she should find her master, she discovered him on the grass amidst the trees in a fainting-fit, his face of a bluish-white. Some acute pain, or spasm, sharper than he had ever felt before, had caused him to lose consciousness, he said when he recovered; and he threatened the woman with unheard-of pains and penalties if she breathed a word to her mistress. Ann Hopley held her tongue accordingly: but when Rose was about again she could see that Adam was not well. And the very impossibility of calling in a medical man to him, without arousing curiosity and comments that might lead to danger, was tormenting her with its own anxiety.

"The baby sleeps well to-night, Rose."

"He has slept better and has been altogether easier since he was baptised," was her answer. "It is just as though he knew he had been made a little Christian, and so feels at rest."

"Goose!" smiled Sir Adam. "Don't you think you are sitting up too late, you young mamma?"

"I am not tired, Adam. I slept well this afternoon."

"It is later than perhaps you are aware of, Rose. Hard upon ten."

"Would you like to have lights?" she asked.

"No. I'd rather be without them."

She also would rather be without them. In this extended cause for fear that was growing up, it seemed safer to be at the open window looking out, than to be shut up in the closed room where the approaches of danger could neither be seen nor heard. Perhaps the same kind of feeling was swaying Sir Adam.

"You are sure you are well wrapped up, Rose?"

"Certain. And I could not take cold in this weather. It is like summer still."

All around was quiet as death. The stars shone in the sky: the gentle breeze, that had ruffled the trees just before, seemed to have died away. Breaking just then upon the stillness, came the sound of the church clock at Foxwood, telling its four quarters and the ten strokes of the hour after it. The same quarters, the same strokes that Miss Blake also heard, emerging from Dame Bell's cottage. The husband and wife, poor banned people, stood on again side by side, they hardly knew how long, hushing the trouble that was making a havoc of their lives, and from which they knew there could be no certain or complete escape so long as time for him should last. Presently he spoke again.

"Rose, if you stay here longer I shall close the window. This night air, calm and warm though it is, cannot be good for you——"

She laid her warning hand upon his arm. The ears of both were quick, but he was speaking at the moment, and so she caught the sound first. A pause of intense silence, their hearts beating almost to be heard; and then the advance of footsteps, whether stealthy ones or not, might be distinctly traced, coming through the maze.

"Go, Adam," she whispered.

But, before Sir Adam could quit the room, the whistle of a popular melody broke out upon the air, and they knew the intruder was Karl. It was his usual advance signal. Ann Hopley heard it below and opened the heavily barred door to him.

'You are late to-night, sir."

"True. I could not come earlier, Ann: it was not safe."

Poor Karl Andinnian! Had he but known that it was not

safe that night, later as well as earlier! That is, that he had not come in unwatched. For, you have understood that it was the night mentioned at the close of the last chapter, when his interview with Mr. Strange had taken place on his return from London, and the detective and Miss Blake had subsequently watched him in.

"Now then, Karl," began Sir Adam, when the room was at length closed and lighted, and Ann Hopley had gone down again, "what was the precise meaning of the cautionary note you sent me to-day?"

"The meaning was to enjoin extra caution upon you," replied Karl, after a moment's hesitation, and an involuntary glance at Rose.

"If you have anything to say and are hesitating because my wife is present, you may speak out freely," cried the very unreticent Sir Adam. Rose seconded the words.

"Speak, Karl, speak," she said, leaning towards him with a painful anxiety in her tone. "It will be a relief to me. Nothing that you or any one else can say can be as bad as my own fears."

"Well, I have found out that that man is a London detective," said Karl, deeming it best to tell the whole truth. "He is down here looking after an escaped fugitive. Not *you*, Adam: one Salter."

"One Salter?" echoed Sir Adam, testily, while Rose started slightly. "Who's he? What Salter? Is there any Salter at Foxwood?"

"It seems that the police in London have been suspecting that he was here, and they sent this detective, who calls himself Strange, to look after him. Salter, however, cannot be found; there's no doubt that the suspicion was altogether a mistake; but, unfortunately, Strange has had his thoughts directed to the Maze, and is looking after it."

"After me?" cried Adam.

"No. I do not believe there exists the smallest suspicion that you are not in the family vault in Foxwood churchyard. He fancies some one is concealed here, and thinks it must be Salter."

"But why on earth should his suspicions be directed to the Maze at all?" demanded Sir Adam, with a touch of his native heat.

"Ah, why! We have to thank Moore for that, and your own incaution, Adam, when you allowed yourself to be seen the night he brought Nurse Chaffen in. It seems the woman has talked of it outside; telling people, and Strange amid the rest, that it was either a real gentleman in dinner attire, or a ghost in the semblance of one. Some have taken unhesitatingly to the ghost theory, believing it to be a remanet of the Throcton times; but detectives are wiser men."

"And so this man is looking after the Maze!"

"Just so. He is after Salter, not after you."

Sir Adam made no immediate observation. Rose, listening eagerly, was gazing at Karl.

"Is it *sure* that Salter is not in the place?" she asked in a low tone. "That he has not been here?"

"Quite sure, Rose. The idea was a misapprehension entirely," replied Karl, returning her meaning glance. "Therefore, you see," he added, by way of giving what reassurance he could, "the man you have so dreaded is not on the track of Adam at all; but on the imaginary one of Salter."

".One scent leads to another," broke forth Sir Adam. "While the fellow is tracking out Salter he may track out me. Who's to know that he has not a photograph of Adam Andinnian in his pocket, or my face in his memory?"

"I should like to ask him the question, whether he knew Sir Adam Andinnian personally; but I fear I dare not," remarked Karl. "A suspicion once awakened would not end. Your greatest security lies in their not knowing you are alive."

"My only security," corrected Sir Adam. "Well, Karl, if that man has his eyes directed to the Maze, it puts an end to all hope of my trying to get away. Little doubt, I suppose, but he is watching the outer walls night and day; perhaps with a dozen comrades to help him."

"For the present, you can only stay where you are," acknowledged Karl. "I have told you all this, Adam, to make you doubly careful. But for your reckless incaution I would have spared you the additional uneasiness it must bring."

"Even though the man does know me, the chances are that he would not find me if he came in," mused Sir Adam aloud. "With my precautions, the task would be somewhat difficult. You know it, Karl."

"Yes, but you are not always using your precautions," returned Karl. "Witness you here, sitting amidst us openly this evening in full dress! *Don't* do in future, Adam; conceal yourself as you best can—I beseech it of you for the love of Heaven. When this present active trouble shall have subsided—if in God's mercy it does so subside—why then you may resume old habits again. At least, there will not be so much risk: but I have always considered them hazardous."

"I'll see," assented Sir Adam. Which was a concession from *him*.

"Be on your guard day and night. Let not one moment of either season find you off it, or unready for any surprise or emergency. Strange talked about applying for a search warrant to examine the house. Should he do so, I will warn you of it, if possible. But your safer course is to be looking for the enemy with every ring that the bell gives, every breath that stirs the trees in the labyrinth, every sound that vibrates on the air."

"A pretty state of things!" growled Adam. "I'm sure I wish I never had come here!"

"Oh, that you had not!" returned Karl.

"It's my proper place, though. It is. My dear little son, heir to all, ought to be brought up on his own property. Karlo, old fellow, that remark must have a cruel ring on your ear: but I cannot put the child out of his birthright."

"I should never wish you to do it, Adam."

"Some arrangement shall be made for the far-off future; rest assured of that, and tell your wife so. In any case, Foxwood will be yours for one-and-twenty years to come, and the income you now enjoy to keep it up with. After the boy shall be of age——"

"Let us leave these considerations for the present," interrupted Karl. "All of us may be dead and buried before then. As for me, I seem not to see a single step before me, let alone a series of years."

"Right, Karl. These dreams lay hold of me sometimes, but it is worse than silly to speak of them. Are you going?"

"Yes. It is late. I should not have come in to-night, but for wishing to warn you. You will try and take care of yourself, Adam?" he affectionately added, holding out his hand.

"I'll take care of myself; never fear," was Sir Adam's light answer as he grasped it. "Look here, brother mine," he resumed, after a slight pause, and his voice took a deeper tone. "God knows that I have suffered too heavily for what I did; He knows that my whole life, from the rising up of the sun to its going down, from the first falling shade of night's dark curtain to its lifting, is one long, unbroken penance : and I believe in my heart that He will in His compassion shield me from further danger. There! take that to comfort you, and go in peace. In your care for me, you have needed comfort throughout more than I, Karl."

Retaining his brother's hand in his, while Karl said goodnight to Rose, Adam went down stairs with him, and beyond the door, after Ann Hopley had unbarred it. It was only since the advent of the new fears that these extra precautions of barring up at sunset had been taken.

"Don't come out," urged Karl.

"Just a step or two."

Karl submitted : he felt secure enough against active danger to-night. But it was in these trifles that Adam's natural incaution betrayed itself.

"Karl, did you tell all you knew?" he began as they plunged into the maze. "Was there more behind that you would not speak before the wife?"

"I told you all, Adam. It is bad enough."

"It might be worse. Suppose they were looking after me, for instance, instead of this fellow, Salter! I shall baffle them; I don't fear."

"Adam, you shall *not* come farther. If the man got in one night, he may get in another. Good-bye."

"Good-bye, dear old anxious fellow!"

"Go in, and get the door barred."

"All right. A last Good-night to you!"

Karl walked on, through the intricacies of the maze. Adam stood listening for a moment, and then turned to retrace his steps. As he did so, the sharp dart of pain he was growing accustomed to went through him, turning him sick and faint. He seized hold of a tree for support, and leaned against it.

"What is it that can be the matter with me?" ran his thoughts after it had subsided, and he was getting out his handkerchief to wipe from his brow the cold drops of agony that had gathered there. "As Ann Hopley says, I ought to see a doctor: but it is not to be thought of; and less than ever now, with this new bother hanging over the house. Hark! Oh, it's only the wind rustling the leaves again."

He stayed listening to it. Listening in a dreamy kind of way, his thoughts still on his malady.

"I wonder what it is? If the pain were in a different direction I might think it was the heart. But it is not *that.* When my father was first taken ill of his fatal illness, he spoke of some such queer attacks of agony. I am over young for his complaint though. Does disease ever grow out of anxiety, I wonder? If so——"

A whirl and a rustle just over his head, and Sir Adam started as though a blow had been struck him. It was but a night owl, flying away from the tree above with her dreary note, and beating the air with her wings; but it had served to startle him to terror, and he felt as sick and faint again as he did just before from the physical pain. What nerves he possessed were on the extreme tension to-night. That Adam Andinnian, the cool-natured equable man, who was the very opposite of his sensitive brother Karl, and who had been unable to understand what nerves were, and to laugh at those who had them—that he could be thus shaken by merely the noise of a night bird will serve to show the reader what his later life had been, and how it had told upon him. He did not let this appear, even to those about him; he kept up his old rôle of cool carelessness—and in a degree he was careless still, and in ordinary moments most incautious from sheer want of thought —but there could be no doubt that he was experiencing to the full all the bitter mockery, the never-ceasing dread and hazard of his position. In the early days, when the attempted escape from Portland Island was only in contemplation, Karl had foreseen what the life must be if he did escape. An existence of miserable concealment; of playing at hide and seek with the law; a world-wide apprehension lying on him always, of being retaken. In short, a hunted man who must not dare to approach the haunts of his fellow-men, and of whom every other man must be the necessary enemy. Even so had it turned out: Adam Andinnian was realizing it to the full. A great horror lay upon him of being recaptured: but it may be questioned whether, had the choice been given him, he would not rather have remained a prisoner than have escaped to this. Even as he stood there now, in the damp still night, with all the nameless, weird surroundings of fancy that night sometimes brings when the spirit is in tune for it, he was realizing it unto his soul.

The glitter of the stars, twinkling in their dusky canopy, shone down upon him through the interstices of the trees, already somewhat thinning their leaves with the approach of autumn; and he remained on, amid the gloom, lost in reflection.

"I should be better off *there*," he murmured, gazing upwards in thought at the heaven that was beyond; "and it may be that Thou, O my God, knowest that, in Thy pitiful mercy. As Thou wilt. Life has become but a weary one here, full of pains and penalties."

"Master!" came to him in a hushed, doubtful voice at this juncture. "Master, are you within hearing? My mistress is feeling anxious, and wants the door bolted."

"Ay, bolt and bar it well, Ann," he said, going forward. "But barred doors will not keep out all the foes of man."

Meanwhile Karl had got through the maze; and cautiously, after listening, let himself out at the gate. No human being, that he could discern, was within sight or hearing; and he crossed the road at once. Then, but not before, he became aware that his agent, Mr. Smith, was in that favourite spot and attitude of his, leaning his arms on the little garden gate, his green glasses discarded—as they generally were after sunset.

"Good-night," said Karl in passing. But some words of the agent's served to arrest his progress.

"Would you mind stepping in for one moment, Sir Karl? I wanted to say just a word to you, and have been watching for you to come out."

"Is it anything particular?" asked Karl, turning in at the gate at once, which Mr. Smith held open.

"I'll get a light, sir, if you will wait an instant."

Karl heard the striking of a match in-doors, and Mr. Smith reappeared in the passage with a candle. He ushered Karl into the room on the left-hand; the best room, that was rarely used.

"This one has got its shutters closed," was the explanatory remark. "I generally keep the others open until I go to bed."

"Tell me at once what it is you want," said Karl. "It is late, and I shall have my household wondering where I am."

"Well, Sir Karl, first of all, I wish to ask if you are aware that you were watched into the Maze to-night?" began Smith. He spoke in the lowest whisper; scarcely above his breath. The agent's one servant had been in bed at the top of the house long before: but he was a cautious man.

"No. Who watched me?"

"Two people, sir. One was Miss Blake, the lady staying

with you at the Court; the other was a confounded fellow who is at Foxwood for no good, I guess, and is pushing his prying nose on the sly into everything."

"Do you mean Mr. Strange?"

"That's the name: a lodger at Mother Jinks's. He and the lady watched you in, Sir Karl; they stood close by the gate among the trees, and then walked off down the road together."

Karl's pulses beat a shade more quickly. "Why should they have been watching me? What could be their motive?"

"Miss Blake did not intend to watch—as I take it. I saw her coming along with a sharpish step from the direction of that blessed St. Jerome's, late as it was—Cattacomb may have been treating his flock to a nocturnal service. When she was close upon the Maze she must have heard your footsteps, for she drew suddenly behind the trees to hide herself. After you were in, she came out of her shelter, and another with her—the man Strange. So he must have been hidden there beforehand, Sir Karl: and, I should say, to watch."

Karl was silent. He did not like to hear this. It seemed to menace further danger.

"I went in to warn Sir Adam against this man," he observed; "to tell him never to be off his guard, day or night. He is a London detective!"

"What—Strange is?" exclaimed the agent, with as much astonishment as his low tones allowed him to express. "A London detective, Sir Karl?"

"Yes, he is."

Mr. Smith's face fell considerably. "But—what is he doing down here?" he inquired. "Who's he after? *Surely* not Sir Adam?"

"No, not Sir Adam. He is after some criminal who—who does not exist in the place at all," added Karl, not choosing to be more explicit, considering that it was the man before him whom he had suspected of being the said criminal, and feeling ashamed of his suspicions now that they were dispelled, and he had to speak of it with him face to face. "The danger is, that in looking after one man the police may come upon the track of another."

The agent nodded his head. "But surely they do not suspect the Maze?"

"They do suspect the Maze," replied Karl. "Owing

to the tattling of the woman Mr. Moore took there—Nurse Chaffen—they suspect it."

Mr. Smith allowed a very unorthodox word to issue through his closed teeth, applied not only to the lady in question, but to ladies in general.

"The man Strange has been down here looking after some one whom he can't find; who no doubt is not in the neighbourhood at all, and never has been," resumed Karl. "Strange's opinion, however, was—and is—that the man is here, concealed. When he heard Chaffen's tale of the gentleman she saw in evening dress at the Maze, but whom she never saw again and therefore concluded he was hidden somewhere about the house not to show himself to her, he caught up the notion that it was the man he was after. Hence his suspicions of the Maze, and his watchings."

"It's a very unfortunate thing!" breathed the agent.

"You see, now, Mr. Smith, how much better it would have been if Sir Adam had never come here. Or, being here, if he had been allowed to go away again."

"He can't attempt it now," was the quiet retort of the agent. "With a detective's eyes about, it would be only to walk straight into the lion's mouth."

"Just so. We all know that."

"I wish to heaven I *could* get him away!" spoke the agent impulsively, and it was evident that his heart was in his words. "Until now I believed he was as safe here as he could be elsewhere—or safer. What the devil brings a confounded detective in this quiet place? The malignant fiend, or some implacable fate must have sent him. Sir Karl, the danger is great. We must not shut our eyes to it."

Alas, Karl Andinnian felt that, and in a more cruel degree than the agent could. It was *his* work; it was he who had brought this hornet's nest about his unfortunate brother's head. The consciousness of it lay heavily upon him in that moment; throat and tongue and lips were alike parched with the fever of remorse.

"May I ask you for a glass of water, Mr. Smith?" broke next from the said dry lips.

"I'll get it for you in a moment, sir," said the agent, rising with alacrity.

Karl heard another match struck outside, and then the steps of the agent retreating in the direction of the pump. In his restlessness of mind he could not sit still, but rose to pace the room. A small set of ornamental book-shelves, hanging against the wall, caught his attention: he halted before it and took down a volume; mechanically, rather than with any motive.

"Philip Salter. From his loving mother."

The words met Karl's eyes as he opened the book. Just for a moment he questioned whether his sight was deceiving him. But no. There they were, in a lady's hand, the ink dry and faded with time. It was Bunyan's "Pilgrim's Progress."

"*Is* it Salter, after all?" mentally breathed Karl.

Mr. Smith came in again with a glass of water as the doubt was running through Karl's mind. Thanking his agent for the water, he drank it at a draught, and sat down with the book in his hand.

"I have been amongst your books, you see, Mr. Smith. A sound old volume, this."

"So it is, Sir Karl. I dip into it myself now and then."

"Did you know this—this Mr. Philip Salter?"—holding the book open at the words.

For answer, the agent threw his eyes straight into Karl's face, and paused. "Did *you* know him, Sir Karl?"

"I never knew him. I have heard somewhat about him."

"Ay, few persons but have, I expect," returned the agent, with a kind of groan. "He was my cousin, sir."

"Your cousin!" echoed Karl.

"My own cousin: we were sisters' sons. He was Philip Salter; I am Philip Smith."

Karl's eyes were opened. In more senses than one.

"The fool that Philip Salter showed himself?" ejaculated Philip Smith—and it was evident by the bitter tone that the subject was a sore one. "I was in his office, Sir Karl, a clerk under him; but he was some years younger than I. He might have done so well: none of us had the smallest idea but what he was doing well. The fall was all through private and illegitimate speculation. He got into a hole where the mire was deep, and he used dangerous means when at his wits' end to get himself out of it. It did for him what you know, and it ruined me; for, being his cousin, men thought I must have known of it, and my place was taken from me."

"Where is he now?" asked Karl.

"I don't know. Sometimes we think he is dead. After his escape, we had reason to believe that he got off to Canada, but we were never made certain of it, and have never heard from him in any way. He may be in some of the backwoods there, afraid to write."

"And this was his book?"

"Yes. Most of his small belongings came into my hands. The affair killed his mother: broke her heart. He was all she had, save one daughter. Sir Karl, do you know what I'd do if I had the power?" fiercely continued Smith. "I would put down by penal laws all these cursed speculators who, men of straw themselves, issue their plausible schemes only to deceive and defraud a confiding, credulous public; all these betting and gambling rogues who lay hold of honest natures to lure them to their destruction. But for them, Philip Salter had been holding up his untarnished head yet."

"Ay," assented Karl. "But that will never be, so long as the greed of gold shall last. It is a state of affairs that can belong only to a Utopian world; not to this."

He put out his hand to Philip Smith when he left—a thing he had never done voluntarily before—in his sensitive regret for having wronged the man in his heart: and went home with his increased burden of perplexity and pain.

CHAPTER XXXII.

ONE DAY IN HER LIFE.

LIFE was to the last degree dreary for Lucy Andinnian. But for the excitement imparted to her mind from that mysterious building, the Maze, and the trouble connected with it, she could scarcely have continued to go on, and bear. It was not a healthy excitement: no emotion can be that, which has either jealousy or anger for its origin. Let us take one day of her existence, and see what it was: the day following the one last told of.

A mellow, bright morning. The pleasant sun, so prolific of his bounties that year, was making the earth glad with his renewed light, and many a heart with it. Not so Lucy's: it seemed to her that never a gleam of gladness could illumine hers again. She sat in her room, partly dressed, after a night of much sleeplessness. What sleep she had was disturbed, as usual, by dreams tinged with the unpleasantness of her waking thoughts. A white wrapper enfolded her, and Aglaé was doing her hair. The woman saw how weary and spiritless her mistress was becoming; but not a suspicion of the true cause suggested itself, for Lucy and her husband took care to keep up appearances, and guarded their secret well. Aglaé attempted to say a word of gossip now and again, but received no encouragement: Lucy was buried in a reverie.

"We are growing more estranged day by day," ran her thoughts. "He went to London yesterday, and never said why; never gave me the least explanation. After he came home at night, and had taken something to eat, he went out again. To the Maze, of course."

"Will my lady please to have her hair in rolls or in plaits this morning?"

"As you please, Aglaé." And, the weary answer given, her thoughts ran on again.

"I fancy Theresa saw him go there. I can't help fancying it. She had all her severe manner on when she came in last night, but was so pityingly kind to me. And I could bear all so much better if she would not be pitiful. It was past ten. That poor Mrs. Bell is likely to die, and Theresa had been to read to her. I kept hoping she would go to bed, and she did not. Is it wrong of *me* to sit up, I wonder, to see what time he comes in?—would Margaret say it was? Theresa got her silks and her work about, and I had mine. He has hardly ever been so late as last night. It was half-past eleven. What right has she to keep him, or he to stay? He said, in a light, indifferent kind of tone, by way of excuse, that he had been talking with Smith, and the time slipped by unheeded. Theresa drew in her lips till she seemed to have none at all, and gave him just one scornful glance. Yes: she had certainly seen him go in elsewhere, and she knew that the excuse was not true. I took my candle, and came up here—and have had one of my most wretched nights again—and neither I nor Aglaé could find that book that comforts me. It was very cruel of Karl to marry me: and yet—and yet—would I be unmarried if I could? Would I break even from this distressing life, if it involved a separation for ever? I fear not. The not seeing him day by day would be a worse fate even than this is."

"Did my lady think to ask Sir Karl whether he had put away that book that is missing from the room?" interposed Aglaé, quite unconscious that her lady had not seen Sir Karl since the book was missed, any more than she herself had: and moreover that he was not likely to see it.

"I have not asked him yet. Perhaps I took it downstairs yesterday."

"Which robe, my lady?"

"The Swiss muslin."

Aglaé left her when she was ready, and Lucy took her Bible for a few minutes, and said her prayers. Never did prayers ascend from a more wrung or troubled heart. The book she had mislaid was one of those little gems of consolation that can only be estimated in *need*. It had been given to Lucy by Miss Sumnor.

She stood a few minutes at the open window, gazing at the sunny morning. The variegated leaves of the changing trees—getting, alas! bare as Lucy's heart felt—the smooth lawn, which Maclean was rolling, the still bright flowers, the sunlight glittering on the lodge! All these fair things were hers; and yet, she could enjoy them not.

She went down: putting away all the sadness from her face that she could put, and looking in her pretty dress as fair as the sunshine. Hewitt came in with the coffee, and Lucy took her place at table. They never waited for Miss Blake. St. Jerome's was exacting, and Mr. Cattacomb somewhat uncertain as to the precise time at which he let out his flock. Hewitt went across the lawn to tell his master, who was talking to Maclean, that the breakfast was ready.

Karl came in through the open doors of the window. She glanced up and hid her eyes again: the more attractive he looked—and he always did look attractive—the greater her sense of pain. The fresh air was sweet and pleasant, and a good fire burnt in the grate.

"Good morning, Lucy."

She put down the sugar-tongs to give him her hand, and wished him good morning in a tone that no eavesdropper could have found fault with. They were quite civil to each other; nay courteous; their intercourse much like that of true friends, or a brother and sister. After playing so long at this for the sake of keeping up appearances to their household and the world, it had become quite easy—a thing of habit.

"What shall I give you?" he asked.

"An egg, please."

"Maclean thinks that fir-tree is dying."

"Which fir-tree?"

"The large one by the ferns. He wants to root it up and make a bed there. What do you think?"

"I don't mind how it is. Is your coffee sweet enough?"

"Yes."

Hewitt appeared with the letters. Two for Miss Blake, one for Lady Andinnian, none for Sir Karl. Lucy read hers; glad of the occupation it afforded: for she did but toy with her breakfast, having little appetite now.

"It is from Mamma," said Lucy. "She is going to stay with my aunt in London. I suppose you did not call on Lady Southall yesterday?"

"I? No."

"You have promised to do so for some time past."

"But I have not been able. When the mind is harassed with worry and business, social calls get put aside. Is Mrs. Cleeve well?"

"Yes, and papa better. He is going to stay at home himself. They desire to be remembered to you."

Karl bent his head in acknowledgment. And thus, talking indifferently of this and that, the meal came to an end. Karl asked his wife if she would go out to look at the fir-tree, and hear what Maclean said—he was always scrupulous in consulting her wishes as the Court's mistress. She brought her parasol at once.

Karl held out his arm, and she took it. As they went down the steps, Miss Blake appeared. They waited to greet her, and to shake hands.

"You must want your breakfast, Theresa. There are two letters for you on the table. Oh, and I have heard from Mamma. She is going to stay with Aunt Southall in London."

Lucy took Karl's arm again, and they went off with the gardener. Miss Blake probably did want her breakfast; but she spared a minute or two to look after them.

"I wonder if anyone was ever so great a hypocrite?" ran her comment. "And to think that I once believed him to be the most noble and best of men. He dared to speak disparagingly of that pure saint, Mr. Cattacomb, the other day. Good patience! what contrasts there are in the world! And the same Heaven made them both, and permits them both! One cannot understand it here. As to Lucy—but I wash my hands of *her*."

Lucy was soon back again. Miss Blake had but read her letters, and begun her breakfast. Karl had passed into his own room.

The morning wore on. Theresa went out again; Karl was shut up, and then he went out; Lucy was left in the house alone. It was usually so. She had given her orders, and no earthly thing else remained to do—save let her heart prey upon itself. When she had pretty nearly gone out of her mind, she put her bonnet on, and betook herself to Mrs. Whittle, the widow of the man who had died suddenly at the station in the summer. Passing out at the extreme gate of the Court, Lucy had but to skirt the wood, and in three minutes was at the cottage: one of a row.

She had taken to come here when she was very particularly miserable—as she felt this day. For the lesson it read to her was most salutary, acting as a kind of tonic. That this poor woman was slowly dying, there could not be much doubt of. She had been in ill health before her husband's death, and the blow struck too severely on the weakened frame. But for Karl and his wife the family must have taken refuge in the workhouse. Lucy went in and sat down on a low wooden stool. Mrs. Whittle, about to-day, was in the easy chair, sent to her from the Court, her three little girls around her, the eldest eight years of age. Two younger children, boys, played on the floor.

"I am teaching them to sew, ma'am," she said to Lucy. "Bessy has got her hand pretty well into it; but the other two haven't. When I lie awake at nights, my lady, and think how little it is they know of any sort of labour yet, and how soon I may be taken from them, and be able to teach no more, my heart fails me. I can only set on to cry, and to pray God to forgive me all my shortcomings."

The tears had come into her eyes, and were falling down her hectic cheeks. She had been very pretty once, but the face was wasted now. Lucy's eyelashes were wet.

"But I think you look better, Mrs. Whittle. And as to short-comings—we all might own to those."

"It seems to me that I could have brought them on better if I'd known what was coming, ma'am. Until that night when my husband was carried home on a shutter, I had not had a thought of death, as being likely to concern any of us at home here. And now the time seems to be coming to an end, and I'm leaving them, and they know nothing."

"I hope you will get better yet," said Lucy.

"I don't think so, ma'am. I should like to if I could. The very distress that is upon me about my children seems as if it kept me back. Nobody can know what it is to leave a family of young children to the world, till they come to it themselves. There's a dreadful yearning upon me always, my lady, an aching like, at the thought of it. Mr. Sumnor, he is very good and kind, and he comes here, and tells me about heaven, and how free from care I shall be, once I get to it. But, oh ma'am, when I must leave these little ones here, with nobody to say a word to keep them from the world's bad ways, how do I know that *they* will ever get to heaven?"

The woman had never spoken out as she was speaking to-day. Generally she had seemed calm and resigned—to get well or to die. Lucy was intensely sorry for her. She would take herself to task for being so miserable with this real distress close at hand, and for at least the rest of the day allow it to read her a salutary lesson. When she said good-bye to the woman, the tears were in her eyes.

Passing in at the small gate again, she made her way to the acacia tree and sat down under it, letting her parasol fall to the ground. Karl, who was at home again, could see her from his window, but he did not attempt to go to her. And so she idled away the morning in weariness.

Theresa appeared at luncheon; but Sir Karl did not. Lucy remembered that a parcel she was expecting from London ought to be at the station, and thought she would go in the pony-chaise for it. It was only an autumn mantle. Anything for a change—for a break in her monotonous life. So the chaise was ordered, and the groom to drive it. It came round, and she was getting in when Karl approached.

"Are you going to drive yourself, Lucy?"

"Oh no. Robert is coming."

"I will go, then. We shall not want you, Robert."

"But I was only going to the station," she said.

"To the station?"

"I think my new mantle may be there."

He drove off, turning towards the station. The mantle was not there: and Karl continued his drive as far as Basham. They said very little to one another. Just a remark on the scenery, or on any object passing: nothing more. Karl pulled up at the saddler's shop, to give some direction about a set of harness that was being made for him. Just as he got into the chaise again, somebody passed and took off his hat, with a "Good afternoon, Sir Karl."

It was Mr. Tatton. Karl wondered what he was doing in

Basham. Of course the detective might be there for fifty things, totally unconnected with his profession: but, nevertheless, the sight of him awoke uneasiness in Karl's mind. When a heavy dread lies upon us, the most trifling event will serve to stir up suspicion and augment fear.

Karl drove home again, and Lucy went up to her little sitting-room. She was owing a letter to Mrs. Cleeve, but held back from writing it. Great though her affection was for her mother, she hated now to write. It was impossible to fill up a letter—as it seemed to Lucy—and yet guard her secret. She could not say "Karl and I are doing this;" or "Karl and I are doing the other:" and yet if she did not say something of this kind of their home life, or mention his name, her fancy suggested that it would look strange, and might arouse doubt. Conscience makes us cowards. She might have sent a letter that day, saying, "I have just got home from a drive with Karl;" and "Karl and I decided this morning to have that old fir-tree by the rocks dug up;" and it would be quite true: but Lucy in her strict integrity so disliked the deceit the words would imply, that she shrank from writing them.

Footsteps on the gravel below: *his* footsteps: and she went to the window to glance out. Yes, he was going straight down the gravel walk, and through the large gates. Going where? Her heart beat a little quicker as the question crept in. To the Maze? The query was always suggesting itself now.

He turned that way—and that was all she could tell, for the trees hid the road from her view. He might be going to his agent's; he might be going to some part or other of his estate; but to Lucy's jealous mind the probability seemed perfectly clear that his destination was that shut-in house, which she already begun to hate so much. And yet—she believed that he did not go in by daytime. Lucy wondered whether Fair Rosamond, who had disturbed the peace of her queen, was half as fair as this Rosamond, now turning her own poor heart to sickness.

More footsteps on the gravel: merry tongues, light laughter. Lucy looked out again. Some of the young ladies from the village had called for Theresa, and they were now going on to St. Jerome's. For laughter such as that, for the real lightness of heart that must be its inevitable accompaniment, Lucy thought she would have bartered a portion of her remaining life.

Aglaé came in, her hands and arms full of clouds of tulle
and blue ribbon.

"Look here, my lady—these English modistes have no taste
at all. They can't judge. They send this heavy satin ribbon,
saying it is the fashion, and they put it in every part of the
beautiful light robe, so that you cannot tell which is robe,—the
tulle, or the ribbon. My lady is not going to wear that, say
I; an English modiste might wear it, but my young lady
never. So I take the ribbons off."

Lucy looked round listlessly. What did all these adorn-
ments matter to her? Karl never seemed to see now what
she was dressed in: and if he had seen, he would not have
cared.

"But what is it you are asking me, Aglaé?"

"I would ask my lady to let me put just a quarter of as
much ribbon on: and silk ribbon, not satin. I have some
silk in the house, and this satin will come in for a heavier
robe."

"Do whatever you like, Aglaé."

"That's well," said Aglaé. "But I wish my lady would not
show herself quite so indifferent," added the woman to herself
as she withdrew. "She could not care less if she were the old
grandmother."

The afternoon passed to its close, Lucy reading a bit and
working a bit to beguile the time. Whether the book or the
work lay before her, her mind was alike far away, brooding
over the trouble that could never leave it. Then she went down
to dinner in her evening dress of silk. No stranger was present:
only herself, Karl, and Theresa. It was generally thus;
neither she nor he had spirits to bring guests about them
often. Theresa told them of a slight accident that had happened at the station that afternoon, and it served for a topic
of conversation. Dinner was barely over when Miss Diana
Moore called in. She was not given to time her visits cere-
moniously; but she was always welcome, for Karl and Lucy
both liked her. Miss Diana generally gave them the news of
the place, and she began now. In some inexplicable manner
the conversation turned on the Maze. At least, something was
said that caused the place to be incidentally mentioned, and it
served to draw Miss Diana's thoughts to what they might
otherwise not have reverted to.

"The senseless geese that people are!" she cried. "Did
you hear of that ghost story that arose about the Maze?"

Karl bit his lip. Lucy looked at Miss Diana: she had heard nothing.

"Mother Jinks told me to my face the other day that there could not be a doubt it was Mr. Throcton's son haunting it. My brother—Mr. Moore—had seen it, she said, as well as Nurse Chaffen: a gentleman in evening dress, who appeared to them and vanished away again. She believed it too."

"I fancy it has been rather more materially accounted for," put in Miss Blake, not at all sorry of the opportunity to give a side fling at Sir Karl.

"Well, what I hear people have found out now is, that the ghost was only Sir Karl Andinnian, who had called in there after or before his dinner," said Miss Diana, laughing. "What do you say to it, Sir Karl?"

Sir Karl did not know what to say. On the one hand it was most essential to do away, if possible, with the impression that any strange gentleman had been at the Maze; on the other, he did not care to admit that he paid evening visits there. Of the two evils, however, the last was the least.

"It may have been myself, Miss Diana. I cannot say, I'm sure. I remember I went over one evening, and stayed a few minutes."

"But it was while Mrs. Grey was ill with fever."

"Just so. I went to enquire after her."

"Well, I suppose it was you, then. I asked William about it, but he is as close as wax when he likes, and professed not to know what I was talking of. One thing is clear, that he could not have recognised you, Sir Karl. It was nearly dark, I believe. That little baby at the Maze is very delicate."

"By the way, Miss Diana, talking of sick people, what does Mr. Moore think of poor Whittle's widow?" asked Sir Karl. "My wife says she is very ill."

The conversation was turned—Sir Karl's object in speaking. Miss Diana talked of Mrs. Whittle, and then went on to other subjects.

But it will be readily seen how cruelly these and similar incidents tried Lucy Andinnian. Had an angel come down from heaven to assure her the gentleman in evening attire was *not* Sir Karl, she would have refused to believe it. Nay, he had, so to say, confessed it—in her presence.

Miss Diana departed. Karl went out with her, and did not come in again. Lucy knew he had gone to the Maze. She went up to her room, and stood there in the dark watching for his return. It was nearly ten when he appeared: he had been spending all that time with her rival!

Even so. Sir Karl had spent it at the Maze. As the autumn evenings grew darker, he could go over earlier and come away earlier. Lucy wondered whether this state of things was to last for ever, and how much longer she could continue to bear and make no sign.

To her weary bed again went she. To the anguish of her outraged heart; to her miserable, sleepless hours, and her still more miserable dreams. Jealousy, as utterly mistaken and foundationless, has too often inflicted torment as lively as this.

It is a "green-eyed monster, which doth make the food it feeds on."

CHAPTER XXXIII.

MRS. CHAFFEN DISTURBED.

WE have now to return to Mr. Strange. That eminent detective was, to tell the truth, somewhat puzzled by his interview with Sir Karl Andinnian, held in the road; thrown, so to say, slightly on his beam ends. The earnest assurances of Sir Karl—that the individual he had been suspecting was the agent Smith, and that there was not, and could not be, any gentleman residing at the Maze—had made their due impression, for he saw that Sir Karl was a man whose word might be trusted. At the same time he detected, or thought he detected, an undue eagerness on Sir Karl's part to impress this upon him; an eagerness which the matter itself did not justify, unless Sir Karl had a private and personal motive for it. Musing on this, Mr. Strange had continued to walk about that evening instead of going on to his lodgings; and when Miss Blake surprised him underneath the trees at the Maze gate—or, rather, surprised herself by finding him there—he had not sought the spot to watch the gate, but as a shelter of seclusion while he thought. The stealthy entrance of Sir Karl Andinnian with a key taken from his pocket, and the whispered communication from Miss Blake, threw altogether another light upon the matter, and served to show what Sir Karl's personal motive might be. According to that lady's hints, Sir Karl was in the habit of stealing into the Maze, and that it was no one but Sir Karl himself who had been seen by Nurse Chaffen.

Mr. Detective Strange could not conceal from his acute brain that, if this were true, his own case was almost as good as disposed of, and he might prepare to go back to town. Salter, the prey he was patiently searching out, was at the Maze or nowhere—for Mr. Strange had turned the rest of the locality inside out, and knew that it contained no trace of him. If the gentleman in the evening dress, seen by Nurse Chaffen, was Sir Karl Andinnian, it could not have been Philip Salter: and, as his sole motive for suspecting the Maze was that worthy woman's account of him she had seen, why the grounds of suspicion seemed slipping from under him.

He thought it out well that night. Well and thoroughly. The tale was certainly likely and plausible. Sir Karl Andinnian did not appear to be one who would embark on this kind of private expedition; but, as the detective said to himself, one could not answer for one's own brother. Put it down as being Sir Karl that the woman saw, why then the mystery of her not having seen him again was at an end: for while she was there, Sir Karl would not be likely to go to the Maze and show himself a second time.

The more Mr. Strange thought it out, the further reason he found for suspecting that this must be the true state of the case. It did not please him. Clear the Maze of all suspicion as to Salter, and it would become evident that they had been misled, and that so much valuable time had been wasted. He should have to go back to Scotland Yard and report the failure. Considering that he had latterly been furnishing reports of the prey being found and as good as in his hands, the prospect was mortifying. This would be the second consecutive case in which he had signally failed.

But it was by no means Mr. Strange's intention to take the failure for granted. He was too wary a detective to do that without seeking for proof, and he had not done with Foxwood yet. The first person he must see was Mrs. Chaffen.

Somewhat weary with his night reflections and not feeling quite so refreshed as he ought to feel, for the thing had kept him awake till morning, Mr. Strange sat down to his breakfast languidly. Watchful Mrs. Jinks, who patronized her easy lodger and was allowed to visit his tea, and sugar, and butter with impunity, observed this as she whipped off the cover from a dish of mushrooms that looked as though it might tempt an anchorite.

"You've got a headache this morning, Mr. Strange, sir. Is it bad?"

"Oh, very bad," said Mr. Strange, who did not forget to keep up his rôle of delicate health as occasion offered opportunity.

"What things them headaches are!" deplored Mrs. Jinks. "Nobody knows whence they come nor how to drive 'em away. Betsy Chaffen was nursing a patient in the spring, who'd had bilious fever and rheumatis combined; and to hear what she said about that poor dear old gentleman's head——"

"By the way, how is Mrs. Chaffen?" interrupted Mr. Strange, with scant ceremony, and no regard to the old gentleman's head. "I have not seen her lately."

"She was here a day or two ago, sir; down in my kitchen. As to how she is, she's as strong as need be: which it's thanks to you for inquiring. *She* never has nothing the matter with her."

"Is she out nursing?"

"Not now. She expects to be called out soon, and is waiting at home for it."

"Where is her home?"

"Down Foxglove Lane, sir, turning off by Mr. Sumnor's church. Bull, the stonemason, lives in the end house there, and she have lodged with 'em for years. Bull tells her in joke sometimes that some of 'em ought to be took ill, with such a nurse as her in the house. Which they never are, for it's as healthy a spot as any in Foxwood."

Mr. Strange had a knack of politely putting an end to his landlady's gossip when he pleased, and of sending her away. He did so now: and the widow transferred herself and her attentions to Mr. Cattacomb's parlour.

People must hold spring and autumn cleanings, or where would their carpets and curtains be? Mrs. Chaffen, though occupying but one humble room (with a choice piece of furniture in it that was called a "bureau" by day, and was a bed by night) was not exempt from the general sanitary obligations. Mrs. Bull considered that she instituted these periodical bouts of scrubbing oftener than there was occasion for, but Betsey Chaffen liked to take care of her furniture— which was her own—and was moreover a cleanly woman.

On this self-same morning she was in the thick of it: her

gown turned up about her waist ; her hands and arms, bare to the elbow, plunged into a bucket of soapsuds; herself on her knees, and the furniture all heaped together, on the top of the shut-up bureau in the corner: when one of the young Bulls came in with the astounding news that a gentleman was asking for her.

"Goodness bless me!" cried the poor woman, turning cold all over, "it can't be that I'm fetched out, can it, Sam?—and me just in the middle of all this mess!"

"He said, was Mrs. Chaffen at home, and could he see her," replied Sam. "He's a waiting outside."

Mrs. Chaffen sat back on her heels, one hand resting on the bucket, the other grasping the wet scrubbing-brush, and her face the very picture of consternation as she stared at the boy. She had believed herself free for a full week to come.

"Is it Mr. Henley himself, Sam?"

"It ain't Mr. Henley at all," said Sam. "It's the gentleman what staying at Mrs. Jinks's."

"What the plague brings him here this morning of all others, when I've got the floor in a sop and not a chair to ask him to set down upon!" cried the woman, relieved of her great fear, but vexed nevertheless to be interrupted in her work, and believing the intruder to be Mr. Cattacomb, come on one of his pastoral visits: for that excellent divine made no scruple, in his zeal, of looking in occasionally on Mr. Sumnor's flock as well as his own. "Parsons be frightful bothers sometimes!"

"'Tain't the parson; it's the t'other one," said Sam Bull.

Mrs. Chaffen rose from her knees, stepped gingerly across the wet floor, and took a peep through the window. There she saw Mr. Strange in the centre of a tribe of young Bulls, dividing among them a piece of lettered gingerbread. Sam, afraid of not coming in for his share of the letters, bolted out of the room.

"Ask the gentleman if he'll be pleased to step in, Sam, and to excuse the litter," she called out after the boy. "I don't mind *him*," she mentally added, seizing upon a mop to mop the wet off the floor, and then letting down her gown, "and he must want something particular of me; but I'd not have cared to stand Cattakin's preaching this busy morning."

Mr. Strange came in in his pleasant way, admiring everything, from the room to the bucket, and assuring her he rather preferred wet floors to dry ones. While she was reaching him a chair, and dusting it with her damp apron, he held out his hand, pointing to where the cuts had been.

"Look here, Mrs. Chaffen. I have been thinking of coming to you this day or two past, but fancied I might see you in Paradise Row; for I'd rather have your opinion than a doctor's at any time. The hand has healed, you see."

"Yes, sir; it looks beautiful."

"But I am not sure that it has healed properly, though it may look 'beautiful,'" he rejoined. "Feel this middle cut. Here; just on the seam."

Mrs. Chaffen rubbed her fingers on the same check apron, and then passed them gently over the place he spoke of. "What do you feel?" he asked.

"Well, sir, it feels a little hard, and there seems to be a kind of knot," she said, examining the place.

"Precisely so. There's a stiffness about it that I don't altogether like, and now and then it has a kind of prickly sensation. What I have been fancying is, that a bit of glass may possibly be in it still."

But Mrs. Chaffen did not think so. In her professional capacity she talked nearly as learnedly as a doctor could have talked, though not using quite the same words. Her opinion was that if glass had remained in the hand it would not have healed: she believed that Mr. Strange had only to let it alone and have a little patience, and the symptoms he spoke of would go away.

It is not at all improbable that this opinion was Mr. Strange's own; but he thanked her and said he would abide by her advice, and gave her a little more gentle flattery. Then he sat down in the chair she had dusted, as if he meant to remain for the day, in spite of the disorder of affairs and the damp floor, and entered on a course of indiscriminate gossip. Mrs. Chaffen liked to get on quickly with her work, but she liked gossip better; no matter how busy she might be a dish of *that* never came amiss; and she put her back against another chair and folded her bare arms in her apron, and gossiped back again.

In a smooth and natural manner, apparently without intent, the conversation presently turned upon the gentleman (or ghost) Mrs. Chaffen had seen at the Maze. It was a theme she had not tired of yet.

"Now you come to talk of that," cried the detective, "do you know what idea has occurred to me upon the point, Mrs.

Chaffen? I think the gentleman you saw may have been Sir Karl Andinnian."

Nurse Chaffen, contrary to her usual habit, did not immediately reply, but seemed to fall into thought.

"Was it Sir Karl?"

"Well now, that's a odd thing!" she broke forth at last. "Miss Blake asked me the very same question, sir—was it Sir Karl Andinnian?"

"Oh, did she. When?"

"When we had been talking of the thing in your rooms, sir—that time that I had been a dressing of your hand. In going down stairs, somebody pulled me, all mysterious like, into the Reverend Cattakin's parlour: I found it was Miss Blake, and she began asking me what the gentleman looked like, and whether it was not Sir Karl."

"And was it Sir Karl?"

"Being took by surprise in that way," went on Mrs. Chaffen, disregarding the question, "I answered Miss Blake that I had not had enough time to notice the gentleman and could not say whether he was like Sir Karl or not. Not having reflected upon it then, I spoke promiscuous, you see sir, on the spur of the moment."

"And was it Sir Karl?" repeated Mr. Strange. "Now that you have had time to reflect upon it, is that the conclusion you come to?"

"No, sir; just the opposite. A minute or two afterwards, if I'd only waited, I could have told Miss Blake that it was not Sir Karl. I couldn't say who it was, but 'twas not him."

This assertion was so contrary to the theory Mr. Strange had been privately establishing that it took him somewhat by surprise.

"Why are you enabled to say surely it was not Sir Karl?" he questioned, laughing lightly, as if the matter amused him.

"Because, sir, the gentleman was taller than Sir Karl. And, when I came to think of it, I distinctly saw that he had short hair, either lightish or greyish: Sir Karl's hair is a beautiful wavy brown, and he wears it rather long."

"Twilight is very deceptive," remarked Mr. Strange.

"No doubt of that, sir: but there was enough light coming in through the passage windows for me to see what I have said. I am quite positive it was not Sir Karl Andinnian."

"Would you swear it was not?"

"No, sir, I'd not swear it: swearing's a ticklish thing:

but I am none the less sure. Mr. Strange, it was not Sir
Karl *for certain*," she added impressively. "The gentleman
was taller than Sir Karl and had a bigger kind of figure,
broader shoulders like; and it rather struck me at the time
that he limped in his walk. That I couldn't hold to, however."

"Just the description of what Salter would most likely be
now," mused the detective, his doubts veering about uncom-
fortably. "He would have a limp, or something worse, after
that escapade out of the railway carriage."

"Well, if you are so sure about it, Mrs. Chaffen, I suppose
it could not have been Sir Karl."

"I can trust my sight, sir, and I *am* sure. What ever
could have give rise to the thought that it was Sir Karl?"
continued she, after a moment's pause.

"Why, you must know, Mrs. Chaffen, that Sir Karl Andinnian is the only man in Foxwood who is likely to put on
evening dress as a rule. And, being a neighbour of Mrs.
Grey's and her landlord also, it was not so very improbable
he should have called in, don't you see?"

Thus enlightened, Mrs. Chaffen no longer wondered how
the surmise had arisen. She reiterated her assertion that it
was not Sir Karl; and Mr. Strange, gliding into the important question of soda for cleaning boards versus soap,
presently took an affable leave.

There he was, walking back again, his thoughts almost as
uncertain as the wind. Was Miss Blake's theory right, or
was this woman's? If the latter, and the man was in truth
such as she described him, taller and broader than Sir Karl,
why then he could, after all, have staked his life upon the
Maze being Salter's place of concealment. What if both
were right? It might be. Sir Karl might be paying these
stealthy visits to Mrs. Grey, and yet be totally ignorant that
any such person as Salter was at the Maze. They would
hardly dare to tell him; and Salter would take care to conceal himself when Sir Karl was there. At any rate, he—
Mr. Strange—must try and put the matter to rest with all
speed, one way or the other. Perhaps, however, that resolution was more easy to make than to carry out. As a preliminary step he took a walk to the police station at Basham;
and was seen in the street there by Sir Karl Andinnian,
when he drove his wife over in the pony-chaise.

CHAPTER XXXIV.

BAFFLED.

THE Maze, in all its ordinary quietness, was lying at rest under the midday sun. That is, as regards outward and visible rest: of inward rest, the rest that diffuses peace in the heart, there was but little. It was the day following the expedition of Mr. Strange to the house of Bull, the stonemason.

Mrs. Grey's baby was lying in its cot. Mrs. Grey, who had been hushing it to sleep in the chamber, prepared to change her morning wrapper for the gown she would wear during the day. A bouquet of fresh-cut flowers lay on the dressing-table, and the chamber window stood open to the free, fresh air. Ann Hopley was in the scullery below, peeling the potatoes for dinner, and the old man-servant was out somewhere over his work. As the woman threw the last potato into the pan, there came a gentle ring at the gate bell. She turned round and looked at the clock in the kitchen.

"Who's that, I wonder? It's too early for the bread. Any way, you'll wait till I've got my potatoes on, whoever you may be," concluded she, addressing the unknown intruder.

The saucepan on, she went forth. At the gate stood an inoffensive-looking young man with a large letter or folded parchment in his hand.

"What do you want?" asked Ann Hopley.

"Is this the Maze?"

"Yes."

"Does a lady named Grey live here?"

"Yes."

"Then I've got to leave this for her, please."

Taking the key from her pocket, Ann Hopley unsuspiciously opened the gate, and held forth her hand to take the parchment. Instead of giving it to her, the man pushed past, inside; and, to Ann Hopley's horror, Mr. Strange and a policeman suddenly appeared, and followed him. She would have closed the gate upon them; and she made a kind of frantic effort to do so: but one woman cannot effect much against three determined men.

"You can shut it now," said Mr. Strange, when they were

inside. "Don't be alarmed, my good woman: we have no wish to harm you."

"What do you want?—and why do you force yourselves in, in this way?" she inquired, frightened nearly to death.

"I am a detective officer belonging to the London police force," said Mr. Strange, introducing himself in his true character. "I bring with me a warrant to search the house called the Maze and its out-door premises"—taking the folded paper from the man's hand. "Would you like me to read it to you before I go on?"

"Search them for what?" asked Ann Hopley, feeling angry with herself for her white face. "I don't want to hear anything read. Do you think we have got stolen goods here?—I'm sure you are enough to scare a body's senses away, bursting in like this!"

Mr. Strange slightly laughed. "We are not looking for stolen goods," he said.

"What for then?" resumed the woman, striving to be calm.

"For some one whom I believe is concealed here."

"Some one concealed here! Is it me?—or my mistress?—or my old husband?"

"No."

"Then you won't find anybody else," she returned, with an air of relief. "There's no soul in the place but us three, and that I'll vow: except Mrs. Grey's baby. And we had good characters, sir, I can tell you, both me and my husband, before Mrs. Grey engaged us. Would we harbour loose characters here, do you suppose?"

It was so much waste of words. Mr. Strange went without further parley into the intricacies of the maze, calling to the policeman to follow him, and bidding the other—who was a local policeman also in plain clothes: both of them from Basham—remain near the gate and guard it against anybody's attempted egress. All this while the gate had been open. Ann Hopley locked it with trembling fingers, and then followed the men through the maze, shrieking out words of remonstrance at the top of her voice. Had there been ten felons concealed within, she made enough noise to warn them all.

'For goodness sake, woman, don't make that uproar!" cried the detective. "We are not going to murder you."

The terrified face of Mrs. Grey appeared at her chamber window. Old Hopley was gazing through the chink of the door of the tool-house, which he was about to clean out. The detective heeded nothing. He went straight to the house door and entered it.

"Wait here at the open door, and keep a sharp look round, inside and out," were his orders to the policeman. "If I want you, I'll call."

But Ann Hopley darted before Mr. Strange to impede his progress—she was greatly agitated—and seized hold of his arm.

"Don't go in," she cried imploringly; "don't go in, for the love of heaven! My poor mistress is but just out of her confinement and the fever that followed it, and the fright will be enough to kill her. I declare to you that what I have said is true. There's no body on these premises but those I've named: my mistress and us two servants, me and Hopley. It *can't* be one of us you want!"

"My good woman, I have said that it is not. But, if it be as you say—that there's no one else, no one concealed here— why object to my searching?"

"For her sake," reiterated the agitated woman; "for the poor lady's sake."

"I must search: understand that," said Mr. Strange. "Better let me do it quietly."

As if becoming impressed with this fact, and that it was useless to contend further, Ann Hopley suddenly took her hands off the detective, leaving him at liberty to go where he would. Passing through the kitchen, she began to attend to her saucepan of potatoes.

Armed with his full power, both of law and of will, Mr. Strange began his search. The warrant had not been obtained from Sir Karl Andinnian, but from a magistrate at Basham: it might be that Mr. Strange did not feel sufficiently assured of Sir Karl's good faith: therefore the Maze was not apprized beforehand.

It was not a large house; the rooms were soon looked into, and nothing suspicious was to be seen. Three beds were made up in three different chambers: the one in Mrs. Grey's room and two others. Was one of these occupied by Salter? The detective could not answer the doubt. They were plain beds in plain rooms, and it might be that the two servants did not sleep together. Knocking at the door, he entered Mrs. Grey's chamber: the baby slept in its cot: she stood at the glass in her dressing-gown, her golden hair falling about her.

"I beg your pardon, madam; I beg your pardon a thousand times," said the detective, with deprecation, as he removed his hat. "The law sometimes obliges us to do disagreeable things; and we, servants of it, cannot help ourselves."

"At least tell me the meaning of all this," she said with ashy face and trembling lips. And he explained that he was searching the house, armed with the authority of a search warrant.

"But what is it you want? *Who* is it?"

Again he explained to her that they were looking after an escaped fugitive, who, it was suspected, might have taken refuge in the Maze.

"I assure you, sir," she said, her gentle manner earnest, her words apparently truthful, "that no person whatever, man or woman, has been in the Maze since I have inhabited it, save myself and my two servants."

"Nevertheless, madam, we have information that some one else has been seen here."

"Then it has been concealed from me," she rejoined. "Will you not at least inform me who it is you are searching for? In confidence if you prefer: I promise to respect it."

"It is an escaped criminal named Salter," replied the officer, knowing that she would hear it from Sir Karl Andinnian, and wishing to be as civil to her as he could.

"Salter!" returned Mrs. Grey, showing the surprise that perhaps she did not feel. "Salter! Why Salter—at least if it is Salter—is the man who lives opposite these outer gates, and goes by the name of Smith. Salter has never been concealed here."

The very assertion made by Sir Karl Ardinnian. Mr. Strange took a moment to satisfy his keen sight that there was no other ingress to this room, save by the door, and no piece of furniture large enough to conceal a man in, and was then about to bow himself out. But she spoke again.

"On my sacred word of honour, sir, I tell you truth. Sir Karl Ardinnian—my landlord—has been suspecting that his agent, Smith, might turn out to be Salter: I suspected the same."

"But that man is not Salter, madam. Does not bear any resemblance to him. It was a misapprehension of Sir Karl's."

"And—do I understand that you are still looking for him here?—in the Maze? I do *not* understand."

"Not looking for that man Smith, madam, but for the real Salter. We have reason to think he is concealed here."

"Then, sir, allow me to affirm to you in all solemnity, that Salter is not, and never has been concealed here," she said with dignity. "Such a thing would be impossible without my knowledge."

He did not care to prolong the conversation. He had his work to do, and no words from her or anyone else would deter him from it. As he was quitting the room, he suddenly turned to ask a question.

"I beg your pardon, madam. Have you any objection to tell me whether your two servants, Hopley and his wife, occupy the same room and bed?"

For a moment or two she gazed at him in silence, possibly in surprise at the question, and then gave her answer almost indifferently.

"Not in general, I believe. Hopley's cough is apt to be troublesome at night, and it disturbs his wife. But I really do not know much about their arrangements: they make them without referring to me."

The detective proceeded on his mission. He soon discovered the concealed door in the evening sitting-room, and passed into the passage beyond it. Ah, if Salter, or any other criminal were in hiding within its dark recesses, there would be little chance for him now! The passage, very close and narrow, had no egress on either side; it ended in a flight of nearly perpendicular stairs. Groping his way down, he found himself in a vault, or underground room. Mr. Strange was provided with matches, and lighted some. It was a bare place, the brick walls dripping moisture, the floor paved with stone. Here he discovered another narrow passage that led straight along, it was hard to say how far, and he had need to strike more matches before he had traversed it. It ended in a flight of stairs: which he ascended, and—found himself in a summer-house at the extreme boundary of the garden.

So far the search had not realized his expectations. On the contrary, it was so unsatisfactory as to be puzzling to his experienced mind. There had been no tracks or traces of Philip Salter; no indication that the passages were ever used; and the doors had opened at his touch, unsecured by bolt or bar.

Taking a look round him while he strove to solve more than one problem, the detective slowly advanced along the garden. All the garden ground surrounding the house, it must be understood, whether useful or ornamental, was *within* the circle of the maze of trees. Turning a corner, after passing the fruit trees and vegetables, he came in view of the lawn and of the greenhouse; also of Ann Hopley, who was plucking some thyme from the herb bed.

"Have you found what you were looking for, sir?" she asked, every appearance of animosity gone, as she raised her head to put the question when he came near.

"Not yet."

"Well, sir, I hope you are satisfied. You may take my word for it that you never will find it."

"Think not?" he carelessly said, looking about him.

"Any way, I am not sorry that you have been through them subterranean places underground," she resumed. "My mistress and I have never ventured to look into them, and she has not much liked the thought of their being there. We got Hopley to go down one day; but his shoulders stuck in a narrow part, and he had to force 'em back and come up again."

The detective stepped into the greenhouse, and stood a moment admiring the choice flowers and some purple grapes ripening above. Ann Hopley had gathered her herbs when he came out, and stood with them in her hand.

"If you'd like to take a few flowers, sir, I'm sure Mrs. Grey would not wish to object. Or a bunch of grapes. There's some ripe."

"Thank you, not now."

He pulled open the tool-house door, only partly closed, and looked in on Hopley. The old man was cleaning it out. Sweeping the floor with a besom and raising a cloud of dust enough to choke a dozen throats, he was hissing and fizzing over his work.

Hopley looked very decrepid to-day: his swollen knees were bent and tottering: his humped back was all conspicuous as he stood; while his throat was enveloped in some folds of an old scarlet comforter.

"Mr. Hopley, I think," said the detective, politely. "Will you please to tell me the name of the gentleman that's staying here?"

But Hopley, bent nearly double over his work, took no notice whatever. His back was towards the detective; and he kept on his hissing and fizzing, and scattering his clouds of dust.

"He does not hear you, sir," said Ann Hopley, advancing. "He's as deaf as a post, and can make out no voice but mine: especially when he has one of his sore throats upon him, as he has to-day. For my part, I think these bad throats have to do with the deafness. He is always getting them."

Stepping into the midst of the dust, she shook her husband by the arm somewhat roughly, and he raised his head with a start.

"Here, Hopley, just listen a minute," she screamed at the top of her voice. "This gentleman is asking you to tell him the name of the gentleman who is staying here—that's it, is it not, sir?"—and Mr. Strange nodded acquiescence. "The name, Hopley, the name."

"I've never see'd no lady here but the missis," said old Hopley at length, in his imperfect articulation, caused by the loss of his teeth, as he touched his broad-brimmed hat respectfully to the stranger, and looked up, leaning on the besom.

"Not a lady, Hopley; a gentleman," bawled Ann.

"I've see'd no gentleman here at all."

"He is rather stupid as to intellect, is he not?" cried the detective to the wife.

She resented the imputation. "Not at all, sir; no more than deaf people always seem to be."

"What gentleman be it?" asked Hopley. "Smith, the agent, comes for the rent at quarter-day, and Sir Karl Andinnian came over one morning about the well."

"Neither of those," roared out Mr. Strange. "The gentleman that's hiding here."

"Not them, Hopley," called Ann in his ear. "The gentleman that's hiding here, he says."

"Hiding where?" asked Hopley. "In them underground places? I never know'd as anybody was hiding in 'em."

"Ask him if he'll swear that no man whatever is in hiding here, Mrs. Hopley."

The gentleman says will you swear that no man is in hiding here at the Maze?" repeated Ann, somewhat improving upon the question.

"I'll swear that there's neither man nor woman in the place, sir, to my knowledge, hiding or not hiding, but us two and the missis," was the answer, given directly to Mr. Strange, and as emphatically as his utterly toothless mouth allowed. "I swear it to my God."

"And you may trust him, sir," said Ann quietly. "I don't

believe he ever told a lie in his life: much less took an oath to one. Hopley's honest and straightforward as the day, though he is a martyr to rheumatism."

Mr. Strange nodded his head to the man and left him to his sweeping. The work and the hissing began again before he was clear of the door. In neither the tool-house nor the greenhouse was any possible chance afforded of concealment—to ascertain which had doubtless been the chief motive for the detective's invasion of them.

"I don't believe the old man knows about it," ran his thoughts; "but the woman *does*."

Ann Hopley carried her herbs indoors, and began picking them. Mr. Strange, calling the policeman to his aid, made as thorough a search out of doors as the nature of the premises and the puzzling maze of trees allowed. There was a closed-in passage of communication through the labyrinth, between the back of the house and the outer circle: but it was built solely with a view to convenience—such as the bringing in of coals or beer to the Maze; or, as Ann Hopley expressed it, the carrying of a coffin out of it. The detective had its doors unbolted and unbarred, and satisfied himself that it afforded no facility for concealment. Borrowing a candle of her, he went again to the secret passages underground, both policemen with him, to institute a more minute and thorough examination.

There ensued no result. And Mr. Detective Strange withdrew his men and finally departed himself; one mortifying word beating its unsatisfactory refrain on his brain:

"BAFFLED."

CHAPTER XXXV.

AT SCOTLAND YARD.

ONCE more on his weary way to London went Karl Andinnian, on the same weary business that he had gone before; but this time he was proceeding direct to the place he had hitherto shunned—Scotland Yard.

The extreme step, taken by the detective, Tatton, in searching the Maze, had alarmed Karl beyond measure. True, the unfortunate fugitive, hiding there, had managed to elude detection: but who could say that he would be able to do so another time, or how often these men of the law might choose to go in? The very fact of their not being actually in search of Sir Adam, but of a totally different individual, made it seem all the more unbearably cruel.

In Mrs. Grey's dire distress and perplexity, she had sent that same night for Karl—after the search—and he heard the whole that had taken place. Adam confessed he did not know what was to be done, or how to avert the fate—recapture—that seemed closely impending; and Rose almost fell on her knees before Karl, imploring him with tears to try and save her husband from the danger. Karl took his remorse home with him: remorse arising from the knowledge that *he* had brought all this about, he, himself, in his insane inquiries after Salter: and, after much anxious consideration, he resolved to go on the morrow to Scotland Yard.

It was past noon when he reached his destination. After he had stated confidentially the nature of his business—that it was connected with the search after Philip Salter, then being carried on at Foxwood by detective Tatton—he was told that it was Mr. Superintendent Game who must see him on the point: but that at present the superintendent was engaged. Karl had to wait: and was kept waiting a considerable time.

Could Karl's eyes have penetrated through two walls and an intervening room, he might have been greatly astonished to see the person with whom the superintendent was occupied. It was no other than Tatton himself. For the detective, taking the night after the search to think over matters, just as Karl had done, had come to the determination of placing the history of his doings at Foxwood before his superiors, and to leave with them the decision whether he should go on with his search, or abandon it. Accordingly, he also had proceeded to London that morning, but by an earlier train; and he was now closeted with Mr. Superintendent Game—who had given him his original instructions, and had, specially, the Salter affair in hand—and was laying before him a succinct narration of facts, together with his various suspicions and his bafflings. Before the interview was over, the superintendent was as well acquainted with the Maze, its rumours and its mysteries, and with sundry other items of Foxwood gossip, as Tatton himself could be.

"A gentleman waiting—had been waiting some time—to see Mr. Game on the Foxwood business," was the interruption that was first brought to them: and both Mr. Game and Tatton felt somewhat surprised thereby. What gentleman could be engaged on the Foxwood business, except themselves?

"Who is it?" asked the superintendent. And a card was handed in.

"Sir Karl Andinnian."

A moment's pause to revolve matters, and then the superintendent issued his fiat.

"See him in five minutes."

The five minutes were occupied with Tatton; but he was safely away ere they had expired, carrying with him his orders to wait; and Sir Karl Andinnian was shown in. The superintendent and the visitor met for the first time, and glanced at each other with some curiosity. The officer saw, in the brother of the noted and unfortunate criminal, a pale, refined, and essentially gentlemanly man, with a sad but attractive face that seemed to tell of sorrow; the other saw a spare man of middle height, who in age might have been his father, and whose speech and manners betokened a cultivation as good as his own.

Taking the seat offered him, Karl entered at once upon his business. Explaining shortly and truthfully the unfortunate suspicion on his own part, that had led to his inquiries about Salter of Mr. Burtenshaw, and to the subsequent despatch of Tatton to Foxwood. He concealed nothing; not even the slight foundation for those suspicions — merely the having seen the name of Philip Salter in a pocket-book that was in the possession of Philip Smith; and related his recent explanation with Smith; when he learnt that he and Salter were cousins. Karl told it all: and the officer saw, and believed, that he was telling it truly. Karl then went on to relate how he had himself sought an interview with Tatton on his last return from London— whither he had gone to try and convince Mr. Burtenshaw that it was *not* Salter —— that he had learnt from Tatton then that his suspicions were directed to a house called the Maze, as the place of Salter's concealment, and that he, Sir Karl, had assured Tatton on his word of honour as a gentleman that it was altogether a mistaken assumption, for that Salter was not at the Maze, and never had been there. He had believed that Tatton was convinced by what he had said: instead of which, he had taken the extreme and, under the circumstances, most unjustifiable step, of proceeding to the house with a search warrant, and two policemen, to the terror of the lady inhabiting it, Mrs. Grey, and her two old servants. It was to report this to Tatton's superiors at head-quarters that he had now come up from Foxwood, Sir Karl added; not, he emphatically said, to complain of Mr. Tatton or to get him reprimanded, for no doubt the man, in doing what he had done, had believed it was but his duty: but to request that instructions might be given him to leave Mrs. Grey in tranquillity for the future. She, feeling much outraged and insulted by the suspicion that she could have a common criminal like Philip Salter concealed in her home, had sent for him, Sir Karl, as her landlord, to beg him to protect her, if in his power, and to secure her from further molestation.

Mr. Superintendent Game listened to Sir Karl's narrative as attentively and with as much apparent interest as though it comprised information that he had never in all his life heard of: whereas, in point of fact, Tatton had just been going over the same facts with him, or nearly the same. He admitted to Sir Karl that it no doubt did seem to Mrs. Grey an unjustifiable step, an unaccountable intrusion; if indeed Salter were not concealed there and she knew nothing of him.

"I assure you, as I assured Tatton, that she does not," spoke Karl, with almost painful earnestness. "There is not an iota of foundation for supposing Salter ever was at Foxwood; certainly he was never at the Maze."

"Tatton is an experienced officer, Sir Karl. You may depend upon it that he had good reasons for what he did."

"That he fancied he had: I admit that. But they were utterly groundless. I should have thought that had any one lady, above another, been exempt from suspicion of any kind, it was Mrs. Grey. She lives a perfectly retired life at the Maze during her husband's absence, giving offence to none. To suppose she would allow the fugitive Salter, a man whom she never knew or saw, to be concealed within her domains is worse than preposterous."

"It is hazardous to answer so far for any one, Sir Karl," was the rejoinder—and Karl thought he detected a faint smile on the speaker's lips. "Especially for a woman. The best of them have their tricks and turns."

"I can answer for Mrs. Grey."

Mr. Superintendent Game, whose elbow as he faced Sir Karl was leaning on a desk-table, took it off and fell to pushing together some papers, as though in abstraction. He was no doubt taking time mentally to fit in some portions of Karl's narrative with the information possessed by himself. Karl waited a minute and then went on.

"I am sure that this lady would be willing to make a solemn affidavit that she knows nothing of Salter; and that he is not, and never has been, concealed there: if by so doing it would secure her exemption from intrusion for the future."

"Yes, no doubt," said the officer somewhat absently. "Sir Karl Andinnian," he added, turning briskly to face him again after another pause, "I assume that your own part in this business was confined to the sole fact of your entering on the misapprehension of taking your agent Smith to be Salter."

"That's all. But do you not see how I feel myself to be compromised: since it was my unfortunate endeavour to set the doubt at rest, by applying to Burtenshaw, that has originated all the mischief and brought the insult on Mrs. Grey?"

"Of course. But for that step of yours we should have heard nothing of Salter in connection with Foxwood."

Karl maintained a calm exterior: but he could have ground his teeth as he listened. It was too true.

"Then, with that one exception, Sir Karl, I am right in assuming that you personally hold no other part or interest in this affair, as regards Salter?"

"As regards Salter? None whatever."

"Well now," resumed the superintendent, in a confidential kind of tone, "we can talk at our ease for a minute. Does it not strike you, Sir Karl, as an impartial and impassioned looker-on, that there is something rather curious in the affair, taking one thing with another?"

"I fail to catch your meaning, sir," replied Karl, gazing at the superintendent. "I confess no such idea has occurred to me. Curious in what way?"

"We shall come to that. Philip Smith has been your agent about six months, I believe."

"About that."

"Whence did you have him? Where did he live before?"

"I really do not know. My mother, the late Mrs. Andinnian, who was occupying Foxwood Court during my absence abroad, engaged him. She became ill herself, was unable to attend to things, and deemed it well to employ some one to look after my interests."

"Report runs in Foxwood—all kinds of gossip have come up to me from the place," the superintendent broke off to add

—"that Smith is only your honorary agent, Sir Karl; that he gives it out he is an old friend of the Andinnian family."

"I can assure you that Smith is my paid agent. He has a house to live in, and takes his salary quarterly."

"The house is exactly opposite the Maze gates?"

"Yes," said Karl, beginning to feel somewhat uncomfortable at the drift the conversation appeared to be taking.

"Is there any truth in the statement that your family knew him in earlier days? You will see in a minute, Sir Karl, why I ask you all this. I conclude there is not."

"I understood my mother to imply in her last illness that she had known something of him: but I was not sure that I caught her meaning correctly, and she was too ill for me to press the question. I had never heard of any Smith myself, and the chances were that I misunderstood her. He makes himself useful about the estate, and that is all I have to look to."

"Report says also—pardon me for recurring to it, Sir Karl—that he makes himself a very easy kind of agent; seems to do as he likes, work or play, and spends most of his time smoking in his front garden, exchanging salutations with the passers-by and watching his neighbour's opposite gate."

Had it been to save his life, Karl Andinnian could not have helped the change that passed over his countenance. What was coming? He strove to be cool and careless, poor fellow, and smiled frankly.

"I fancy he is rather idle—and given to smoke too much. But he does well what he has to do for me, for all that. Mine is not a large estate, as you may be aware, and Sir Joseph left it in first-rate condition. There is very little work for an agent."

"Well, now, I will ask you a last question, Sir Karl. Do you think Smith's residence at Foxwood is in any way connected with the Maze?"

"Connected with the Maze!" echoed Sir Karl, his face never betraying the uneasiness that his beating and terrified heart was beginning to feel all too keenly.

"That is, connected with its tenants."

"In what way would it be possible?"

"Look here. Philip Smith presented himself at Foxwood Court about six months ago, soliciting the agency of your estates from Mrs. Andinnian—as there is little doubt he did so present himself to her, and solicit. Now, it was a very singular thing for him to do, considering that his previous life (as I happen to know, had in no way whatever qualified him for the situation. He knew no more of land, or the duties of a land-agent, than does this inkstand on my table. Why did he attempt to take such a place?"

"For the want of something else to do, probably," replied Karl. "He told me himself the other day, that his cousin's fall ruined him also, by causing him to be turned from his situation. As to the duties he has to perform for me, a child might be at home in them in a week."

"Granted. Let us go on. Mr. Smith's installation at your place as agent was closely followed by the occupancy of the Maze, Mrs. Grey and her servants arriving as its tenants. Was it not so, Sir Karl?"

"I—think it was," assented Karl, appearing to be recalling the past to his memory, and feeling himself in a bath of horror as he saw that the all-powerful man before him, powerful to know, to rule, and to act, was quite at home behind the scenes.

"Well, I cannot help thinking that the one may have been connected with the other; that Smith's appearance at your place, and the immediately following occupancy of the Maze, may have been, so to say, connecting links in the same chain," continued the superintendent. "A doubt of it was floating in my mind before I had the honour of seeing you, Sir Karl: but I failed to detect any adequate cause; there was none on the surface. You have now supplied that, by telling me who Smith is—Salter's relative."

"Indeed I cannot understand you," said Karl, turning nevertheless from hot to cold.

"The Maze is a place—what with its surrounding labyrinth of trees and its secret passages and outlets—unusually favourable for concealment. A proscribed man might hide himself there for years and years, and never be discovered unless suspicion were accidentally drawn on him. I think that the chances are that Salter is there; and that his cousin, Smith, is keeping guard over him for his protection, while ostensibly fulfilling only the duties of your agency. They may have discovered in some way the desirable properties of the Maze and laid their plans to come to it accordingly."

It was so faithful a picture of what Smith was really doing at Foxwood—though the one he was watching over was a very different man from Salter—that Karl Andinnian almost thought some treacherous necromancy must have been at work. All he could do was, to speak forcibly against the view, and to declare that there could not be any foundation for it.

"That is only your opinion against mine, Sir Karl," observed the superintendent courteously. "You may rely upon it, I think, that the fact of Salter's being there would be kept from you, of all people."

"Do you forget the slur you would cast on Mrs. Grey?"

"As to that, Salter may be some relative of hers. Even her husband—even her brother. I remember it was said, at the time his case fell, that he had one sister. In either case, of course Mrs. Grey—the name she goes under—would not allow the fact of his concealment there to transpire to you."

How could Karl meet this? Sitting there, in his perplexity and pain, he could not see a step before him.

"You have forgotten that Tatton has searched the Maze from roof to basement, Mr. Superintendent."

"Not at all. It tells nothing. There are no doubt other hidden places that he did not penetrate to in that first search At best, it was but a superficial one."

That "first" search. Was all security slipping from Karl's feet, inch by inch?

"Believe me, you are wrong," he said; "your notion is an utterly mistaken one. I assure you on my word of honour, as truly and solemnly as I shall ever testify to any fact in this world, that Salter is not within the Maze; that he never has been. Mind you, sir, I *know* this. I go over occasionally to see poor Mrs. Grey in her loneliness, and am in a position to speak positively."

An unmistakable smile sat on the officer's face now. "Ay," he said, "I have heard of your occasional nocturnal visits to her, Sir Karl. The young lady is said to be very attractive."

At the first moment Sir Karl did not detect the covert meaning. It came to him with a rush of indignation. The superintendent had rarely seen so haughty a face.

"No offence, Sir Karl. 'T was but a joke."

"A joke I do not like, sir. I am a married man."

"Est ce que cela empêche"—the other was beginning: for the conclusion he had drawn, on the score of Sir Karl's evening visits was a very decided one; but Karl put a peremptory stop to the subject. He deemed the superintendent most offensively familiar and unwarrantably foolish; and he resented in his angry heart the implied aspersion on his brother's wife, the true Lady Andinnian, than whom a more modest and innocent-natured woman did not exist. And it never entered into the brain of Karl Andinnian to suspect that the same objectionable joke might have been taken up by people nearer home, even by his own wife.

The interview came to an end. Karl went away, uncertain whether he had made sufficient impression, or not, to ensure the Maze against intrusion for the future. The superintendent did not say anything decisive, one way or the other, except that the matter must be left for his consideration. It might all have been well yet, all been well, but for this new complication, this suspicion rather, touching Smith and Salter jointly! He, Karl, had given the greatest rise to this, he and no other, by stating that day that the men were cousins. He asked himself whether Heaven could be angry with him; for, whatever step he took for good only seemed to lead to mischief and make affairs worse. One assurance he did carry away with him: that the young lady at the Maze might rest content: her peace personally should not be molested. But that was not saying that the house should not be.

After Sir Karl's departure, the superintendent's bell rang and Tatton was recalled. A long conversation ensued. Matters known were weighed; matters suspected were looked at: and Mr. Tatton was finally bidden back to Foxwood.

Karl had gone direct from Scotland Yard to take the train. A fast one, which speedily conveyed him home. He walked from the station, and was entering his own gates when Hewitt —who seemed to have been gossiping at the lodge with the gardener's wife, but who had probably been lingering about in the hope of meeting his master—accosted him; and they went up the walk together.

"I am afraid something is amiss at the Maze, sir," began the man, looking cautiously around and speaking in a low tone.

"Something amiss at the Maze!" echoed Karl, seized with a terror that he did not attempt to conceal.

"Not *that*, sir; not the worst, thank Heaven! Sir Adam has been taken ill."

"Hush, Hewitt. No names. Ill in what way? How do you know it?"

"I had been to carry a note for my lady to old Miss Patchett, Sir Karl. Coming back, Ann Hopley overtook me; she was walking from the station at a fine rate. He·master had been taken most alarmingly ill, she said; and at any risk a doctor must be had to him. They did not dare to call in Mr. Moore, lest he might talk to the neighbours, and she had been to the station then to telegraph for a stranger."

"Telegraph where?"

"To Basham, sir. For Dr. Cavendish."

Karl drew a deep breath. It seemed to be perplexity on perplexity: and he saw at once how much danger this step must involve.

"What is the matter with him, Hewitt? Do you know?"

"It was one of those dreadful fainting-fits, sir. But they could not get him out of it, and for some time thought he was really dead. Mrs. Grey was nearly beside herself, Ann said, and insisted on having a doctor. He is better now, sir," added Hewitt, "and I think there's no need for you to go over unless you particularly wish. I went strolling about the road, thinking I might hear or see something more, and when Ann Hopley came to the gate to answer a ring, she told me he was quite himself again but still in bed. It was the pain made him faint."

"I cannot think what the pain is," murmured Karl. "Has the doctor been?"

"I don't think he has yet, Sir Karl."

Karl lifted his hat to rub his aching brow. He saw his wife sitting under one of the trees, and went forward to join her. The wan, weary look on her face, growing more wan, more weary, day by day, struck on him particularly in the waning light of the afternoon.

"Do you do well to sit here, Lucy?" he asked, as he flung himself beside her, in utter weariness.

"Why should I not sit here?"

"I fancy the dew must be already rising."

"It will not hurt me. And if it did—what would it matter?"

The half reproaching, half indifferent accent in which it was uttered, served to try him. He knew what the words implied—that existence had, through him, become a burden to her. His nerves were strung already to their utmost tension; the trouble at his heart was pressing him sore.

"Don't *you*, by your reproaches, make matters worse for me Lucy, to-day. God knows that I have well-nigh more than I can bear."

A A

The strangely-painful tone, so full of unmistakable anguish, aroused her kindly nature. She turned to him with a sigh.

"I wish I could make things better for both of us Karl."

"At least, you need not make them worse. What with one thing and another——"

"Well?" she said, her voice softened, as he paused.

"Nothing lies around me, Lucy, but perplexity and dread and pain. Look where I will, abroad or at home, there's not as much as a single ray of light to cheer my spirit, or the faintest reflection of it. You cannot wonder that I am sometimes tempted to wish I could leave the world behind me."

"Have you had a pleasant day in town?" she asked, after a little while.

"No, I have had an unsatisfactory day in all ways. And I have come home to find more to try me: more dissatisfaction *here*, more dread abroad. 'Man is born to trouble as the sparks fly upwards.' Some of us are destined to realise the truth in ourselves all too surely."

He looked at his watch, got up, and walked in-doors without another word. Lucy gazed after him with yearning eyes; eyes that seemed to have some of the perplexity he spoke of in their depths. There were moments when she failed to understand her husband's moods. This was one.

CHAPTER XXXVI.

ILL-OMENED CHANCES.

KARL ANDINNIAN was tempted bitterly to ask of his own heart whether he could have fallen under the displeasure of Heaven, so persistently did every fresh movement of his, intended for good, turn into an increased bank of danger. Poor Sir Adam had more need to question it than he; for nothing but ill-omened chances seemed to pursue him.

It is quite probable that when Ann Hopley and her flurried mistress decided to telegraph for Dr. Cavendish of Basham, they had thought, and hoped, that the doctor would come back by train, pass quietly on foot into the Maze, so pass out again, and the public be none the wiser. Dr. Cavendish, however, who was from home when the telegram arrived, drove over later in his gig; and the gig, with the groom in it, paced before the Maze gate while the doctor was inside, engaged with his patient.

Just then there occurred one of those unhappy chances. Mr. Moore, the surgeon, happened to walk by with his daughter, Jemima, and saw the gig—which he knew well—waiting about. It took him by surprise, as he had not heard that any one was ill in the vicinity. The groom touched his hat, and Mr. Moore went up to him.

"Waiting for your master, James? Who is he with? Who is ill?"

"It's somebody down yonder, sir?" replied the man, pointing back over his shoulder to indicate the Maze; but which action was not intelligible to the surgeon.

"Down where? At the Court?"

"No, sir. At the Maze."

"At the Maze! Why, who can be ill there?" cried Mr. Moore.

"I don't know, sir. Master had a telegram, telling him to come."

At that moment Dr. Cavendish was seen to leave the gate and come towards his gig. Mr. Moore walked quickly forward to meet him, and the gig turned.

"I suppose you have been called to Mrs. Grey, doctor," observed the surgeon, as he shook hands. "Has she had a relapse? I wonder she did not send for me. I have but just given up attending her."

"Mrs. Grey?" returned the doctor. "Oh no. It is a gentleman I have been called to see."

"What gentleman?" asked the surgeon in surprise. "There's no gentleman at the Maze."

"One is there now. I don't know who it is. Some friend or relative of the lady's probably. Ah, Miss Jemima! blooming as ever, I perceive," he broke off, as the young lady came slowly up. "Could you not give some of us pale, over-worked people a receipt for those roses on your cheeks?"

"What is it that's the matter with him?" interposed the surgeon, leaving his daughter to burst into her giggle.

Dr. Cavendish put his arm within his friend's, led him beyond the hearing of Miss Jemima, and said a few words in a low tone.

"Why, the case must be a grave one!" exclaimed Mr. Moore aloud.

"*I* think so. I don't like the symptoms at all. From some cause or other, too, it seems he has not had advice till now, which makes it all the more dangerous."

"By the way, doctor, as you are here, I wish you would spare five minutes to see a poor woman with me," said Mr. Moore, passing from the other subject. "It won't hinder you much longer than that."

"All right, Moore. Who is it?"

"It's the widow of that poor fellow who died from sun-stroke in the summer: Whittle. The woman has been ailing ever since, and very grave disease has now set in. I don't believe I shall save her; only yesterday it crossed my mind to wish you could see her. She lives just down below there; in one of the cottages beyond Foxwood Court."

They got into the gig, the physician taking the reins, and telling his groom to follow on foot. Miss Jemima was left to make her own way home. She was rather a pretty girl, with a high colour and a quantity of light brown curls, and her manners were straightforward and decisive. When the follies and vanities of youth should have been chased away by sound experience, allowing her naturally good sense to come to the surface, she would, in all probability, be as strong-minded as her Aunt Diana, whom she already resembled in many ways.

The autumn evening was drawing on: twilight had set in. Miss Jemima stood a moment, deliberating which road she should take; whether follow the gig, and go home round by the Court, or the other way. Of the two, the latter was the nearer, and the least lonely; and she might—yes, she might—encounter Mr. Cattacomb on his way to or from St. Jerome's. Clearly it was the one to choose. Turning briskly round when the decision was made, she nearly ran against Mr. Strange. That gentleman had just got back from London, sent down again by the authorities of Scotland Yard, and was on his way from the station. The Maze had become an object of so much interest to him as to induce him to choose the long way round, that would cause him to pass its gates, rather than take the direct road to the village. And here was another of those unfortunate accidents apparently springing out of chance; for the detective had seen the gig waiting, and halted in a bend of the hedge to watch the colloquy of the doctors.

"Good gracious, is it you, Mr. Strange?" cried the young lady, beginning to giggle again. "Why, Mrs. Jinks declared this afternoon you had gone out for the day!"

"Did she? Well, when I stroll out I never know when I may get back: the country is more tempting in autumn than at any other season. That was a doctor's gig, was it not, Miss Jemima?"

"Dr. Cavendish's of Basham," replied Miss Jemima, who enjoyed the honour of a tolerable intimacy with Mrs. Jinks's lodger—as did most of the other young ladies frequenting the parson's rooms.

"He must have come over to see some one. I wonder who is ill?"

"Papa wondered, too, when he first saw he gig. It is somebody at the Maze."

"Do you know who?"

"Well, they seem to talk as if it were a gentleman. I did not much notice."

"A gentleman?"

"I think so. I am sure they said 'he' and 'him.' Perhaps Mrs. Grey's husband has arrived. Whoever it is, he must be very ill, for I heard papa say the case must be 'grave,' and the doctor called it 'dangerous.' They have gone on together now to see poor Hannah Whittle?"

Not since he had had the affair in hand, had the detective's ears been regaled with so palatable a dish. That Philip Salter had been taken ill with some malady or another, sufficiently serious to necessitate the summoning of a doctor, he fully believed. Miss Jemima resumed.

"I must say, considering that papa is medical attendant there, Mrs. Grey might have had the good manners to consult him first."

"It may be the old gardener that's ill," observed the detective slowly, who had been turning his thoughts about.

"So it may," acquiesced Miss Jemima. "He's but a poor creahy old thing, by all accounts. But no—they would hardly go to the expense of telegraphing for a physician for him, with papa at hand."

"Oh, they telegraphed, did they?"

"So the groom said."

"The girl is right," thought the detective. "They'd not telegraph for Hopley. It is Salter. And they have called in a stranger from a distance in preference to Mr. Moore close by. The latter might have talked to the neighbours. You have done me a wonderful service, young lady, if you did but know it."

Mr. Strange did not offer to attend her home, but suffered her to depart alone. And Miss Jemima, who was rather fond of a little general flirtation though she did perhaps favour one swain above all others, resented the slight in her heart. She consoled herself after the manner of the fox when he could not reach the grapes.

"He's nothing but a bear," said she, tossing her little vain head, as she tripped away in the deepening gloom of the evening. "It is all for the best. We might have chanced to have met Mr. Cattacomb, and then he would have looked daggers at me. Or—my goodness me!—perhaps Aunt Diana."

Mr. Strange strolled on, revolving the aspect of affairs in his official mind. His next object must be to get to speak to Dr. Cavendish and learn who it really was that he had been to see. Of course it was not absolutely beyond the cards of possibility that the sick man was Hopley. It was not impossible that Mrs. Grey might have some private and personal objection to the calling in again of Mr. Moore; or that the old man had been seized with some illness so alarming, as to necessitate the services of a clever physician in preference to those of a general practitioner. He did not think any of this likely; but it *might* be; and only Dr. Cavendish could set it at rest.

Perhaps some slight hope animated him that he might obtain an immediate interview with Dr. Cavendish on the spot, as he returned from Mrs. Whittle's cottage. If so, he found it defeated. The gig came back with the two gentlemen in it, and it drove off direct to the village, not passing Foxwood Court at all, or the detective; but the latter was near enough to see it travel along. Mr. Moore was dropped at his own house, and the groom—who had been sent on there—taken up; and then the gig went on to Basham.

"I must see him somehow," decided the detective—"and the less time lost over it, the better. Of course a man in the dangerously sick state this one is represented to be, cannot make himself scarce as quickly as one in health could; but Salter has not played at hide-and-seek so long to expose himself unnecessarily. He would make superhuman efforts to elude us, and rather get away dying than wait to be taken. Better strike while the iron is hot. I must see the doctor to-night."

He turned back to the station; and was just in time to watch the train for Basham go puffing out.

"That train has gone on before its time!" he cried in anger.

After reference to clocks and watches, it was found that it had gone on before its time by more than a minute. The station-master apologised: said the train was up three or four minutes too early; and, as no passengers were waiting to go on by it, he had given the signal to start rather too soon. Mr. Strange gave the master in return a bit of his mind; but he could not recall the train, and had to wait for the next.

The consequence of this was, that he did not reach Basham until past nine o'clock. Enquiring for the residence of Dr. Cavendish, he was directed to a substantial-looking house near the market-place. A boy in buttons, who came to the door, said the Doctor was not at home.

"I particularly wish to see him," said Mr. Strange. "Will he be long?"

"Well, I don't know," replied the boy, indifferently; who, like the rest of his tribe, had no objection to indulge in semi-insolence when it might be done with safety. "Master don't never hardly see patients at this hour. None of 'em cares to come at night-time."

"I am not a patient. My business with Dr. Cavendish is private and urgent. I will wait until he comes in."

The boy, not daring to make objection to this, ushered the visitor into a small room that he called the study. It had one gas-light burning; just enough to illumine the book-shelves and a white bust or two that stood in the corners on pedestals.

Here Mr. Strange was left to his reflections.

He had plenty of food for them. That Salter was at the Maze, he felt as sure of as though he had already seen him. Superintendent Game had informed him who Smith the agent had acknowledged himself to be—Salter's cousin—and stated his own views of the motives that induced his residence at Foxwood. This was an additional thread in the web of belief Mr. Strange was weaving; a confirmatory link that seemed all but conclusive. In the short period that elapsed between his interview with Nurse Chaffen, chez elle, and his run up to London, he had seen his friend Giles, the footman, and by dint of helping that gentleman to trace days back and recall events, had arrived at a fact that could neither be disputed nor controverted—namely, that it could not have been Sir Karl Andinnian who was seen at the Maze by her and the surgeon. On that evening, Sir Karl, his wife, and Miss Blake had gone to a dinner party at a few miles distance. At the self-same minute of time that the event at the Maze took place, they were seated with the rest of the company at the dinner table, Mr. Giles himself standing behind in waiting. This was a fact: and had Miss Blake taken a little trouble to ascertain from Nurse Chaffen *which* evening it was that the mysterious gentleman had presented himself to view, and then recalled the day of the dinner, she would have discovered the fallacy of her belief in supposing him to have been Sir Karl.

Mr. Strange had, however, discovered it, and that was unfortunately more to the purpose. Whatever might be the object of Sir Karl's private visits to the Maze—and up to that point Mr. Strange's opinion did not change, and he had laughed quietly over it with the superintendent—it was not Sir Karl who was seen that night. It was a great point to have ascertained: and the detective thought he had rarely held stronger cards at any game of chance than were in his hands now. That Mrs. Grey would prove to be Salter's sister, he entertained no doubt of.

But the waiting was somewhat weary. Ten o'clock struck. Unless Dr. Cavendish made his appearance shortly, Mr. Strange would lose the last train, and have the pleasure of walking all the way from Basham. He was standing before one of the busts—the late Sir Robert Peel's—when the door opened, and there entered a quiet, lady-like woman, with cordial manners and a homely face. It was Mrs. Cavendish.

"I am so sorry you should have to wait so long for my husband," she said. "If I knew where he was gone, I would send to him: but he did not happen to tell me before he went out. Your business with him is of importance, I hear."

"Yes, madam: of importance to myself. Perhaps he will not be much longer now."

"I should think not. Will you allow me to send you in a glass of wine?"

He thanked her, but declined it; and she went away again. A short while, and a latch-key was heard in the house door, denoting the return of its master. Some few words were exchanged in the hall between Dr. Cavendish and his wife—and the former entered: a short, quick-speaking man, with grey whiskers.

As a matter so much of course that it hardly needs mentioning, the detective had to be no less crafty in conducting this interview than he was in some other matters. To have said to Dr. Cavendish, "I want from you a description of the patient you were called to see to-day, that I may ascertain whether it be indeed an escaped criminal of whom I am in search," would have been to close the doctor's mouth. It was true that he might open his cards entirely and say, "I am Detective Tatton from Scotland Yard, and I require you, in the name of the law, to give me all the information you can about the patient:" and, in that case it was possible that the doctor might deem himself obliged to give it. But he preferred to keep that master-stroke in hand, and try another way.

He possessed pleasant manners, and had a winning way with him—it has been already said; he spoke as a gentleman. Sitting down close to the doctor, he began enquiring in an earnest tone after the new patient at the Maze, and spoke so feelingly about patients in general, that he half gained the physician's heart.

"You are some close friend of the gentleman's?" observed Dr. Cavendish. And the word "gentleman" set the one great doubt at rest.

"I am most deeply interested in him," said the detective: and the unsuspicious doctor never noticed the really sophistical nature of the answer.

"Well, I am sorry to tell you that I think him very ill. I don't know what they can have been about, not to call in advice before." And in a few short words he stated what disease the symptoms seemed to threaten.

It startled the detective. He was sufficiently acquainted with surgery to know that it was one of difficulty and danger.

"Surely, Dr. Cavendish, he is not threatened with *that?*"

'I fear he is."

"Why, it will kill him! It is not curable, is it?"

"Rarely, if ever, when once it has certainly set-in."

"And it kills soon."

"Generally."

Mr. Strange looked very blank. To hear that his prize might escape him by death—or might die close upon his capture, was eminently unsatisfactory. It would be a termination to the great affair he had never thought of; would tarnish all the laurels in a business point of view: and he was, besides, not a hard-hearted man.

"He is young for that kind of thing, is he not, doctor?"

"Yes. Rather so."

"What brings it on, sir, in general?"

"Oh, various causes."

"Will trouble induce it?—I mean *great* trouble; anxiety; care?"

"Sometimes. Especially if there should be any hereditary tendency to it in the system."

"Well, I did not expect to hear this."

"Are you his brother?" asked the Doctor, seeing how cut-up the visitor looked. "Not that I detect any likeness."

"No, I am not his brother; or any other relative. Do you consider it a hopeless case, Dr. Cavendish?"

"I have not said that. I should not be justified in saying it. In fact, I have not yet formed a positive opinion on the case, and cannot do so until I shall have examined further into it. All I say at present is, that I do not like the symptoms."

"And—if the symptoms turn out to be what you fear; to threaten the malady you speak of—what then?"

"Why then there will be very little hope for him."

"You are going over to him again, then?"

"Of course. To-morrow. He is not in a state to be left without medical attendance."

"How long do you think it has been coming on, doctor?"

"I cannot tell you that. Not less than a twelve month, if it be what I fear."

Mr. Strange played with his watch-chain. He wanted the description of the man yet—though, in fact, he felt so sure as hardly to need it, only that detectives do not leave anything to chance.

"Would you mind telling me what you think of his looks Dr. Cavendish?"

"Oh, as to his looks, they are the best part about him. His face is somewhat worn and pallid, but it is a very handsome face. I never saw a nicer set of teeth. His hair and short beard seem to have gone grey prematurely, for I should scarcely give him forty years."

"He is only five-and-thirty," spoke the detective, thinking of Salter. And that, as the reader may recall, was also about the age of Sir Adam.

"Only that? Then in looks he has prematurely aged."

"In his prime, say two or three years ago, he was as good-looking a man as one would wish to see," observed the detective, preparing to give a gratuitous description of Salter. "A fine, tall, upright figure, strongly-built withal; and a pleasant, handsome, frank face, with fine dark eyes and hair, and a colour fresh as a rose."

"Ay," acquiesced the physician: "I only saw him in bed, and he is now much changed, but I should judge that would be just the description that once applied to him. You seem to hint at some great trouble or sorrow that he has gone through: he gives me just that idea. Of what nature was it?—if I may ask."

"It was trouble that was brought on by himself—and *that* is always the most trying to bear. As to its nature—you must pardon me for declining to particularise it, Dr. Cavendish, but I am really not at liberty to do so. Do not put the refusal down to discourtesy. The trouble is not yet over: and the chances are that you will certainly hear all about it in a day or two."

Dr. Cavendish nodded. He assumed the words to imply that the patient himself would enlighten him. As to the detective, his mission was over; and well over. He had learnt all he wanted: what he had suspected was confirmed.

"That beautiful young woman, living alone at the Maze—what relative is she of his?" asked the doctor, as his visitor rose and took up his hat.

"His sister," was the rather hazardous answer.

"Oh, his sister. Mr. Moore could not make out who the patient was. He thought it might be the husband who had returned. When I asked his name, to write a prescription for the chemist, Mrs. Grey said I might put it in hers—Grey."

"I thank you greatly for your courtesy, Dr. Cavendish."

"You are welcome," said the doctor. "Mind, I have not expressed any certain opinion as to his non-recovery. Don't go and alarm him. What I have said to you was said in confidence."

"You may depend upon me. Good night."

Mr. Detective Strange had to walk from Basham, for the last train was gone and his return half-ticket useless. Basham police station was nearly opposite the doctor's, and he stepped in there to leave a message on his way. In the satisfaction his visit had afforded him, he did not at all mind the night-walk: on the morrow, the long-sought-for Salter, who had dodged them so vexatiously, would be in their hands, the prey would have fallen. A satisfaction, however, that was not without alloy, in the damping circumstances that encompassed the man's state of health. And for that he could but feel compassion.

Midnight was chiming from the clock at Foxwood as he

reached the Maze—for he preferred to take that round-about way. Halting at the gate, he looked about and listened for a minute or two. Then he let himself in with his master-key, and went through the labyrinth.

The house lay in silence. All seemed still as the grave. There was no light, no sound, no token of illness inside; no, nor even of inmates. He gently put the said key in the entrance-door to see if it would yield. No: the door was not only locked but bolted and barred. He went to the summer-house, leading up from the underground places, and found the trap-door there also bolted and barred within. All was as secure as wary hands could make it.

"And it is welcome to remain so until to-morrow," breathed the detective as he turned to thread his silent steps back through the maze; "but then, Mr. Philip Salter, you are mine. Neither bolts nor bars can save you then."

And he finally let himself out again at the gate with that ingenious instrument, the key. To be polite, we will apply a French name to it, and call it a passe-partout.

But Mr. Cavendish, reflecting afterwards upon the interview, rather wondered who the stranger was, and whence he had come; and remembered then that he had totally omitted to ask his name.

CHAPTER XXXVII.

ANN HOPLEY STARTLED.

The morning sun was chasing the dew from the grass: and the lawn of the Maze, glittering so brightly in the welcome rays, told no tales of the strange feet that had, unbidden and unsuspected, trodden it in the night. Mrs. Grey, looking wondrously pretty and delicate in her white morning gown, with her golden hair as bright as the sunshine, sat at breakfast in a little room whose window was beside the entrance porch. Her baby, wide awake, but quiet and good, lay covered up on the sofa in its night-dress. She was talking to it as she ate her breakfast, and the wide-open little eyes were turned to her as if it understood.

"Good little darling! Sweet, gentle baby! It does not scream or fight as other babies do: no, never. It is mamma's own precious treasure—and mamma is going to dress it presently and put on its pretty worked robe. Oh, baby, baby!"

she broke off, her mood changing, and the distress at her heart rising to the surface, above the momentary make-believe dalliance, "if we could but be at rest as others are! We should be happier than the day has hours in it."

The accession of illness, attacking Sir Adam on the previous day, the great risk they ran in calling in a doctor to him, had shaken poor Rose's equanimity to the centre. She strove to be brave always, for his sake; she had been in the habit of keeping.in as well as she could the signs of the dread that ever lay upon her, and she had done so in a degree yesterday. But in the evening when the doctor had safely gone, and the day and its troubles were over, she had yielded to a sudden fit of hysterical weeping. Her husband came into the room in the midst of it. He partly soothed, partly scolded her: where was the use of fretting, he asked; better take matters as they came. With almost convulsive efforts she swallowed her sobs and dried her eyes; and turned the tables on him by gently reproaching him with getting up, when Dr. Cavendish had peremptorily enjoined him to stay in bed. Sir Adam laughed at that: saying he felt none the worse for his fainting fit, or whatever it was, and was not going to lie a-bed for all the doctors in Christendom.

The cheery morning sun is a great restorer—a gladdening comforter: and Rose felt its influence. During her sleepless night, nothing could be more disheartening, nothing more gloomy than the view pervading her mind: but this morning, with that glorious light from heaven shining on all things, she and the earth alike revived under it. One great thing she felt incessant thankfulness for; it was a real mercy—that that miserable visitation of the detective and his policemen had not been delayed to the day of Sir Adam's illness. Had they caught him in bed, no earthly power, she thought, could have saved him. Karl, stealing over for a few minutes at night, to see for himself what this alarm of increased illness of his brother's could mean, had warned them both to be prepared, for he had reason to fancy the search might be repeated.

"This spot is getting more dangerous day by day," murmured Rose to herself, pouring out another cup of tea. "Oh, if we could but get away from it! London itself seems as though it would be safer than this."

She proceeded with her meal very slowly, her thoughts buried in schemes for their departure. Of late she had been ever weaving a web of possibility for it, a cunning plan of action: and she thought she had formed one. If necessary, *she* would stay on at the Maze with her baby—oh, for months—for years even—so that Adam could but get away. Until this man, the detective—more feared by her, more dreadful to contemplate than any man born into the world yet—should take his departure from the place, nothing might be attempted: they could only remain still and quiet; taking what precautions they could against surprise and recapture, and she praying always that her husband might be spared this last crowning calamity: beyond which, if it took place, there would never more be anything in this world but blank despair.

Ann Hopley was upstairs, making the beds, and attending to matters there generally. Until her room was ready, and the fire had burnt up well to dress the baby by, Mrs. Grey would stay where she was: consequently she was at full liberty to linger over her breakfast. There was something in the extreme quietness of the little child and in its passive face, that to a more experienced eye might have suggested doubts of its well-being: a perfectly healthy infant is apt to be as troublesome as it can be. Mrs. Grey suspected nothing. It had improved much since its baptism, and she supposed it to be getting strong and healthy. A soft, sweet, plaintive note escaped the child's lips.

"Yes, my baby. Mamma has not forgotten you. The room will soon be warm, and baby shall be dressed. And then mamma will wrap it up well and wrap herself up, and sit out of doors in the sunshine. And papa——"

The words broke off in a low wail of horror; her heart seemed to die away in the faintness of sick despair. Something like a dark cloud had passed the window, shutting out for a moment the glad sunshine on the grass. It was Mr. Detective Strange; and, following closely on his heels, were the two same policemen, both of them this time in official clothes. They had come through the maze without warning, no doubt by the help of the passe-partout, and were making swiftly for the entrance-door—that lay open to the morning air. Her supposition was that they had fathomed Adam's system of concealment.

"God help us! God save and protect us!" breathed the poor wife, clasping her hands, and every drop of blood going out of her ashy face.

Mr. Strange, who had seen her through the window, was

in the room without a moment's delay. He was courteous as before: he meant to be as considerate as the nature of his mission allowed him to be: and even before he had spoken a word, the keen, practised eye took in the visible signs. The small parlour, affording no possibility for the concealment of Salter; the baby on the sofa: the breakfast, laid for one only, of which Mrs. Grey was partaking.

He was very sorry to be obliged to intrude upon her again: but he had orders once more to search the Maze, and could but obey them. And he begged her to believe that she herself, individually, should be subjected to no annoyance or restraint.

She made no answer: she could collect neither thoughts nor words to do so in her terrible fear. Mr. Strange retreated with a bow and closed the door again, making a mental comment upon her evident distress, her ghastly looks.

"There's no mistake, I think, that he is ready to our hands this time: her face alone would betray it. The curious thing is—where was he before?"

Ann Hopley had finished the rooms, and was kneeling before the fire in her mistress's chamber, coaxing an obstinate piece of coal to burn, and blowing at it with her lips with all her might, when a slight noise caused her to turn. There stood Mr. Strange, a policeman at his elbow. She had not heard the entrance. Up she got, and stood staring; unable to believe her eyes, and startled almost into screaming. But she knew how much lay upon her—almost life or death.

"Goodness bless me!" cried she, speaking freely, as she strove to brave it out, and shaking inwardly. "Whatever brings you folks here again?"

"We have to go through the house once more."

"How did you get in?"

"Quite legally," replied Mr. Strange. "I have to do my duty."

So entirely was she unprepared for this, and perhaps fearing that in her state of dismayed perplexity she might let fall some dangerous word of admission, feeling also that she could do no good to her master by staying, but might do harm, Ann Hopley withdrew, after giving the fire a gentle lift with the poker, and went down to the kitchen with a cool air, as if resolved not to let the affair interrupt her routine of work. Taking up a small basket of what she would have termed "fine things," recently washed, consisting

of caps and bits of lace, and such like articles pertaining to
the baby, she carried it out of doors beyond the end of the
lawn, and began putting the things on gooseberry bushes to
dry. Old Hopley was pottering about there, doing something to the celery bed. The policeman left on guard below,
and standing so that his sight could command all things,
surveyed her movements with a critical eye. She did not go
out of his sight, but came back with the basket at once.
While spreading the things, she had noted him watching
her.

"I daresay I'm a kind of genteel prisoner," ran her
thoughts. "If I attempted to go where those ugly eyes of
his couldn't follow me, he might be for ordering me back,
for fear I should give warning to the master that they are
here. Well, we can do nothing; it is in Heaven's hands;
better they came in to-day than yesterday!"

Mr. Detective Strange had rarely felt surer of anything
than he was that he should find Philip Salter in bed, and capture him without the slightest difficulty in his sick state. It
was not so to be. Very much to his amazement, there
appeared to be no sign whatever of a sick man in the place.
The rooms were all put in order for the day, the beds made;
nothing was different from what it had been at the time of
his previous entrance. Seek as he would, his practised eye
could find no trace—nay, no possibility—of any hidden
chamber. In fact, there was none.

"Where the deuce can the fellow be?" mused Mr. Strange,
gazing about him with a thoughtful air.

The underground places were visited with as little success,
though the search he made was minute and careful. He could
not understand it. That Salter had not been allowed time to
escape out of doors, so rapid was their first approach, he knew;
but, nevertheless, the trees and grounds were well examined.
Hopley lifted his poor bent back from his work in the celery-
bed—from which, as the watching policeman could have
testified, he had not stirred at all—to touch his straw hat when
the detective passed. Mr. Strange answered by a nod, but did
not accost him. To question the deaf old man would be only
waste of time.

There was some mystery about all this: a mystery he—
even he—could not at present fathom. Just one possibility
crossed his mind and it was exceedingly unwelcome—that
Salter, alarmed by the stir that was being made, had in truth

got away. Got away, in spite of the precautions that he, Strange, in conjunction with the police of Basham, had been for the past day or two taking, secretly and unobserved.

He did not believe it. He did not wish to believe it. And, in truth, it seemed to him not to be possible, for more reasons than one. A man in the condition of health hinted at by Dr. Cavendish would be in no state for travelling. But still—with the Maze turned, as he honestly believed, inside out and showing no signs or trace of Salter, where was he?

This took up some time. Ann Hopley had got her preparations for dinner forward, had answered the butcher's bell and taken in the meat: and by and by went across the garden again to cut two cauliflowers. She was coming back with them in her apron, when Mr. Strange met her, and spoke.

"I have a question or two to put to you, Mrs. Hopley, which I must desire of you to answer—and to answer correctly. Otherwise I shall be obliged to summon you before the magistrates and compel your answers on your oath. If you are wise, you will avoid giving me and yourself that trouble."

"As far as answering you goes, sir, I'd as soon answer as be silent," she returned, in a temperate but nevertheless injured tone. "But I must say that it puts my temper up to see an innocent and inoffensive young lady insulted as my poor mistress is. What has she done to be signalled out for such treatment? If she were not entirely unprotected here, a lone woman, you'd not dare to do it. You told her the other day you were in search of one Salter: and you know that you looked in every hole and corner our house has got, and must have satisfied yourself that no Salter was here. And yet, here you come in, searching again!"

"It was not Salter, I suppose, who was ill yesterday; for whom Dr. Cavendish was telegraphed?" rejoined Mr. Strange, significantly, having allowed her speech to run on to its end. "Perhaps you will tell me that?"

"Salter! That I'll take my oath it was not, sir."

"Who was it, then?"

"Well, sir, it was no one that you could have any concern with."

"I am the best judge of that. Who was it? Remember, I ask you in the name of the law, and you must answer me."

"That gentleman came down on a short visit to my mistress, and was taken ill while he stayed. It frightened us out of our senses; it was a fainting fit, or something of that sort, but he looked for all the world like a man dead; and I ran off and telegraphed for a doctor."

The detective's eyes were searching Ann Hopley through and through. She did not flinch: and looked innocent as the day.

"What has become of him?"

"He went away again last night, sir."

"Went away, did he!" in a mocking tone of incredulity.

"He did, sir. After the doctor left, he got up, and dressed, and came down, saying he was better. He didn't seem to think much of his illness; he had been as bad, he said, before. I confess I was surprised, myself, to hear he was going away, for I thought him not well enough to travel. But I believe he was obliged to go."

"What was his name?"

"I did not hear it, sir. He was here but a few hours in all."

"Look here, Mrs. Hopley: if you will tell me where that gentleman came from, and what his name is, I will give you five sovereigns."

Her eyes opened, apparently with magnitude of the offer.

"I wish I could, sir. I'm sure I should be glad to earn all that, if it were in my power; for I don't believe Hopley will be able to work over-much longer, and we are laying up what little we can. I think he came from London, but I am not sure: and I think he's going off to some foreign country, for he and my mistress were talking of the sea. She wished him a good voyage and a safe landing. I heard her."

The detective paused. Was this true or false? "What was his name? Come, Mrs. Hopley?"

"Sir, I have said that I did not hear his name. He came without our expecting him, or I might have heard it beforehand. My mistress called him Edward: but of course that must be his Christian name. I understood him to be some relation of hers."

"I wonder what Hopley could tell me of this?" cried the detective, looking at her.

"Hopley could tell you nothing—but of course you are welcome to ask him if you please. Hopley never saw him at all, as far as I know; and I did not say anything to the old man about it. If you question Hopley, sir, I must help you —yor'd be a month making him hear, yourself."

"How is it that you keep your husband in ignorance of things?—as you seem to do."

"Of what things, sir?" rejoined the woman. "I'm sure I don't keep things from him: I have no things to keep. It's true I didn't tell him of this. I was uncommonly tired last night, for it had been a trying day, and I was full of work besides; and it takes no little exertion, I can testify, to make Hopley understand. One can't gossip with him, as one can with people who have got their hearing."

This was no doubt true. The detective was frightfully at fault, and did not conceal from himself that he was. The woman seemed so honest, so open, so truthful; and yet he could have staked his professional fame that there lay mystery somewhere, and that the sick man had *not* gone away. Instinct, prevision—call it what you will—told him that the man was lying close to his hand—if he could only put that hand out in the right direction and lay it on him. Bending his head, he took a few steps about the grass: and Ann Hopley, hoping she was done with, went into the kitchen with her cauliflowers.

Letting them fall on to the dresser out of her apron she gave a sharp look around, indoors and out. The detective was then conversing with his two policemen, whom he had called up. Now was her time. Slipping off her shoes—though it was not likely her footsteps could be heard out on the lawn—she went across the passage and opened the door of the little room: from which Mrs. Grey, in her fear and distress, had not dared to stir.

"Mistress," she whispered, "I must give you the clue of what I have been saying, lest they come and ask you questions too. It would never do for us to have two tales, you one and me another. Do you mind me, ma'am?"

"Go on, Ann. Yes."

"The sick gentleman came unexpectedly yesterday, and was taken sick here. You and me got frightened, and sent telegraphing off for a doctor. He got up after doctor left— said he was better—didn't seem to think much of his illness, said he had been as bad before. Went away again at night; *had* to go; was going off to sea. I thought, as I heard you wish him a good voyage and safe landing. I didn't know his name, I said; only heard you call him Edward: thought it was some near relation of yours.—Can you remember all this, ma'am?"

"Oh yes. You had better go back, Ann. If they see you talking to me—oh, go back! Ann, I—I feel as though I should die."

"Nay, but you must keep up," returned the woman in a kind tone. "I'll bring you in a beat-up egg with a drop of wine in it. And, ma'am, you might say he was your brother if they come to close questioning: or brother-in-law. Don't fear. I'd lay all I'm worth they won't light upon the master. Twice they went within a yard or two of him, but——"

There was some noise. Ann Hopley broke off, closed the door softly, stole back again, and slipped her feet again into her shoes. In less than a minute, when one of the men sauntered up, throwing his eyes through all the windows, she was in the scullery pumping water over her cauliflowers with as much noise as she could make.

Ann Hopley had judged correctly. Mr. Strange went to the little room, knocking for permission to enter, and there held an audience of its mistress. The baby lay on her lap now, fast asleep. His questions were tended to get a confirmation—or contradiction—of the servant's ready tale. Mrs. Grey, though in evident tremor, and looking only fit for a ghost, had caught the thread of her lesson well, and answered correctly. Some particulars she had to improvise; for his questions were more minute than they had been to Ann Hopley.

His name?—Grey. What relation?—Brother-in-law. What did he come down for?—To say good-bye before embarking for Australia. Where would he take ship?—She did not know; forgot: oh, now she remembered, it was Gravesend. Was she in the habit of seeing him?—Not often. He was never long together in one place, always travelling about. But was he in a fit state to travel? She did not know. She had thought he looked very ill and begged him to remain at least until to-day, but he said he could not as he might lose his ship. Did he come down to Foxwood by train?—Oh yes, by train: there was no other way. And go up by train?—To be sure. *Which* train?—One of the evening trains: thought it was past eight when he left the Maze.

"It's the time for my mistress to take her egg," interposed Ann Hopley at this juncture, entering the room with the said egg in a tumbler. "I suppose she's at liberty to do it."

To this last little fling Mr. Strange answered nothing. Ann Hopley put the tumbler on the table and withdrew. Poor

Mrs. Grey looked too weak and ill to lift it to her lips, and let it stay where it was.

"Can it possibly be true that you are still in search of Philip Salter?—here?" she asked, raising her troubled eyes to the detective's.

"It is quite true," he replied.

"And that you really believe him to be concealed here?"

"Madam, I could stake my life upon it."

She shook her head in feeble impotence, feeling how weak she was to combat this fixed belief. It was the old story over again. Nevertheless she made one more effort. Mr. Strange was watching her.

"Sir, I do not know what to say, more than I said before. But I declare to you once again, as solemnly as I can ever speak anything in this life, as solemnly as I shall one day have to answer before my Maker, that I know nothing of Philip Salter. He never was here at all to my knowledge, later or earlier. Why will you not leave me in peace?"

Mr. Detective Strange began to think that he should have to leave her in peace. Twice had he carried this fortress by storm to search at will its every nook and corner: and searched in vain. Armed with great power though he was, the law would not justify these repeated forcible entries, and he might be called to account for exceeding his duty. But the man was there—as surely as that the sun was in the heavens: and yet he could not unearth him. He began to think there must be caves underground, impenetrable to the eye of man, with some invisible subtle entrance to them through the earth itself—and perhaps a subterranean passage communicating with Mr. Smith's abode opposite.

And so, the second search ended as the first had done—in signal failure. Once more there was nothing left for the detective but to withdraw his men and himself, and to acknowledge that he was for the time defeated.

CHAPTER XXXVIII.

UP THE SPOUTS AND DOWN THE DRAINS.

TURNING his face towards the railway station after quitting the Maze with the view of making some enquiries, as to what passengers had alighted there the previous day and had gone back again—not that he believed one syllable of the tale told him—Mr. Strange encountered the gig of Dr. Cavendish bowling down. The physician recognised him and pulled up.

"What's this I hear, sir, about my patient's having gone off again?" cried the doctor in a sharp tone.

"I have heard the same," replied Mr. Strange. "But I don't believe it."

"Oh then—you were not privy to it? You did not send him?"

"Not I, Dr. Cavendish. I went to the Maze betimes this morning to—to pay him a visit; and I was met with a tale that the bird had flown."

"I can tell you, sir, that he was in a *most unfit* state to travel," said the doctor with angry emphasis. "I don't know what the consequences will be."

"Ay, if he had gone. But it's all moonshine."

"What do you mean by 'moonshine?' Has he gone, or has he not?"

"They say at the Maze he has; but I am sure he has not," was the answer. "There was a motive for his being denied to me, Dr. Cavendish; and so—and so—when I went in this morning they concocted an impromptu tale of his departure. That's what I think."

"They must have concocted it last night then," said the doctor. "The letter, informing me of the circumstance, was posted last night at Foxwood—and therefore must have been written last night."

"Did they write to tell you he had gone?" asked the detective, after a slight pause.

"Mrs. Grey wrote. I got it by the post this morning. She would not trouble me to come over again, she said, as my patient had found himself obliged to leave last night. But I *have* troubled myself to come," added the doctor, wrathfully, "and to see about it; for, of all mad acts, that man's getting up from his bed yesterday, and starting off by a shaking railway train was the maddest. Drive on, James."

The groom touched the horse at the short command, and the animal sprang forward. Mr. Strange thought he would let the station alone for a bit, and loiter about where he was. This letter, written last night, to tell of the departure, somewhat complicated matters.

A very short while, and the doctor came out again. Mr. Strange accosted him as he was about to step into his gig.

"Well, Dr. Cavendish, have you seen your patient?"

"No, I have not seen him," was the reply. "It is quite true that he is gone. I find he is embarking on a sea voyage, going off somewhere to the other end of the world, and he had to go up, or forfeit his passage-money."

"They told you, then, what they told me. As, of course, they *would*," he added inwardly.

"But there's something in it I don't altogether understand," resumed the doctor. "Not a syllable was spoken by the patient yesterday to denote that he was on the move, or that he had been on the move, even only to journey down from London. On the contrary, I gathered, or fancied I gathered, from the tenor of his remarks that he had been for some time stationary, and would be stationary for an indefinite period to come. It was when I spoke to him about the necessity of keeping himself quiet and free from exertion. What I don't understand is, why he should not candidly have told me that he had this voyage before him."

Mr. Strange did not answer. Various doubts were crowding upon him. *Had* the man got away? in disguise, say? But no, he did not think it.

"By the way, you did not tell me your name," said the doctor, as he took his seat in the gig.

"My name! oh, did I not? My name is Tatton."

Dr. Cavendish bent down his head and spoke in a low tone. His groom was adjusting the apron.

"You hinted last night at some great trouble that this gentleman was in, Mr. Tatton. I have been wondering whether that has to do with this sudden departure—whether he had reasons for being afraid to stay?"

"Just the question that has occurred to me, Dr. Cavendish," confessed the detective. "If he has gone away, it is fear that has driven him."

The gig bowled onwards. Mr. Strange stood still as he looked after it: and had the pleasure of seeing Mr. Philip Smith smoking his long pipe at his own window, and regarding the landscape with equanimity. He went on the other way.

"Good morning, Mr. Tatton."

Mr. Tatton turned on his heel and saluted the speaker, Sir Karl Andinnian, who had followed him up. There was a degree of suppressed indignation in Karl's face, rarely seen.

"Is this true that I have just heard, Mr. Tatton," he began, calling the man by his true name—"that you have been again searching the Maze? My butler informs me that he saw you and two policemen quit it but now."

"It is true enough, Sir Karl. Salter is there. At least, he was there yesterday. There cannot be the slightest doubt that the sick man to whom Dr. Cavendish was called was Salter. I obtained a description of him from the doctor, and should have recognized it anywhere."

What was Karl to say? He could not attempt to deny that a sick man had been there. It was an unfortunate circumstance that Sir Adam, in regard to height and colour of hair, somewhat answered to the description of Philip Salter.

"Sir Karl, you must yourself see that there's a mystery somewhere," resumed the detective, who (having taken his clue from Superintendent Game) honestly believed that the baronet of Foxwood Court cared not a rap for Salter, and had no covert interest in the matter, beyond that of protecting his tenant at the Maze. "Some one who is never seen by the public is living at the Maze, that's certain; or, at any rate, dodging us there. Remember the gentleman in evening attire seen by the surgeon and nurse; and now there's this gentleman sick abed yesterday. These men could not be myths, Sir Karl. Who, then, are they?"

From sheer inability to advance any theory upon the point, lest he should do mischief, Karl was silent. These repeated trials, these shocks of renewed dread, were getting more than he knew how to bear. Had they come upon Adam this morning? He did not dare to ask.

"As to the tale told me by the woman servant and Mrs. Grey—that the sick gentleman was a relative who had come down by train and left again, it will not hold water," contemptuously resumed the detective. "Men don't go out for a day's journey when they are as ill as he is—no, nor take long sea voyages. Why, if what Dr. Cavendish fears is correct, there cannot be many weeks of life left in the man he saw yesterday; neither, if it be so, can the man himself be unconscious of it."

Karl's heart stood still with its shock of pain.

"Did Dr. Cavendish tell you that, Mr. Tatton?"

"Yes. Well, now, Sir Karl, that man is at the Maze still—I am convinced of it; and that man is Salter."

"What did you find this morning?"

"Nothing. Nothing more than I found before. When I spoke of the sick man, and asked where he was, this cock-and-bull tale was told me; which of course they had got up among themselves."

"As I said before, Mr. Tatton, I feel certain—I am certain—that you will never find Salter at the Maze, from the simple fact that he is not there to find—I am sure of it. I must most earnestly protest against these repeated annoyances to my tenant, Mrs. Grey; and if you do not leave her alone for the future, I shall see whether the law will not compel you. I do not—pray understand—I do not speak this in enmity to you, but simply to protect her."

"Of course I understand that, Sir Karl," was the ready answer. "There's no offence meant, and none taken. But if you could put yourself in my place, you'd see my difficulty. Upon my word, I never was so mystified before. *There Salter is.* Other people can see him, and have seen him; and yet when I search I find no traces of him. A thought actually crossed my mind just now, whether there could be a subterranean passage from the Maze to Clematis Cottage, and that Salter makes his escape there to his cousin on occasion. I should like to search it."

"Come and do so at once," said Karl, half laughing. "Nothing convinces like ocular demonstration. I give you full permission, as owner of the cottage; I doubt not Smith will, as its tenant. Come and ask him."

The detective was in earnest, and they crossed over. Seeing them making for the gate, Mr. Smith came out of his house, pipe in hand. It was one of those long church-wardens. Karl spoke a few words of explanation: Mr. Detective Tatton suspected there might be secret rooms, or doors, or fugitives hidden in Clematis Cottage, and would like to search it. After the first momentary look of surprise, the agent remained unruffled.

"Pass on, sir," said he, extending the thin end of his pipe to indicate the way. "You are welcome. Go where you please: search into every nook and corner; up the spouts and down the drains. If you surprise old Betty, tell her you're the plumber."

Mr. Strange took him at his word. Karl and the agent waited in the sitting-room together.

"Is it after Sir Adam, sir?" breathed the agent.

"No. No suspicion of him. It's after the other I told you of. Hush! Better be silent."

The agent put his pipe away. Karl stood at the front

window. Old Betty, the ancient servant, came in with a scared face. She was a little deaf, but not with a deafness like Hopley's over the way.

"It's all right, Betty," called out her master. "Only looking to the drains and spouts."

Satisfied in one sense of the word—for in truth it was readily seen by the most unprofessional eye that there were no means afforded for concealment in the shallow-built cottage—the officer soon joined them again. He had not had really a suspicion of the cottage, he said by way of apology: it was merely a thought that crossed him. Mr. Smith, however, did not seem inclined to take the matter quite indifferently now, and accosted him.

"Now that you are satisfied, sir, perhaps you will have no objection to tell me who the individual may be, that you have fancied I would harbour in my house. I heard before from Sir Karl that you were after some one."

From the tone he spoke in, a very civil tone, tinged with mockery, the detective caught up the notion that Smith already knew; that Sir Karl must have told him: therefore he saw no occasion for observing any reticence.

"When you know that we are looking for Philip Salter, you need not be so much surprised that we have cast a thought to this house as Salter's possible occasional refuge, Mr. Smith."

The very genuine astonishment that seized hold of Smith, pervading his every look, and word, was enough to convince those who saw it that he was unprepared for the news.

"Philip Salter!" he exclaimed, gazing from one to the other, as if unable to believe. "*Philip Salter!*" Why, is he here? Have you news that he is back in England?"

"We have news that he *is* here," said the detective blandly. "We suspect that he is concealed at the Maze. Did you not know it, Mr. Smith?"

Mr. Smith sat down in the chair that was behind him, as if sitting came easier than standing, in his veritable astonishment.

"As Heaven is my judge, it is a mistake," he declared. "Salter is not at the Maze; never has been. We have never heard that he is back in England."

"Did you know that he left England?"

"Yes. At least, we had good reason to believe that he got away shortly after that dangerous escape of his. It's true it was never confirmed; but the confirmation to his family lies in the fact that we have never since heard of him, or from him."

"Never."

"Never. Were he in England we should have been sure to have had some communication from him, had it only been an application for aid—for he could not live upon air; and outlets of earning are here closed to him. One thing you and ourselves may alike rest assured of, Mr. Detective—that, once he got safely away from the country he would not venture into it again."

What with one disappointment and another, the detective almost questioned whether it was not as Smith said; and that Salter, so far as Foxwood was concerned, would turn out to be indeed a myth. But then—who was this mysterious man at the Maze? He was passing out with a good day when Mr. Smith resumed.

"Have you any objection to tell me what gave rise to your suspicion that Salter was at Foxwood? Or in England at all?"

But the officer had tact; plenty of it; or he would not have done for his post; and he turned the question off without any definite answer. For the true originator of the report, he who had caused it to reach the ears of Great Scotland Yard, was Sir Karl Andinnian.

Very conscious of the fact was Karl himself. He raised his hat from his brow as he went home, to wipe away the fever-damp gathered there. He remembered to have read somewhere of one of the tortures devised by inquisitionists in the barbarous days gone by. An unhappy prisoner would be shut in a spacious room; and, day by day, watched the walls contracting by some mysterious agency, and closing around him. It seemed to Karl that the walls of the world were closing around him now. Or, rather, round one who had become dearer to him in his dread position than himself —his most ill-fated brother.

At home or abroad there was not a single ray of light to illumine or cheer the gloom. Abroad lay apprehension; at home only unhappiness, an atmosphere of estrangement that seemed to have nothing homelike or true in it. Karl went in, expecting to see the pony-chaise waiting. He had been about to drive his wife out; but, alarmed by the report whispered to him by Hewitt, and unable to rest in tranquillity, he had gone forth to see what it meant. But the chaise was not there. Maclean was at work on the lawn.

"Has Lady Andinnian gone?" he enquired, rather surprised—for Lucy had not learned to drive yet.

"My leddy is somewhere about the garden I think, Sir Karl," was the gardener's answer. "She sent the chay away again."

He found his wife sitting in a retired walk, a book in her hand, apparently reading it. Lucy was fading. Her face, worn and thin, had that indescribable air of pitiful sadness in it that tells of some deep-seated, ever-present sorrow. Karl was all too conscious of it. He blamed her for her course of conduct; but he did not attempt to conceal from himself that the trouble had originated with him.

"I am very sorry to have kept you waiting, Lucy," he began. "I had to go to Smith's on a little matter of business. You have sent the chaise away."

"I sent it away. The pony was tired of waiting. I don't care to go out at all to-day."

She spoke in an indifferent, almost a contemptuous tone. We must not blame her. Her naturally sweet temper was being sorely tried: day by day her husband seemed to act so as to afford less promise of any reconciliation.

"I could not help it," was all he answered.

She glanced up at the weary accent. If ever a voice spoke of unresisted despair, his did then. Her resentment vanished: her sympathy was aroused."

"You look unusually ill," she said.

"I am very ill," he replied. "So ill that I should be almost glad to die."

Lucy paused. Somehow she never liked these semi-explanations. They invariably imbued her with a sense of self-reproach, an idea that she was acting harshly.

"Do you mean ill because of our estrangement?"

"Yes, for one thing. That makes all other trouble so much worse for me that at times I find it rather difficult to put up with."

Lucy played with her book. She wished she knew where her true duty lay. Oh how gladly, but for that dreadful wrong ever being enacted upon herself, would she fall upon his arm and whisper out her beseeching prayer: "Take me to you again, Karl!"

"Should the estranged terms we are living on, end in a

total and visible separation, you will have the satisfaction of remembering in your after life, Lucy, that you have behaved cruelly to me. I repeat it: cruelly."

"I do not wish to separate," murmured Lucy.

"The time may soon come when you will be called upon to decide, one way or the other; when there will be nothing left to wait for; when all will be known to the world as it is known to us."

"I cannot understand you," said Lucy.

"Let it pass," he answered, declining as usual to speak openly upon the dreaded subject; for, to him, every word so spoken seemed fraught with danger. "You can guess what I mean, I daresay: and the less said the better."

"You seem always to blame me, Karl," she rejoined, her voice softening almost to tears.

"Your own heart should tell you that I have cause."

"It has been very hard for me to bear."

"Yes; no doubt. It has hurt your pride."

"And something besides my pride," rejoined Lucy, with a faint flush of resentment.

"What has the bearing and the pain for you been, in comparison with what I have had to bear and suffer?" he asked with emotion. "I, at least, have not tried to make it worse for you, Lucy, though you have for me. In my judgment, we ought to have *shared* the burden; and so made it lighter, if possible, for one another."

Ay, sometimes she had thought that, herself. But then her womanly sense of insult, her justifiable resentment, would step in and scatter the thought to the winds. It was too bad of Karl to reflect on her "pride."

"Is it to last for ever?" she asked, after a pause.

"Heaven knows!" he answered. "Heaven knows that I have striven to do my best. I have committed no sin against you, Lucy, save that of having married you when—I ought not. I have most bitterly expiated it."

He spoke like one from whom all hope in life has gone; his haggard and utterly spiritless face was bent downwards. Lucy, her love all in force, her conscience aroused, touched his hand.

"If I have been more harshly judging than I ought, Karl, I pray you and heaven alike to forgive me."

He gave no answer: but he turned his hand upwards so that hers lay in it. Thus they sat for some time, saying nothing. A singing bird was perched on a tree in front of them; a light cloud passed over the face of the blue sky.

"But—you know, Karl," she began again in a half whisper, "it has not been right, or well, for—for those to have been at the Maze who have been there."

"I do know it. I have repeatedly told you I knew it. I would almost have given my life to get them out. It will not be long now, I fear, one way or the other: the climax I have been dreading seems to be approaching."

"What climax?"

"Discovery. Bringing with it disgrace, and pain, and shame. It is when I fear that, Lucy, that I feel most bitterly how wrong it was of me to marry. But I did not know all the complication: I never anticipated the evils that would ensue. You must forgive me, for I did it three-parts in ignorance."

He clasped her hand as he spoke. Her tears were gathering fast. Karl rose to depart, but she kept his fingers in hers, her tears dropping as she looked up at him.

"I ask, Karl, if we are to live this kind of life for ever?"

"As you shall will, Lucy. The life is of your choosing, not of mine."

One long look of doubt, of compassion, of love, in each other's eyes; and then the hand-clasp that so thrilled through each of them was loosed; the fingers fell apart. Karl went off to the house, and Lucy burst into a storm of sobs so violent as to startle the little bird, and stop its song.

CHAPTER XXXIX.

TAKEN FROM THE EVIL TO COME.

DREADFUL commotion at Mrs. Jinks's. Young ladies coming in, all in excitement; the widow nearly off her head. Their pastor was ill.

On a sofa before his parlour fire he lay extended, the Reverend Guy; his head on a soft pillow, his feet (in embroidered slippers) on an embroidered cushion. The room was quite an epitome of sacred decorations; crosses lay embedded amid ferns; illuminated scrolls adorned the walls. Something was wrong with the reverend gentleman's throat: his hands and brow were feverish. Whether it was merely a relaxed throat, or a common soreness, or a quinsy threatening him, could not be decided in the general dismay. Some thought one way, some another; all agreed in one thing—that it must be treated promptly. The dear man was passive as any lamb in their ministering hands, and submitted accordingly. What rendered the case more distressing and its need of recovering treatment all-urgent, was the fact that the morrow would be some great day in the calendar, necessitating high services at St. Jerome's. How were they to be held when the chief priest was disabled? Damon Puff was all very well; but he was not the Reverend Guy Cattacomb.

The Widow Jinks, assuming most experience by reason of years, and also in possessing a cousin who was a nurse of renown, as good as any doctor on an emergency, had recommended the application of "plant" leaves. The ladies seized upon it eagerly: anything to allay the beloved patient's sufferings and stop the progress of the disorder. The leaves had been procured without loss of time; Lawyer St. Henry's kitchen garden, over the way, having had the honour of supplying them; and they were now in process of preparation in the ladies' fair hands. Two ladies were picking, three boiling and bruising, four sewing, all inwardly intending to apply them. The Widow Jinks had her hands full below: gruel, broth, jelly, arrowroot, beef-tea, custard puddings, and other things, being alike in the course of preparation over the kitchen fire: the superabundant amount of sick dainties arising from the fact that each lady had ordered that which seemed to her best. What with the care of so many saucepans at once, and the being called off perpetually to answer the knocks at the front door, the widow felt rather wild; and sincerely wished all sore throats at Jericho. For the distressing news had spread; and St. Jerome's fair worshippers were coming up to the house in uninterrupted succession.

It fell to Miss Blake to apply the cataplasm. As many assisting, by dint of gingerly touching the tip of the reverend gentleman's ears, or holding back his shirt collar, as could get their fingers in. Miss Blake, her heart attuned to sympathy, felt stirred by no common compassion. She was sure the patient's eyes sought hers: and, forgetting the few years' difference in their ages, all kinds of flattering ideas and sweet hopes floated into her mind—for it was by no means incumbent on her to waste her charms in wearing the willow for that false renegade—false in more ways than one— Karl Andinnian.

Looking on passively, but not tendering her own help amid so many volunteers, sat Jemima Moore in a distant chair her face betokening anything but pleasurable ease. There were times when she felt jealous of Miss Blake.

The leaves applied, the throat bound up, and some nourishment administered in the shape of a dish of broth, nothing remained to be essayed, save that the patient should endeavour to get some sleep. To enable him to do this, it was obvious, even to the anxious nurses themselves, that he should be left alone. Miss Blake suggested that they should all make a pilgrimage to St. Jerome's to pray for him. Eagerly was it seized upon, and bonnets were tied on. A thought crossed each mind almost in unison—that *one* at least might have been left behind to watch the slumbers: but as nobody would help another to the office, and did not like very well to propose herself, it remained unspoken.

"You'll come back again!" cried the reverend sufferer, retaining Miss Blake's hand in his, as she was wishing him good-bye.

"*Rely* upon me, dear Mr. Cattacomb," was the response—and Miss Blake regarded the promise as sacred, and would not have broken it for untold gold.

So they trooped out: and Mr. Cattacomb, left to himself and to quiet, speedily fell into the desired sleep. He was really feeling ill and feverish.

The time was drawing on for the late afternoon service, and Tom Pepp stood tinkling the bell as the pilgrims approached. Simultaneously with their arrival, there drove up an omnibus, closely packed with devotees from Basham, under the convoy of Mr. Puff. That reverend junior, his parted hair and moustache and assumed lisp in perfect order, conducted the service to the best of his ability; and the foreheads of some of his fair hearers touched the ground in humility when they put up their prayers for the sick pastor.

The autumn days were short now; the service had been somewhat long, and when St. Jerome turned out its flock, evening had set in. You could hardly see your hand before you. Some went one way, some another. The omnibus started back with its freight: Mr. Puff, however (to the utter mental collapse of those inside it), joined the pilgrims on their return to Mr. Cattacomb's. Miss Blake went straight on to Foxwood Court: for, mindful of her promise to the patient, she wished to tell Lady Andinnian that she should not be in to dinner.

Margaret Sumnor was staying with Lucy: her invalid sofa and herself having been transported to the Court. The rector and his wife had been invited to an informal dinner that evening; also Mr. Moore and his sister: so Miss Blake thought it better to give notice that she should be absent, lest they might wait for her. Jemima Moore, a very good-natured girl on the whole, offered to accompany Miss Blake, seeing that nobody else did; for they all had gone off in the clerical wake of Mr. Puff. As the two ladies left the Court again, after leaving the message, they became aware that some kind of commotion was taking place before the Maze gate. It was too dark to see so far, but there was much howling and groaning.

"Do let us go and see what it is!" cried Miss Jemima. And she ran off without further parley. The irruption into the Maze of Mr. Detective Tatton—who was by this time known in his real name and character—had excited much astonishment and speculation in Foxwood; the more especially as no two opinions agreed as to what there was within the Maze that he could be after. The prevailing belief amid the juvenile population was, that a menagerie of wild beasts had taken up its illegitimate abode inside. They collected at hours in choice groups around the gate, pressing their noses against the ironwork in the hope of getting a peep at the animals, or at least of hearing them roar. On this evening a dozen or two had come down as usual. Tom Pepp, having cut short the ringing out, in his ardour to make one, had omitted to put off the conical cap.

But these proceedings did not please Sir Karl Andinnian's agent at Clematis Cottage. That gentleman, after having warned the boys sundry times to keep away, and enlarged on the perils that indiscriminate curiosity generally brought to its indulgers, had crossed the road to-night armed with a long gig-whip, which he began to lay about him kindly. The small fry, yelling and shrieking, dispersed immediately.

"Little Simpletons!" cried Miss Jemima Moore, as the agent walked back with his whip, after explaining to her. "Papa says the police only went in to take the boundaries of the parish. And—oh! There's Tom Pepp in his sacred cap! Miss Blake, look at Tom Pepp. Oh! oh, if Mr. Cattacomb could but see him!"

Miss Blake, who never did things in a hurry, walked leisurely after the offending boy, intending to pounce upon him at St. Jerome's. In that self-same moment the Maze gate was thrown open, and Mrs. Grey, her golden hair disordered, herself in evident tribulation, came forth wringing her hands, and amazing Miss Jemima more considerably than even the whip had amazed the boys.

What she said, Jemima hardly caught. It was to the effect that her baby was in convulsions; that she wanted Mr. Moore on the instant, and had no one to send.

"I'll run for papa," cried the good-natured girl. "I will run at once; I am his daughter. But you should get it into a warm bath, instantly, you know. There's nothing else does for convulsions. I would come and help you if there were any one else to go for papa."

In answer to this kind suggestion, Mrs. Grey stepped inside again, and shut the gate in Miss Jemima's face. But she thanked her in a few heartfelt words, and begged her to get Mr. Moore there without delay: her servant was already preparing a bath for the baby.

Jemima ran at the top of her speed, and met her father and aunt walking to Foxwood Court. The doctor hastened to the Maze, leaving his sister to explain the cause of his absence to Sir Karl and Lady Andinnian.

Dinner was nearly over at the Court when the doctor at length got there. The baby was better, he said: but he was by no means sure that it would not have a second attack. If so, he thought it could not live: it was but weakly at the best.

As may readily be imagined, scarcely any other topic formed the conversation at the dinner-table. Not one of the guests seated round it had the slightest notion that it was, of all others, the most intensely unwelcome subject to their host and hostess: the one, in his dread to hear the Maze alluded to at all; the other, in her bitter pain and jealousy. The doctor enlarged upon the isolated position of Mrs. Grey, upon her sweetness and beauty, upon her warm love for her child, and her great distress. Sir Karl made an answering remark when obliged. Lucy sat in silence, bearing her cross. Every word seemed to be an outrage on her feelings. The guests talked on; but, somehow, each felt that the harmony of the meeting had left it.

Making his dinner of one dish, in spite of the remonstrances of Sir Karl and the attentions of Mr. Giles and his fellows, the doctor drank a cup of coffee, and rose to leave again. His

sister, begging Lady Andinnian to excuse her, put on her hat
and shawl, and left with him.

"Are you going over to the Maze, William?" she asked
when they got out.

"I am, Diana."

"Then I will go with you. That's why I came away. The
poor young thing is alone, save for her servants, and I think
it only a charity that some one should be with her."

The surgeon gave a grin of satisfaction in the darkness of
the night. "Take care, Diana," said he, with assumed gravity.
"You know the question the holy ones at St. Jerome's are
raising—whether that lovely lady is any better than she
should be."

"Bother to St. Jerome's," independently returned Miss
Diana. "If the holy ones, as you call them, would expend a
little more time in cultivating St. Paul's enjoined charity, and
a little less in praying with those two parsons of theirs, Heaven
might be better served. Let the lady be what she will, she is
to be pitied in her distress, and I am going to her. Brother
William!"

"Well?"

"I cannot think what is the matter with Lady Andinnian.
She looks just like one that's pining away."

The evening went on at the Court. Miss Blake came back,
bringing the news that the Reverend Mr. Cattacomb's throat
was easier, which was of course a priceless consolation. At
ten o'clock Mr. and Mrs. Sumnor took their departure, Sir
Karl walking with them as far as the lodge. Lost in thought,
he had gone out without his hat: in returning for it he saw
his wife at one of the flower-beds.

"Lucy! Is it you, out in the damp? What do you
want?"

"I am getting one of the late roses for Margaret," was the
answer. "She likes to have a flower to cheer her when she
lies awake at night. She says it makes her think of
heaven."

"I will get it for you," said Karl. And he chose the best
he could in the starlight, and cut it.

"Lucy, I am going over the way," he resumed in a low
tone, as they turned to the steps, "and I cannot tell when I
shall be back. Hewitt will sit up for me."

Of all audacious avowals, this sounded about the coolest to
its poor young listener. Her quickened breath seemed to

chafe her; her heart beat as though it would burst its bounds.

"Why need you tell me of it?" she passionately answered, all her strivings for patience giving way before the moment's angry pain.

Karl sighed. "It lies in my duty to do what I can, Lucy: as I should have thought you might see and recognize. Should the child have a relapse in the course of the night, I shall be there to fetch Moore: there's no one else to go."

Lucy let fall the train of her dress, which she had been holding gathered round her, and swept across the hall; vouchsafing back to him neither look nor word.

The chamber lay in semi-light: with that still hush pervading it, common to rooms where death is being waited for, and is seen visibly approaching. Mr. Moore's fears had been verified. The infant at the Maze had had a second attack of convulsions, and was dying.

It lay folded in a blanket on its mother's lap. The peaceful little face was at rest now; the soft breathing, getting slower and slower, alone stirring it. Miss Diana, her hat thrown off, sat on her heels on the hearth-rug, speaking every now and then a word or two of homely comfort: the doctor stood near the fire looking on; Ann Hopley was noiselessly putting straight some things in a corner.

With her golden hair all pushed from her brow, and her pretty face, so delicate and wan, bent downwards, she sat, the poor mother. Save for the piteous sorrow in the despairing eyes, and a deep sobbing sigh that would arise in the throat, no sign of emotion escaped her. She knew the fiat—that all hope was over. The doctor, who saw the end getting nearer and nearer, and was aware that such ends are sometimes painful to see, even in an infant—the little frame struggling with the fleeting breath, the helpless hands fighting for it—had been anxious that Mrs. Grey should resign her charge to some one else. Miss Diana made one more effort to bring it about.

"My dear, I know you *must* be tired. You'll get the cramp. Let me take the baby, if only for a minute's relief."

"Do, Mrs. Grey," said the doctor.

She looked up at them with beseeching entreaty; her hand tightening involuntarily over the little treasure.

"Please don't ask me," she piteously said. "I must have him to the last. He is going from me for ever."

"Not for ever, my dear," corrected Miss Diana. "You will go to him, though he will not return to you."

The door softly opened, and some one came gently in. Absorbed by the dying child, though she was, and by the surroundings it brought, Mrs. Grey glanced quickly up and made a frantic movement to beckon the intruder back, her face changing to some dread apprehension, her lips parting with fear. She thought it might be one who must not dare to show himself if he valued life and liberty: but it was only Karl Andinnian.

"Oh Karl, he is dying!" she cried in the hasty impulse of the moment—and the dry eyes filled with tears. "My darling baby is dying."

"I have been so sorry to hear about it, Mrs. Grey," returned Karl, who had his wits about him if she had not, and who saw the surprise of the doctor and Miss Diana, at the familiarity of the address. "I came over to see if I could be of any use to you."

He fell to talking to Mr. Moore in an under-tone, giving her time to recover her mistake; and the hushed silence fell on the chamber again. Karl bent to look at the pale little face, soon to put on immortality; he laid his hand lightly on the damp forehead, keeping it there for a minute in solemn silence, as though breathing an inward prayer.

"He will be better off there than here," whispered he to the mother, in turning to leave the chamber. "The world is full of thorns and care, as some of us too well know: God is taking him from it."

Pacing a distant room like a caged lion, was Sir Adam Andinnian. He wheeled round on his heel when his brother entered.

"Was ever position like unto mine, Karl?" he broke out, anger, pain, impatience, and most deep emotion, mingling together in his tone. "Here am I, condemned to hide myself within these four walls, and may not quit them even to see my child die! The blackest criminal on earth can call for his friends on his death-bed. When are that offensive doctor and his sister going?"

"They are staying out of compassion to Rose," spoke Karl, in his quiet voice. "Oh, Adam, I am so sorry for this! I feel it with my whole heart."

"Don't talk," said Adam, rather roughly. "No fate was ever like my fate. Heaven has mercy for others: none for me. Because my own bitter punishment was not enough, it must even take my son!"

"It does seem to you cruel, I am sure. But God's ways are not as our ways. He is no doubt taking him in love, from the evil to come. When we get up Above there ourselves, Adam, we shall see the reason of it."

Sir Adam did not answer. He sat down and covered his face with his hand, and remained in silence. Karl did not break it.

Sounds by-and-by. The doctor and his sister were departing, escorted by Ann Hopley—who must see them out at the gate and make it fast again. Adam was bursting from the room: but his brother put his arm across the entrance.

"Not yet, Adam. Not until Ann is in again, and has the door fast. Think of the consequences if you were seen!"

He recognized the good sense, the necessity for prudence, fierce as a caged lion though his mood indeed was. The bolts and bars were shot at last, and Adam went forth.

In its own crib lay the baby then, straight and still. The fluttering heart had ceased to beat; the sweet little peaceful face was at rest. Rose knelt by her own bed, her head muffled in the counterpane. Sir Adam strode up to his child and stood looking at it.

A minute's silence, deep as that of the death that was before him, and then a dreadful burst of tears. They are always dreadful when a man sheds them in his agony.

"It was all we had, Karl," he said between his sobs. "And I did not even see him die!"

Karl took the strong but now passive hands in his. His own eyes were wet as he strove to say a word of comfort to his brother. But these first moments of grief are not best calculated for it.

"He is happier than he could ever have been here, Adam. Try and realize it. He is already one of God's bright angels."

And my young Lady Andinnian, over at Foxwood Court, did not choose to go to bed, but sat up to indulge her defiant humour. Never had her spirit been so near open rebellion as it was that night. Sir Karl did not come in: apparently he meant to take up his abode at the Maze until morning.

"*Of course* he must be there when his child is dying!" spoke she to herself, as she paced the carpet with a step as impatient and a great deal more indignant than those other steps that had paced that night. "Of course *she* must be comforted! While I——"

The words were choked by a flood of emotion. Bitter reflections crowded on her, one upon another. The more earnestly and patiently she strove to bear and *for*bear, the more cruelly seemed to rise up her afflictions. And Lucy Andinnian threw herself in abandonment, wondering whether all pity had quite gone out of heaven.

CHAPTER XL.

NEWS FOR MR. TATTON.

WHAT Mr. Detective Tatton's future proceedings would have been, or to what untoward catastrophe, as connected with this history, they might have led, had his stay at Foxwood been prolonged to an indefinite period, cannot here be known. He remained on. Social matters had resumed their ordinary groove. The Maze was left undisturbed; Mr. Cattacomb was well again; St. Jerome's in full force.

It might be that Mr. Tatton was waiting—like a certain noted character with whom we all have the pleasure of an acquaintance—for "something to turn up." That he was contemplating some grand coup, which would throw his prize into his hands, while to the world and Mrs. Jinks he appeared only to be enjoying the salubrious Kentish air, and amusing himself with public politics generally, we may rest pretty well assured of. But this agreeable existence was suddenly cut short.

One morning, when Mr. Tatton's hopes and plans were, like Cardinal Wolsey's greatness, all a-ripening, he received a communication from Mr. Superintendent Game at Scotland Yard, conveying the astounding intelligence that the real Philip Salter had not been in Foxwood at all, but had just died in Canada.

Mr. Tatton sat contemplating the letter. He could not have been much more astonished had a bombshell burst under him. Of the truth of the information there could be no question: its reliability was indisputable. One of the chief officers in the home police force, who was in Canada on business, and had known Salter well, discovered him in the last stage of a wasting sickness, and saw him die.

"I've never had such a fool's game to play at as *this*," ejaculated Mr. Tatton, when sufficiently recovered to speak; and never wish to have such another. What the deuce, then, is the mystery connected with the Maze?"

Whatever it might be, it was now no business of his; though could he have afforded to waste more time and money, he would have liked very well to stay and track it out. Summoning the Widow Jinks to his presence, he informed her that he was called away suddenly on particular business; and then proceeded to pack up. Mrs. Jinks resented the departure as quite a personal injury, and wiped the soft tears from her eyes.

On his way to the station he chanced to meet Sir Karl Andinnian: and the latter's heart went up with a great bound. The black bag in Mr. Tatton's hand, and the portmanteau being wheeled along beside him, spoke a whole volume of hope.

"Good morning, Sir Karl. You have misled us finely as to the Maze."

"Why, what do you mean, Mr. Tatton?" asked Karl.

"Salter has turned up in Canada. Or, one might perhaps rather say, turned down; for he is dead, poor fellow."

"Indeed!"

"Indeed and in truth. One of our officers is over there, and was with him when he died. It was too bad of you to mislead us in this way, Sir Karl."

"Nay, you misled yourselves."

"A fine quantity of time I have wasted down here! weeks upon weeks; and all for nothing. I never was so vexed in my life."

"You have yourself to blame—or those who sent you here. Certainly not me. The very first time I had the honour of speaking to you, Mr. Tatton, I assured you, on the word of a gentleman, that Salter was not at Foxwood."

"Well, come, Sir Karl—what is the secret being enacted within the place over yonder?" pointing his finger in the direction of the Maze.

"I am not in the habit of inquiring into the private affairs of my tenants," was the rather haughty answer. "If there be any secret at the Maze—though I think no one has assumed it but yourself—you may rely upon it that it is not in any way connected with Salter. Are you taking your final departure?"

"It looks like it, Sir Karl"—nodding towards the luggage going onwards. "When the game's at the other end of the world, and dead besides, it is not of much use my staying to search after it in this. I hope the next I have to hunt will bring in more satisfaction."

They said farewell cordially. The detective in his natural sociability; Karl in his most abundant gratitude for the relief it would give his brother. And Mr. Detective Tatton, hastening on in the wake of the portmanteau, took the passing up-train, and was whirled away to London.

A minute or two afterwards Karl met his agent. He was beginning to impart to him the tidings about Salter, when Smith interrupted him.

"I have heard it, Sir Karl. I got a letter from a relative this morning, which told me all. The information has taken Tatton off the land here, I expect: I saw you speaking to him."

"You are right."

"As to poor Salter, the release is probably a happy one. He is better off than he ever could have been again in this world. But what on earth put Scotland Yard on the false scent that he was at Foxwood will always be a problem to me. Tatton's gone for good, I suppose, sir?"

"He said so."

"And Sir Adam is, in one sense, free again. There will be less danger in his getting away from Foxwood now, if it be judged desirable that he should go."

Karl shook his head. There was another impediment now to his getting away—grievous sickness.

That Sir Adam Andinnian, the unfortunate fugitive, hiding in peril at the Maze, had some very grave disorder upon him, could no longer be doubtful to himself or to those about him. It seemed to develop itself more surely day by day. Adam took it as calmly as he did other evils; but Karl was nearly out of his mind with distress at the complication it brought. Most necessary was it for Adam to have a doctor; to be attended by one; and yet they dare not put the need in practice. The calling in of Dr. Cavendish had entailed only too much danger and terror.

The little baby, Charles Andinnian, was lying at rest in Foxwood churchyard, within the precincts consecrated to the Andinnian family. Ann Hopley chose the grave, and had a fight over it with the clerk. That functionary protested he would not allot it to any baby in the world. She might choose any spot except that, but that belonged to the Foxwood Court people exclusively. Ann Hopley persisted the baby should have that, and no other. It was under the weeping elm tree, she urged, and the little grave would be shaded from the summer's sun. Sir Karl Andinnian settled the dispute. Appealed to by the clerk, he gave a ready and courteous permission, and the child was laid there. Ann Hopley then paid a visit to the stone-mason, and ordered a little white marble stone, nothing to be inscribed on it but the initials "C. A." and the date of the death. Poor Rose had only her sick husband to attend to now.

He was not always sick. There were days when he seemed to be as well, and to be almost as active, as ever; and, upon that, would supervene a season of pain, and dread, and danger.

One afternoon, when Karl was driving his wife by in the pony-chaise, Ann Hopley had the gate open, and was standing at it. It was the day following the departure of Mr. Tatton. Something in the woman's face—a kind of mute, appealing anguish—struck Karl forcibly as she looked at him. In the sensation of freedom and of safety brought by the detective's absence, Karl actually pulled up.

"Will you pardon me, Lucy, if I leave you for one moment? I think Ann Hopley wants to speak to me."

He leaped out of the little low chaise, leaving the reins to Lucy. Her face was turning scarlet. Of all the insults he had thrust upon her, this seemed the greatest. To pull up at that very gate when *she* was in the carriage! Mr. Smith and his churchwarden-pipe were enjoying themselves as usual at Clematis Cottage, looking out on the world in general; and no doubt (as Lucy indignantly felt) making his private comments.

"He is very ill again, sir," were the few whispered words of Ann Hopley. Can you come in? I am not sure but it will be for death."

"Almost immediately," returned Karl; and he stepped back to the chaise just in time. Lucy was about to try her hand at driving, to make her escape from him and the miserable situation.

Since the night of the baby's death, Karl and his wife had lived a more estranged life than ever. Lucy avoided him continually. When he spoke to her, she would not answer beyond a monosyllable. As to any chance of explanation on any subject, there was none. It is true he did not attempt any; and if he had, she would have waived him away, and refused to listen to it. This day was the first for some time that she had consented to let him drive her out.

It had happened on their return. Lucy's eminently ungracious manner as he took his seat again would have stopped his speaking, even if he had had a mind to speak; but he was deep in anxious thought. The resentful way in which she had from the first taken up the affair of his unfortunate brother, served to tie his tongue always. He drove in home, stood to help her out—or would have helped, but that she swept by without touching him—left the pony to the waiting groom, and walked back to the Maze.

Adam was in one of his attacks of pain, nay, of agony. It could be called nothing less. It was not, however, for death; the sharpness of the paroxysm, with its attendant signs, had misled Ann Hopley. Rose looked scarcely less ill than her husband. Her most grievous position was telling upon her. Her little child dead, her husband apparently dying, danger and dread of another sort on all sides. More like a shadow was she now than a living woman.

"Do you know what I have been thinking, Rose?" said Karl, when his brother had revived. "That we might trust Moore. You hear, Adam. I think he might be trusted."

"Trusted for what?" returned Adam; not in his sometimes fierce voice, but in one very weak and faint.

He was lying on the sofa. Rose sat at the end of it, Karl in a chair at the side.

"To see you; to hear who you are. I cannot help believing that he would be true as steel. Moore is one of those men, as it seems to me, that we might trust our lives with."

"It won't do to run risks, old fellow. I do not want to be captured in my last hours."

Karl believed there would be no risk. Mr. Moore was a truly good man, sensible and benevolent. The more he dwelt on the idea, the surer grew his conviction that the surgeon might be trusted. Rose, who was almost passive in her distress, confessed she liked him. Both he and his sister gave her the impression of being, as Karl worded it, true as steel. Ann Hopley was in favour of it too. She put the case with much ingenuity.

"Sir, I should think there's not a doctor in the world—at least, one worthy the name—who would not keep such a secret, confided to him of necessity, even if he were a bad man. And Mr. Moore's a good one."

And the decision was made. Karl was to feel his way to the confidence. He would sound the surgeon first, and act accordingly.

"Not that it much signifies either way," cried Sir Adam, his careless manner reviving as his strength and spirits returned. "Die I soon must, I suppose, now; but I'd rather die in my bed here than on a pallet in a cell. So, Karlo, old friend, if you like to see what Moore's made of, do so."

"I wish it had occurred to me before," cried Karl. "But indeed, the outer dangers have been so imminent as to drive other fears away."

"It will never matter, bon frère. I don't suppose all the advice in the kingdom could have saved me. What is to be, will be."

"Master," put in Ann Hopley, "where's the good of your taking up a gloomy view of it, all at once? *That's* not the way to get well."

"Gloomy! not a bit of it," cried Sir Adam, in a voice as cheery as the lark's on a summer's morning. "Heaven is more to be desired than Portland Prison, Ann."

So Karl went forth, carrying his commission. In his heart he still trembled at it. The interests involved were so immense; the stake was so heavy for his unfortunate brother. In his extreme caution, he did not care to be seen going to the surgeon's house, but sent a note to ask him to call at the Court.

It was the dusk of evening when Mr. Moore arrived. He was shown in to Sir Karl's own room. Giles was appearing with two wax-lights in massive silver candlesticks, but his master motioned them away.

"I can say what I have to say better by this light than in a glare," he observed to the doctor: perhaps as an opening preliminary, or intimation that the subject the interview was not a pleasant one. And Giles shut them in alone. Karl sat sideways to the table, his elbow leaning on it; the doctor facing him with his back to the window.

"Mr. Moore," began Karl, after a pause of embarrassment, "did it ever occur to you to have a secret confided to your keeping involving life or death?"

Mr. Moore paused in his turn. The question no doubt caused him surprise. He took it—the "life or death"—to be put in a professional point of view. A suspicion came over him that he was about to be consulted for some malady connected with the (evident) fading away of Lady Andinnian.

"I do not suppose, Sir Karl, there is a single disease that flesh is heir to, whether secret or open, but what I have been consulted upon in my time."

"Not disease," returned Karl hastily, finding he was misunderstood. "I meant a real actual secret. A dangerous secret, involving life or death to the individual concerned, according as others should hold it sacred or betray it."

A longer pause yet. Mr. Moore staring at Karl through the room's twilight.

"You must speak more plainly, Sir Karl, if you wish me to understand." And Karl continued thoughtfully, weighing every word as he spoke it, that it might not harm his brother.

"The case is this, Mr. Moore. I hold in my keeping a dangerous secret. It concerns a—a friend: a gentleman who has managed to put himself in peril of the law. For the present he is evading the law; keeping himself, in fact, concealed alike from enemies and friends, with the exception of one or two who are—I may say—helping to screen him. If there were a necessity for my wishing to confide this secret to you, would you undertake to keep it sacred? Or should you consider it lay in your duty as a conscientious man to betray it?"

"Goodness bless me, no!" cried the doctor. "I'm not going to betray people: it's not in my line. My business is to heal their sickness. You need not fear me. It is a case of debt, I suppose, Sir Karl?"

Karl looked at him for a moment steadily. "And if it were not a case of debt, but of crime, Moore? What then?"

"Just the same. Betraying my fellow men, whether smarting under the ban of perplexity or of sin, does not rest in my duty, I say. I am not a detective officer. By-the-way, perhaps that other detective—who turns out to be named Tatton, and to belong to Scotland Yard—may have been down here looking after the very man."

Mr. Moore spoke lightly. Not a suspicion rested upon him that the sad and worn gentleman before him held any solemn or personal interest in this. Karl resumed, his voice insensibly taking a lower tone.

"An individual is lying in concealment, as I have described. His offence was not against you or against me. Therefore, as you observe, and as I judge, it does not lie even in our duty to denounce him. I am helping to screen him. I want you to undertake to do the same when you shall know who he is."

"I'll undertake it with all my heart, Sir Karl. You have some motive for confiding the matter to me."

"The motive arises out of necessity. He is grievously ill; in urgent need of medical care. I fear his days are already numbered: and in that fact lies a greater obligation for us to obey the dictates of humanity."

"I see. You want me to visit him, and to do what I can for him. I am ready and willing."

"He is—mind, I shall shock you—a convicted felon."

"Well?—he has a body to be tended and a soul to be saved," replied the surgeon, curiously impressed with the hush of gravity that had stolen over the interview. "I will do my best for him, Sir Karl."

"And guard his secret?"

"I will. Here's my hand upon it. What would my Maker say to my offences at the Last Day, if I could usurp His functions and deliver up to vengeance my fellow-man?"

"I may trust you, then?"

"You may. I perceive you are over anxious, Sir Karl. What more assurance can I give you? You may trust me as you trust yourself. By no incautious word or action of mine shall his peril be increased, or harm come nigh him: nay, I will avert it from him, if I can. And now—who is he? The sick man at the Maze—to whom Mr. Cavendish was called? Taking one thing with another, that Maze has been a bit of a puzzle in my mind lately."

"The same."

"Ay. Between ourselves, I was as sure as gold that some one was there. Is it Mr. Grey? The poor young lady's husband; the dead baby's father?

"Just so. But he is not Mr. Grey."

"Who is he, then?"

Karl glanced around him, as though he feared the very walls might contain eaves-droppers. Mr. Moore saw his dread.

"It is a most dangerous secret," whispered Karl with agitation. "You will keep it with your whole heart and life?"

"Once more, I will; I will. You cannot doubt me. Who is it?"

"My brother. Sir Adam Andinnian."

The doctor leaped to his feet. Perhaps he had a doubt of Karl's sanity. He himself had assisted to lay Sir Adam in his grave.

"Hush!" said Karl. "No noise. It is indeed my most unfortunate brother."

"Did he come to life again?—Did Sir Adam come to life again?" reiterated the wondering surgeon in his perplexity.

"He did not die."

They went together to the Maze after dark, Karl letting the doctor in with his own key. The whole history had been revealed to him. Nothing was kept back, save a small matter or two connected with the means of Sir Adam's daily concealment: of those, no living soul without the Maze was cognisant, save three: Karl, Hewitt, and Smith the agent. Mr. Moore was entrusted with it later, but not at first. During the lifetime of a medical man, it falls to his lot to hear some curious family secrets, as it had fallen to Mr. Moore; but he had never met with one half so strange and romantic as this.

Sir Adam had dismissed the signs of his illness, and—it will hardly be credited—attired himself in evening dress. With the departure of Mr. Tatton, old habits resumed their sway, with all their surrounding incaution. Mr. Moore saw the same tall, fine man, with the white and even teeth, that he had caught the transient glimpse of in the uncertain twilight some weeks before. The same, but with a difference: for the face was shrunken now, little more than half the size it had been then. In the past week or two he had changed rapidly. He met them when they entered—it was in the upstairs sitting-room: standing at the door erect, his head thrown back. Mr. Moore put out his hand; but the other did not take it.

"Do you know all, sir?" he asked.

"All, Sir Adam."

"And you are not my enemy?"

"Your true friend, Sir Adam. Never a truer one shall be about you than I."

Their hands met then. "But I am not Sir Adam here, you know; I am Mr. Grey. Ah, doctor, what a life it has been!"

"A life that has done its best to kill him," thought the

doctor, as he sat down. "Why did you not call me in before?" he asked.

"Well, we were afraid. You would be afraid of everybody if you were in my place and position. Besides, this disease, whatever it may turn out to be, has developed itself so rapidly that but little time seems to have been lost. I do not see how you will come in now, if it is to be a daily visit, without exciting the curiosity of the neighbourhood."

"Oh, nonsense," said the surgeon. "Mrs. Grey has a renewal of illness and I come in to see her, the curious neighbours will understand, if they are exacting upon the point. Or old Hopley, your gardener—I'm sure his rheumatism must need a doctor sometimes."

Sir Adam laughed. "Hopley will do best," he said. "And then you know, doctor, if—if the worst comes to the worst; that is, the worst so far as sickness is concerned, I can be carried out as Hopley."

"What do you think of him, Mr. Moore?" inquired Karl gravely when the interview was over.

"I will tell you more about it when I have seen more of him," was the surgeon's answer. But his face and tone both assumed, or seemed to Karl to assume, an ominous shade as he gave it.

CHAPTER XLI.

MRS. CLEEVE AT FAULT.

MRS. CLEEVE was at Foxwood. She had been staying in London with her sister, Lady Southall, and took the opportunity to come down to see her daughter. Lucy's appearance startled her. As is well known, we are slow to discern any personal change either for the better or the worse in those with whom we live in daily intercourse: it requires an absence of days or weeks, as the case may be, to perceive it in all its naked reality. Mrs. Cleeve saw what none around Lucy had seen—at least, to the extent—and it shocked and alarmed her. The face was a sad, drawn face; dark rims encircled the sweet brown eyes; the whole air and bearing were utterly spiritless.

"What can be the matter with you, my dear?" questioned Mrs. Cleeve, seizing on the first opportunity that they were alone together.

"The matter with me, mamma!" returned Lucy, making

believe not to understand why the question should be put: though her face flushed to hectic. "Nothing is the matter with me."

"There most certainly is, Lucy: with your health or with your mind. You could not be as you are, or look as you do, unless there were."

"I suffered a great deal from the heat," said poor Lucy.

"My dear—you are suffering from something else; and I think you should enlighten me as to its nature. After that fever, even, you did not look as you are looking now."

But not an iota of acknowledgment from her daughter could Mrs. Cleeve obtain. Lucy would not admit that aught was amiss in any way; at least, that she was conscious of it. Mrs. Cleeve next appealed to Miss Blake.

But that young lady, absorbed by her own pursuits and interests; by the Reverend Mr. Cattacomb and the duties at St. Jerome's, had really not been observant of Lucy's fading face. She could be regardful enough in a contemptuous sort of way of Sir Karl's delinquencies, and of what she looked upon as his wife's blind infatuation; she did not omit to note the signs of trouble and care too evidently apparent in him, and which she set down as the result of an uneasy conscience: but she had failed to note them in Lucy. One cause of this perhaps was, that in her presence Lucy invariably put on an air of lightness, not to say gaiety: and Miss Blake was rarely at home, except at meals; if she did not get an hour there, she was up to the ears in silks and church embroidery. What with Matins and Vespers, and the other daily engagements at St. Jerome's; what with looking after St. Jerome's pastors; what with keeping the young fry in order, including Tom Pepp, and seeing to the spiritual interests of their mothers, Miss Blake had so much on her hands that it was no wonder she was not very observant of Lucy.

"I do not think there is anything particular the matter with Lucy," was the answer she made to Mrs. Cleeve.

"You must see how ill she looks, Theresa."

"She is not ill. At least, that I know of. She eats her dinner and dresses, and goes out, and has company at home. I really had not observed that she was looking ill."

"She talks of the heat," continued Mrs Cleeve; "but that is all nonsense. Extreme heat may make a person thin, but it cannot make them sad and spiritless."

"Lucy is neither sad nor spiritless—that I have noticed."

"Perhaps you have not noticed, Theresa. You have so many out-of-door pursuits, you know. I suppose," continued Mrs. Cleeve, with some hesitation, and lowering her voice to a confidential tone, as she put the question, "I suppose there is nothing wrong between Lucy and her husband?"

"Wrong in what way, do you mean?" rejoined Miss Blake.

"Any misunderstanding, or unpleasantness."

"I should say *not*," returned Miss Blake, with some acrimony. "It is rather the other way. Lucy is blindly, absurdly infatuated with Sir Karl. If he boxed her on the one ear, she would only offer him the other."

"It cannot be that, then," sighed Mrs. Cleeve. "I only thought of it because there was nothing else I could think of. For I cannot help fancying, Theresa, that the malady is on her spirits more than on her health. I—I wonder whether that ague-fever left unsuspected consequences behind it that are developing themselves now?"

Theresa, her attention given to the employment in her hand —a cross she was working in gold thread to adorn some part or other of Mr. Cattacomb's canonicals—a great deal more than it was given to the conversation, allowed the doubt to pass undiscussed. Mrs. Cleeve had always been accustomed to worry herself over Lucy: Theresa supposed it was the habit of mothers to do so, who had an only daughter. So the subject of Lucy's looks dropped for the time.

"What is that for?" resumed Mrs. Cleeve, directing her attention to the small gold cords.

"This? Oh, a little ornament I am making. Please don't touch it, Mrs. Cleeve, or you will entangle the threads."

Thus rebuked, Mrs. Cleeve sat for some moments in silence, inhaling the fresh air through the open window, and the perfume of the late flowers. The mignonnette, in its large clusters, seemed as though it intended to bloom on until winter.

"Theresa, how much longer do you intend to remain here?" she suddenly asked. "Your stay has been a very protracted one."

Theresa was aware of that. She was slightly suspicious that Sir Karl and his wife had begun to think the same thing, though in their courtesy they were not likely to let it appear. In truth the matter was causing her some little reflection: for she would willingly have made the Court her permanent home. While Mr. Cattacomb remained at St. Jerome's, *she* should remain. It might have been somewhat of a mistake to institute St. Jerome's, and to bring Mr. Cattacomb to it: Miss Blake could recognize it now: but as that step had been taken, she meant to abide by it.

"I am not likely to leave at present," she replied. "It would be very dull for Lucy to be here without me. As the winter weather comes on, my out-door duties will be somewhat curtailed, and I shall be able to give her more of my time. Lucy would be lost by herself, Mrs. Cleeve. She was always rather given to moping."

Yes. There was no doubt Lucy did "mope." Mrs. Cleeve sighed deeply. A cloud lay on Foxwood Court, and she could not trace out its source.

The cloud, she thought, lay on Sir Karl as well as on Lucy. That is, his sadness, his weary face, and his evident preoccupation were quite as visible to Mrs. Cleeve as were her daughter's. But for Theresa's emphatic assurance to the contrary, she might still have doubted whether the cloud did not lie between *them*. She was a single-minded, kind-hearted, simple-natured lady, not given to think ill, or to look out for it: but in this case she did try to observe and notice. She could not help seeing how seldom Karl and his wife were together. Karl would drive Lucy out occasionally; but as a rule they saw but little of him. He was generally present at meals, and always sociable and kind, and he would come into the drawing-room when visitors called, if at home; spending his other time chiefly in his own room, and in walking out alone. Later in the evenings he would usually be absent: Mrs. Cleeve noticed that. She had seen him walk across the lawn in the gloom to one of the little gates; she had seen him come in again after an hour or two's interval; and she wondered where he went to.

The truth was, Karl was obliged to go to the Maze more frequently than he used to go, or than was at all prudent. Mr. Moore had not yet pronounced the fatal fiat on Sir Adam that Dr. Cavendish had—doubtfully—imparted to Mr. Detective Tatton; but he concealed from none of them that the case was one of extreme gravity; ay, and of danger. That Sir Adam grew more attenuated might be seen almost daily; he himself assumed that he had but a short span left of life; and he would not allow Karl to be for one single evening absent. Sometimes in the day Karl also went there. The conviction that Adam would not be long among them lay on every heart more or less: and it will be readily understood that Karl should sacrifice somewhat of caution to be with him while he might.

"Karlo, brother mine, you'll come over to-morrow morning?" Sir Adam would say, when their hands met for the evening farewell—and he would keep the hand until the answer should be given.

"If I can, Adam."

"That won't do. You must. Promise."

"I will, then. I will, if I can do it with safety."

And of course he had to go. Under other and happier circumstances, he would never have quitted the invalid night or day.

The lack of what Karl considered "safety," as he spoke it in his answer to Adam, would have consisted in the highway before the Maze gates being peopled; in his being seen to enter. It was so very unfrequented a road that not a soul would pass up or down for a quarter of an hour together; nay, for half a one; and, as a rule, Karl was safe. But he exercised his precaution always. He would saunter towards the gate, as though merely taking a stroll on the shady side path; and then, the coast being clear, ring—for by day-time he never used his own key. His ears and eyes alike on the alert; he, if by mal-chance some solitary passenger should appear, would saunter over to Mr. Smith and talk to him: and then slip in when the intruder should have passed, Ann Hopley having the door by that time ready to open. Karl would use the same precaution coming out: and hitherto had escaped observation. It was not always to be so.

The time passed on; Sir Adam fluctuating; some days fearfully ill, some days feeling well and hearty; and Mrs. Cleeve continuing at Foxwood, for she could not bear to leave Lucy.

Karl went across one morning soon after breakfast. His brother had been very ill indeed the evening before: so ill that Karl had brought most unpleasant thoughts away with him. He was ringing at the gate when it suddenly opened; Ann Hopley was letting out Mr. Moore.

So far as *his* visits went, there had been no trouble. Foxwood had taken care to inform itself as to what patient at the Maze Mr. Moore was again in regular attendance upon, and found it to be Hopley the gardener. The old man had caught an attack of rheumatic fever, or some other affection connected with age and knee joints—said the Miss Moores to the rest of the fair flock going to and from St. Jerome's. There was neither interest nor romance attaching to the poor old man; so the doctor was at liberty to pass in and out at will, without the slightest thought being given to it. In the doctor's day-book the patient was entered as "James Hopley, Mrs. Grey's servant." The doctor's assistant, a fashionable young man from London, who wore an eye-glass stuck in his eye, could have the pleasure of reading it ten times a day if he chose.

"How is he?" asked Karl of Mr. Moore.

"Oh, better this morning—as I expected he would be," was the surgeon's answer. "But I have ordered him to lie in bed for the day. This time I think he will obey me, for he feels uncommonly weak."

"Every fresh attack makes him weaker," observed Karl.

"Why of course it does: it must do so. I don't half like the responsibility that lies on me," continued the doctor. "We ought to have another opinion."

"How can it be had?" remonstrated Karl.

"There it is—how? I wish he could be in London under the constant care of one of its practised men."

"We wish this, and wish the other, Mr. Moore," said Karl, sadly, "and you know how impossible it is for us to do more than we are doing. Answer me truly—for I think you can answer. Would there be a fair chance of his recovery if we had other advice than yours? Would there be any better chance of it?"

"Honestly speaking, I do not think there would. I believe I am doing for him all that can be done."

Ann Hopley drew the gate open again, and the doctor went out. Karl passed on through the labyrinth.

Sir Adam liked to use his own will in all respects, and it was the first time he had made even a semblance of obeying Mr. Moore's orders of taking rest by daytime. He looked very ill. The once handsome face seemed shrunk to nothing; the short hair was almost white; the grey-blue eyes, beautiful as Karl's, had a strangely wistful, patient look in them.

"I thought you would be here, Karlo. I have wanted you ever since daylight."

"Are you feeling better, Adam? Free from pain?"

"Much better. Quite free from it."

"Moore has been saying he wishes we could get you to London, that you might have more skilled advice."

"What nonsense!" cried Adam. "As if any advice could really avail me! He knows it would not. Did it avail my father, Karl?"

Karl remained silent. There was no answer he could make.

"Sit down, old fellow, and tell me all the news. Got a paper with you?"

"The papers have not come yet," replied Karl, as he drew a chair to the bedside.

"Slow coaches people are in this world! I shall get up presently."

"No, Adam, not to-day. Moore says you must not."

"Good old man! he is slow too. But he won't keep me in bed, Karl, when I choose to quit it. Why should I not get up?" continued Sir Adam, his voice taking a tone of its old defiance. "I am the best judge of my own strength. If I lay here for a month of Sundays, Karl, it would not add a day to my life."

Perhaps that was true. At any rate, Adam was one whom it was of no use to urge contrary to his will.

"What's the old adage, Karlo?—'a short life and a merry one?' Mine has not been very merry of late, has it?"

"I wish we could get you well, Adam."

"Do you? We are told, you know, that all things as they fall, are for the best. The world would say, I expect, that this is for the best. I wonder sometimes, though, how soon or how late the enemy would have shown itself, had my life continued smooth as yours is."

Smooth as yours is! The unconscious words brought a pang to Karl's heart; they sounded so like mockery. Heaven alone knew the distress and turbulence of his.

"I got Moore into a cosy chat the other day," resumed Sir Adam: "the wife was safe away, trimming the plants in the greenhouse—Rose is nearly as good a gardener as I am, Karl."

"I know she is fond of gardening."

"Ay, and has been amidst it for years, you see. Well—I led Moore on, saying this, and asking the other, and he opened his mind a bit. The disease was in me always, he thinks, Karl, and must inevitably have come out, sooner or later. It was only a question of time. I have said so myself of late. But I did not look to follow the little olive branch quite so quickly."

"We may keep you here a long while yet, Adam. It is still possible, I hope, we may keep you for good. Moore has not said to the contrary."

"You think he knows it, though?"

Karl was really not sure. His own opinion was this—that Adam had less chance of getting well where he was, than he would have had under those of the London faculty whose speciality embraced that class of disease.

"Shall you put on mourning for me, old fellow? It will be a risk, won't it? I shan't care to be held up to the world as Adam Andinnian, dead, any more than I do, alive. You'll not care to say, either, 'This black coat is worn for that brother of mine: the mauvais sujet who set the world all agog with his scandal.'"

What kind of a mood was Sir Adam in this morning? Karl's grey eyes questioned it. One of real, light, careless mockery?—or was it an underlying current of sadness and regret making itself too uneasily felt in his heart?"

"Don't, Adam. It jars on every chord and pulse. You and I have cause to be at least more sober than other men."

"What have I said?" cried Sir Adam, half laughing. "That you may have to put on mourning for me. It is in the nature of things that the elder should go before the younger. You look well in black, too, Karl; men with such good-looking faces as yours always do."

"I hope it will be a long while before I have to wear it," sighed Karl, perceiving how hopeless it was to change his brother's humour.

"I'd bet Foxwood with you that it will be before Christmas."

"Adam, is it right to speak in this way?"

"Is it particularly wrong?"

"Why do you do it?"

"Need of change, I suppose. I have had a solemn night of it, old fellow: and I hardly know yet whether I was asleep or awake. It was somewhat of both, I expect: but I thought I was amidst the angels. I can see them now as they looked; a whole crowd of them gathered about my bed. And, Karlo, when a man begins to dream of angels, and not to be able to decide afterwards whether it be a dream or a shadowed reality, it is a pretty sure sign, I take it, that no great time will elapse before he is with them."

Adam talked himself into a doze. With his worn and haggard face turned to the wall, he slept as peacefully as a child. Karl stole away, and went into the greenhouse. Rose was there amid the plants; the sunlight, shining on her beautiful hair, turned it into threads of gold. She lifted her white face, with its sad expression.

"I knew you were with him, Karl, so I did not come in. Don't you think he looks very, very ill this morning?"

"Yes, he certainly does. He is asleep now."

"Asleep! In the day time!"

"He had a bad night, I fancy."

"Do you think there's hope, Karl?" she piteously asked—almost as if all hope had left herself.

"I don't know, Rose. Mr. Moore has not told me there is none."

"Perhaps it is that he will not say," she rejoined, resting her elbow on the green steps amid the plants, and her cheek on her hand. "I seem to see it, Karl; to see what is coming. Indeed, you might tell me the truth. I shall not feel it quite so much as I should had our circumstances been happier."

"I have told you as far as I know, Rose."

"There's my little baby gone: there's my husband going: all my treasures will be in the better world. I shall have nothing to do but live on for, and look forward to, the time when I may go to them. Six months ago, Karl, had I known Adam must die, I think the grief would have killed me. But the apprehension we have undergone the last few weeks—Adam's dread, and my awful fear for him—has gone a great way to reconcile me. I see—and I think he sees—that Death would not be the worst calamity. Better for him to be at rest than live on in that frightful peril night and day; each moment as it passes one of living agony, lest the next should bring the warders of Portland Island to retake him. No wonder it is wearing him out."

Karl went away echoing the last sentence; every word she had spoken leaving its echo of pain on his heart. No: it was no wonder that fatal illness had seized on Adam Andinnian before its time.

Well, on this day Karl was not to escape unnoticed so easily. Ann Hopley unlocked the gate, and then both of them stood listening according to custom. Not a sound broke the stillness, save the furious chirping somewhere of two quarrelsome sparrows: not a step could be heard awaking the echoes of the ground. Ann Hopley drew back the half of the gate, and Karl went forth.

Went forth to find himself, so to say, in the very arms of Mrs. Cleeve and Miss Blake. They were standing quite still (which fact accounted for their footsteps not being heard) gazing at these same two fighting birds in the hedge. What with Karl's naturally nervous organization, and what with the dread secret he had just left, every drop of blood went out of his face. But he did not lose his presence of mind.

"Looking on at a fight, Mrs. Cleeve!" he exclaimed in a light tone. "Birds have their hasty passions as well as men, you see. You wicked combatants! Let one another's heads alone. They'll not look any the better without feathers."

One of the noisy birds, as if in obedience, flew away to a distant tree; the other followed it. Karl stayed talking for a minute with the ladies; heard that they had come out for a little walk; and then he went on to his home. Mrs. Cleeve, as she continued her way, glanced inquisitively at the iron gate in passing.

"Do the same people live there still, Theresa? Let me see —a Mrs. Grey, was it not?"

"Oh yes, she lives there," slightingly returned Miss Blake. "She had a baby at the close of summer, but it died."

"A baby! Why, she was a young widow? Stay—no— what was it?—Oh, her husband was abroad. Yes, I remember now. Has he come home yet?"

"As much as he ever will come, I expect," observed Miss Blake. "The girl has just as much a husband as I have, Mrs. Cleeve."

"Why, what is it that you would imply?" cried Mrs. Cleeve, struck with the words and the tone.

"I once, quite accidentally, heard her sing, 'When lovely woman stoops to folly!' You know the song? It was, in one sense of the word, sung in character."

"Oh, dear!" cried Mrs. Cleeve! "But,—but what does Sir Karl do there?"

"Sir Karl? Oh—he is her landlord."

The taunting way in which Miss Blake said it, turned Mrs. Cleeve's delicate cheeks to a rosy red. All kinds of unpleasant thoughts began crowding into her mind.

"Theresa, what do you mean?" she asked, her voice dropping with its own dread. "*Have* you any meaning?"

And the chances were—taking into consideration the love of gossip and of scandal so inherent in woman—that Theresa Blake would there and then have disclosed that she had a meaning, and what the meaning was: but in that self-same moment she happened to turn her eyes on Mr. Smith, the agent. He was leaning over his garden gate, playing with a bunch of late roses; and he gravely lifted his hat to Miss Blake as she looked at him.

There was something in the grave look, or in the sight of the man himself, or in the roses, telling of summer, that recalled most vividly to Miss Blake's mind the private conversation she had once held with Mr. Smith, and the caution he had given her. At any rate, Jane Shore and the lighted taper, and the white sheet, and all the other accessories, rose up before her mental vision as plainly as one can see into a mirror. The penance looked no more palatable to Miss Blake now than it had then. As well keep clear of such risks, great and small. She changed her tone.

"I really don't know anything about the young woman, Mrs. Cleeve. Pray do not take up a mistaken notion. She is Sir Karl's tenant; that is all."

"But if she is not—quite—quite circumspect in her conduct, it must be rather unpleasant to have her close to the Court," said Mrs. Cleeve.

"Oh, she lives a perfectly retired life."

"She is very pretty, I think?"

"Beautiful as an angel."

Nothing more passed. The two sparrows came flying to a proximate tree, and began fighting again. But an uneasy impression was left on Mrs. Cleeve's mind; for she could not forget the strangely-significant tone in which Miss Blake had spoken, and its too sudden change to cautious indifference.

Karl was pacing one of the broad paths that evening in his grounds, when he found himself joined by Mrs. Cleeve. She had thrown a warm shawl over her grey silk evening dress. He gave her his arm. The shadows were deepening: the evening star was already twinkling in the clear sky.

"I want to tell you of a little plan I have formed, Sir Karl, and to get your assent to it. It cannot have escaped your notice that Lucy is looking very ill."

"I have seen it for some time," he answered.

"And I should have spoken to you of it before," resumed Mrs. Cleeve, "only that Lucy herself seems so much annoyed when I allude to it; telling me that nothing is the matter with her, and begging me not to take up fancies. Are you aware of anything being wrong with her general health?"

"No, I am not: there is nothing wrong with it that I know of," returned Karl, unpleasantly conscious that he was not likely to know more about his wife's general health than any other of the Court's inmates.

"Well, what I wish to do is this: to take Lucy to town with me when I leave, and let some physician see her."

"But you are not leaving us yet?"

"Not just yet, perhaps; but when I do go. In fact, I really must take her. I could not be easy to go back home and leave Lucy looking as she is, without having some good medical opinion. Have you any objection to this?"

"Not the slightest. I do not fancy any physician could do much good to Lucy—she has certainly, as I believe, no specific disease—but I think change of air and scene may be of much benefit to her. I am glad that she should go."

"Well, now that I have your permission, Sir Karl, I shall know how to act. Lucy has been telling me that she does not need a physician, and will not see one; and that she does not care to go to London. But that we have never had consumption in our family, I should fear it for Lucy."

Karl was silent. That Lucy had taken the unfortunate secret to heart in a strange manner, and that it was telling upon her most unaccountably, he knew.

"It is rather ungrateful of her to say she does not care to go to London, considering that she has never stayed with her aunt since that time of illness at Winchester," resumed Mrs. Cleeve. "Though, indeed, Lucy seems to have no energy left, and her cheerfulness appears to me more sham than reality. Lady Southall is anxious for her to go up with me."

"Are you intending to stay again with Lady Southall yourself."

"I shall now; as long as Lucy does. And, armed with your authority, I shall insist on Lucy's going up with me. I wish you would come too, Sir Karl; my sister would be so glad to see you."

With his unfortunate brother dying at the Maze, it was not possible for Karl to quit Foxwood. But he was exceedingly glad that Lucy should be absent for a time. It would leave him more at liberty. At least, in spirit. With Lucy's intense contempt and hatred for the Maze and its troubles, Karl never went there but he was conscious of feeling something like a school-boy, who is in mischief away from home.

"I cannot leave home just now," said Karl. "But you must tell Lady Southal that I shall be most happy to take a future opportunity of paying her a visit."

"Are you busy, that you cannot leave?"

"My uncle Joseph's papers are not arranged yet; I am anxious to get on with them," he said, by way of excuse. And in truth that, so far, was so. In his mind's terrible distress the sorting of the papers had been much neglected.

"At least, you will come to town to fetch Lucy home?"

"Of course I will."

The affair decided, they strolled the whole length of the walk in silence. Karl's thoughts were no doubt busy: Mrs. Cleeve was wishing to say something else, and did not quite know how to begin.

"What a nice evening it is!" cried Karl. "How fair the weather continues to be!"

"Yes. But the hedges are showing signs of winter. I noticed it particularly when I was out with Theresa this morning. That was the Maze, I think, that we saw you coming out of."

Karl assented. There was no help for it.

"Does the young lady live there alone still?"

"She has her servants with her."

"But not her husband."

"Mr. Grey, it is understood, spends a good deal of his time in travelling."

"Sir Karl, I think I must ask you plainly; I have been wanting to ask you," she said, taking courage. "Is there any reason for supposing that this lady is not—is not quite what she ought to be?"

"Why, what do you mean?" returned Karl, standing still in his surprise. "Are you speaking of Mrs. Grey?"

"It is almost impossible to avoid attaching some doubt to a young and lovely woman, when she lives so unaccountably secluded a life," returned Mrs. Cleeve, calling up the most plausible excuse she could for her suspicions.

"The very fact of her keeping herself so secluded ought to absolve Mrs. Grey from it," said Karl warmly. "She is a good and honourable lady."

"You feel sure of that?"

"I am sure of it. I know it. Believe me, dear Mrs. Cleeve, that Lucy herself is not more pure and innocent than that poor lady is," he added, taking Mrs. Cleeve's hands in his earnestness, in his anxiety to convince her. "She has had great trouble to try her; she may be said to live in trouble: but heaven knows how good she is, and how persistently she strives to be resigned, and endure."

Mrs. Cleeve kept the sensitive hands in hers; she saw how worthy of trust he was in his earnestness; and every doubt went out of her.

"I am very glad to hear it. I hope she and you will pardon my foolish thoughts. You go to see her sometimes, I believe?"

"When I think I can be of any use, I go. Her husband was once my dear friend: I go there for his sake."

"Why does he not live here with her?"

"He cannot always do quite as he would. Just now he is in bad health."

"And she lost her baby, I hear."

"Yes. It was a great grief to both of them."

The sounding of the dinner-gong stopped the questioning. We may be assured Karl lost no time in conducting Mrs. Cleeve to the house.

CHAPTER XLII.

AT THE RED DAWN.

FOXWOOD was going on quietly with the approach of winter. Mrs. Cleeve had gone to London with her daughter; leaving Miss Blake to keep house at the Court. Some ladies, fearing the world's chatter, might have objected to remain with so young and attractive a man as Sir Karl Andinnian; Miss Blake was a vast deal too strong-minded for any thought of the kind. She was busy as ever with St. Jerome's and its offices; but she nevertheless kept a tolerably keen look-out on the Maze and on Sir Karl's movements as connected with it. He went there more than he used to do: by day now as well as by night: and she wondered how long the simple neighbourhood would keep its eyes closed to facts and figures, that, to her, were so offensively plain.

There had been a sharpish frost in the night, but the glorious morning sun had chased its signs away. At midday it was shining hotly; and Karl was almost glad of the thin screen of leaves left in the labyrinth as he made his way through it. Some days had passed now since Adam had

had any sharp amount of illness: he was wasting away rapidly, and that was the worst outward sign. But his will in these intervals of ease was indomitable, and it imparted to him a fictitious strength.

As Karl came in view of the lawn, he saw Rose standing by one of the distant beds, talking to Hopley. The old man was digging; and had bent himself nearly double over his work. Karl crossed over, a reprimand on his lips.

"Adam, you should not. You promised me you would not again take a spade or other gardening implement in your hand. Your strength is not equal to it, and it must do you harm."

"Just hark at him, Rose. It would not be Karlo if he did not find fault with me. What shall you do for somebody to croak at, brother mine, when I am gone?"

Was it Hopley who spoke?—or was it Sir Adam? The falling-in mouth and the speech, the crooked back, the tottering and swelling knees, the smock-frock and the red comforter and the broad straw hat, all were Hopley's. But the manner of speech and the eyes too, now you came to see them as he looked up at Karl, were Sir Adam's.

Yes. They were one and the same. Poor old Hopley the gardener was but Sir Adam in disguise. With the padded knees and the false hump he had managed to deceive the world, including Mr. Detective Tatton. He might not perhaps have so surely deceived Mr. Tatton, had the latter been looking after Sir Adam Andinnian and been acquainted with his person. But the decrepid gardener bore no resemblance to Philip Salter: and, that fact ascertained, it was all that concerned Mr. Tatton.

It may be remembered that when Mrs. Andinnian was staying at Weymouth, she and her servant, Ann Hopley, were in secret communication with one of the warders of Portland Prison: in point of fact, they were negotiating with him the possibilities of Sir Adam's escape. This man was James Hopley; a warder—as Karl had taken him to be —and also Ann's husband. In the scuffle that took place the night of the escape, the man really killed was the other prisoner, Cole: and it was he who was taken to Foxwood and lay buried in its churchyard. Hopley was drowned.

At that period, and for some little time before it, Philip Smith was at Portland Prison. Not as a prisoner: the man had never in his life done aught to merit incarceration: but

seeking employment there, through the interest of one of the
chief warders, who was a friend of his—a man named O'Brian.
From the date of the frauds of Philip Salter, Philip Smith
had been—as he considered it—a ruined man: at any rate he
was unable to obtain employment. A ruined man must not be
fastidious, and Smith was willing and was anxious to become
a warder if they would make him one. It was while he was
waiting and hoping for the post, and employed sometimes as
an assistant, and thoroughly trusted, that the attempted
escape of the prisoners occurred. Smith was one of those
who put off in the boat after the fugitives: the other two
being Hopley and O'Brian. In the scuffle on the Weymouth
shore, Sir Adam was wounded and left for dead. O'Brian
saw him lying there apparently dead, and supposed him to be
so. O'Brian, however, afterwards received a blow that
stunned him—for the night was dark, and friends and foes
fought indiscriminately—and Smith contrived to get Adam
away into a place of concealment. It is very probable that
Smith foresaw in that moment how valuable a prize to him
the living and escaped Sir Adam might become. O'Brian
really believed him to be dead, and so reported him to the
authorities. A dead man is worthless, and Sir Adam was
allowed to be retained by his friends for interment: the
beaten and disfigured Cole, shot in the face, being looked
upon as Sir Adam.

After that, the path was easy. Sir Adam, very badly
injured, lay for many weeks hidden away. Smith continued
at Portland Prison unsuspected, keeping his own counsel, and
visiting Sir Adam cautiously at intervals. As soon as it was
practicable for Sir Adam to be moved, the step was ventured
on. He was got away in safety to London, and lay in retirement there, in a house that had been taken by Smith: his
wife (formerly Rose Turner) coming up to join him; and
Ann Hopley, faithful to Sir Adam's fortunes through all,
waiting on them. She had no one else left to be faithful
to now, poor woman. Smith managed everything. He had
withdrawn himself from Portland Island, under the plea that
he could no longer, in consequence of his disabled arm, aspire
to a wardership—for his arm had been damaged that fatal
night, and it was thought he would never have the full use of
it again. The plea was unsuspiciously recognised by the
prison authorities; Smith retained his friendship with O'Brian,
and occasionally corresponded with him, getting from him

scraps of useful information now and then. From that time his services were devoted to Sir Adam. It was he who communicated between Sir Adam and his mother; for letters they did not dare to transmit. It was he who first disclosed to Mrs. Andinnian the fact that Miss Rose Turner was her son's wife; it was he who made the arrangements for Sir Adam's taking up his abode at the Maze, and provided the disguise to arrive at Foxwood in, as the decrepid old husband of the servant, Ann Hopley. To do Mr. Smith justice, he had fought against the scheme of coming to the Maze; but Mrs. Andinnian and Adam were both bent upon it; and he yielded. Adam and his wife had stayed in London under the name of Mr. and Mrs. Grey, and she retained it.

Amidst the injuries Sir Adam received, was one to the mouth and jaw. It destroyed those beautiful front teeth of his. After his recovery he sought the services of a clever but not much known dentist named Rennet, went to the pain of having the rest of his teeth extracted, and an entire set of false ones made. Two sets, in fact. The journey Rose took to London, when Miss Blake espied her with Karl, was for the purpose of getting one of these sets of teeth repaired, Sir Adam having broken the spring the night before.

The teeth had to be conveyed personally to Mr. Rennet and brought away; for Adam and his wife were too cautious to entrust him with their address.

And now it will be seen how Sir Adam had concealed himself at the Maze. In the daytime he was the toothless, humpbacked, infirm old Hopley, working at his garden with enlarged knees and tottering steps: as soon as dusk came on, his false padding was thrown off—with his smock-frock and coarse clothes, and he was the well-bred gentleman, Sir Adam Andinnian, in his evening attire and with his white and even teeth. His assumed rôle was maintained always during the day: his meals were taken in the kitchen, to be safe in case of any possible surprise, Ann attending upon him with all respect. The delay in admitting Nurse Chaffen, kept waiting once on the wrong side of the kitchen door, was caused by "Hopley's" taking out his set of teeth and putting on his broad-brimmed hat: for it was convenient to assume the teeth during the short period devoted to dinner. The deafness was of course assumed as an additional precaution. Thus he had lived in a state of semi-security, tending his flowers, and occupied with the care of his garden generally, an employment that he loved so well. The day that General Lloyd's party went in, Karl was transfixed with apprehension and amazement to see Hopley showing himself. Adam enjoyed it: it was so like him to brave things; and he feared no danger from a pleasure party like that.

Well, I think that is all that is needed in the way of explanation; and we can go on. Karl was looking at the digging with regretful eyes.

"You ought to be glad to see me at work again, Karl, instead of groaning over it," cried Sir Adam.

"And so I should be, Adam, only that I fear you will feel its effects unpleasantly by and by."

"I asked him not to do it, but he only laughed at me," said Rose.

"Somebody must do it. I can't see the garden quite neglected. Besides, if I am well enough to work there's no reason why I should not. I am not sure, Karl, but I shall cheat you now."

"Cheat me?"

"By getting well. What should you say to that?"

"Thank heaven for it: and do my best to get you away to a place of safety."

"By George, old fellow, I don't know that I shan't. I am feeling as blithe as a bee. Rose, take yourself a trifle further off, out of the mould."

He was throwing about the spadefuls almost as well as he had ever thrown them in his strength. Rose was cheated into something like hope, and her face for the moment lost its sadness.

"I wish to goodness I had a draught of beer," cried Adam. "Where's Ann, I wonder."

Karl went to fetch it. Ann Hopley shook her head at the idea of hope, when Karl spoke of it as she gave him the beer.

"You never see any person, who was to live on, have the look in his face that he has, sir."

"He looks fairly well to-day."

"And so he will continue to look at times to the last, as it strikes me. I have had a good deal of experience in illness, sir. As to his talking about getting well—why, sir, you know what he is: saying this and that without meaning it. There's no doubt he feels pretty sure himself how it will be."

Karl sighed as he went back with the beer. Yes, there was no real hope.

That same night—or rather on the following morning, for the dawn was more than glimmering—Karl in his bed began to dream that he was out in a shower of hail. It seemed to be falling with great violence; so much so that a sharper crash awoke him. Lying awake for a moment and questioning where he was, he found the noise to be reality. The hail was beating on the chamber window.

Was it hail? Scarcely. It was crashing but on one window, and only came at intervals. It sounded more like gravel. Karl rose and opened the window. Smith the agent stood underneath. A prevision of evil shook Karl as he leaned out.

"He is very ill indeed, sir," said Smith in the lowest whisper possible to be heard, and extending his finger to indicate the Maze. "Mr. Moore's there and thinks it will be for death. I thought you would like to know it."

"How did you hear it?" asked Karl.

"Ann Hopley ran over and knocked me up, that I might go for the doctor."

"Thank you," replied Karl. "I'll be there directly."

Now it so happened that for some purposes of cleaning—for the Maze was not exempt from those periodical visitations any more than the humble dwelling of Mrs. Chaffen—Miss Blake's chamber had been temporarily changed to the one next to that recently occupied by Lady Andinnian. Miss Blake was in the habit of sleeping with her window open; and, not being asleep at the time, she had heard Mr. Smith's footsteps and the crashes at Sir Karl's window. Of course she was curious as to what could cause the noise, and at first thought of housebreakers. Had Mr. Smith chanced to turn his head in the right direction during the colloquy with Sir Karl, he might have seen an elaborately night-capped head peeping forth cautiously.

"Why, it is Mr. Smith!" thought Miss Blake, as he walked away. "What an extraordinary thing! He must have been calling up Sir Karl."

Listening inside as well as out, Miss Blake heard the bell that was in Hewitt's chamber ring gently; and, after a minute or two, the latter proceeding to his master's room. Then they both went down together, and Hewitt let Sir Karl out at the hall door, and came upstairs again. Miss Blake, after a good deal of self-puzzling, arrived at the conclusion that the affair must be in some way connected with poachers—who had been busy on the land latterly—and returned to her bed.

With death on his face, and a look of resignation than which nothing could be more peaceful, lay Sir Adam for the last time. His weary life, with all its bitter turmoil, was nearly at an end; night *here* was closing, morning *there* was opening. Karl's grey eyes were wet as he bent over him.

"Don't grieve too much," said Adam with a smile, as he put his cold hand into Karl's clasp. "You know how much better off I shall be. Rose knows it."

"You were so full of hope yesterday, Adam."

"Was I? It cheated the wife into a few hours of pleasantness, and did its mission. I did not think I took *you* in. Why, Karlo, I have just been waiting from day to day for what has now come: moreover, I have seen how much best it all is *as* it is than anything else would be. I would not accept life if you'd give it to me, unless the whole time since that Midsummer Eve could be blotted out."

Karl swallowed a sob.

"You don't know what it has been, Karl. No one can know what it is, to live under a hanging sword, as I have, unless they experience it. And few in this world can do that. It was all a mistake together. The shooting of Scott when I ought to have horsewhipped him; the escape from Portland; the taking up my abode here; everything: and these mistakes, Karl, have to be worked out. I have paid for mine with life."

Karl did not answer. He was only nervously pressing the wasted hand in his.

"It is all, I say, for the best. I see it now. It was best that the little lad should go; it is best that I should; it is best that you should be the true owner of Foxwood. It would have been too much of a complication otherwise. The boy could never have put forth a claim to it while I lived; and, after that, people might but have pointed their scornful finger at him as the son of a convict. I thank God for taking him."

"Should you talk so much, Adam?"

"I don't know. A man in my condition, about to leave the world behind, prefers to talk while he can. You will take care of my wife, Karl. There was no settlement, you know and——"

"I will take care of her to the best of my power, Adam," came the earnest interruption. "She shall have a proper and suitable jointure as the widowed Lady Andinnian."

"No, Karl; not that. She and I have talked over the future

at odd moments, and we do not wish it. Rose does not mean to acknowledge her marriage with me, or to live in any kind of state in accordance with it. She will be Mrs. Grey to the end. Unless, indeed, any occasion were to arise, such as a tarnishing breath of scandal brought against this past period of her life. Then, of course, the truth must be declared, and you, Karl, would have to come forward and testify to it. I leave that in your hands."

"With every surety," assented Karl.

"A few hundreds a year, say four or five, are all that she will want from you, or take. Her late uncle's money must come to her sometime, and that of itself would be almost enough. She purposes to live a retired life with her aunt; and I think it will be the happiest for her. In my desk, Karl, you will find a paper in my handwriting, setting forth all these wishes of hers and mine; it will serve as a direction for you. —No," he went on, after a pause, "for her own peace, the world must never know her as Lady Andinnian. She dreads it too much. See you not the chief reason? She would have to stand before the public convicted of perjury. That past trial is rarely out of her mind, Karl—when she appeared falsely as Miss Rose Turner. The foolish things people do in their blindness! It was my fault. *Her* fault lay only in obeying me: but your charitable people would not accept that as an excuse. Be it as it may, Karl, Rose's life henceforth will be one of modest position and strict retirement. Ann Hopley goes with her."

Looking at the matter from all points of view, it might be, as Sir Adam said, for the best.

"And you will be Sir Karl in reality as well as in seeming, brother mine; and Foxwood will be your true home and your children's after you. That is only justice. When you arranged to marry Lucy Cleeve, you deemed yourself to be the inheritor, and she deemed it. My death will set all right. And now about Smith, Karl. The man did me a great service, for I should have been retaken but for him; and he has been faithful to me since. I should like you to allow him something in the shape of an annuity—a hundred and fifty pounds a year, or so. Not the cottage: he will not stay in this neighbourhood when I am gone. It was through me that his arm got injured: which, of course, partly incapacitates him for work; and I think I am bound to provide for him."

"It shall be done," said Karl. "Ungrudgingly."

"I have mentioned it in the paper, and the sum. He—he—he—"

Sir Adam's hesitation was caused by faintness. He broke down, and for the time said no more. Nor did he recur to the subject again.

The day went on, Adam partially sleeping through it. At other times he lay in a kind of stupor. Mr. Moore attended at intervals; but nothing further could be done. At dusk Hewitt came over for a last sight of his old master; for a last farewell: and he sobbed bitterly as he took it.

Karl did not go home—at which Miss Blake was in much private wonder. Discarding the poacher theory, she shrewdly suspected now that he must be at the Maze, taking the opportunity of his wife's absence to play the gay bachelor away from home. She asked Hewitt, she questioned Giles; Giles knew nothing, Hewitt fancied Sir Karl might be "detained at Basham" on some business.

And so, the night set in. When quite awake Adam had the full possession of his senses, and exchanged a few words, sometimes with his wife, sometimes with Karl. About three o'clock he fell into a calm sleep. Karl watched on; Rose, weak and sick and weary, dropped into a doze in a distant chair. Ann Hopley was in the kitchen below.

Save for the faint sighing of the wind as it swept round the house, stirring the branches of the trees, there was no sound to be heard. Stillness reigned unbroken in the dying chamber. How many of us have kept these watches! But who has kept them as this was being kept by Karl Andinnian!

With that bitter aching of the heart known but to few, and which when felt in its greatest intensity is the saddest pain the troubles of the world can give, Karl sat gazing on his brother. In his love for him, every pang endured by Adam in the past was a sting for himself, every hazard run, had reflected on him its dread apprehension. He sat thinking of what might have been; looking on what was: and an awful regret, than which nothing like unto it could be ever again experienced, tore at his heart-strings for the wasted life, cut short ere it had reached its prime. More than willingly in that moment would Karl have given his own remaining days to undo what his brother had done, and to restore to him freedom and honour. It might not be. Adam's course was run: and he was passing away in obscurity from the world in which he had virtually no longer a place. Never for a moment did the immunity from perplexity it would bring to himself or the release from the false position he had been compelled to assume, occur to Karl; or, if it did, it was not dwelt upon: all of self and self-interest was lost in the regret and grief for his brother. He saw Adam living at Foxwood Court with his wife, its master: held in repute by men; he saw himself settled near with Lucy, his fortunes advanced by his brother's aid to a position not unacceptable to Colonel Cleeve; he saw his mother alive still and happy: a united family, enjoying comfort the one with the other. This might have been. His mother dead of a broken heart; Adam, dying before his eyes, an escaped fugitive; his own life blighted with pain and sorrow unutterable for Adam's sake, his wife estranged from him —this was what was. Be you very sure that no earthly pang could be keener than that despairing heart-ache felt by Karl Andinnian.

How many a night at that still hour had Adam lain in his terror, listening to this moaning wind with supernaturally quick ear, lest it should be only covering other sounds—the approach of his deadly enemies! How many times in a night had he quitted his bed, his heart beating, and stolen a cautious peep beside the blind to see whether they might not be there, in battle array, waiting until the dawn should come and they might get in to take him! Ah, it was all at an end now; the fever, and the fear, and the wasting restlessness. Why! if the men were drawn up round his bed, they would not care to touch him. But the terror from force of habit stayed with him to the last.

Adam started up. How long he had slept, and how the night was going, Karl in his abstraction hardly knew. Adam's eyes looked somewhat wild in the shade of the night-light, and he put up his feeble hand.

"What is it?" asked Karl gently.

"I thought they were here, Karl; I saw them in the room," he whispered—and his eyes went round it. "They had muskets, I think. Was it a dream?"

"Nothing but a dream, Adam. I am with you. Rose is asleep in the arm-chair."

"Ay. I have not dreamt of them for a week past. Stay by me, Karlo."

Karl would have risen to administer some cordial: but Adam was holding his hand in a tight grasp; had shut his eyes, and seemed to be dropping asleep again.

He slept about half-an-hour. Karl could not stir for fear of disturbing him: and his imprisoned arm went from a state of pins and needles into the cramp. When Adam awoke, there was a smile on his face and a peaceful rest in his eyes. He was quite collected.

"Karl, I dreamt of them again: but they had turned to angels. They were here, all about my bed. Oh Karl, I wish you could see them as I saw them! you'd never be afraid of anything more in this world. What's that?"

Karl turned round: for Adam's eyes were fixed on something or other behind him. He could see nothing save a streak of light, herald of the dawn, that came in at the side of the blind.

"Do you mean the light, Adam? It's the dawn breaking."

"Ay. *My* dawn. Draw up the blind, Karl."

Softly, not to awake Rose, Karl drew it up. Rose-coloured clouds, heralds of a beauteous sunrise, flooded the East. Adam lay and gazed at it, the smile on his face changing to a rapt look that seemed to speak of heaven, more than of earth.

"It will be better there than here, Karl. For me."

"Better for all of us."

"I am very happy, Karl. The world is fading from me: heaven opening. Forgive me all that I have cost you."

Karl's heart and eyes were alike full.

"Just as the men who had troubled me were changed into angels, so my fear has changed to rest. The angels are about the bed still, Karl; I know they are; waiting for me. The same lovely light shone on them that is shining yonder; and they told me without words that they were come to bear me up to God. I read it in their tender faces—so full of pitying love for me. It won't be so very long, Karl: you'll come later."

Karl's tears were falling on the up-turned face.

"I should like to have seen your wife, Karl; just once. Tell her so, with my love. Ask her to forgive me the worry I know I have caused her."

"I will, I will."

"Oh, Karl, it has been a dreadful life for me; you know it has. I began to think that God had forgotten me—how foolish I was! He was full of mercy all the while, and kept me here in safety, and has now changed it all into peace. Listen, Karl! there's a sound of sweet music."

Karl could hear nothing but the wind.

"It is the angels singing," whispered Adam, a smile of ineffable beauty on his face. "They sing on the journey, you know. Good-bye, Karl, good-bye!"

Karl bent his face, his tears streaming, his heart aching. These partings are too bitter to be told of. This was most essentially so.

"Where's Rose, Karl?"

She was already by Karl's side. He yielded his place to her, and went down to Ann; and there sobbed over the kitchen fire as a woman might have done.

But in the midst of it all, he could say as his brother had done, "Thank God." If ever a poor, sinful, weary man had need to rejoice that he was removed to that better world, it was Adam Andinnian.

Rose's bell called Karl up again. The last moment was at hand. Ann Hopley followed: and they all stood round the bed and saw him die. The red clouds had dispersed; the sun was just showing itself above the verge of the horizon.

CHAPTER XLIII.

LAID TO HIS REST.

FOXWOOD heard the news. Mrs. Grey's shaky old gardener was dead, James Hopley. Mr. Moore, when applied to for particulars, went into a learned dissertation on chronic rheumatism, and said that he was not able to save him.

Ann Hopley astonished the undertaker. She gave orders for three coffins; and they must be of the best, she said, if it cost her a hundred pounds. Her poor husband and she had saved money, and she should like to spend it on him.

There was again a battle with the clerk. It had been bad enough when Ann Hopley chose the ground for Mrs. Grey's little child, within the precincts of that belonging to the Andinnian family; but to insist upon it that her own husband, a servant, should also lie there, was a piece of presumption the equal of which the clerk had never before heard of. However, Sir Karl, not waiting to be appealed to this time, called on the clerk, and said the woman might bury her husband there if she pleased; he did not think it right in people to assume exclusiveness after death, whatever they might do in life. The clerk lifted his hands when Sir Karl's back was turned: radical notions such as these would tend to demoralize the best conservative community.

It was while his brother was lying dead, that Sir Karl—truly Sir Karl now—heard from his wife. She was ready to come to Foxwood, as Mrs. Cleeve was about to return to Winchester, and she appointed the following day, Tuesday, for Sir Karl to fetch her. It happened to be the day fixed for the funeral, and Karl wrote back to say that he could not leave home that day, but would fetch her on the Wednesday instead. To this he received no reply; and he of course intended to abide by it.

Tuesday came. About twelve o'clock in the day the funeral turned out of the Maze gates; sundry curious ones amid the juvenile population being assembled to witness the exit. A funeral was not an every-day event at Foxwood: and, besides, the Maze had been exciting interest of late. It was a simple funeral. The plumed hearse and one mourning coach; the undertaker and carriers walking. In the coach went Ann Hopley, smothered in a hood, with Hewitt to bear her company. Foxwood said it was very neighbourly and civil of the butler: but Miss Blake felt sure he had received private orders from Sir Karl, and she wondered what Sir Karl was coming to.

Now Lucy, Lady Andinnian, looking at things through a mist, as she had been looking, poor wife, for some time past, was very resentful that Sir Karl would not fetch her on the day she named. She reasoned with herself that his refusal must arise from one of two causes: either he was neglectfully indifferent; or else he had some engagement with Mrs. Grey: for, of deterring occupation, she believed he possessed none. Proudly angry, she determined to take her own way, and return home without him.

Accordingly, on the Tuesday she started with her maid from London. But, like many a one who does things in offhand inexperience, she made a mistake, and took the wrong train. That is, she took one that did not stop at Foxwood. Lucy discovered this after she was in the carriage, and found they must get out at Basham. Leaving Aglaé and the luggage to wait for the next train, which would not be up for two hours, Lucy took one of the waiting flies, and drove on.

Lucy was full of thoughts and anticipations. She wondered where her husband was, what she should find him doing, and what excuse he would make. It lasted her all the way: and they were close on Foxwood village before anything occurred to arouse her. She woke up from her thoughts to find the driver, who was a Foxwood man, had come very nearly to a standstill, and was staring at a funeral procession just then entering the churchyard.

The first object that caught Lucy's eye was Hewitt. Hewitt attired as a mourner, and following the coffin. For a moment Lucy's heart beat quicker, and her gaze was strained: who could it be that was inside? Gradually her eyes took in the whole of the scene: the spectators collected in the distance, watching; the person enveloped in a silk hood and cloak at Hewitt's side: Mr. Sumnor in his surplice.

All in a moment, as it seemed, just as the clergyman began to read, springing she could not tell from whence, there advanced Sir Karl Andinnian. He was in black attire, but wore neither crape band nor scarf; and it might have been thought he was only an ordinary spectator. Hewitt, however, drew a step back to give his master the place of precedence, as though out of proper respect, as did Ann Hopley: and Sir Karl took off his hat and stood there, close to the coffin, his head bent low.

"How very strange it is!" thought Lucy. "Who can be in the coffin?—and who is the woman in the black silk cloak and hood? There is Mr. Smith, the agent, too!—he is standing near with *his* hat off now."

"Lucy! Can it be you? We did not expect you until to-morrow."

The voice was Miss Blake's. St. Jerome's devotees were no more free from curiosity than their inferiors; and a few of them had chanced to be taking a walk past the churchyard just at the critical moment; of whom Miss Blake was one.

"I thought I would come to-day, and not give Sir Karl the trouble of fetching me," replied Lucy. "Aglaé is coming on from Basham by the next train with the luggage. How are you, Theresa? Will you come inside?"

Miss Blake's answer was to open the fly door, seat herself by Lady Andinnian, and turn her gaze on the churchyard. The scene bore a charm for her as well as for Lucy.

"Why, that's Sir Karl there!" she exclaimed in surprise, the spectators' heads having intercepted her view while on the ground.

"Yes," assented Lucy. "And there's Hewitt—and Sir Karl's agent—and a mourner with her face hidden. Who is it that is being buried, Theresa?"

"Why, it's only the old gardener at the Maze. As to Hewitt, I suppose he had to go to keep the woman in countenance. The old man was her husband, you know."

"But what should bring Sir Karl there?"

"And standing first, as though he were chief mourner!" commented Miss Blake, devouring the scene with her condemning eyes, and giving the reins to her thoughts. "*I* don't know why he is there, Lucy. There are several things that I have not attempted to understand for some time past."

"Is not that the part of the churchyard where the Andinnians lie?—where their vault is?"

"It is. But Hopley is being buried there, you see: and that infant, that you know of, was buried there. The clerk is in a fine way over it, people say: but Sir Karl ruled that it should be so."

Thoughts connected with Mrs. Grey, and the inexplicable manner in which Sir Karl seemed to yield to her humours, even to the honouring of her servants, flashed into Lucy's brain. It did not tend to appease her previous anger against him.

"Why could not Sir Karl come for me to-day, Theresa?"

"It is of no use to ask me, Lucy. Sir Karl does not explain his motives to me. This funeral perhaps kept him," added Miss Blake sarcastically, unconscious how very near she was to the truth. "After you left, he seemed almost to live at the Maze. Last week he was there, as I believe, for a whole day and a whole night. I *must* speak, Lucy. Out of regard to decency, that girl ought to quit the Maze, or you quit Foxwood."

"Drive on," cried Lucy to the coachman, in a tone as though the world and all things in it were grating on her. And the man did not dare to disobey the sharp command.

But Miss Blake preferred to get out; and did so. She had said what she did say from good motives: and she took credit for not making worse of the account—as she might have done. Not a word would she say about his being called up in the night—and she knew now that it was to the Maze he was summoned. With her whole heart she pitied Lucy.

"May I be forgiven if my duty ought to lie in silence!" she muttered as she joined the Miss St. Henrys and others in the crowd. "Lucy seems to have no friend about her in the world but me."

The interment was over. The procession—what was left of it—went its way back again, Hewitt and Ann Hopley side by side in the coach. Sir Karl strolled away over the fields, and presently found himself joined by Mr. Smith.

"So your mission at Foxwood is over," he sadly cried to the latter. "I have no more need to make believe I want an agent now."

"Ay, it's over, Sir Karl. Better for him, almost, that he had fallen in the fray off Weymouth; that I had never saved him; than have lived to what his life has since been."

"Better for him had he never come to the Maze," rejoined Sir Karl.

"It was none of my doing. As you know, sir."

"No: but you opposed his leaving it."

"As he was here, I did. I had but his interest at heart, Sir Karl: although I know you have thought the contrary. The chances were that he could not have got away in safety. In his own person he dared not have risked it; and a decrepid figure like Old Hopley's must have attracted attention. But for that detective's pitching upon Foxwood to make a hunting place of, I believe Sir Adam would have been most secure here."

"Well, it is over, with all its risks and chances," sighed Karl. "He did not forget you when he was dying. His wish was, that you should enjoy a moderate annuity during your life: which I have undertaken to pay."

The agent's thanks, and they appeared very heartfelt and genuine, were cut short by the approach of Mr. Moore. He joined them as they walked along; and the conversation fell on the illness of the deceased.

"There was no real hope from the beginning, once the disease had fairly set in," cried the surgeon. "There never is. In Sir Adam's case, the terrible anxiety he endured day and night brought it on, and caused it to develop with unusual rapidity: there was not a shadow of chance for him."

"You did not tell me that," said Karl.

"I was not quite sure of it myself at first: though I suspected it. I did not tell you, you say, Sir Karl: well, no, not in so many words: but your own eyes might have seen it as its progress went on. Sir Adam knew it himself, I fancy, as surely as I."

"Do you remember saying you wished he could have further advice?" asked Karl. "Did not that prove that you had hope?"

"I wished it chiefly for the satisfaction of those connected with him. All the advice in the world could not—as I suspected then, and soon saw—have availed to save his life. We sometimes say of people, death has been a happy release for them. In his case, Sir Karl, it has been most unquestionably so: he is at rest."

CHAPTER XLIV

REPENTANCE.

DOWN on her knees, in self-abasement, the tears of contrition raining from her eyes, her face scarlet in its agony of shame, cowered Lucy Andinnian at her husband's feet. She would not let him raise her. It seemed to her that a whole lifetime of repentance could never wash out her sin.

The elucidation of the misunderstanding that had kept them apart for months was taking place.

On the day after the funeral, Karl sought his wife in the dressing-room to tell her of what had occurred. She had scarcely spoken a word to him since her return, or allowed him to speak one to her. Very briefly, in half a dozen words, he informed her his brother was dead, and delivered the message Adam had left for her. For a few minutes Lucy's bewilderment was intense; and, when she did at length grasp somewhat of the truth, her confusion and distress were pitiable.

"Oh, Karl, Karl, do you think you will ever be able to forgive me? What can I do?—what can I do to atone for it?"

"You must get up, Lucy, before I say whether I forgive you or not."

"I cannot get up. It seems to me that I ought never to get up again. Your *brother* at the Maze!—your brother's wife! Oh, what must you have thought of my conduct? Oh, Karl, why do you not strike me as I lie?"

Sir Karl put forth his arms and his strength, and raised her to the sofa. She bent her face down on its pillow, to weep out her tears of shame.

"Come, Lucy," he said, when he had waited a few minutes, sitting beside her. "We shall not arrive at the end in this way. Is it *possible* that you did not know my brother was alive?"

"How could I know it, Karl?" she asked, amid her streaming tears. "How was I likely to know it?"

"You told me you knew it. You said to me that you had discovered the secret at the Maze. I thought you were resenting the fact of his being alive. Or, rather, of my having married you, knowing that he was."

"Why should I resent it? How could you think so? Was *that* the secret you spoke of in Paris the night before our wedding?—that Adam was alive."

"That, and no other. But I did not know then that he was married—or suspect that he ever would marry. I learnt that fact only during my mother's last illness."

"Oh, Karl, this is dreadful," she sobbed. "What must you have thought of me all this time? I almost wish I could die!"

"You still care for me, then; a little?"

With a burst of anguish she turned and hid her face upon his breast. "I have only loved you the better all the while," she whispered.

"Lucy, my dear, I say we shall not get to the end in this way. Look up. If you were in ignorance of my brother's existence, and of all the complications for you and for me that it involved, what then was it that you were resenting?"

"Don't ask me, Karl," she said, her face growing scarlet again. "I could not tell you for the very shame."

He drew a little away, making a movement to put her from him. Never had his countenance been so stern to her as it was now; never could he be so little trifled with.

"If there is to be an explanation between us, Lucy, it must be full and complete. I insist upon its being so. If you refuse to give it now—why I shall never ask you for it again. Do you not think you owe me one?"

Again she bent her face upon him. "I owe you everything, Karl; I owe you more reparation than I can ever pay. Never, as long as our lives shall last, will I have a secret from you again, heaven helping me. If I hesitate to tell you this, it is because I am ashamed for you to know how foolish I could be, and the wicked thoughts I could have."

"Not more foolish or wicked, I dare say, than I was for

making you my wife. Speak out, Lucy. It must be so, you see, if there is to be a renewal of peace between us."

Keeping her head where it was, her face hidden from him, Lucy whispered her confession. Karl started from her in very astonishment.

"Lucy! You could think that! Of me!"

She put up her hands beseechingly. "Oh, forgive me, Karl; for the sake of the pain, forgive me! It has been killing me all the while. See how worn and thin I am."

He put his arm out and drew her to his side. "Go on, my dear. How did you pick up the notion?"

"It was Theresa." And now that the ice was broken, anxious to tell all and clear herself, Lucy described the past in full: the cruel anguish she had battled with, and her poor, ever-to-be renewed efforts to endure patiently, for his sake and for God's. Karl's arm involuntarily tightened around her.

"Why did you not speak to me of this at once, Lucy?" he asked, after a pause. "It would have cleared it up, you see."

"I did speak to you, Karl; and you seemed to understand me perfectly, and to accept it all as truth. You must remember your agitation, and how you begged me not to let it come to an exposure."

"But I thought you alluded to the trouble about my poor brother: that it was the fact of his being alive you had discovered and were resenting. *That* was the exposure I dreaded And no wonder: for, if it had come, it would have sent him back to Portland Island."

Lucy wrung her hands. "What a miserable misapprehension it has been!—and how base and selfish and cruel I must have appeared to you! I wonder, Karl, you did not put me away from you for ever!"

"Will you go now?"

She knew it was asked in jest: she probably knew that neither would have parted from the other for the wealth of the world. And she nestled the least bit closer to him.

"Karl!"

"Well?"

"Why did you not tell me about your brother when you found I knew nothing, and was resenting it? If I had but known the real truth, we never should have been at issue for a day."

"Remember, Lucy, that I thought it was what you knew, and spoke of. I thought you knew he was alive and was at the Maze with his wife. When I would have given you the whole history from the first, you stopped me and refused to hear. I wished to give it; that you might see I was less to blame than you seemed to be supposing. It has been a wretched play at cross-purposes on both sides: and neither of us, that I see, is to blame for it."

"Poor Sir Adam!" she cried, the tears again falling. "Living in that dreadful fear day after day! And what must his poor wife have suffered! And her baby dying, and now her husband! And I, instead of giving sympathy, have thought everything that was ill of her, and hated her and despised her. And, Karl—why, Karl—*she* must have been the real Lady Andinnian."

He nodded. "Until Adam's death, I was not Sir Karl, you see. The day you came with her from Basham, and they told her the fly, waiting at the station, was for Lady Andinnian, she was stricken with terror, believing they meant herself."

"Oh, if I had known, all this time!" bewailed Lucy. "Stuck up here, in my false pride and folly, instead of helping you to shield them and to lighten their burthen! I cannot hope that you will ever quite forgive me in your heart, Karl."

"Had it been as I supposed it was, I am not quite sure that I should. Not quite, Lucy, even to our old age. You took it up so harshly and selfishly, looking at it from my point of view, and resented it in so extraordinary a fashion, so bitter a spirit——"

"Oh don't, don't!" she pleaded, slipping down to his feet again in the depth of her remorse, the old sense of shame on her burning cheeks. "Won't you be merciful to me? I have suffered much."

"Why, my darling, you are mistaking me again," he cried tenderly, as he once more raised her. "I said, 'Looking at it from my point of view.' Looking at it from yours, Lucy, I am amazed at your gentle forbearance. Few young wives would have been as good and patient as you."

"Then do you really forgive me?" she asked, raising her eyes and her wet cheeks.

"Before I answer that, I think I must ask whether you forgive my having married you—now that you know all."

"Oh, Karl!"

She fell upon his shoulder, her arms round his neck. Karl caught her face to his. He might take what kisses he chose from it again.

"Karl, would you please let me go to see her?" she whispered.

"See whom?" asked Karl, in rather a hard tone, his mind pretty full just then of Miss Blake.

"Poor Lady Andinnian."

"Yes, if you will," he softly said. "I think she would like it. But, my dear, you must call her 'Mrs. Grey,' remember. Not only for safety, but that she would prefer it.'

They went over in the afternoon. Miss Blake, quite accidentally this time, for she was returning home quietly from confession at St. Jerome's—and a wholesale catalogue of peccadilloes she must have been disclosing, one would say, by the length of the hearing—saw them enter. It puzzled her not a little. Sir Karl taking his wife *there!* What fresh ruse, what further deceit was he going to try? Oh, but it was sinful! Worse than anything ever taken for Mr. Cattacomb's absolution.

Lucy behaved badly: without the slightest dignity whatever. The first thing she did was to burst out crying, and kiss Mrs. Grey's hand: as if—it really seemed so to Mrs. Grey—she did not dare to offer to kiss her cheek. Very sad and pretty looked Mrs. Grey in her widow's mourning.

It was a sad interview: though in some respects a soothing and satisfactory one. Lucy explained, without entering into any details whatever, that she had not known who it was residing at the Maze, or she should have been over before, Karl and Sir Adam permitting her. Rose supposed that for safety's sake Karl had deemed it well to keep the secret intact. And there the matter ended.

"You will come and stay with me at the Court before you leave," pleaded Lucy.

Rose shook her head. "It is very kind of you to wish it, Lady Andinnian; very kind indeed under the circumstances; but it could not be. I shall not pass through these gates until I pass through them with Ann Hopley for good. That will be very soon."

"At least, you will come and stay with us sometime in the future."

"I think not. Unless I should get a fever upon me to see the spot once more that contains my husband and child. In that case, I might trespass on you for a day or two if you would have me. Thank you very much, Lady Andinnian."

"You will let me come over again here before you leave?"

"Oh, I should be pleased—if Sir Karl has no objection. Thank *you*, Karl," she added, holding out her hands to him, "thank you for all. You have been to us ever the most faithful friend and brother."

The church bell at Foxwood was ringing for the late afternoon service as they quitted the Maze—for Mr. Sumnor, in spite of his discouragement and the non-attendance, kept on the daily service. The ting-tang was sounding from St. Jerome's; and several damsels, who had come round by the Court to call for Miss Blake, were trooping past. Lucy bowed; Karl lifted his hat: he had ceased to care who saw him going in and out of the Maze gate now.

"Karl," said Lucy, "I should like to go to prayers this evening. I shall take no harm: it is scarcely dusk yet."

He turned to take her. Mr. Sumnor and the clerk were in the church; hardly anybody else—just as it had been that other evening when Lucy had crept in. Even Miss Diana was off to St. Jerome's, in the wake of her flighty nieces. Lucy went on to her own pew this time.

Oh, what a contrast it was!—this evening and that. Now she was utterly still in her rapt thankfulness; then she had lain on the floor, her heart crying aloud to God in its agony. What could she do to show her gratitude to Him, who had turned the darkness into this radiant light? She could do nothing. Nothing, save strive to let her whole life be spent as a thank-offering. Karl noted her excessive stillness, her blinding tears; and he probably guessed her thoughts.

While he was talking with Mr. Sumnor after the service, Lucy went in to the vicarage. Margaret, lying in the dusk, for the room was only lighted by its bit of fire, could not see who had entered.

"Is it you, Martha?" she said, thinking it was her sister. "You are back early."

"It is I—Lucy," said Lady Andinnian. "Oh, Margaret, I was obliged to come to you just for a minute. Karl is outside, and we have been to church. I have something to tell."

Margaret Sumnor put out both her hands in token of welcome. Instead of taking them, Lucy knelt by the reclining board, and brought her face close to her friend's, and spoke in a hushed whisper.

"Margaret, I want to thank you, and I don't know how. I have been thinking how impossible it will be for me ever to thank God: and it seems to be nearly as impossible ever to thank you. Do you remember what you once said to me, Margaret, about bearing and waiting? Well, but for you, I don't think I *could* have borne or waited, even in the poor way I have; and—and——"

She broke down: sobs of emotion checked her utterance.

"Be calm, my dear," said Margaret. "You have come to tell me that the trouble is over."

"Yes: God has ended it. And, Margaret, I never need have had a shade of it: I was on a wrong track all the while. I—I was led to think ill of my husband; I treated him worse than any one will ever know or would believe: while he was good and loyal to the core in all ways, and in the most bitter trouble the world can inflict. Oh, Margaret, had I been vindictive instead of patient—I might have caused the most dire injury and tribulation, and what would have been my condition now, my dreadful remorse through life? When the thought comes over me, I shiver as I did in that old ague fever."

A fit of shivering took her actually. Miss Sumnor saw how the matter had laid hold upon her.

"Lucy, my dear, it seems to me that you may put away these thoughts now. God has been merciful and cleared it to you, you say; and you ought to be happy."

"Oh, so merciful!" she sobbed. "So happy! But it might have been otherwise, and I cannot forget, or forgive myself."

"Do you remember, Lucy, what I said? That some day, when the cloud was removed, your heart would go up with a bound of joyous thankfulness?"

"Yes. Because I did—and have done—as Margaret told me; and endured."

The affair had indeed laid no slight hold of Lucy. She could not forget what might have been the result, and quite an exaggerated remorse set in.

A few nights afterwards Karl was startled out of his sleep

by her. She had awakened, it appeared, in a state of terror, and had turned to him with a nervous grasp as of one who is drowning. Sobbing, moaning, she frightened her husband. He would have risen for a light, but she clung to him.

"But what has alarmed you, Lucy?—what is it?" he reiterated.

"A dream, Karl; a dream," she sobbed, in her bitter distress. "I am always thinking of it by day, but this time I dreamt it; and I awoke believing it was true."

"Dreamt what?" he asked.

"I thought that cruel time was back again. I thought that I had not been quiet and patient, as Margaret enjoined, leaving vengeance to God, but had taken it into my own hands, and so had caused the Maze's secret to be discovered. You and Adam had both died through it; and I was left all alone to my dreadful repentance, on some barren place surrounded by turbid water."

"Lucy, you will assuredly make yourself ill."

"But, oh Karl, if it had been true! If God had not saved me from it!"

CHAPTER XLV.

ONLY A MAN LIKE OTHER MEN.

THEY stood together in the north parlour: Sir Karl Andinnian and Miss Blake. In the least severe terms he knew how to employ, Sir Karl was telling her of her abuse of his hospitality—the setting his wife against him—and intimating that her visit to them had better for the present terminate.

It took Miss Blake by surprise. She had remarked a difference in their behaviour to one another, in the past day or two. Lucy scarcely left Sir Karl alone a minute: she was with him in his parlour; she clung to his arm in unmistakable fondness in the garden; her eyes were for ever seeking his, with a look of pleading, deprecating love. "They could not have been two greater simpletons in their honeymoon," severely thought Miss Blake.

Something else had rather surprised her. Walking past the Maze on this same morning, she saw the gate propped open, and a notice, that the house was to let, erected on a board.

The place was empty; the late tenants of it, the lady and her maid, had departed. Turning to ask Mr. Smith the meaning of this, she saw a similar board at his house: Mr. Smith was packing up, and Clematis Cottage was in the market.

"Good gracious! Are you going to leave us, Mr. Smith?" she asked, as that gentleman showed himself for a moment at the open window, with an armful of books and papers.

"Sorry to say that I am, madam. Business is calling me to London."

"I hear that Mrs. Grey has left, too. What can have taken her away?"

"Can't tell," said Mr. Smith. "Does not care to stop in the house, perhaps, after a death has taken place in it. Servants must die as well as other people, though."

Without another word to her, he went to the back of the room with his load, and began stuffing it into a trunk with his one arm. Miss Blake summed up the conclusion in her mind.

"Sir Karl must have summarily dismissed him."

Little did she foresee that Sir Karl was about, so to say, summarily to dismiss herself. On this same day it was that he sought the interview with her. When the past was touched upon by Karl, and her part in it, Miss Blake, for once in her life, showed signs that she had a temper. Her face turned white.

"You might have done me incalculable mischief, Miss Blake: mischief that could never be repaired in this world," he said, standing to face her. "I do not allude to the estrangement that might have been caused between myself and my wife, but evil of a different nature. What could possibly have induced you to take up so outrageous a notion in regard to me?"

Miss Blake, in rather a shrill tone—for she was one of those unfortunate individuals whose voices grow harsh with annoyance—ventured upon a disparaging word of Mrs. Grey, but evaded the true question. Karl did not allow her to go on.

"That lady, madam," he said, raising his hand with a kind of solemnity, "was good and pure, and honourable as is my own wife; and my dear wife knows it now. She was sacred to me as a sister. Her husband was my dear and long-tried friend: and he was for some months in great trouble and distress. I wished to do what I could to alleviate it: my visits there were paid to *him*."

"But he was not living there," rejoined Miss Blake, partly in hardy contest, partly in surprise.

"Indeed he was living there. He had his reasons for not wishing to make any acquaintance in the place, and so kept himself in retirement; reasons in which I fully acquiesced. However, his troubles are at an end now; and—and the family have ceased to be my tenants."

Whether Miss Blake felt more angry or more vexed, she was not collected enough at the moment to know. It was a very annoying termination to her long and seemingly well-grounded suspicions. She always wished to do right, and had the grace to feel somewhat ashamed of the past.

"What I said to Lucy I believed I had perfectly good grounds for, Sir Karl. I had the interests of religion at heart when I spoke."

"Religion!" repeated Sir Karl, his lips involuntarily curling. "Religion is as religion does, Miss Blake."

"After all, she did not heed me; so, if it did no good, it did no harm. Lucy is so very weak-minded——"

"Weak-minded!" interposed Sir Karl. "If to act as she did—to bear patiently and make no stir under extreme provocation, trusting to the future to right the wrong—if this is to be weak-minded, why I thank God that she is so. Had she been strong-minded as you, Miss Blake, the result might have been terribly different."

Miss Blake was nettled. Her manner froze.

"I see what it is, Sir Karl; you and your wife are so displeased with me that I feel my presence in your house is no longer welcome. As soon as I can make arrangements I will quit it—thanking you both for your hospitality."

She paused. Sir Karl paused too. Perhaps she had a faint expectation that he would hasten to refute the decision, and request her to stay on. But he did nothing of the kind. On the contrary, he, in a word or two of politeness, acquiesced in the proposal of departure, as though it admitted of no question.

"I should not have trespassed upon you so long—in fact, I should not have stayed at all after your first return here with Lady Audinnian, but for St. Jerome's," she rejoined, her temper getting up again; while there ran in her mind an undercurrent of thought, as to whether she could find suitable lodgings in Foxwood.

"You will not have to regret that, in leaving," he observed. "I am about to do away with St. Jerome's."

"To do away with St. Jerome's!"

"In a week's time from this it will be shut up, and all the nonsense within its walls cleared away."

"The nonsense!" shrieked Miss Blake.

"Why you cannot call it sense—or religion either. To tell you the truth, Miss Blake, the place has been an offence to me for some time. It has caused a scandal——"

"For shame, Sir Karl Andinnian! Scandal, indeed!"

"And this little bit of fresh scandal that has arisen now, people don't like at all," quietly persisted Sir Karl. "Neither do I. So, to prevent the bishop coming down upon us here, I close the place."

Miss Blake compressed her lips. She could have struck him as he stood.

"What do you mean by a 'fresh' scandal, pray?"

"Well, the story runs that Mr. Cattacomb was seen to kiss one of the young ladies in the vestry."

Miss Blake started, Miss Blake shrieked, Miss Blake wondered that the very ceiling did not drop upon the bold false tongue. To do her justice, she believed St. Jerome's pastor was by far too holy a man for any wickedness of the sort. Not to speak of restraining prudence.

"Sir Karl, may you be forgiven! Where do you expect to go to when you die?"

"To the heaven, I hope, that our merciful God has provided for us," he answered, meeting the query solemnly and with some emotion. "Some of those dearer to me than life have gone on thither to wait for me."

At which Miss Blake drew up her pious head, and intimated that she feared it might be another kind of place, unless he should mend his manners. And Sir Karl closed the interview, leaving her to understand that she had received her congé.

The circumstance to which he alluded was this. A day or two before, some prying boys, comrades of Tom Pepp's, were about St. Jerome's as usual. For, ever since its establishment, the place had been quite a point of attraction to these young reptiles; and, keep off they would not. On the morning in question, during a grand church cleaning, Mr. Cattacomb disturbed the ladies by coming in to search for a book he had left in the vestry, and Miss Jemima Moore followed in to help him look for it. Hovering around the vestry window and the walls generally, these wicked boys, a slight inlet of view was discovered, in consequence of the blind's being accidentally drawn somewhat aside. Of course as many eyes were applied to the chink as could find space; and they had the pleasure of seeing the parson steal a kiss from the blushing cheek of Miss Jemima. Rare nuts for the boys to crack! Before the day had closed, it was being talked of in Foxwood, and reached the ears of Miss Diana. She handed the case over to the doctor.

Down he went to St. Jerome's on the following morning, and caught Mr. Cattacomb alone in the vestry, just getting into his sheepskin. Mr. Moore wasted no time in circumlocution or superfluous greeting.

"You were seen to kiss my daughter yesterday, young man."

To be pounced upon in this unprepared manner is enough to try the nerves of almost any hero; what must it have been then for a modest young clergyman, with a character for holiness, like Guy Cattacomb? He stammered and stuttered, and blushed to the very roots of his scanty hair. The tippet itself turned of a rosy hue.

"No equivocation, sir. Do you acknowledge it, or do you not?"

Gathering up his scared wits and a modicum of courage in the best way he could, the Reverend Guy virtually acknowledged it to be true. He added that he and Miss Jemima were seriously attached to each other; that he hoped sometime to win her for his wife; and that a sense of his utter want of means had alone prevented his speaking to the doctor.

"Now, look here," said the surgeon, after a pause of consideration, perceiving from the young man's earnest manner that this was the actual state of the case, "I say *No* to you at present. It lies with yourself whether I ever say yes. If you and she care for one another, I should be the last to stand in your way, once you have proved yourself worthy of her. Get rid of all the rubbish that's filling up your foolish brain;" —and he gave his hand a sweep around—" become a faithful, honest clergyman of the Church of England, serving your Master to the best of your power; and then you may ask for her. A daughter of mine shall never tie herself to a vain fop. No; though I had to banish her to the wilds of Kamschatka, to prevent it."

"I'll do my best, sir, to become what you will approve of," returned the parson, humbly, " if you will only give me hope of Miss Jemima."

"It is because I think you have some good in you that I do give you hope, Mr. Cattacomb. The issue lies with you."

Now, this was what Sir Karl alluded to. When it fell to Miss Blake's lot to find it was true and to hear the particulars, she thought, in her mortification, that the world must be drawing to an end. At least, it was signally degenerating. That adored saint to have turned out to be only a man after all—with all a man's frail nature! All Miss Blake's esteemed admirers seemed to be slipping from her one by one.

She, and the congregation generally, were alike incensed. Mr. Cattacomb, lost to any future hopes, fell in their estimation from fever-heat down to zero: and they really did not care much, after this, whether St. Jerome's was shut up or not. So Sir Karl and Farmer Truefit found their way was made plain before them.

"What a heap of silk we have wasted on cushions and things for him!" cried Charlotte St. Henry, in a passion. "And all through that sly little cat, Jemima Moore!"

CONCLUSION.

A SWEET calm day in early spring. Sir Karl and his wife stood on the steps of their house, hand in hand, ready to welcome Colonel and Mrs. Cleeve, who were driving up to pay a long visit. Lucy had recovered all her good looks; Karl's face had lost its sadness.

Things had been getting themselves straight after the dark time of trouble. Some pleasant neighbours were at the Maze now; Clematis Cottage was occupied by Margaret Sumnor. There was a new vicar of Foxwood. Mr. Sumnor, who had not been without his trials in life, had died in the winter. His widow and second family went to reside in London;

Margaret, who had her own mother's fortune now—which was just enough to live upon quietly—removed to Clematis Cottage, to the extreme delight of Lady Andinnian. St. Jerome's had been converted into a school-room again: its former clergymen had retired into private life for a season, and no more omnibus-loads of young ladies came over from Basham. Sir Karl was earning popularity everywhere. Caring earnestly for those about him, actively promoting the welfare of all, unceasingly and untiringly, generous in aiding, chary of fault-finding, Sir Karl Andinnian was esteemed and beloved even more than Sir Joseph had been. Nothing educates and softens the human heart like the sharp school of adversity.

"Lucy, you are a puzzle to me," said Mrs. Cleeve, when she had her daughter to herself upstairs. "In the autumn you were so ill and so sad; now you are looking so well and so radiantly happy."

"I am quite well, mamma, and happy."

"But what was the cause of your looking so ill then?"

Lucy did not answer, evading the question in the best way she could. The past time would be ever sacred between herself and her husband.

"Well, I cannot understand it," concluded Mrs. Cleeve. "I only hope you will continue as you are now. Sir Karl looks well, also; almost as he did when we first knew him at Winchester, before his brother brought that trouble on himself and all connected with him. To tell you the truth, Lucy, I thought when I was last here that you were both of you on the high road to consumption. Now you both look as though you were on the road to—to——"

"A fine old age," put in Lucy, as her mother broke down for want of a simile. "Well, mamma, I hope we are—if God shall so will it."

"And—why you have made this into a dressing-room again!" cried Mrs. Cleeve, as Lucy took down her hair, and rang for Aglaé.

"Yes; I wanted it as one when I went back to my own room."

"What do you do with the other room—the one you slept in?" questioned Mrs. Cleeve, throwing open the door as she spoke—for she had a great love of seeing into house arrangements. "You have had the bed taken away!"

"The room is not being used at present," replied Lucy. "Karl—Karl——"

"Karl—what?" asked Mrs. Cleeve, wondering at the sudden timidity, and looking round. Lucy's sweet face was blushing.

"Karl thinks I shall like to make it the day nursery, later on."

"Oh, my dear! I am glad to hear *that*."

Lucy burst into tears of emotion. A very slight occurrence served still to bring back the past and its repentance.

"Mamma, you do not know, you can never know, how good God has been to me in all ways; and how little I deserved it."

And so we leave all things at peace. The dark storms had rolled away and given place to sunshine.

THE END.

www.ingramcontent.com/pod-product-compliance
Lightning Source LLC
Chambersburg PA
CBHW022140300426
44115CB00006B/270